CRITICAL ESSAYS ON THE PHILOSOPHY OF R. G. COLLINGWOOD

CRITICAL ESSAYS
ON THE
PHILOSOPHY OF
R. G. COLLINGWOOD

EDITED BY

MICHAEL KRAUSZ

CLARENDON PRESS · OXFORD

1972

Oxford University Press, Ely House, London, W.1

GLASGOW NEW YORK TORONTO MELBOURNE WELLINGTON
CAPE TOWN IBADAN NAIROBI DAR ES SALAAM LUSAKA ADDIS ABABA
DELHI BOMBAY CALCUTTA MADRAS KARACHI LAHORE DACCA
KUALA LUMPUR SINGAPORE HONG KONG TOKYO

PRINTED IN GREAT BRITAIN
BY WILLIAM CLOWES & SONS LIMITED
LONDON, COLCHESTER AND BECCLES

PREFACE

SOME THIRTY years ago R. G. Collingwood urged that critics write not about him but about the subjects he raised. It has since become clear, however, that many subjects about which Collingwood wrote can be treated more adequately by considering Collingwood's own suggestive contributions.

The following collection provides critical assessment of a wide range of Collingwood's philosophical contributions, including those to philosophical method, philosophy of mind, philosophy of religion, philosophy of art, philosophy of history, philosophy of education, metaphysics, and ethics and politics. Philosophical persuasions of contributors vary widely, as did the philosophical sources of Collingwood's inspirations. The essays do not attempt primarily to offer histories of Collingwood's intellectual development, and they do not discuss—except where philosophically relevant—Collingwood's historical and archaeological works.[1]

All essays in this volume appear in print here for the first time, and were commissioned especially for this volume by the Clarendon Press, Oxford.

The comprehensive Collingwood bibliography at the end of this volume draws extensively upon the bibliography in Lionel Rubinoff's *Collingwood and the Reform of Metaphysics* (Toronto, 1970).

Thanks are due to Lionel Rubinoff, Sherman Stanage, Gerald Stormer and Peter Cirzan for bibliographical suggestions, and to J. Terry Nutter for technical assistance. Special thanks are due to Mark Thornton who compiled the indexes.

M. K.

Bryn Mawr, Pa.

---

[1] For a bibliography of Collingwood's historical and archaeological works, see I. M. Richmond, *Proceedings of the British Academy*, XXIX (1943), pp. 481-5.

CONTENTS

LIST OF ABBREVIATIONS

The following abbreviations of Collingwood's works will be used:

RP   *Religion and Philosophy* (1916)
SM   *Speculum Mentis* (1924)
OPA   *Outlines of a Philosophy of Art* (1925)
RFCI   'Reason is Faith Cultivating Itself' (1927)
FR   'Faith and Reason' (1928)
EPM   *An Essay on Philosophical Method* (1933)
IN   *The Idea of Nature* (written 1933–4; published 1945)
PNP   'The Present Need of a Philosophy' (1934)
IH   *The Idea of History* (written 1936–9; published 1946)
PA   *The Principles of Art* (1938)
A   *An Autobiography* (1939)
EM   *An Essay on Metaphysics* (1940)
FN   'Fascism and Nazism' (1940)
FML   *The First Mate's Log* (1940)
NL   *The New Leviathan* (1942)

With the exception of *NL*, these abbreviations will be followed by page numbers. *NL* will be followed by paragraph numbers, as used in *The New Leviathan*.

I

COLLINGWOOD AND PHILOSOPHICAL METHOD

ALAN DONAGAN

IN THIS paper, I examine what Collingwood wrote about philosophical method, in the light of his maturing philosophical practice. In 1939 he described his only extended methodological study, the *Essay on Philosophical Method* (1933), as 'my best book in matter', and as 'in style ... my only book, for it is the only one I ever had the time to finish as well as I knew how' (*A*, 118).[1] It embodies his critical reflections on what he had done in his earlier philosophical writings, especially *Speculum Mentis* (1924). In his later writings, its precepts are followed with least deviation in the *The Idea of Nature* (1946), most of which he wrote immediately after completing it.

From first to last, Collingwood conceived philosophy as autonomous theoretical inquiry, from the subject-matter of which nothing is excluded. Its autonomy distinguishes it from the special sciences, whether exact or empirical—if it is true, as it has been widely taken to be, that those sciences accept certain principles of reasoning, and certain assumptions or data, as unquestionable; with the consequence that the direction of reasoning in them is irreversible (*EPM*, 152–3, 166–7). Collingwood himself neither accepted nor rejected this view of the special sciences (*EPM*, 9–10), but he had no doubt he could prove it false of philosophy. In philosophy, he maintained, there is no principle and no assump-

---

[1] In 1939 Collingwood had published, besides the *Essay on Philosophical Method*, four philosophical books: *Religion and Philosophy* (1916); *Speculum Mentis* (1924); *Outlines of a Philosophy of Art* (1925); and *The Principles of Art* (1938).

tion that may not be questioned (*EPM*, 21–3, 159). How is this possible?

That no fact is excluded from the subject-matter of philosophy does not imply that every fact is of philosophical interest. That wombats are native to Australia is a fact which can enter into philosophical reflection in various ways, for example, in epistemo-logical theories of how such facts can be known; but a man is not philosophically the poorer for ignorance of it. The kinds of fact which, in Collingwood's view, command the attention of philosophers have to do with the fundamental forms of human experience. In the Prologue to *Speculum Mentis*, which has some claim to be the finest passage of prose in his early writings, he followed 'existing and traditional philosophies' in provisionally recognizing five fundamental forms of experience: art, religion, science, history, and philosophy (*SM*, 57). By a 'form of experience' he meant 'an activity of the whole self, in which every faculty, if it is permissible to distinguish faculties, is engaged', and which claims to be cognitive, that is, to be 'in some sense a kind of knowledge' (*SM*, 39). Existing philosophical traditions allocate every fact to one or another of these forms of experience; and philosophy is distinct from the other forms in this if in no other way: that whereas, except for art which is wholly unreflective, each form of experience arises out of reflection on those lower than itself; philosophy alone must reflect, not only on all the lower forms of experience, but also on itself.

In post-Renaissance European civilization, the various forms of experience have commonly been pursued independently of the others, and those who devote themselves to one such form are as a rule hostile to the others. Collingwood confessed himself a disciple of Hegel and Ruskin in diagnosing these tendencies as symptoms of a deep-seated disease of modern life: namely, disintegration of the unity of mind or spirit (*SM*, 27, 30–5).[1]

---

[1] See also his lecture *Ruskin's Philosophy* (Kendal, 1922), pp. 17–19. When he wrote, the essential unity of mind (or culture), while largely lost in practice, was seldom denied in theory. Today, as Lord Snow's *The Two Cultures and the Scientific Revolution* (Cambridge, 1959) and its progeny bear witness, that unity is commonly found theoretically incomprehensible.

Despite brutal religious persecution, and endemic poverty and violence, the medieval mind, as revealed in its art, feels itself 'surrounded, beyond the sphere of trial and danger, by a great peace, an infinite happiness'; and this happiness 'characteristically present in the medieval mind, is characteristically absent from the modern' (*SM*, 25–6). Its loss was necessary. Medieval man possessed it only because in him the various forms of experience, even religion, were little developed, and could consequently be experienced as at bottom the same. But they are not: the differences between them 'appear all too sharply when they reach maturity' (*SM*, 29). Compared with modern man, medieval man was a child; and, for the race as well as for individuals, there is no return to childhood (*SM*, 23, 29). Yet the mind *is* one. What the Middle Ages felt, and what Hegel and Ruskin took for a principle, is true. One task of philosophy, in its examination of all the forms of experience, including itself, is to show how that principle can be true (*SM*, 36).

How, then, do the various forms of experience differ from one another? Classification, according to traditional theory, consists in dividing a *summum genus*, by its peculiar differentiae, into species.[1] These become subaltern genera for further division, and so on until *infimae species* are reached; to one or another of which, but to no more than one, every member of the summum genus must belong. At each level of the division, co-ordinate species exclude one another, and the same *fundamentum divisionis* is applied throughout.

If the *summum genus* to be classified is experience, the *fundamentum divisionis* by which it is divided into species is naturally presumed to be either something in the subject of experience, e.g., that each form or species of experience is the work of a distinct mental faculty; or something in the object of experience, that is, differences among what the experiencing mind is directed upon.

---

[1] To Collingwood, the traditional theory of classification was part of what every undergraduate trained in philosophy knew. What he wrote about it accords exactly with H. W. B. Joseph's account of it in *Introduction to Logic* (2nd edn., Oxford, 1916), ch. 5. Essentially the same account may be found in R. M. Eaton, *General Logic* (New York, 1931), pp. 282–6.

Collingwood could accept neither of these alternatives. Believing the whole mind to be present in everything it does, he could not assign different forms of experience to different faculties; and believing that a form of experience is wholly the work of the mind, he could not seek a *fundamentum divisionis* outside the experiencing mind altogether.

The peculiar character of the *fundamentum divisionis* of the classification of experience in *Speculum Mentis* underlies its more superficial peculiarities, which in the *Essay on Philosophical Method* Collingwood declared to be characteristic of all philosophical classifications.

The first peculiarity of philosophical classification is that co-ordinate classes overlap (*EPM*, 31–3). In fact, the logical standard of classification is seldom satisfied in the empirical sciences: zoological classifications usually employ several *fundamenta divisionis*, and consequently do not exclude the possibility of overlapping classes.[1] Collingwood announced in advance that he would welcome such information, as confirming from the side of the empirical sciences his view that overlapping classes are admissible in philosophy (*EPM*, 9–10). Yet, since he himself neither asserted nor denied that classes overlap in the empirical sciences, for him the question does not arise whether the reasons for it in the empirical sciences are the same as the reasons for it in philosophy.

As might have been expected, thay are not the same. The logical principle of a single *fundamentum divisionis* in a classification is disregarded in the empirical sciences; for, since the variety of natural species falls far short of logical possibility, to apply that principle would yield a multitude of empty classes. Thus zoologists classify mammals as vertebrates which, *inter alia*, possess hair and suckle their young, and birds as feathered vertebrates.[2] To require a single *fundamentum divisionis*, whether mode of nurturing young or nature of pelt, would produce two distinct successive classifications, and would provide for a class of feathered vertebrates that

---

[1] Joseph, op. cit., p. 119; Eaton, op. cit., pp, 285–6.

[2] The example is a simplified version of one of Eaton's. See Eaton, op. cit., pp. 285–6. Joseph gives another (op. cit., pp. 120–1).

suckle their young, a class that is believed to be empty. Overlap of classes, when an anomalous species is discovered, is the price not unwillingly paid for this economy.

With philosophy it is otherwise. The classes with which it is concerned are not empirical. In no branch of philosophy is careful attention to historical fact more important than in political philosophy; yet political philosophers would not be entitled to neglect a possible species of polity on the ground that there are no instances of it. But that is not the bottom of the matter. The exact or mathematical sciences, like philosophy, are concerned with possible worlds, and not merely with the actual one. And something like an overlap of classes occurs in one of the most fundamental classifications of mathematics, that of number itself. In the hierarchy of numbers—natural numbers, signed integers, rational numbers, real numbers, complex numbers—each higher species of number contains a sub-set corresponding to each lower species. Thus the rational number $+2/+1$, and the signed integer $+2$, correspond to the natural number 2. It would not be unnatural to say that the class of natural numbers is completely overlapped by the class of signed integers, and that of signed integers by that of rational numbers.[1]

The classes of numbers are generated by mathematical operations all of which can be carried out on natural numbers: addition, subtraction, multiplication, division, exponentiation, and the extraction of roots. Let us say that a set of numbers is 'closed' under a given mathematical operation, if carrying out that operation on one of its members always yields another of its members. Except for special cases involving 0, the set of natural numbers is closed under the operations of addition, multiplication, and exponentiation, but not under the operation of subtraction. The set of signed integers is closed under the operation of subtraction, as well as under all the operations under which the set of natural numbers is closed, but not under the operation of division. In turn, the set of rational numbers is closed under the operation of division, but not

---

[1] In this and the following paragraph, I depend on the valuable discussion of the classification of numbers by William and Martha Kneale, in their *Development of Logic* (Oxford, 1962), pp. 392–5.

under that of extracting roots; that of real numbers is closed under the operation of extracting any root of any positive number; and that of complex numbers is closed for all the operations mentioned without restriction. Most mathematical classifications, e.g. that of conic sections, whether in solid geometry, projective geometry, or algebra, satisfy the traditional requirements: thus, the differentia of one species excludes that of another, a figure having the differentia of an ellipse *cannot* have that of a parabola. But the classification of numbers is a scale, in which the higher classes not merely overlap, but in a sense contain the lower.

Collingwood's principal examples of overlapping classes in philosophy, which are drawn from ethics, are very like this. The genus *bonum* is traditionally divided into the species *iucundum*, *utile*, and *honestum*, which not only overlap—some pleasant things are useful or expedient, some useful or expedient things are right; but constitute a scale of forms, in which the higher contain the lower—the useful or expedient contains whatever is genuinely good in the pleasant, and the right whatever is genuinely good in the useful or expedient (*EPM*, 86–8). And Collingwood held that this explains the overlap of classes in philosophy: '[t]he higher of any two adjacent forms overlaps the lower because it includes the positive content of the lower as a constituent element within itself'(*EPM*, 90).

It is here perhaps that philosophical classifications, as Collingwood conceived them, differ from the mathematical classification of numbers. The higher classes of numbers in a sense contain the lower, but cannot be said to be opposite to them, or more real. The rational number corresponding to the signed integer $+2$ is neither its opposite in any sense, nor more real than it. In a philosophical scale of forms, however, the higher forms express the generic essence more adequately than the lower. A less adequate expression can be considered as opposed to a more adequate, and, as such, opposed to the genus itself: thus mere pleasure, considered as opposed to utility, is not good but bad. And, so considered, the less adequate expressions of the generic essence are false expressions of it (*EPM*, 84–5). The lower forms on a philosophical scale, which, as opposed to the higher, are false expressions of the generic essence, may therefore be considered, by contrast with the higher, as mere *appearances* of the generic essence, and hence as less real than the higher (*EPM*, 88–91).

Professor Louis O. Mink has drawn attention to the fact that Collingwood's theory in the *Essay on Philosophical Method* partly describes and partly corrects his practice in *Speculum Mentis*.[1] In *Speculum Mentis*, as we have seen, he divided the genus experience into five overlapping species: art, religion, science, history, and philosophy. The forms which determine membership of these species constitute a scale, in which the lower realize the generic essence less adequately than the higher. Yet, as Mink points out, there is a discrepancy between what Collingwood says about philosophy in the two books, which arose out of his recognition of the obvious fact that there are incompatible philosophical positions or systems. The highest form of experience is not anything or even everything than can reasonably claim to be a philosophy: it is *true* philosophy; and each of the various false philosophical positions dogmatically asserts the universality and adequacy of one of other of the lower forms of experience. In *Speculum Mentis*, Collingwood denied that the dogmatic philosophical systems occupy a place in a scale of forms.

These dogmatisms [he wrote] are only the negative moments of the dialectic of experience, dead by-products of the forms of consciousness which produce them, blind alleys in the process of thought. You cannot work forward out of them: you must retreat backwards from them and begin afresh from another form of experience (*SM*, 263).

In the *Essay on Philosophical Method* he repudiated this. If we take the state of philosophy at any given time, he declared, we shall find it to be composed of 'various philosophies . . . vary[ing] in the degree to which they deserve the title philosophy of the present day'; nevertheless, 'ideally a place can be found even for the crudest and least philosophical of them in a scale . . . travelling downward towards zero but never reaching it . . .' (*EPM*, 196).

[1] Louis O. Mink, *Mind, History, and Dialectic: the Philosophy of R. G. Collingwood* (Bloomington, Ind., and London, 1969), pp. 73–8. Despite some disagreements, which will appear in the sequel, my debt to Mink's work is large.

Philosophy proper, as expounded in *Speculum Mentis*, is philosophy that is true to the tradition of Hegelian idealism. By the 1930s, Collingwood came to resent the label 'idealist', perhaps because a reviewer described *Speculum Mentis* as 'the usual idealistic nonsense'; and in his *Autobiography* he even denied that *Speculum Mentis* was 'idealistic' (*A*, 56). Now that virtually all Collingwood's early writings are accessible, it is discreditable that recent commentators should repeat this fantasy. In his papers 'Croce's Philosophy of History,'[1] and 'Can the New Idealism Dispense with Mysticism?',[2] Collingwood wrote as a professed idealist; and in *Speculum Mentis* itself, while it is true that he confessed that 'the foundations laid by the great German idealists' were unsound (*SM*, 286), he put it down to their failure to be idealist enough, 'to live up to the example of Descartes and see the objective fact as the inseparable correlative of the subject's thought' (*SM*, 287). Although he unsparingly criticized his German, British, and even his Italian idealist predecessors, far from objecting to their idealism, or proposing a new philosophy that should be neither idealist nor realist, he called instead for an idealism purged of every vestige of realism (*SM*, 288).

Just as logical positivism is grasped most clearly as the rejection of metaphysics as the logical positivists understood it, so the idealism of *Speculum Mentis* is best approached through its negation—realism as Collingwood understood it. Admirers of *Speculum Mentis* have been curiously reluctant even to review what Collingwood said in it about realism. First, he distinguished between the genus realism, and its species. Generically, realism is 'identical with dogmatism or error in general' (*SM*, 281); and dogmatism or error in general is abstract thinking (*SM*, 252): 'knowledge polarizes itself into abstract or erroneous and concrete or true' (*SM*, 313). Collingwood characterized abstraction in general most fully when analysing the different relations of religion and science to 'abstractions'.

---

[1] *Hibbert Journal*, xix (1921), 263–78; reprinted W. Debbins (ed.), R. G. Collingwood, *Essays in the Philosophy of History* (Austin, Tex., 1965).

[2] *Aristotelian Society*, Supp. Vol., iii (1923), 161–75; reprinted in L. Rubinoff (ed.) *Faith and Reason, Essays in the Philosophy of Religion by R. G. Collingwood* (Chicago, 1968).

To abstract is to consider separately things that are inseparable; to think of the universal, for instance, without reflecting that it is merely the universal of its particulars, and to assume one can isolate it in thought and study it in this isolation. This assumption is an error. One cannot abstract without falsifying. To think apart of things that are together is to think of them as they are not, and to plead that this initial severance makes no difference to their inner nature is only to erect falsification into a principle (*SM*, 160).

'To think apart of things that are together': that is the generic essence of realism, or of dogmatism.[1] Its specific forms are differentiated by the different 'things that are together' one can consider separately: 'there are as many types of dogmatism as there are types of abstraction' (*SM*, 254).

In *Speculum Mentis*, as we have seen, four species of realism or dogmatism are identified and attacked, each one corresponding to one of the lower forms of experience, which, 'by a single, blind, abstract act of will' it declares to be identical with experience itself (*SM*, 259). They are as follows:

(1) *Aesthetic Philosophy*, or 'the abstract assertion of immediacy, the denial of thought' (*SM*, 262–3). By abstracting the immediacy of thought from its character as affirmation, the aesthetic philosopher 'reduces all problems to terms of imagination or intuition' (*SM*, 262). Obviously, this is inconsistent: it affirms that there are no affirmations.

(2) *Religious Philosophy*. This may take the form either of theism

---

[1] Neither the plain meaning of the passage quoted, nor its importance, has been recognized by some commentators. Mink, for example, has expressed the opinion that all Collingwood meant by 'the error of "abstraction"' is the 'failure of [each of the lower forms of experience] to recognize the extent to which it has determined what it supposes itself to have found' (*Mind, History, and Dialectic*, p. 47). Such failure is only one of the specific forms which, in Collingwood's view, the generic error of abstraction may take. Overlooking this, Mink went on to declare that in *Speculum Mentis* ' "abstraction" has a quite different sense' from what it does in *The New Leviathan* (op. cit., 264, note 'Abstraction'). However, Mink himself holds that in *The New Leviathan*, 'abstraction' means 'the activity of selective *attention*, which divides or separates features within the objective field of *consciousness* at any level' (ibid.); and that is no more than a technical rendering of the formulation in *Speculum Mentis*, 'thinking apart of things that are together'.

or of atheism. Theism is the affirmation of the existence of the object of the religious consciousness, that object being conceived abstractly, as distinguished both from other objects, e.g., as mind opposed to matter (*SM*, 266), and from the religious consciousness itself (*SM*, 268). Atheism, the denial that the abstract object affirmed by theism exists at all, is plainly committed to the intelligibility of the same abstractions. The 'poverty and squalor of both disputants' can be overcome only by critically investigating the nature of the religious consciousness, and destroying the abstractness of its object by discovering that it is only metaphorical (*SM*, 270).

(3) *Scientific Philosophy*. With this species, the abstractness of realism becomes explicit; for it is the affirmation that the true account of reality must be abstract, that is, must be 'in terms of abstract concepts' (*SM*, 271). 'The essence of this dogmatism', Collingwood declared, 'is to regard generalizing, abstracting, as synonymous with knowing, which implies the conception of the ultimate reality as an abstract reality' (*SM*, 279); and he objected that at least one reality is not abstract, namely, the scientist's own thinking (*SM*, 273, 277–8).

(4) *Historical Philosophy*, or 'modern realism'. This, the highest form of realism, recognizes that what is real is not the abstract concept, but something concrete, which it disastrously identifies with the facts of history or of perception (*SM*, 282). Such facts cannot be concrete; for they are conceived in abstraction from, and so as independent of, the knower who knows them (*SM*, 282–3). Modern realism is therefore 'a confused running to and fro, between two principles, the abstract concept and the concrete fact' (*SM*, 285). It can only be overcome by an idealism more radical than Hegel's, in which no intimation is tolerated that mind may be external to its objects. Mind's object is—itself (*SM*, 286–7, 292–5).

In the lower forms of experience, so far as we are conscious of them, our mind carries out one abstract operation or another on objects other than itself. The different species of realism or dogmatism are affirmations that some one of these lower forms of experience is what experience essentially is. The truth, which can be grasped only by the most thoroughgoing idealism, is that experience is mind concretely thinking itself.

And what is that? In *Speculum Mentis*, Collingwood in the end has nothing to offer beyond the *via negativa* of his comprehensive denunciation of realism. Concrete or true knowledge is *not* knowledge of something other than the external worlds of art, religion, science, and history: rather, 'the construction of external worlds . . . is the only way by which the mind can possibly come to that self-knowledge which is its end' (*SM*, 315). This is because 'concrete knowledge . . . is abstract knowledge freed from its own abstractness by simply recognizing that abstractness' (*SM*, 315). Collingwood illustrated what he meant by the figure of a mirror: in the four lower forms of experience the mind appears to be confronted with an external reality, but that apparent external reality is its own mirror-image (*SM*, 316).

The decisive objection to this scheme is so obvious that we need not dwell upon it. Was Collingwood's description of modern realism as 'a confused running to and fro, between two principles, the abstract concept and the concrete fact' an unconscious reflection of it, only slightly distorted? In *Speculum Mentis* he repeatedly asserted, as fundamental truths, both that the mind cannot know itself except by abstraction, and that, since to abstract is to falsify, the mind must free itself from the abstractness of the external worlds it constructs by 'recognizing their abstractness' and hence their falsity. That this to and fro process of 'the creation and destruction of external worlds' might be taken for 'a mere futile weaving and unweaving of Penelope's web, a declaration of the mind's inability to produce solid assets, and thus the bankruptcy of philosophy', Collingwood was too acute to overlook (*SM*, 316); but his argument against so taking it, that mind's self-knowledge is not an accumulation of information, but a developed power to solve new problems (*SM*, 316-7), is empty. On his own showing, the only problems mind has to solve either fall within the lower forms of experience, in which case their solutions are abstract, and augment our store of abstract information; or else they are philosophical, and are solved by identifying and rejecting one specific form of abstraction or another. We must remember that to reject an abstraction is not to deny a proposition and so affirm its contradictory, but to repudiate as illegitimate the concepts employed in both. So, when we reject the abstraction of religious philosophy, we repudiate both theism and atheism. A philosopher who can claim no more than a practised skill in unmasking hidden abstractions has no more to show, in the way of solid assets, than a theologian whose sole boast is that he can smell out any heresy, however plausible, provided only that its contradictory be a heresy too.

Corruptio in principiis est pessima. The flaw in *Speculum Mentis* is in its foundation, the anti-realist principle that to abstract is to falsify, that to think apart of things that are together is to think of them as they are not. Of Homer's prayer that strife might perish from among gods and men, Herakleitos acidly observed that Homer did not see that he was praying for the destruction of the universe; for without strife, all things would pass away. A similar verdict must be passed on the idealist aspiration to overcome abstraction: the idealists have not seen that they are calling for the destruction of all thought whatever; for without abstraction, there can be no thought.

The implicit argument in *Speculum Mentis* for its anti-realist principle (cf. *SM*, 160) is a sophism. When I say, 'That cat's head is too small for its body', I 'consider separately' or 'think apart', its head and its body. To infer, as Collingwood did, that in so doing I 'think of them as they are not', or that I carry out an 'initial severance' upon them, may be an agreeable pleasantry, but it is not a serious argument. Considering things separately is not the same as considering them to be separate or even separable; nor is thinking apart of things that are together the same as thinking that they are apart. Collingwood did not acknowledge this in print until his last book, *The New Leviathan*, and then he did not mention that the doctrine denounced as Bradley's and Bergson's had also been his own.

To fancy [he wrote] that when thought begins making abstractions it condemns itself to live in a world of abstractions and turns its back on reality is as foolish as to fancy that an unborn child, when it begins building itself a skeleton, turns its back on flesh and blood . . . [T]he

life of thought is a symbiosis of immediate experience with abstractions
. . . It is a further development of the same foolish fancy when people
obsessed with this fancy (like F. H. Bradley . . . and H. Bergson . . .)
look forward to a divine event whereby thought shall not only return
to the womb but there digest its own skeleton (*NL*, 7.64–.66).

The process by which Collingwood renounced the anti-abstraction
principle underlying his theory of concrete thinking in *Speculum
Mentis* is one of the two keys to understanding how his conception
of philosophical method developed.

The first intimations of doubt appeared in *Speculum Mentis*
itself. The idealist conception of philosophy expounded in it
cannot even be stated without employing abstract concepts like
abstract and *concrete* (cf. *SM*, 315). Nor was Collingwood blind to
the abstractness of his catalogue of realist errors.

[A]n exhaustive table of errors [he confessed] . . . would be a system of
pigeon-holes in which we could without more ado arrange all philosophies except our own, and so excuse ourselves from any further
criticism of them: 'So-and-so is a scientific dogmatist: fundamental
error, abstraction of universal from particular: necessary consequences,
this and that': nothing more need be said. So-and-so's philosophy is
thus disposed of because it is a mere instance of a type, not an individual
but an abstract particular (*SM*, 288).

As a description of his own table of errors, this is exact. But
Collingwood did not put his finger on where his table went wrong.
It was not in disposing of so-and-so's philosophy as an instance of
a type; for pointing out an error in an individual philosophy
necessarily and inevitably classifies it as belonging to the type of
philosophy that makes that error. You cannot identify errors
except by abstraction. Collingwood's table is wrong because it
refutes itself: tables of error are necessarily abstract, but his is a
table of the supposed error of making abstractions.

Collingwood was slow to expose the fundamental mistake of
Speculum Mentis—its anti-abstraction principle—in its full universality (or abstraction). In the *Essay on Philosophical Method* he
retracted his reprobation of 'realistic or dogmatic' philosophies as
absolutely false, and acknowledged them as constituting a scale of
forms. For ethics, as Mink has pointed out, he worked out some

of the consequences of this, abandoning the 'absolute ethics' of *Speculum Mentis*, and adopting much of the realist W. D. Ross's teaching about the forms of goodness (*EPM*, 70–91).[1] In metaphysics, however, he seems to have moved (whether forwards or backwards we need not decide) from the negativism of *Speculum Mentis* to a conventional absolutism. Accepting that tradition is right in treating the object of philosophical inquiry from three points of view, as *unum* (in metaphysics), *verum* (in logic), and *bonum* (in ethics), he considered the task of metaphysics (which he also described as 'a special study of the existential aspect of that same subject matter whose aspect as truth is studied by logic and its aspect as goodness by ethics'—*EPM*, 127) to be to think out 'the idea of an object that shall completely satisfy the demands of reason'[2] (*EPM*, 125; cf. 33). Of such an object, St. Anselm's ontological proof, properly understood, holds good (*EPM*, 125). Although Collingwood is sometimes said to have meant no more than that, in reflecting on his own thinking, a thinker cannot rationally doubt that his thinking exists; in other words, to have vindicated the ontological proof by reducing it to a Cartesian *Cogito*; his text makes nonsense of such reductions. What the ontological proof proves, he wrote, is 'that essence involves existence, not always, but in one special case, the case of God in the metaphysical sense: the *Deus sive Natura* of Spinoza, the Good of Plato, the Being of Aristotle: the object of metaphysical thought' (*EPM*, 127). If the various metaphysical systems that have appeared in the history of thought are forms on a scale of attempts to think out the idea of an object that shall fully satisfy the demands of reason, it can hardly be in doubt that Collingwood placed the systems of Hegel and his successors near the summit of that scale.

[1] *Mind, History, and Dialectic*, pp. 55, 70–3.
[2] Cf. F. H. Bradley, *Appearance and Reality* (2nd. edn., corr., Oxford, 1930), pp. 506–7: 'In this attempt to attribute diversity and avoid contradiction what in the end would satisfy the intellect supposing that it could be got? This question, I think, is too often ignored. Too often a writer will criticize and condemn some view as being that which the mind cannot accept, when he apparently has never asked himself what it is that would satisfy the intellect, or even whether the intellect could endure its own implied alternative. What in the end, then, let us ask, would content the intellect?'

Partly for this reason, Sir Malcolm Knox considered the *Essay on Philosophical Method* to represent the zenith of Collingwood's metaphysical achievement.[1] In Collingwood's work as a whole, it was transitional. In *The Principles of Art*, which was written in 1937, Collingwood for the first time explicitly acknowledged that thought or intellection, unlike sensation and imagination,[2] is analytic and abstract (*PA*, 252–4, cf. 158–9). If his analyses in *The Principles of Art* of sensation, imagination, and thought are true, then non-abstract or 'concrete' thinking is impossible. It is not, therefore, surprising that when he wrote about metaphysics in his next two books, the *Autobiography* and the *Essay on Metaphysics*, he jettisoned the implicit idealist absolutism of the *Essay of Philosophical Method*. What in the earlier book he had referred to as '. . . the Being of Aristotle: the object of metaphysical thought' (*EPM*, 127), he ridiculed in the *Essay on Metaphysics* as 'a subject-matter entirely devoid of peculiarities; a subject-matter, therefore, containing nothing to differentiate it from anything else, or from nothing at all' (*EM*, 14). And he explained that this was because the pure Being of Aristotle was what he had denied it to be in the *Essay on Philosophical Method*, a 'universal' representing 'the limiting case of the abstractive process' (*EM*, 14). Why did Collingwood, after denying in the *Essay on Philosophical Method* that the highest term in the classification of beings is 'the most abstract of all abstractions; simple abstract being', and endorsing the concept of it as overlapping or transcending or diffusing itself across the divisions of the categories (*EPM*, 33), take for granted in the *Essay on Metaphysics* that it could only be simple abstract being? I know of only one answer: that he believed what he had written in the earlier book to presuppose that there could be a non-abstract idea of pure Being; and that he had come to reject that presupposition.

If Collingwood's disillusionment with the anti-abstraction principle of *Speculum Mentis* is one key to understanding his mature

---

[1] In his editorial preface to R. G. Collingwood, *The Idea of History* (Oxford, 1946), xvi, xx.

[2] In *NL* his predominant view is that, except for first-order consciousness, imagination too involves abstraction. See my *The Later Philosophy of R. G. Collingwood* (Oxford, 1962), pp. 47–56.

philosophical method—and also, incidentally, to the almost complete freedom of his later writings from idealist jargon: 'identity in difference', 'concrete universal', and so forth—a second key is a conviction which underlies *Speculum Mentis*, and which he never doubted in his life: that the whole mind is active in each and every form of human experience. *Speculum Mentis* is not merely sceptical about the four lower forms of experience, it roundly affirms that they are all forms of error. Although this doctrine is not formally inconsistent with the principle of the unity of the mind, their conjunction gives rise to serious difficulties. Why should the mind, by whose own standards (especially the anti-abstraction principle) the lower forms of experience are condemned, nevertheless persist in them? The answer, 'Because only so can it create the reflections by which it knows itself', does no more than raise a more difficult question, 'Why must every reflection by which the mind knows itself be false?' The answer to that, 'Reflections are false because they are reflections', raises the most intractable difficulty of all, that there must be something radically wrong with the mind if it sets itself a task (to know itself by creating reflections of itself) which by its very nature cannot be performed (because reflections as such are false). If that is what mind is, then it is contemptible.

Whether or not he followed out this line of thought, Collingwood abandoned the view that the lower forms of consciousness are necessarily erroneous even before he renounced the anti-abstraction principle. In *The Idea of Nature*, the body of which he wrote immediately after completing the *Essay on Philosophical Method*, and in the lectures written in 1936, which form the bulk of *The Idea of History*, he throughout treated natural science and history as self-critical inquiries in which truth is attainable and sometimes attained. Along with *The Principles of Art* these two books are the most read of all Collingwood's writings, and his reputation with the educated public rests chiefly on them. They provide an example of partial immunity to what he himself had diagnosed as the disease of modern life; a divided mind and culture. In them, while thoroughly revising his analyses in *Speculum Mentis* of art, natural science, and history, he not only confirmed his earlier conclusion that each is a distinct and autonomous activity, but also demonstrated that none of them can be seriously or effectively pursued without the others: none, in short, can claim to be a complete way of life. An artist with no tincture of natural science is impoverished not merely as a man but as an artist; and a natural scientist with no tincture of art is impoverished as a scientist. Nor can one responsibly engage in art, science, or history, without doing what Collingwood called 'second-degree' thinking about the nature of aesthetic, scientific, and historiographical experience (*IH*, 1–3). Since such second-degree thinking is philosophical, serious work in art, science, and history must have a philosophical side.

Certain of the themes in the *Essay on Philosophical Method* are illustrated in Collingwood's later writings on art, natural science, and history. As species of experience, although distinct, they overlap one another; and they even constitute a scale of forms; art being the non-theoretical foundation of all intellectual activity, natural science and history being thought of the first degree, and philosophy thought of the second degree, with history and philosophy overlapping one another in an especially complicated way. This scheme is further modified and refined in *The New Leviathan*. Yet the patterns of philosophical thought laid down in the *Essay on Philosophical Method* do not obtrude in Collingwood's later writings; they are, for example, irrelevant to his theory of historical explanation, and to his analysis of expression in art.

One principle of method, which in the *Essay on Philosophical Method* Collingwood treated as peculiar to philosophy, is that philosophy has no data, and recognizes no unquestionable foundations. The direction of reasoning in philosophical inquiry is always reversible: it must indeed make assumptions, and reason from them; but it not only can but must turn back and investigate those assumptions in the light of what follows from them. This principle, however, is now generally recognized to apply to all branches of inquiry: to mathematics, natural science, and history, equally with philosophy.

Yet Collingwood's mature philosophical method, if I am right about it, was seriously incomplete. His abandonment of the anti-abstraction principle left him with no coherent method of inquiry in what he himself recognized as the traditional core of philosophy: metaphysics, logic, and ethics. The *Essay on Philosophical Method* is a prolegomenon to an unwritten idealist investigation of all three. In ethics, it draws heavily on the Kantian tradition that has provided the foundation for much of the best recent work. In logic, it is jejune: Collingwood did not recognize what mattered in the logical work of his contemporaries. In metaphysics, it outlines an idealist programme, which he could not carry out when he concluded that the idealist Absolute was a chimaera. Except for meditating an historicist 'reform of metaphysics', which, as I have argued elsewhere, is incoherent in itself, and which, except in name, is absent from *The New Leviathan*,[1] he was at a loss for an alternative. The failure of absolute idealism indeed points in a direction that is now being followed: to return to the problems left unresolved by Kant, the Hegelian 'solutions' of which proved disastrous; but Collingwood did not himself follow it.

The collapse of Collingwood's programme for metaphysics left him without a philosophy of religion. Since he seems never to have doubted that religion was necessary to a full human life, or that Christianity was the only religion with which what he called 'the modern European mind' could be content, it follows that his philosophy is, on its own terms, incomplete even as a second degree inquiry into all forms of first degree experience.

There is, I believe, a deeper reason for Collingwood's failure in his study of religion than any particular philosophical error, however radical. Although Christianity was the only religion he studied at all closely, throughout his philosophical accounts of it, from *Religion and Philosophy* to *Speculum Mentis*, from *Speculum Mentis* to *Faith and Reason*, and from *Faith and Reason* to the *Essay on Metaphysics* and *The New Leviathan*, one thing remained constant: he could not accept it on his own terms. This is what he found to say, in *Speculum Mentis*, about the Christian 'drama of the fall and redemption of man':

In the beginning, by an absolute act which was not itself subject to any determination of time or space, God created the heavens and the earth

[1] See my *The Later Philosophy of R. G. Collingwood*, pp. 262–84.

... But the world is no mere toy shaped by God ... His spirit moves upon the face of the waters ... and ... becomes the soul of life in the man whom he creates in his own image ... Now man, by his misguided thirst for knowledge, partakes of that knowledge which is forbidden, namely error, or the human wisdom which negates God's wisdom ... His error is implicit just because it is complete. It can only become explicit if God reveals himself afresh ... This, in the fullness of time, is granted ... Now in this imagery there is one flaw, namely the transcendence of God ... But this is exactly where the truth of our religious imagery shines most brilliantly. It is God who accepts the burden of error, takes upon himself the moral responsibility for the fall, and so redeems not his creature but himself (*SM*, 302–3).

Consider now what any ordinary Christian believes that Christian redemption is redemption from. John Bunyan depicted it allegorically as follows:

I dreamed, and behold *I saw a Man cloathed with Rags, standing in a certain place, with his Face from his own House, a Book in his hand, and a great Burden upon his Back,* I looked, and saw him open the Book, and read therein, and as he read he wept and trembled, and not being able longer to contain, he brake out with a lamentable cry, saying, *What shall I do?*[1]

I submit that to interpret this passage in terms of Collingwood's notions about the fall and redemption of man would be less blasphemous than laughable.

If Christianity is, as Collingwood thought, the only religion which satisfies the modern European mind, then religion cannot be reduced to imagery the real meaning of which is some metaphysical truth that can, without residue, be stated and defended philosophically. Natural theology may be possible, but it cannot be enough. For a philosopher who accepts Christianity, metaphysics must be, in matters of divine revelation, *ancilla theologiae;* it cannot be wholly autonomous. Collingwood's lifelong attempt to expound the Christian faith in terms of a metaphysics one principle of which was its own autonomy was ultimately inconsistent.

---

[1] John Bunyan, *Grace Abounding and The Pilgrims Progress*, ed. John Brown (Cambridge, 1907), p. 142.

II

PHILOSOPHY OF MIND:
AN APPRAISAL OF COLLINGWOOD'S
THEORIES OF CONSCIOUSNESS,
LANGUAGE, AND IMAGINATION

W. VON LEYDEN

AN APPRAISAL of Collingwood's philosophy of mind must begin with his attitude towards psychology. One reason for this is his view that the proper object of consciousness in its simplest form is feeling, and that the proper study of feeling is psychology. Secondly, as a result of his preoccupation with the various lower- and higher-order acts of consciousness, he was led to include in his philosophy of mind accounts of the 'unconscious' and what he called the 'preconscious'. Finally, though he maintained that psychology lacked the normative, 'criteriological' function of a science of thought, he valued it as the revelation of important facts about consciousness,[1] and was clearly intrigued by the pronouncements of Freud and other practising psychologists. One might say that the tragedy of his last years of ill health, which eventually reduced him to the helplessness of an infant, was redeemed by the use he made of this experience both as a philosopher of mind and a student of psychology. He could now, while completing *The New Leviathan*, check from his own predicament his views on body and mind, the 'chaos of consciousness'[2] and the birth of language.[3]

---

[1] For the distinction see *PA*, 171, n.

[2] For the phrase see *NL*, 8.47–.48; 7.69.

[3] This, I think, is the import of one of the letters he wrote to me after he had resigned from his Oxford Chair. The letter is dated 31 May 1941: '... There is much that I should like to talk to you about, but I cannot write except in a scrawl barely legible to myself and not at all to anyone else; and this machine, which I am trying to use instead of a pen, is a tedious thing and difficult to keep under

That psychology should have an impact on philosophy should surprise no one, not even a contemporary philosopher. It is embedded in the work of Russell, Wittgenstein, and Wisdom no less than that of Price and Ryle. *The Concept of Mind* concludes with a chapter entitled 'Psychology', in which Ryle explains that his book could properly be described as an essay in philosophical psychology, and where he refers to Freud as 'psychology's one man of genius'. As will appear later on in my discussion, there are a number of parallels as well as contrasts between Collingwood's and Ryle's philosophies of mind. In order to prepare the way for an assessment of these, Collingwood's views on feeling and the unconscious should first be investigated.

Man's mind, on Collingwood's view,[1] is made of thought, theoretical and practical. There are two things, he considers, which belong to mind—consciousness and feeling. Consciousness belongs to it as a *constituent*, i.e. in the way in which a man belongs to a family or a page to a book. Feeling[2] belongs to mind as an *apanage*, i.e. in the way in which an estate belongs to a family or a card in the library catalogue to a book. Of course, in one sense of the word 'body', feelings are 'bodily', and as such are described by doctors, physicists, or neuro-physiologists. Body in this sense is the object of a story concerning man with which Collingwood, though he considers it an all-important story, is not concerned as a philosopher. Instead he looks upon body in another sense—the sense in which body has to do with pleasures, feelings, sensations,

---

control. I should like to ask you to come and see me here; it is not very far from Oxford; but then I can't talk except a little and stumblingly, like a man using a language to which he is strange'.

'All this is explanation, not complaint. I lead an interesting, sufficiently active, and on the whole happy life. The work I watch myself doing day by day to restore the adjustment of mind and body is I can't tell you how interesting, though mostly "unconscious": I congratulate myself that I have trained myself, all my life, to "keep on good terms with my own unconscious" as a psychologist once put it to me . . ..'

[1] I refer here to a number of views expounded by Collingwood in *NL*, chs. I and III–V, without giving detailed references for each.

[2] For the fact that both 'feeling' and 'sensation' are words used in more than one sense see *PA*, 160–4, 172–3. Cf. Ryle's *The Concept of Mind* (London, 1949), pp. 199–203, 210 f., 240–4.

and emotions as studied by anyone who reflects upon the contents of consciousness in its simplest form. Thus there is a psychological or mental sense of 'body' as opposed to the medical or physical sense. Since Collingwood was no believer in any of the traditional mind–body theories, according to which body and mind are two *different* (either interacting or correlated) *parts* of man, but instead considered the two as one and the same thing, the whole of man, as known in two different ways,[1] the use of the word 'body' with which he is concerned belongs to the study of man as undertaken by the sciences of mind. The adjustment of body and mind, particularly at the low level to which he had sunk when writing the letter quoted previously, thus turns out to be 'indirect' (*NL*, 2.4–.49); it consists of the relation between two descriptions of a man in terms of the two senses of 'bodily' explained above.

Another terminological point which should be clarified is Collingwood's definition of feeling as belonging to mind as its *apanage*. This word is in one sense misleading. What is characteristic of feeling is that it is the proper object of consciousness in its simplest form, and that in this capacity it is as basic and necessary as a lower-order action is a necessary condition (or presupposition, in both Ryle's and Collingwood's terminology)[2] of a higher-order action. In one passage (*NL*, 5.1 and 5.11; see also 4.85 and 4.86) Collingwood himself refers to an apanage as a foundation, explaining that thought and knowledge rest on a 'bodily' foundation in the psychological sense of the word. Elsewhere (*NL*, 5.19) he speaks of feeling as 'an *indispensable* apanage'.[3] And in the important 'Retrospect'[4] of Part I of *The New Leviathan* he states that A, i.e. first-order consciousness correlated with feeling, is logically prior to B, i.e. second-order consciousness correlated with appetite, and so on, the implication being that A is a necessary but not a sufficient condition of B. Restated in the form of his

[1] The view was rightly hailed as a 'great philosophical advance' by Ryle, in his Inaugural Lecture *Philosophical Arguments* (Oxford, 1945), p. 4.

[2] *Concept of Mind*, ch. VI, sect. 6; *NL*, 9.43 and 9.47.

[3] My italics.

[4] Ch. IX. This chapter divides Collingwood's preceding inquiry into mind proper (or 'what mind does', not 'what mind is', 9.16) from his subsequent discussion of the passions of the mind and morality.

'Law of Contingency' (*NL*, 9.48), the implication is that the earlier terms in a series of mental functions do not determine the later, even though some of the primitive elements may *survive*[1] in forms of higher-order consciousness such as desire, choice, or utility. To call feeling an apanage of mind is of course acceptable, if all that is meant is that it *happens* to consciousness at a particular level of its development. But then, since a feeling and the consciousness of it cannot really be separated, feeling itself may be regarded as the basis of mind.

In connection with his doctrine of feeling Collingwood holds a number of further views. Though these may have lost some of their significance in the eyes of contemporary philosophers, I propose nevertheless to deal with the more relevant of them. In the first place he argues that one cannot determine whether feeling is active or passive (*NL*, 5.4–42). Between these alternatives feeling, as Plato put it,[2] 'wanders about'. To argue, as Locke did,[3] that feelings and sensations are passive because they are 'caused in the mind' by the operation of 'external causes', is to substitute physical or physiological inquiries for the relevant psychological or philosophical ones. The substitution is tantamount to what Collingwood calls the 'Fallacy of Swapping Horses' (*NL*, 2.71)— his name for a category-mistake—which he rightly intimates Locke himself recognized and repudiated, when he proposed not to 'meddle with the physical consideration of the mind . . .'.[4] Another point Collingwood raises is the 'Fallacy of Misplaced Argument' (*NL*, 4.71–.75; 5.43–.49). This consists in arguing about a feeling immediately given,[5] rather than appealing to the

---

[1] For the 'Law of Primitive Survivals' see 9.5 and 9.51. The survival of any given primitive feeling in a higher-order consciousness is made particularly easy by what Collingwood refers to as the 'tenacity' of feeling (*NL*, 5.17).

[2] *Republic*, 479 E.

[3] *Essay*, Bk. II, ch. viii.

[4] *Essay*, Introduction, sect. 2.

[5] For the 'immediately given' see *NL*, 4.22. Wittgenstein's well-known opposition to the doctrine of immediacy expressed itself in his contention that the elements of experience get their significance not from any self-intimating, self-sufficient nature of their own, but from their setting in a general pattern of actions and events—a form of life (*Philosophical Investigations* (Oxford, 1953), Pt. I, para. 583; Pt. II, p. 226).

way in which it presents itself to the person experiencing it. It follows that such questions as whether a feeling (a) is or is not active, (b) arises within or from without, or (c) is or is not what it appears to be, are questions that do not arise at this level of consciousness.

A further argument is that feeling is a 'field', a 'confused mass' (NL, 5.6 and 5.61; 7.24). What is articulated within it is that it is a here-and-now with a focal region and a penumbral region (NL, 4.44–.45), but as yet without edges either around the field or between its two regions. Edges occur only with an act of selective attention (NL, 4.33; 4.5; 5.63; 7.3–.32), which introduces lines of demarcation within the field, singling out the focal region as, say, 'this red patch' and ignoring or 'repressing' (NL, 4.51–.52; 7.3) the background. The distinction between what is 'circumscribed' and what is left 'blunt' or 'diffuse' is *made*, at the second stage of mental life, by a second-order act of consciousness, whereas what is *given* (NL, 4.52–.53; 7.31) at the first stage is the original consciousness of the here-and-now of feeling. While the second stage is possible for a mind but not necessary (NL, 7.28–.29), the first is necessary, though it may not always be possible to penetrate to it. However, just as an experienced painter learns to 'recover the innocence of the eye' (NL, 4.55), so should a skilled psychologist or philosopher be able to re-establish this primitive and basic stage.[1] Colour-patches, Collingwood maintains, are often described as though they were themselves *'given* in sensation and not (as they really are) *made* by selective attention' (NL, 7.31).[2] In his opinion, anyone describing them in this way has not penetrated further than the level at which colour-patches are *found* ready-made. There is the deeper level, at which the work of making them is done, and there is the basic level, with which we have been

[1] As Virginia Woolf points out, novelists such as Joyce, and presumably herself, convey this 'uncircumscribed spirit', 'life itself' ('Modern Fiction', in *The Common Reader* (London, 1925; Harmondsworth, Pelican Books, 1938), pp. 149–50). She also remarks (p. 151) that the modern novelist finds relevant material in the 'dark places of psychology'. Impressions for her are 'evanescent'— the expression Collingwood uses in describing feeling, which includes sensation (NL, 5.5).

[2] My italics.

concerned hitherto, at which the work of selective attention has not yet begun.

As part of his views on feeling as a here-and-now Collingwood also maintains that at this primitive, merely psychical,[1] level of experience a feeling exists when it is felt, and that there is in fact an interpenetration of the activity of feeling and the thing felt, of sensation and sensum. Therefore at this level a person's immediate experience is too close to him to become knowledge (NL, 4.29–.4). Conversely, knowing a sensuous-emotional experience is not part of the experience itself. It is only if the original experience is attended to that the 'block' (PA, 204) of feeling or sentience is split in two—not only into what is selected and what is ignored but also into sensation and its sensum, with the added qualification that at this level feeling or sentience has changed its character of feltness and immediacy and has become 'known' sentience or feeling. While this second-order consciousness can tell what a given feeling is, e.g. whether the noise I hear is in my head or made by something outside me (NL, 4.33), mere feeling cannot arrive at this distinction by itself (NL, 4.4; 9.41).

Next Collingwood asks 'are there objects of feeling or sensation?' and after prolonged discussion (NL, 5.2–.39) decides, with the help of Ockham's Razor, that there are not. He finds it preferable to say that the grammar of the sentence 'I see a blue colour' is like the grammar of 'I feel a transient melancholy' or 'I go a fast walk', than to say that it is like the grammar of 'I kick a bad dog'. I regard it as by no means out of place to recall Ryle's view here that, while observations have objects, viz. things or episodes, sensations have not.[2] One of Ryle's reasons for the distinction is that 'I had a twinge' does not assert a cognitive or any other relation to an object, as 'I had a hat' does. Another is that one can make mistakes of observation, but that it is meaningless to talk of correct

---

[1] For the expresion see PA, 164, 203–4, 228 ff., and 234 ff.

[2] Concept of Mind, ch. VII. By sensation Ryle means both the sophisticated sense of the word, according to which perceiving trumpets or trees involves having auditory or visual sensations, and the unsophisticated sense, according to which sensing or feeling is itself a species of perceptions, viz. tactual, kinaesthetic, or temperature perceptions, as well as pains and discomforts (op. cit., pp. 200, 240 ff.).

or incorrect, veridical or non-veridical sensations. Hand in hand with Ryle's assertion that sensations are neither proper objects of observation nor themselves observings of objects goes his denial that there is an antithesis of 'inside' to 'outside' applying to sensations. I mention these parallels between Ryle's and Collingwood's terminology for what they are worth, at the same time suggesting that they indicate at least a minimum measure of affinity between their two doctrines.

Since one of Collingwood's conclusions about feeling is that it exists when it is felt or when it is present to consciousness in its simplest form, it might appear surprising that he should raise the question *whether feelings can be unconscious?* (*NL*, 5.8)[1]. However, this question occurs at the end of his list of ambiguities concerning feeling; hence the answer obviously depends on certain qualifications. In the sense explained so far, the expression 'unconscious feeling' is meaningless. So is the claim that a man may *know* that he has feelings of which he is unconscious. And if *he* cannot know, no one else can. None the less, psychologists maintain that some feelings are unconscious, and since on Collingwood's premisses psychologists are experts in the study of feeling, they ought to know. The dilemma is resolved in the following way (see *NL*, 5.8–.94; 6.23; 6.28; 7.24).

Collingwood rejects as nonsensical the way in which traditional psychologists have talked of people *feeling* something, of which they are at the same time unaware. Instead he accepts two senses of the word 'unconscious' as defined by Freud—the descriptive and the dynamic. Unconscious in the descriptive sense is what, though latent, may become conscious. For example, a man may be cold or want something, before he first notices the cold or his want: he might then be cold 'preconsciously' or have a 'preconscious' appetite.[2] Collingwood accepts this terminology, because it falls in with his view of mind as constituted by different forms or orders of consciousness, anyone of which may be referred to as preconscious in relation to a higher-order consciousness. The reason, I

---

[1] 'Unconscious' is always used here passively, i.e. that of which something else is not conscious.

[2] For a man's preconscious or latent appetite and will see *NL*, 11.18 and 13.63.

suppose, why the preconscious is referred to as the 'descriptive' meaning of the word 'unconscious' is that it represents a process which we assume to be active *at a certain time*, although at that time it is latent and thus without a descriptive content.[1] The dynamic sense of 'unconscious', for both Freud and Collingwood, is the opposite of the process of selective attention at the level of second-order consciousness, i.e. a withdrawal of attention leading to the repression and disowning of an experience, and hence to what Collingwood calls a 'corrupt consciousness' (*PA*, 216–21, 224, 282–5). One point should be noted in connection with repression. Even if a person were not in some sense conscious of his repressed feelings, they would sooner or later express their *strength* (e.g. in dreams, or a slip of the tongue). The dynamic sense of the term 'unconscious' is derived from this inferred efficacy of certain important regions of the mind upon thoughts and forms of behaviour which cannot be accounted for in terms of explicitly conscious experience.[2]

Now the descriptive (unlike the dynamic) sense of 'unconscious', i.e. the preconscious, is not bound to any particular level of consciousness; in fact, as has been shown, it may describe a condition prior to mere feeling or to first-order consciousness. I mention the point in order to ward off confusion, particularly that which seems to me to occur in Alan Donagan's otherwise excellent book *The Later Philosophy of R. G. Collingwood*.[3] Equating the preconscious with what Collingwood in *The Principles of Art* calls the merely psychical level of experience, or bare feeling, he replaces in several quotations from *The Principles of Art* (*PA*, 230, 236–7)[4] the expression 'psychical' by the word 'preconscious', which occurs nowhere in *The Principles of Art* and in Collingwood's terminology is not equivalent to 'psychical'. The reasons for my contention are as follows: in *The Principles of Art* Collingwood places the 'psychical level' below that of consciousness or thought,

[1] For the terminology see Freud's *New Introductory Lectures on Psycho-Analysis*, transl. by W. J. H. Sprott, 3rd ed. (London, 1946), Lecture XXXI, pp. 94 ff.

[2] See A. C. MacIntyre, *The Unconscious* (London, 1958), ch. II.

[3] (Oxford, 1962), ch. II, sect. 6.

[4] In Donagan, op. cit., pp. 44–6 and *passim*. See also *PA*, 283, lines 2–6, and Donagan, p. 127, lines 17–21.

which is characterized by selective attention. Hence the psychical
level is what *The New Leviathan* calls 'simple consciousness' or
'first-order consciousness', and is below the level of what is called
there 'second-order consciousness'. On the other hand, Collingwood nowhere identifies the preconscious exclusively with any
particular level, and when he speaks of feeling as preconscious
(*NL*, 6.28, 6.38), he regards the level at which it *becomes* conscious
as first-order consciousness or the merely psychical level—'the
first stage of mental life'—where the principle of selective attention
is not as yet operative.[1] Consequently, a preconscious (i.e. unnoticed) condition of feeling *precedes* the psychical level of experience, or bare feeling. It is true of course that the psychical level is a
preconscious condition of experience before it is 'reflected' on by
(second-order) consciousness. However, when Collingwood talks
of it in *The Principles of Art*, he means what he calls 'simple consciousness' in *The New Leviathan*, and he does *not* mean what he
defines there as the preconscious.

The point I am trying to make is important for an understanding
of the arguments advanced in *The New Leviathan* about the 'birth'
of language in preconscious conditions of feeling. In his chapter on
language (ch. 6) Collingwood explains that there is a tendency to
hold that consciousness of a feeling precedes its naming. In his
opinion, anyone holding such a view is putting the cart before the
horse. The correct view, according to him, is that consciousness is
itself a linguistic act, and may indeed be the effect of such an act.
The man who is cold 'preconsciously' will not feel the cold unless
and until he names it, either by saying 'cold' or giving an expressive
shiver (*NL*, 6.23–.28).[2] This doctrine has a far-reaching implication:
thought, knowledge, reason, and mind are all the product of some
linguistic activity. It also follows that the origin of language in its
most primitive form, i.e. before it is learned, lies in an expressive
activity, which might not be always reasonable, and might in fact
be illogical, unorganized, and unplanned (*NL*, 6.58; 7.24). Except

[1] The levels at which feeling becomes conscious, i.e. is first noticed (first-order
consciousness) and then reflected on by the operation of selective attention
(second-order consciousness), are clearly distinguished in *NL*, 4.22–.24, 5.9–.92,
6.28–.36, 7.24, and 7.31.

[2] See also *IH*, Pt. V, 306.

for the second corollary, Collingwood's theory was inspired by Hobbes (*NL*, 6.42–.57) and appears to have been developed independently of Wittgenstein. When it comes to the alleged preconscious source of language itself, his doctrine is largely the product of conjecture, both on his part and that of his commentators. I propose to advance some suggestions of my own here and, in order to avoid ambiguity, make explicit some preliminary distinctions.

One point to be kept in mind is that language need not be speech, and that cries, gesture-language, and changes in the muscular, circulatory, or glandular system are all exemplifications of expressive activities which, according to Collingwood, precede consciousness and thought. A further point is that any of these primitive or automatic forms of expression may occur not only in babies but also in adults. Thirdly, in the case of *speech* itself, one might wish to distinguish its basic status at the adult level from that when one begins to learn one's mother tongue. Finally, speaking of the preconscious origin of language might mean either (1) naming, when one is an adult, a feeling or something one sees or hears, which was unnoticed before being named; or (b) naming for the first time, i.e. when one is a baby, a feeling or something seen or heard, the like of which has never been noticed before. While in the former case the preconscious source of language is that of a *learned* language, in the latter it is that of an as yet *unlearned* language.

Except for the first, Collingwood makes none of these points of difference as explicit as one might wish. In pronouncing Hobbes's doctrine right he does so after reflecting on the normally preconscious act of naming—an 'experiment . . . not easy to make' (*NL*, 6.56). Which level, precisely, is he talking of here, that of an adult, or of a baby, or both? Similarly, when he speaks of the skill of an observer 'reading like an open book the psychical emotions of *every one with whom we have to do*' (*PA*, 230),[1] he does not distinguish the primitive emotions of babies from those involved in adult crowd behaviour. How then can we fathom his views on the birth of language in early infancy? Had he lived, he might have sided with the later Wittgenstein;[2] alternatively, his sympathies

---

[1] My italics.
[2] See for instance *NL*, 6.16; 13.41–.43; *PA*, 1–2.

could have fallen in with Noam Chomsky's more recent views. My reasons for the latter conjecture are that Collingwood did not wholly share Wittgenstein's view of language-learning as a process of becoming conditioned by a given environment to a customary, and chiefly in this sense correct, verbal behaviour. Instead he might have sympathized with Chomsky's assumption that children are born already equipped with an unconscious knowledge of a common 'deep structure' of languages, which is subsequently transformed into the appropriate surface structures of a fully developed surrounding language.[1]

Putting aside conjecture, I will mention a point Collingwood makes about the basic status of *learned* language. He argues that in order to perceive a mountain, knowledge of the word 'mountain' or some similar *general* noun word is indispensable (*NL*, 6.26). The theory he opposes here is that a person is conscious of a mountain in the first place and then recalls that its general name is 'mountain'. He rightly rejects this theory and suggests that it is derived from a false analogy with cases essentially different, such as when an explorer first sees an unrecorded mountain and then decides to give it a particular *proper* name, or wonders what special type of mountain it is, e.g. volcanic or metamorphic. Collingwood's point (if I am right in my interpretation of it) could also be put in this way. Identifying a particular as the same as certain other similar things presupposes seeing it as a certain such-and-such or X, where 'X' is a common noun like 'mountain'. Wittgenstein had probably something similar in mind when he urged that, even if I may be aware of something as *this* and then remember afterwards what it is called (e.g. 'red'), 'this' and 'what' can have meaning only in terms of a description or the correct use of some general words in a given language.[2] 'You cannot, in such cases, get behind language.'[3]

---

[1] Cf. *NL*, 7.24 (especially the phrase '. . . *found* language of some kind . . .'—my italics). See also *PA*, 237, n. 1.

[2] *Philosophical Investigations*, Pt. I, paras. 369–81. The passage can be seen as a reply to the far less radical thesis advanced by Collingwood in *PA*, 212–13. There he holds that the ability to say of what *kind* a thing is, e.g. 'this is a patch of red', succeeds the ability to utter the more primitive phrase '*this* is how I feel'.

[3] Donagan, op. cit., p. 43.

Collingwood appears to have a further affinity with Wittgenstein in his theory of the origin of language at the stage where a person *begins* to learn it. He argues that a child does not learn the words 'fire', 'milk', or 'toe' by its mother pointing to the fire, holding up the milk, or touching its toe. He rejects this *prima facie* plausible theory of ostensive definition on two grounds (*PA*, 227). First the gestures of pointing are themselves in the nature of a language, whose meaning will have to be taught in its turn. In other words, as Wittgenstein was to explain in great detail,[1] no ostensive definition as such contains a clue to what it is to mean in any given case. For example, pointing to the fire might mean 'observe its glow', 'look at its size', 'feel its warmth', or 'guess what is burning'. Collingwood's second reason for rejecting the theory is that gestures of pointing are usually part of a 'flood of talk' and that, in any case, when a mother points to the fire, she probably says 'pretty'; when holding up the milk, she might say 'nice'; and when touching her child's toe, she recites 'this little pig went to market'. What stands out in the flood of talk surrounding the child is its mother's expression of her feelings, to which the child replies with gurglings and cooings before it starts imitating her phrases in garbled form.

The process of a child learning its mother tongue is thus, on Collingwood's view, in the nature of 'tumbling to' the language —a phrase he unfortunately failed to define more fully. In his opinion, a child also begins in the cradle to express more subtle and differentiated emotions, which reveal its growing pride, will-power, and ability to draw attention to its feelings (*PA*, 236). The development from the simple origin to the more sophisticated uses of language is illustrated in Collingwood's example of a mother removing her child's bonnet with the words 'Hatty off!'—a situation soon 'improved' upon by the child taking its own bonnet off and throwing it out of the perambulator with the exclamation 'Hattiaw!', thereby expressing its sense of triumph both over its mother and the symbol of its babyhood (*PA*, 227–8, 239–41). The example illustrates the basis of self-conscious and purposive

[1] Op. cit., Pt. I, paras. 28 ff., 198–201, 454 f.; *The Blue Book*, pp. 1 ff., 33–4.

utterance in contrast to the involuntary cry of pain or hunger at the purely psychical level of experience.

According to Collingwood self-consciousness or second-order consciousness presupposes, in addition to selective attention and a more highly developed ability to use language, one other important factor—imagination. His most detailed discussion of this concept is contained in the central part (Book II) of *The Principles of Art*, where it represents the link between his theories of emotion and aesthetic expression (see *PA*, 151). I will deal with his analysis, one of his more notable contributions to the philosophy of mind, in the remaining part of this essay.

The theory of imagination which Collingwood advances is extraordinarily complex. The different lines of inquiry he pursues and his attempt at combining them will, I hope, emerge clearly in the course of my exposition. First, however, certain preliminary points will have to be considered.

Collingwood has no doubt whatever that an imaginary no less than a real experience is *sensed* so that, if the two are said to differ, the difference must lie in something other than the sensory element. For him the meaning of 'real' in this context differs from that of 'imaginary' not unlike the way in which 'real *property*' differs from 'personal *property*' (*PA*, 173–4). That is to say, the difference between real and imaginary sensations must differ significantly from that between real diamonds and imitation diamonds, since on his view imaginary experiences are sensations, whereas imitation diamonds are not diamonds. This point must be borne in mind; it will reappear in my appraisal of Collingwood's theory in the light of Ryle's argument that sensations differ from images just as what is real and genuine differs from what is sham and counterfeit.[1] The question which immediately arises, once real and imaginary experiences are regarded as sensory, is how is one to tell the difference between the two. Since Collingwood's two solutions to this problem are inspired by clues derived from the history of the issue from Descartes to Kant, the historical basis of his inquiry should be remembered throughout (*PA*, 174ff.).

After noting Descartes' denial that sensation can be distinguished from imagination, Collingwood remarks that both Hobbes and

[1] *Concept of Mind*, pp. 245 ff.

Spinoza used one term only, designed to cover sensation as well as imagination.[1] Locke, he holds, is the first to introduce a distinction, at least with regard to complex ideas:[2] if these have a 'foundation in nature' (as in the case of gold), they are on his view 'real', and if not (as in that of centaurs) they are 'fantastical'. Locke's attempt to buttress this distinction by introducing the notion of a causal relation between physical objects and real ideas is rejected by Collingwood, since for him the crux of the problem is to show that the distinction, if it exists at all, can be stated and verified purely in terms of ideas. He discovers the germ of this 'introspection theory' already in Locke's description of fantastical ideas as ideas which the mind 'makes to itself,' thereby displaying an *activity* and 'some kind of liberty'[3] on its part. Berkeley's contribution here, as Collingwood explains, can be subdivided into three aspects, of which the first two are versions of the introspection theory, while the third, to be dealt with later, is called by Collingwood the 'relation theory'. Berkeley formulates his introspection theory in the proposition that 'the ideas of sense are more strong, lively, and distinct than those of the imagination.'[4] This might mean either that a real sound is loud and an imaginary one weak; or that a real sound forces itself upon us, whereas an imaginary one can be evoked or suppressed at will. The first version of the theory is already adumbrated in Hobbes's notion of imagination as 'more obscure' and 'weaker' than when a thing is sensed, just 'as the voyce of a man is in the noyse of the day'.[5] Hume subsequently summarized the two versions in the statement that 'impressions' and 'ideas' differ from one another 'in the *degrees* of *force and liveliness* with which they *strike upon* the mind.[6]

[1] This covering term is not 'sensation', as one might expect from the drift of Collingwood's argument, except when Hobbes calls imagination 'nothing but *decaying sense*' (*Leviathan*, ch. 2). In general Hobbes refers to the appearance of sensible qualities as 'Fancy, the same waking, that dreaming' (ibid., ch. 1, and *NL*, 4.48). For Spinoza all sense-perception is *imaginatio* (*Ethics*, Pt. II, prop. xvii, schol.).

[2] *Essay*, Bk. II, ch. xxx, sect. 1.

[3] Ibid., sects. 2–3.

[4] *The Principles of Human Knowledge*, sects. xxx and xxxvi.

[5] *Leviathan*, ed. Pogson Smith (Oxford ,1909), ch. 2, p. 14.

[6] *Treatise of Human Nature*, ed. Selby-Bigge, Bk. I, Pt. I, sect. i, p. 1 (my italics).

Now Collingwood rejects both versions, not because, as for Ryle,[1] an imagined sound is no *sound* (either loud or faint), nor 'seeing' a colour in one's mind a species of seeing colours, but because the theory, in both its versions, allows of exceptions and is in this sense false. Dreams, visions, and all sorts of emotional imaginings can be clear and very lively; they can also, no less than real sense-impressions, force themselves upon the mind, as when the sight of a horrible accident haunts an eye-witness for days, in spite of his efforts to banish it. Hume admitted almost as much when he pleaded that the cases mentioned are exceptions to the rule. His mistake was not to have realized that, no matter how rare, exceptions have to be taken seriously.

In reformulating the introspection theory Collingwood offers his first solution to the problem concerning the status of imagination. He acknowledges indebtedness to Hume in drawing attention to the fact that, when perceptions are related by association or by means of the understanding, the relation is not between *impressions* but *ideas*.[2] Combining this doctrine with his own theory of the evanescence of feelings (*NL*, 5.5–.57; *PA*, 168–70, 198, 201–3, 206 ff.), i.e. the observation that feelings (including sensations) begin to perish soon after they have come into existence, he argues that, if two feelings or sensations are compared with one another, at least one will have vanished and, in order to be compared with the other, must be held before the mind. In this capacity it is in certain ways like a feeling, in others unlike it. It is unlike it in that it is not actually sense-given, but presented in the form of an idea or image of something that has been or could be sensed, but at present is not. Now Collingwood's thesis is that in imagining and attending, a person is using some kind of liberty (admittedly less than in choosing and thinking), whereas an actual feeling or sensation, though itself not entirely unfree, is in an important sense something he cannot help having. As *idées fixes* and the haunting vision of a past accident show, a man's control over imaginary experiences by a deliberate act of will can be equally

---

[1] *Concept of Mind*, p. 250. See also Wittgenstein, *The Blue Book*, pp. 40–1.

[2] *A Treatise of Human Nature*, Bk. I, Pt. I, sects. iv and v. For a qualification see Bk. II, Pt. I, sect. iv. Cf. *PA*, 200–1, 202–3, 207–8, 223 n. 1.

limited (*PA*, 179). Whereas such experiences may remain *intense*, they still show little of the violence or power which crude sensation has in *determining our thoughts and actions* (*PA*, 209). The point is that, while an imaginary experience, like a real sensation, may be vivid, it has not much influence on the mental or behavioural context in which it occurs. In imagining, then, we are at least to that extent free, and in this sense the experience differs in kind from any real experience.

Next Collingwood takes up for criticism Berkeley's relation theory. According to this theory 'ideas of sense have likewise a steadiness, order, and coherence, and are not excited at random . . . but in a regular train or series'.[1] Berkeley calls the rules for consistency and order in any such series the laws of nature. In Collingwood's terminology, if sense-data are related to each other by such fixed rules of appearance, they belong to 'families';[2] if they are not so related, they are 'wild'. It follows that for Berkeley illusions and hallucinations are in some new sense exceptional. Collingwood's criticism of this point is that, if I discover that the crouching animal I seem to see in a dark corner of my garden is the product of an illusion or of my imagination, I need not for that reason deny that what I seem to see does obey certain (psychological or even physical) laws, and therefore belongs fundamentally to a 'family' and is no exception to the rule: the crouching animal has 'appeared' before, at dusk and when I felt tired.

Collingwood's own view, which he traces back to Kant, is that, if relationships are to serve as a basis for the distinction between the real and the imaginary, they must consist in the ways in which the various types of experience are related to an altogether different order of consciousness—the interpretative function of thought. If looked upon in this light, imagination differs from sensation in kind no less than in degree (*PA*, 187 and n.1).[3] In Collingwood's

---

[1] *Principles*, sect. xxx.
[2] A term he borrows from H. H. Price, *Perception* (London, 1932), ch. VIII, and *passim*.
[3] For Collingwood's view that differences of degree involve differences of kind see his *EPM*, 54 ff., 69 ff. As a general principle, and particularly for the purpose of distinguishing between sensation and imagination, one should regard the two types of difference as mutually exclusive.

opinion, an imagined colour is still a *colour* and in this capacity sensed. However, it differs from a visible colour not in that it is wild, but in that it is as yet uninterpreted by the understanding. One of his reasons for arguing that imagination is in itself indifferent to the distinction between real and unreal is that I may imagine behind the oak tree on the lawn some grass (which is in fact there) and also a lawn-mower (which is not); yet there is nothing in the two things imagined, which indicates that one is real and the other not (*PA*, 136–7; see also *IH*, 241). Sensory experience in general (i.e. before it is interpreted by thought) is as such equally indifferent to the distinctions between real and unreal, true and false, veridical and illusory (*PA*, 194; also *NL*, 4.33).[1] However, once thought attempts to interpret a sensory experience, one correctly interpreted becomes real, being in this capacity firmly placed in its context and in this sense strong. On the other hand, a falsely interpreted sensation will turn out to be illusory. This means that, before the process of interpretation begins, the imaginary animal in the corner of my garden 'is there', though only in the sense that I see it; so is a rainbow, the content of a dream, and the notorious pink rats. When I discover that the animal does not move when I shout, nor has a continuous surface when I draw nearer, I infer that what I saw was unreal. Without such contextual data, I might (erroneously) take it for real, thereby falling victim to an illusion.[2]

Collingwood's doctrine of imagination may now be summarized, particularly in connection with what he says about attention and thought at the level of second-order consciousness. Though closely related to sensation, imagination differs radically from it in that imaginary colours, and so on, instead of being really seen, are colours anticipated, recalled, or, particularly for purposes of identification and comparison, held before the mind and 'attended to' (*PA*, 203 ff.).[3] One characteristic of attending is

---

[1] Cf. Ryle, *Concept of Mind*, pp. 152, 204, 237–8.

[2] On Collingwood's view, the interpretative criterion which applies to illusions also applies to day-dreaming and make-believe, all of which (because they have an opposite, called 'real') must be distinguished from imagining, which is not amenable to the distinction between real and unreal (*PA*, 135–8, 286).

[3] Compare with Ryle's 'heed concepts', together with his warning against misdescribing heed in the contemplative idiom, *Concept of Mind*, pp. 135 ff.

that it is the performance of an act of a different logical order from that of pure sensation, just as looking is of a different logical order from seeing, and listening from hearing (*PA*, 203–4, 206).[1] Another is that attending is the basis of the interpretative work of thought.[2] Now thinking, on Collingwood's premises, is 'bipolar', i.e. it admits of the distinction between thinking truly and 'misthinking', interpreting correctly and misinterpreting, and in general between 'success' and 'failure'—a distinction absent from mere feeling and sensation, but not from looking or listening. Unlike seeing and hearing, but not unlike thought, attention is also a 'task' activity, and the word 'attending' a 'try' verb.[3] Moreover, unlike impressions, attention is not a response to a stimulus. A man may deliberately refuse attention to a loud sound and concentrate on a faint one or a tune running in his head. Hence attention, being master in its own house, can 'domesticate' feeling, regardless of its intensity, whereas at the level of merely psychic experience feeling dominates. When on the strength of attention and imagination a person becomes more active and free, his feelings become correspondingly less violent.[4]

Collingwood's doctrine at this point is modelled on the insight of two classical philosophers, Spinoza and Hobbes, whose influence is manifest in the bearing of his views on imagination and attention on his moral philosophy. The problem of ethics, for Spinoza, lies in the question 'How can man become free?' The answer, he argues, must show how men, who in general are the slaves of their impressions and emotions, can gain control of their sensations and feelings. His own clue is that, as soon as a man forms a clear

---

[1] Cf. Ryle, *Concept of Mind*, pp. 149–51, and *passim*.

[2] 'Attention is going on concurrently with intellection', *PA*, 204.

[3] The words in quotation marks are Collingwood's own, used in connection with his analysis of thought (*PA*, 157). They may be compared with the similar, though far more technical, terminology which Ryle (*Concept of Mind*, pp. 130, 149–53) uses in his analysis of task verbs (e.g. 'look'), as opposed to achievement words (e.g. 'see') and their antithesis, 'missed-it' words (e.g. 'misspell').

[4] Compare here Collingwood's example of the difference between a child howling automatically from mere rage at the psychic level and its howl, 'audibly different to an experienced ear', at the self-conscious level, when it is anxious to draw the attention of others to its anger, before attending to it itself, thereby putting a stop to its howl altogether (*PA*, 208, 217, 236).

and distinct *idea* of a feeling which is a passion, it ceases to be a passion and becomes an expression of the mind's activity.[1] Hobbes's argument, endorsed by both Collingwood and leading contemporary philosophers, is that though a man's action would always be causally determined, he is not always acting under constraint, nor are his actions always impeded from outside. Hence a man is free whenever he is not compelled or hindered by others.[2] Collingwood's point in this context is that a man acquires freedom by dominating his feelings and the impressions he 'undergoes'. The process consists in a voluntary act[3] and can be achieved by means of attention, the forming of images, and also by the use of speech.

I will now evaluate Collingwood's complex analysis of the concept of imagination. In my view one should compare his theory, particularly its controversial aspect, with Ryle's, which is both straightforward and plausible. The part of Collingwood's analysis which is open to criticism is its central assumption that, at least from one point of view, an idea does not differ in its own intrinsic nature from the corresponding impression (*PA*, 236). In other words, what we imagine are *the very same kinds of things* (*PA*, 222; also 206–7, 209) (i.e. colours, sounds, anger, etc.) which are present in our real experiences. The assumption, it might be argued, is a specification of what Collingwood subsequently formulated as the 'Law of Primitive Survivals' (*NL*, 9.5–.51), according to which, when A (e.g. sensation) is modified into B (e.g. imagination), there survives in any example of B an element of A in its primitive and pure, i.e. unmodified, state. Now this assumption is disputable and has in fact been rejected by Ryle,[4] who insists that there is nothing in an imaginary sound or colour which 'corresponds to that element in perceiving [a sound or colour] which is *purely sensuous*'.[5] A tune heard and a tune running in someone's head are

---

[1] *Ethics*, Pt. V, prop. iii (my italics). See *PA*, 219; *NL*, 13.45.

[2] Hobbes, *Leviathan*, ch. 21; *Of Liberty and Necessity*, in *English Works*, ed. W. Molesworth (London, 1840), iv, 229–78. Cf. *NL*, 13.17–.45; 13.7 ff.

[3] For the use of the words 'act' or 'action' for the will see *NL*, 13.86–.88.

[4] *Concept of Mind*, ch. VIII, sects. 1–6.

[5] Ibid., p. 265 (my italics). None of the points concerning imagination discussed here are to be found in Ryle's contribution to the symposium 'Imaginary Objects' in *Aristotelian Society*, *Supp. Vol.*, xii (1933).

neither two indistinguishable instances of 'fancy' or 'imaginatio' (as for Hobbes and Spinoza), nor two species of a sound perception (as for the British Empiricists), nor again is the one either stronger or weaker than the other. According to Ryle, the traditional problem can be resolved, once it is recognized that an imaginary sound is no *sound*, nor an imaginary colour a *colour*. As little as there can be competition between a murder and a mock-murder (since the latter is no murder nor a species of murder), can there be competition between a noise and an imaginary noise (the latter being no noise nor a species of noise). Accordingly, an imaginary noise cannot be either ear-splitting or faint, nor can it drown or be drowned by a real noise. 'Seeing' snakes in *delirium tremens* or 'hearing' a tune in my head is something 'totally different in kind' from seeing or hearing.[1]

From my discussion of Collingwood's theory it appears that he would like to have it both ways. As part of his introspection theory he admits that in imagination an impression is attended to, retained before the mind, and in the process changed into something 'very different', 'something with a character of its own' (*PA*, 202, 222, 223). He also affirms that in imagination 'colours and sounds, in their capacity as sensa, have ceased to be seen or heard'. And in more than one passage he explicitly states that real colours, sounds, etc., and imaginary colours, sounds, etc., are 'two *kinds* of things' which 'must' be distinguished (*PA*, 202).[2] As part of his relation theory he likewise concedes that the difference between real and imaginary is one of degree (which for him involves a difference of kind) (*PA*, 187, n. 1). On the other hand, as we have seen, his doctrine is that, from one point of view, an attended or even an imaginary colour is still colour, and that in fact what we imagine are the 'very *same kinds* of things' which are present to us in mere sensation.

I will make a few comments on this ambiguous doctrine so as to explain (though not necessarily to justify) it. First, on Collingwood's theory, there ought to be *two* senses of what in imaginary experiences is 'seen' or 'heard', one I call the maximum sense and

---

[1] *Concept of Mind*, p. 246.
[2] My italics.

the other the minimum. Suppose I am attending, as I am when I am listening or looking (which on Collingwood's introspection theory should present me with the ideas or images of certain things). In such a case I may be said to have an auditory or visual experience of something, which in most cases could also be said to be audible or visible. This is what I call the maximum sense of the view that a sensuous element is involved in imagination. If, on the other hand, I recall a sound or colour or evoke it at will, I may still be said (in one sense at least) to have an auditory or visual experience, though what I experience can no longer be said to be audible or visible. This is the minimum sense of saying that a sensuous element is involved in imagination. A similar principle applies in the case of Collingwood's relation theory. Whereas the animal I 'see' crouching in a dark corner of the garden is not only a visual experience, but also (in one sense) visible, snakes 'seen' in *delirium tremens*, though a visual experience, are not visible. I suggest that the minimum sense is a basis from which to resolve the *prima facie* inconsistency in Collingwood's views on the sensuous element in imagination. He himself accepts this sense in his rejection of the 'pseudo-aesthetic' conception of a work of art, according to which a piece of music, for example, is a series of audible noises, rather than (as it should be from the point of view of art proper) something 'never sensuously or "actually" heard at all', 'which may exist solely in the musician's head' (and that of the understanding member of the audience) (*PA*, 151; see also 139 and 141-3). If, as on this view, the sensuous element of a tune is merely an experience listened to and appreciated *in the mind*, what exactly *is* this element, if it is not an experience of something actually audible? The answer, I suggest, is that it is an experience of something which is potentially audible and, above all, has been audible in the past.

Secondly, then, if what is meant by a merely auditory experience is the 'survival' of a sound heard in the past, how is this survival to be explained? Ryle's answer is that it consists in learning and not forgetting how a certain tune sounds. Imaging, for him, is precisely one of the ways in which a perceptual lesson has been learned, retained and subsequently applied in appropriate forms, e.g. by recognizing a tune, humming it, or going through it in one's head.[1] An alternative answer is that the survival of a past perceptual experience is to be explained by means of *traces*—a concept which both Ryle and Collingwood associate with Hume's doctrine that all ideas and images are derived from impressions.[2] Whilst Collingwood hesitatingly accepts the trace theory, Ryle repudiates it as part of the para-mechanical myth. And there are indeed difficulties in the theory, if only because it entails the 'Fallacy of Swapping Horses'. However, all that is needed to solve the question under discussion is to show that some meaning can be given to Collingwood's assertion that imagining is grounded in some sensuous (e.g. auditory or visual) experience, without there *actually* being anything audible or visible. If sensation is given this minimum meaning, then his view that ideas of sense survive in, and consequently cannot be distinguished from, those of the imagination becomes in some sense acceptable, and at the same time compatible with his justified contention that *in other respects* (e.g. those formulated in his introspection and relation theories) real sensation or mere feeling differs from imagining in *kind*. Certainly in this capacity the concept of imagination plays its role as the basis of Collingwood's aesthetics, ethics, and theory of history.[3]

I may add (what must have become apparent throughout) that for the purpose of elucidation and appraisal Collingwood's philosophy of mind might profitably be studied in conjunction with Ryle's. If held up beside the latter, it shows shortcomings; on the other hand, apart from the implicit criticisms of it in *The Concept of Mind*, its impact appears to have survived in some of Ryle's own positive pronouncements.

[1] *Concept of Mind*, pp. 265–6, 268–70, 271–2.
[2] Ibid., pp. 271–2; *PA*, 210–11.
[3] For the indispensable role of imagination as part of historical thought see *IH*, Pt. V, para. 2, 'The Historical Imagination.'

III

A CRITICAL OUTLINE OF
COLLINGWOOD'S PHILOSOPHY
OF ART

PETER JONES

1. *Sources of Collingwood's Aesthetic Views*

Collingwood mentions Plato, Vico, Coleridge, Hegel, and Croce as sources for his views on art; but he also acknowledged a general debt to the Romantic movement, and in his later work Spinoza and Hobbes emerge as influences, particularly on his theory of expression.[1] Collingwood admitted that his views accorded with those of many of his contemporaries, and although it is difficult to establish who influenced whom, reference may be made to two authors who anticipated his views in some respects, even if they did not precisely influence them. In *The Theory of Beauty*,[2] Collingwood's Oxford tutor E. F. Carritt admitted that he was himself following Croce in maintaining that every man

---

[1] Vico and Croce are acknowledged in *SM*, 74, and writers of the Romantic movement, ibid., 38; Coleridge and Croce are acknowledged in the Preface to *OPA*, and Vico is again mentioned in *PA*, 80, 138n. Collingwood may have owed his original acquaintance with Vico to Croce's commentary which Collingwood translated as *The Philosophy of Giambattista Vico* (London, 1913). In Croce's work Collingwood is closest to the first three chapters of the first two editions of *Aesthetic;* G. N. G. Orsini, *Benedetto Croce Philosopher of Art and Literary Critic* (Carbondale, 1961), has pointed out that Croce radically altered his views later. For Plato, see Collingwood's 'Plato's Philosophy of Art', *Mind*, xxxiv (1925), now reprinted in *Essays in the Philosophy of Art*, ed. A. Donagan (Bloomington, Ind., 1964) (abbreviated henceforth as *E*). The similarity between Collingwood and the Romantics is well brought out by consulting J. S. Mill's 'The Two Kinds of Poetry', and 'What is Poetry?' in *Mill's Essays on Literature and Society*, ed. J. B. Schneewind (London, 1965). *EPM* contains several references to Spinoza, but not to his theory of emotions which influenced Collingwood in *PA* (see pp. 177, 219). The influence of Hegel, most marked in *SM* gradually diminished.

[2] London, 1914.

is an artist in so far as he uses language; in addition, he drew attention to Nettleship's remarkable analysis of 'expression', which reappears almost unchanged in Collingwood's writings.[1] I. A. Richards, in *Principles of Literary Criticism*,[2] anticipated Collingwood in holding that emotions are 'felt as clearly marked colourings of consciousness', and in the view that we 'imaginatively construct' works of art, which are thus not to be identified with physical objects; but although Collingwood agreed with him that art is not play, amusement or relaxation, it should be observed that he disagreed with Richards' account of language. T. M. Knox has suggested that Vernon Blake's *Relation in Art* (1925) may have influenced Collingwood's later work,[3] and it may be wondered whether S. Alexander was also an influence, in view of Collingwood's description of his essays on aesthetics as 'the most important contribution to the philosophy of art that England has made since the eighteenth century'.[4] But in both cases it seems more likely that their views merely coincided rather than that they influenced each other, because Collingwood had himself already expressed similar views. Two other references to sources may be made, however, the first to an author whom Collingwood did acknowledge—the Neapolitan philosopher Giambattista Vico (1668–1744). On the premiss that there are three degrees of knowledge—bare feeling, confused perception, and reflective clarity—Vico argues that poetry is concerned with feelings and the particular, whereas philosophy is concerned with reflection and the universal.[5] The faculty genetically prior to reflection, and to which poetry, more accurately, may be said to belong, is imagination. Poetry is caused by the impetus of violent passions, and is born of the natural need of expression; the most obvious means of expression is

[1] Carritt (5th ed., pp. 15 n., 180 n.) quoted from *Philosophical Lectures and Remains of R. L. Nettleship*, ed. A. C. Bradley and G. R. Benson (London, 1897), especially pp. 130–6.

[2] London, 1924.

[3] T. M. Knox, review of W. M. Johnston, *The Formative Years of R. G. Collingwood* (The Hague, 1967), in *Philosophical Quarterly*, xix (1969), 166.

[4] Collingwood's review of S. Alexander, *Art and Instinct*, (Oxford, 1927), in *Journal of Philosophical Studies*, iii (1928), 370–3.

[5] G. B. Vico, *The New Science*, (3rd. ed., 1744), transl. T. G. Bergin and M. H. Fisch (New York, 1961), Bk. I, Axioms L, LII, LIII; Bk. II, sect. 2; Bk. III, sect. 1.

gesture. A theory of poetry is inseparable from a theory of language. Knowledge, in the first place, is self-consciousness. One man can 'feel' the expressions of another's gestures only by 'individualizing' them. All these views are found in Collingwood.

The last undoubted source of Collingwood's aesthetic views is a book by his father, who was Ruskin's secretary. In *The Art Teaching of John Ruskin*,[1] W. G. Collingwood imposed his own philosophical concepts and structure on Ruskin's writings, admitting that his master's philosophy was 'latent'; as a result his exposition distorts Ruskin's views to the extent that it clarifies them, and this is the major reason for claiming that the direct influence on R. G. Collingwood was his father, and not Ruskin himself. In W. G. Collingwood's account of Ruskin's views on art, we find emphasis upon the concept of imagination (*AT*, 62, 99, 133–5, 167, 169, 173, 177); the view that art is language, or expression of emotion (*AT*, 31, 42, 49); a claim that there is a double distinction between art and sham art, and between art and great art (*AT*, 38, 88, 135); the assertion that art is not craft, amusement, emotional intoxicant, or imitation (*AT*, 153, 167); the view that individualization is the essence of art (*AT*, 87, 98–100, 112), and the view that three stages of art correspond to three stages of knowledge; the views that the sensibility of the artist is controlled in some way by his audience (*AT*, 177), and that there is a close relation between art and morality (*AT*, 169). All these views reappear in the writings of R. G. Collingwood and, in large measure, may be taken as an advance summary of them. The eclecticism and familiar conclusions of his aesthetic views may explain, in part, their comparative neglect by Collingwood's contemporaries; such neglect was an injustice, however, to Collingwood's attempt to support and interrelate his conclusions, and to this attempt we must turn, beginning with an outline of his declared positions.

2. *An Outline of Collingwood's Early Views*

In a lecture delivered in 1919 Collingwood had commended Ruskin for having stressed the strong connection between art and

---

[1] London, 1891 (hereafter abbreviated *AT*). See my 'Collingwood's debt to his Father', *Mind*, lxxviii (1969).

morality, and the view that any theory of art is based upon a theory of mind. His own theory is set out in *Speculum Mentis* (1924), and *Outlines of a Philosophy of Art* (1925);[1] in the rewritten version of the latter book, *The Principles of Art* (1938), the theory of mind is modified in some respects, and in *The New Leviathan* (1942) further modifications carry implications for aesthetic theory although there is little discussion of art itself. In his early writings Collingwood argued that the first step to knowing what you mean is knowing that you mean something (*SM*, 90, 102; *OPA*, 129); thinking or perception presupposes a phase of consciousness in which no distinctions are made between truth and falsity, and such a phase is imagination (*OPA*, 55). To imagine is to isolate an object from its context; similarly, to apprehend something aesthetically is to isolate it in its uniqueness and wholeness, and the aesthetic experience is simply awareness of what we immediately apprehend, ignoring its relations to other things (*OPA*, 139; *SM*, 60–5). Works of art may thus be defined as acts of imagination, which cease to exist as soon as the existence of anything else is recognized simultaneously with their own (*SM*, 69; *OPA*, 68). It follows that works of art do not live on canvas or in libraries (*SM*, 67; *OPA*, 129-30), for, if art is the activity of imagining, everything becomes a work of art by being cut off from its surroundings and treated as an indivisible unity. Art is instrumental in the sense that it is undertaken for the purposes of discovery, for, in the absence of imagining one does not know what a thing is like (*SM*, 69; *OPA*, 129); the acts of painting, writing, sculpting, and so on, are themselves means to imagining (*SM*, 67), and their actual course is determined by the abstract notion of relevance; in *SM*, 97 the activity said to account for this is conceiving, which somehow precedes imagining, but this explanation is later dropped. Although Collingwood seems to be close to some of the earlier pronouncements of Croce at this stage, he closely follows A. C. Bradley[2] in urging that the meaningfulness which is

[1] Now reprinted in *Essays in the Philosophy of Art*, ed. Donagan, to which my page numbers refer. The 1919 lecture on Ruskin is reprinted in the same volume.
[2] A. C. Bradley, 'Poetry for Poetry's Sake' (1901), in *Oxford Lectures on Poetry* (London, 1909).

a characteristic of all art cannot be torn from the imaginative setting in which it is embedded, or stated in any other terms. In this sense works of art are self-explanatory. What can be explained, however, are the processes by which an artist reached a particular point of view, because, from the genetic standpoint, an artist's works are necessarily the imaginative resultant of his whole previous experience (*OPA*, 152, 94)–indeed, the artistic problem might be said to be that of concentrating his whole experience into a single imaginative view of reality (*SM*, 79; *OPA*, 67, 94, 121). Since imagination is the activity of presenting to oneself a complete, self-contained monadic world, which exists only in that act, we can say that works of art are monads (*SM*, 71; *OPA*, 66). But not only does the artist not know he is imagining; there can be no act of pure imagination, for imagination and cognition are factors in every cognitive act (*SM*, 72, 83), from which it follows by definition that there is an aesthetic factor in all experience. Empirically, the facts of communication, the society of artists and physical artifacts, establish that art is not pure imagination (*SM*, 99), and is in error when it thinks otherwise; the conceptual evidence that art is confused thinking, in respect to its own status, is deduced from the claim that the outcome of art, and the next stage of knowledge, is clear thinking (*SM*, 108, 250–1, 206–8, 219, 242; *OPA*, 62). Art is thus to be defined not only as the activity of imagining, but also as error (*OPA*, 62). It should be noted that to imagine a thing as a whole is also to see it as beautiful (*SM*, 60–5, 84, 94; *OPA*, 52). Although an element of thinking controls imagining, the self-consciousness required to know this belongs to a higher stage of knowledge than art (*OPA*, 92–3); Vico, and Plato before him, were right in holding that poetry is the spiritual kingdom of the child, and poetic speech the natural speech of children (*SM*, 58, 104; *OPA*, 59).

3. *An Outline of Collingwood's Later Views*

Collingwood described philosophical inquiry as an attempt to know better what in some sense we know already (see *EPM*, 11, 161, 200, 214). Accordingly, he not only describes his aim in *The Principles of Art* as the clarification of ideas we already possess, but he also defines art as the bringing to consciousness or clarification of what we half-consciously know. The exclusive purpose of art is the discovery of what one feels, and this is achieved by the activity of expressing. Following F. H. Bradley and some of his eighteenth-century predecessors, Collingwood distinguishes expressing, which individualizes, from describing, which classifies and hence generalizes.[1] An 'activity', to judge from isolated remarks, is something we try to do, in order to bring about change, even if we do not fully succeed (EPM, 4; PA, 196–7, 280–2); and 'expressing' is defined as 'becoming conscious' (PA, 282). There are two jointly necessary conditions for the occurrence of art: certain unexpressed emotions, and the wherewithal to express them (PA, 130; cf. E, 231). There are also two necessary conditions of expression, together with two accompanying characteristics of success. The necessary conditions are, firstly, that an agent must try to express, for there can be no expression by accident or unintentionally; it is something he has to do, not something that escapes from him or happens to him passively. Secondly, the agent must have an uncorrupt consciousness, a notion which is introduced in connection with sincerity (e.g. PA, 315). Given that a man is trying to express, only a corrupt consciousness can prevent success; if he possesses such a consciousness, however, he will deny what he feels. Collingwood holds that such corruption is always partial, for a man who continually suppressed his emotions would be literally insane; further, we can always establish that we are suffering from corrupt consciousness, although sometimes we do not do so, by comparing our state with memories of uncorrupt consciousness. It should be noted that no mistakes can be made about instances of uncorrupt consciousness; that every sane agent logically must have one veridical memory of uncorrupt consciousness which is the model against which he can measure subsequent lapses into corruption; and thirdly, that it would seem that everybody's first mental state must be one of uncorrupt conscious-

---

[1] F. H. Bradley, *The Principles of Logic* (London, 1883, 2nd ed. 1922), vol. i, Bk. I, ch. 1, pp. 29 ff. Collingwood uses much of the vocabulary of J. Ward, *Psychological Principles* (Cambridge, 1918). Ward had been an astute critic of Bradley.

ness, since any corruption could never be known. The notion of suppressed or repressed emotion is thus seen to be parasitic upon expression of emotion, and cases of success precede cases of failure. It should be remembered that Collingwood regards expression as a natural condition of childhood, both literally and metaphorically. The first accompanying characteristic of expression is a feeling of alleviation from the perturbation which was the occasion of expression. A perturbation may persist, may cease, or may be alleviated; only the last guarantees and attends expression. Secondly, other people should be able to judge that a man's expression is appropriate to his emotion, and they can do this because emotions are to an extent shared, and because they are tied to beliefs and thoughts.

The whole of the summary exposition so far will become a little clearer when we turn to Collingwood's theory of mind which underpins the conclusions. One preliminary remark is in order, however, to forestall repetition of misapplied objections to his position. As a partial account of the unreflective spontaneity detectable in all the greatest works (*PA*, 29), Collingwood asserted that artists do not know in advance what is going to come of their activities (*PA*, 129); and it must be presumed that he meant by this that artists are unable to predict to the very last detail the outcome of their activities, not that they do not have a general idea of it in advance. At the same time, Collingwood felt that the fact that artists are prone to say, at a particular stage in their work, 'This is just right', seemed to imply some foreknowledge in virtue of which we may all compare what 'we want . . . with what we have done' (*OPA*, 118). Such comparison is incompatible, of course, with the doctrine that only in expressing does a man discover, and in a sense create, what is to be expressed. It may be urged in Collingwood's defence that he has no need of the view that what an artist is now prepared to accept must be equated with what he formerly wanted. But he disregarded the view that reasons which justify what the artist has done must be distinguished from causal explanations of it (the best reasons may be thought of, on occasions, after the work is finished), because he held that works of art are concerned with bringing to consciousness what is immediate, and 'immediacy means absence of reasons' (*OPA*, 140). Only a causal explanation, therefore, is in place, which means in the present case the statement that the artist's experiences were of a certain sort upon a given occasion, in virtue of numerous factors best captured by the phrase 'his previous life-history'.

The theory of mind articulated in Book II of *The Principles of Art* is deduced by conceptual analysis. The most general verb denoting experience is 'to feel', and its proper objects are feelings; these may be known in varying degrees from relative unconsciousness to full classification. Classification logically presupposes individuation, which results from attention, and individuation presupposes vague awareness. The notion of awareness, however, entails the independence, and perhaps also the prior existence (*PA*, 163), of its objects, and so a level of experience is postulated which is, in some sense, below the level of consciousness—there could be no empirical evidence for this logical postulate, of course (*PA*, 205). This level of 'bare feeling' seems to contradict Collingwood's persistent denial of any atomistic attempt to postulate pure sensations, and his assertion that all knowledge is fundamentally interpretation, thought having for its objects only other thoughts.[1]

It will be convenient to summarize the amplified account of feelings given in *The New Leviathan*, taking note of important differences. Consciousness is defined as the essential constituent of mind (*NL*, 4.19); its proper objects, feelings, consist (as Descartes and more recently Hegel and Bradley held) of both a sensuous and emotional element which are materially indistinguishable (*PA*, 162; *NL*, 3–4). Earlier he had explicitly held that feelings were both states and objects of consciousness (*OPA*, 138). It is impossible to argue about feelings because, as the foundation of experience, they are immediately given in the sense that they exist only while being sensed (*PA*, 168; *NL*, 4.7). Feeling is a field upon which we direct our attention, and in so doing create focal and penumbral regions. Contrary to the view in *PA*, feelings are said not to have objects (*NL*, 5.2), but to be modes, whose names function adverbially (*NL*, 5.47). A man makes himself conscious of his feelings by naming them (*NL*, 6.2), which contradicts his earlier view that

---

[1] Collingwood, *Proceedings of the Aristotelian Society*, xxiv (1923–4), 74.

naming is a classifying activity belonging to a higher level of consciousness than the level to which expression belongs (*PA*, 203). Language in its simplest form is a mere 'register' of feelings, where 'language' is defined as any system of bodily movements intended by the agent as having meaning (*NL*, 6). The painter's problem is to establish 'the field to primitive consciousness before the act of isolation took place' (*NL*, 4.55), and the importance of isolation, necessary as it is for subsequent classification, is that the act of attention which brings it about alters the object by circumscribing it (*NL*, 7.3). Attention does not precede but is the logical foundation of intellection (*PA*, 204); consciousness is not something other than thought, but simply a level which is not yet intellect (*PA*, 215).

Collingwood holds that there are three stages in the life of a feeling, and there is an emotion corresponding to each level and which has its own kind of expression. By expressing the emotional element appropriate to each level, the non-emotional residue is raised to a higher level of consciousness. This metaphorical account is not further elucidated, but it should be observed that wherever Collingwood detects complex phenomena he always postulates a logically simpler state which is its foundation, and which sometimes seems to precede it temporally (cf. *PA*, 236). For example, the evidence of the data below the level of consciousness is derived from the analysis of the concept of attention, which requires the independence of its objects; yet it is unclear what elements in that analysis justify the predication of discreteness, perpetual flux, immediate evanescence, and non-recurrence to the basic data (*PA*, 159–64).

4. *Consciousness, Attention, Imagination*

Since sensa form a continuous flow, on the account given, and all sensa have emotional charges, there is no room for doubt whether one is feeling an emotion at any particular time; 'having an emotion' cannot discriminate one state from another. An oppressive perturbation is the first indication to any man of his emotion; he discovers what this is, and in so doing alleviates the oppression, by attending to it or raising it to consciousness.

Comment on these two concepts is called for. Collingwood uses the terms 'theoretical' and 'practical' to characterize aspects of activities; to refer to the theoretical aspect is to refer to the changes the activity produces in the agent himself, the practical aspect referring to changes brought about in the world. Hence, theoretically considered, an artist is one who comes to know himself, and, practically, he is one who alters his world by putting into practice the thoughts he has discovered (PA, 290-1; cf. OPA, 50-1). Similarly, the activity of attending has the two sides (PA, 222): theoretically we become aware of our field of view; practically, we assert our mastery over our feelings, no longer being subject to them as passions. Attention, awareness and consciousness seem to be synonyms (PA, 222-3; cf. NL, 4.25), although later, attention is said to be the practical aspect only of consciousness (NL, 4.33); but in any case Collingwood has conflated what must be separated. Momentary feelings catch our attention, and preclude our attending to them; we are passive. Feelings we can attend to must be continuous. Collingwood in part allows for this by remarking that 'sustained sensation' is pure sensation modified by consciousness (PA, 209).[1] On the other hand he mistakenly assumes that attending is an activity on a par with looking and listening, rather than a notion referring to the circumstances in which activities occur, and to be analysed adverbially. To become aware of a feeling is to feel it, but not to attend to it; we can become aware only of what lasts for some time. Becoming aware and becoming conscious are alike reception concepts denoting results, or knowledge acquired through attention, but they are not achievements we can try for.[2] Collingwood is right to introduce the notion of correctness at his second level, for 'no sensation can force us to make a mistake about it' (PA, 190); being conscious of a thing entails both attention and knowledge, for one cannot be conscious of what is not the case. But the concepts of attention and becoming conscious should not be equated with each other: although we can only attend to and become conscious of what is continuous, becoming conscious

---

[1] Compare Wittgenstein, The Blue and Brown Books (Oxford, 1958), 174: 'Attending to the feeling means producing or modifying it.'
[2] I am indebted here to A. R. White, Attention (Oxford, 1964).

is more passive, being a reception in which something catches our attention. Collingwood could justifiably postulate a continuous flux of sensa to which we could attend, but cannot argue that we attend to atomic constituents of that flow. Momentary sensations may be noticed or felt, and if they are not felt they are not had; continuing states, on the other hand, can be had unfelt but cannot therefore be noticed—we can forget our jealousy and our hunger, but not their stabs and pangs. It may be thought, however, that these curt legislations are as unsatisfactory as Collingwood's own; but either set must be judged on its ability to cover the phenomena at issue.

It is unfortunate that Collingwood gave no extended account of emotions, other than that they appear at all levels of consciousness and in all experience, and seem to be felt as sensations. And although he intentionally adopted the most general term 'feel' to characterize experience, he failed to remark differences in what we are said to feel, for example, bodily sensations, conditions, and emotional states. It is true that one may know nothing more about a feeling than that one has it, for one can be conscious of strange and indescribable feelings which catch our attention; but there can be no reason, other than a misplaced desire for simplicity and symmetry, to urge that this is the first stage in all experience. One important difference resides in the presence and nature of the object of a feeling, as Thomas Reid[1] pointed out (and cf. *NL*, 5.35); to feel a twinge of rheumatism is to refer to no object, but to feel a pang of jealousy entails thought about somebody of whom one is jealous. Emotions of this sort are characterized by their objects, not by inner sensations; we could not differentiate, for example, disdain, contempt, and derision of X by means of inner sensations. We can be mistaken about our emotions precisely because we can distinguish what we feel and what we know; whereas we cannot distinguish, say, feeling a twinge and knowing what we feel, because there are no alternative descriptions to the one we have already given. And the very same distinction between having, and being aware of having, an experience necessitates some mode of symbolism for the purpose of individuating the object of

[1] T. Reid, *Essays on the Intellectual Powers of Man* (1785), Essay II, ch. 16.

awareness; this role is fulfilled by expression. Prince Myshkin, when he did not know he was in love, was not a man who had feelings of love of which he was unconscious, but rather a man who did not realize that his conscious feelings were those of love.

The consequences of these observations for Collingwood's argument must now be assessed. Some feelings force themselves upon our attention, and of these we become conscious, but we cannot actively attend to them. Of some feelings one cannot become conscious, because this latter notion entails knowledge; I cannot become conscious of my ignorance, slowness, inadequacy, if I am none of these things, even though I can feel my inadequacy and so on. One can attend only to those feelings that are continuous and of which one is already conscious in some way; Collingwood is thus right to talk of focusing at the level of consciousness. Now if art is identified with the expression of feeling, it cannot be the expression of any or all feelings, because some of these force themselves upon our attention. In an earlier essay Collingwood agreed with Ruskin that art arose when one felt strongly *about* something (*E*, 33), which entails a use of 'feeling' which has objects; and although he always held that imagination or consciousness must have objects (*SM*, 70; *NL*, 5.26), he came to hold the mistaken view that feeling itself had no objects (*NL*, 5.2). This aside, he would say that art, as such, was impervious to any distinction between the cause and object of an emotion, since he argued that art was the expression of experience in its immediacy, before it was classified or related to a context; all such questions, since they concern relations, belong to a higher level of consciousness. It should be stressed that Collingwood did not deny that most emotions are tied to thoughts, and have objects (cf. *PA*, 232, 277). But even on the supposition that art is the discovery of whatever the agent himself feels, whether or not those feelings have reference in some way to the external world, it must still be with only a sub-class of feelings that art is concerned, namely, those we can actively attend to, not those which catch our passive attention. Thus, expression cannot be a necessary step to knowledge since this last case shows how we can attain knowledge without it. And there is, in fact, a further restriction upon expression because Collingwood asserts that an artist should be concerned with emotions which he shares with his audience (*PA*, 312).

It may be argued that Collingwood sought to avoid the issues just raised, and in particular the need to give an account of emotions, by maintaining that emotions and ideas are alike only known in, and uniquely characterized by, their expression. For there is a necessary and asymmetrical relation between an emotion and the act expressing it (*PA*, 229, 235, 286), and 'the expression of any given thought is effected through the expression of the emotion accompanying it' (*PA*, 225, 267). The necessity of any expression arises because an emotional charge cannot be felt (*PA*, 238) and thus cannot be known, until it is expressed; what is known depends on the way it is expressed, and thus the expression defines an emotion for what it is. This is the sense in which expression creates what it expresses, and the meaning of the claim that there are no unexpressed feelings (*PA*, 245). It is because of this intimate connection that Collingwood deems it appropriate to ascribe defects of the artist's products to the processes by which they came about (*PA*, 123), and to claim that to praise a work is always 'to praise the artist as such' (*OPA*, 74). An important corollary follows: the emotions we have are determined by the languages we have for expression; thus, the English tongue expresses English emotions; the French, French; music, musical, and so on. All this is in accord with an earlier observation, to which we shall return, that a man's expression is conditioned by his whole previous experience (*OPA*, 94). If it is only by expressing that a man becomes conscious of what he feels, it is not clear how Collingwood would account for a man's recognition of his past states, when, say, he comes to reflect upon descriptions of his behaviour offered by observers. He might say that third-person accounts, based on observation of the agent's behaviour, are in such cases inferences from the agent's betrayals of his emotion; and that he himself achieves expression only when he becomes aware, at whatever time, of his states. Nevertheless, on the view that feelings are evanescent and only propositions about them can be remembered or reflected upon (*NL*, 5.54, 11.18), it is doubtful whether Collingwood's position is here coherent.

Collingwood insisted that an account of art can be given only in the light of a general theory of imagination and language (*PA*, 305). In the early period, as we have seen, to imagine is to isolate, and is an activity presupposed by conceptual thinking. Works of art are defined as functions of the mental activity of imagining and cease to exist with the cessation of that activity. In the later work 'attending' replaced 'isolating' as a central term, and the term 'imagine' and its correlates continued to undergo strain, primarily because 'imagination' was used to denote both the level of an activity and its products. As the name of a level, it was synonymous with 'consciousness', but it also denoted the feelings after consciousness had processed them; that is, imaginations were the proper objects of consciousness (*PA*, 215). At the same time, however, Collingwood used the phrase 'imaginary object' in the same sense. Just as we feel feelings, and think thoughts, so we imagine imaginings; just as the proper object of thinking is a thought, so the proper object of imagining is an imaginary object (*OPA*, 52; *PA*, 173). (He merely asserted, without elucidation, that the relations between activity and object in these cases were importantly different (*PA*, 160).) Hence, by simple transposition, art comes to have imaginary objects as its proper objects; for, although the proper objects of awareness are feelings, awareness is imagination, and imagination is art. Such legislation once more conflates what ought not be conflated. Omitting the consequences of the fact that isolation may be a result of attention, but is not synonymous with it, we should note that whereas attending requires the independence of its objects, imagining does not. In part, Collingwood embraced this point by holding that when imagining we are impervious to the ontological status of the object of imagination (*PA*, 136); but he also confused the matter by insufficiently grasping the ambiguity of any such phrase as 'the object of imagination'. This phrase may be used, and Collingwood generally so used it, to denote the object in imagination, that is, the imagined object having only the properties it is imagined as having (cf. *NL*, 10.33). On the other hand, in contrast to this sense, the phrase may be used to denote the object imagined; in this sense the object may be individuated by means other than the particular one under which it was imagined.

In one sense of the fashionable but obscure terminology, Collingwood holds that a work of art is the 'intentional' object of
imagining; and if it is urged that intentionality always entails
thought, and that intentional objects are inescapably propositional
in nature,[1] he would accept the former and reject the latter claim
(cf. *NL*, 10.26). Being an act of consciousness, the imaginative
construction which is the work of art is an act of thought, but
because it is below the level of intellect it is not yet propositional
(*PA*, 287; *NL*, 10.51). Since the greatest works of art may be
described as the expression of intellectual emotions, however, it
may be wondered whether Collingwood should not agree to the
propositional nature of intentional objects (*PA*, 292–7), in spite of
his rejection of the analogy between imagining and entertaining
hypotheses on the ground that the expressive element of the former
is missing from the latter (*PA*, 286).

Two major features of Collingwood's account may be noted.
He has provided material for an illuminating account of the
ontological status of a work of art as an intentional object. An
intentional object of thought can be individuated only by the
descriptions under which one thought of it; more generally, and
in accord with Collingwood's views, an intentional object of
consciousness can be individuated only in its expression; or, again,
we can become aware of our immediate states only through
language, which, in its primitive expressive form, is art. It is
because a man's knowledge of his states depends on these acts of
expression, that Collingwood asserts 'his world is his language'
(*PA*, 291). Furthermore, because the sole objective of expression
is the clarification of a man's states, questions about their appropriateness to the external world arise only subsequently. It may
transpire, for example, that awareness or clarification of one's
states reveals that they are confused or ill-adapted to their occasion.
Against these aspects of his arguments, however, must be set the
fact that Collingwood does nothing to show how anyone makes
the step from knowledge about himself to justified belief about the
external world (*PA*, 292); any more than he shows how it is possible
for non-conceptual expressive language to give way to conceptual

[1] W. Kneale, *Aristotelian Society, Supp. Vol.*, xlii (1968).

language which in his view is exclusively conventional. In addition, even if he was justified in rejecting some familiar uses of the phrase 'work of art' in favour of his own, he was not justified in ignoring various senses and respects in which works of art are said to be 'imaginative' or are said to show 'imagination' and 'imaginativeness'. In Collingwood's view, to say that art is imaginative[1] is to say that it belongs to the second level of experience; to say that art is expressive is to say that it discharges the emotional aspect of feeling as a means of knowing what it is, and as a means to ensuring its progress to the next level of experience, intellect. To say that art is meaningful is not to say that it has conceptual or contextual reference, for these belong to the next level; it is to say that it is knowledge of the immediate experience, of the individuality, of emotions (*PA*, 269, 289).

5. *Expression*

Collingwood holds that persons are connected by linguistic relations, because, independently of language, no one can compare emotions (*PA*, 248–9). How, then, is one person to understand another's expression? At first, he argues that written or printed words are only hints or traces which a reader must use in order to create in his own imagination the original gesture-situation which constituted expression (*PA*, 243). But for this to be done there must be conventions for connecting traces with the expression, and expression with the emotion, and any conventions, since they entail rules, must belong to the level of intellect, which would preclude the operation from taking place on the level of imagination (*PA*, 251). More seriously, an audience would need to know in advance which phenomena constituted the traces or relevant aspects of them, since not everything a man does is correctly described as the successful outcome of his attempt to do it, and not everything he does counts as expressions of his feelings. Collingwood quotes three conditions for understanding another's gesture, however (*PA*, 251): a hearer must have had relevant impressions of his own,

[1] See T. Mischel, *Australasian Journal of Philosophy*, vol. xxxix (1961), and J. Bailey, ibid., vol. xli (1963).

which he can convert into ideas; to do this he must have an un-corrupt consciousness; similarly, the speaker must have an un-corrupt consciousness. To construct another's idea from the evidence of his words (*PA*, 243) seems to imply that there is a unique emotion for each set of words, and a unique idea for each set of words: and this is a tenet, indeed, which follows from Collingwood's definition of expression. Nevertheless, it is granted that there is no absolute assurance that one man has understood another (*PA*, 251, 309); closely following Nettleship,[1] Colling-wood asserts that there is only a relative, empirical assurance, depending upon how the linguistic relationship develops between them. It should be noted that the view that to understand another's ideas one must have had analogous experience is a legacy from the Humean doctrine of 'impressions', which served the dual purpose of accounting for the acquisition of knowledge, and also for the meaningfulness of concepts. And Collingwood would seek in vain to avoid the 'private-meaning' doctrine by appealing to yet another Humean tenet, namely, that, contingently, people just do have the same experiences on the whole and this secures com-munication. But having defined 'understanding' so that its achievement can never be certain, Collingwood is faced by the problem of how an artist can know whether he is pursuing his task successfully (*PA*, 281).

Two criteria are offered, one internal, the other external. Some of our feelings, remaining in the penumbral region outside the focus of our attention, pass us by; but in the focused area we may succeed or fail in becoming conscious of what we feel. Failure, which is caused by corrupt consciousness (*PA*, 216–20, 280–5), is a denial of one's feelings, a form of self-deception. The account is not entirely satisfactory since, given that a man is trying to express his feelings, the only evidence of a corrupt consciousness is his failure in the attempt; corruption is thus postulated as the cause of something which is the sole evidence of its presence. Furthermore, if a corrupt consciousness is a necessary condition of failure or incapacity to express, it would seem that all audiences of works of art suffer from corruption since, by definition, they have not

---

[1] *Philosophical Lectures and Remarks of R. Nettleship*, pp. 130–6.

themselves expressed their own emotions in this context. Self-deception might well be analysed, however, in terms of a half-realization and suppression, or a refusal to recognize the object and nature of one's feelings. Collingwood does not discuss the extent to which attention to his field of feelings is a matter of the agent's will; but since a man's perturbation might remain after failure to alleviate it, he could always know that he had deceived himself in some way. If this were so, Collingwood would still be able to distinguish cases where a man refuses to act in the light of self-knowledge from cases where he denies what he knows; provided, that is, that perturbation is not allowed just to go away without the intervention of the agent. On the basic premiss, however, that the vast majority of our feelings must remain in the penumbral region outside the focus of attention, it is surely certain that countless perturbations will just disappear without their nature becoming evident. Now the internal criterion of successful expression is that an agent feels positive alleviation from the oppressive perturbation which was a condition of expressing; alleviation is not itself a feeling requiring expression, although it may be felt as a sensation—for example, weeping, although not part of the definition of the emotion it accompanies, is nevertheless felt. A man with a corrupt consciousness cannot erroneously think he felt alleviation, however, because consciousness does not err by referring things to the wrong concept (*PA*, 216); rather, disowning arises from diverting one's attention, not from a mistaken judgement.

One further observation is pertinent. Following many of his philosophical predecessors, including Coleridge,[1] Collingwood argued that to express an emotion and to express it well are the same thing, since to express badly is failing to express; a bad work of art is an unsuccessful attempt (*PA*, 282). It becomes clear that works of art are thus to be defined in terms of attempts or tryings; and this is in accord with the view that art is an activity. Modifying the terminology we may say that whereas all works of art are cases of attempts to express, or express*ings*, only good works of art

[1] S. T. Coleridge, 'On the Principles of Genial Criticism', in *Biographia Literaria*, ed. J. Shawcross (Oxford, 1949), ii, 232.

are successful attempts, or express*ions*. It should be noted that Collingwood avoids the objection that we cannot tell whether the expressed emotion is the same as what was formerly unexpressed, by holding that we simply become more aware of what we were already vaguely aware of; in the sense that awareness modifies, it also creates its objects, which is why there are no unexpressed emotions. 'Expression' is an achievement concept for Collingwood, and his problem is to show how we are able to recognize failures in the attempt; there must be different criteria for the trying, on the one hand, and the success, on the other. In his earlier work Collingwood held that failure to express would be indistinguishable from success at doing something else (*OPA*, 69). Normally, it might be argued that the only way to distinguish not-doing from refraining-from-doing is by reference to the agent's intentions; but although expressing is something intended, the intention cannot be individuated before fulfilment, except by the general characterization of trying to become conscious of obscure feelings. It may have been because of such considerations that Collingwood felt the need to bolster the internal criterion of alleviation with the external criterion of the audience's judgement. An artist is said to take into account his audience's limitations, which then operate as conditions determining the subject-matter or meaning of his work (*PA*, 311–12). It is unclear how an artist could know if he shared emotions with an audience which had not expressed them: if they had been expressed his own efforts would be supererogatory; and any comparison, even if possible, would belong to the level of intellect, not to the imaginative level on which the artist works. Further, 'subject-matter' is inconveniently defined as 'the emotion it expresses' (*PA*, 293), from which it follows that nothing could condition the subject-matter except the mode of expression. Collingwood has a much stronger reason for introducing an audience's judgement, however; he wants to avoid having two different theories of aesthetic experience, one for the artist, the other for the audience (*PA*, 301). In particular, he wants to avoid holding that externalization of the aesthetic experience is unnecessary for the artist, but necessary for the audience because without it they cannot create for themselves the inner aesthetic experience. Omitting the problem of how they identify his failure, it is argued that they can understand what he has done, when he succeeds, if their experience is identical with his, because they come to grasp the nature of their own emotions. Much remains obscure in this view, but one comment may be made. Before the outcome, an artist only knows of his attempts to remove a perturbation (*PA*, 129); even if it is caused by, or is in some way related to, outside objects, he does not yet know this. But as an audience we are bound to describe his activity, not in terms of his private states to which we have no access, nor in terms of his tryings which no longer exist,[1] but in terms of their putative outcome. Collingwood seems to be trying to deny the ineradicable distinction between first-person and third-person statements, and behind this move lurks the assumption, once more, that concepts are meaningful only to those who have had the experience they denote. And yet if Collingwood allows that others may judge an artist better than the artist himself can (*PA*, 314), his own self-knowledge cannot be a necessary condition of others' knowledge of him; and the distinction is re-introduced.

Although Collingwood insists that to possess and to use a language are the same (*PA*, 250), it is not quite clear how primitive thoughts primitively betrayed in natural, unlearnt behaviour (by a baby, say) give way to more sophisticated thought and the expression of it.[2] In what sense are expressions appropriate to emotions (*PA*, 238)? Since it is not self-contradictory for a man to exhibit anger behaviour or love behaviour and yet not be angry or in love, the connection between his states and his gestures characteristically regarded as their expression cannot be necessary, contrary to Collingwood's view (e.g. *PA*, 299). But it is in virtue of very strong conventional correlations that others would be justified in such a case in saying that the man was angry or in love. Usually, it is necessary to know the agent's beliefs and thoughts in a particular context seen under a particular description, before

---

[1] See E. Hanslick, *The Beautiful in Music* (1857), ed. M. Weitz (Indianapolis, Ind., 1957), ch. 3, pp. 59, 60.

[2] Collingwood anticipated some views of Wittgenstein; see, for example, *Zettel* (Oxford, 1967), paras. 191, 513, 534, 549.

we can assess the appropriateness of the description of his expression as an expression of the emotion X. It is important to ask what sorts of mistakes are possible for an owner about his emotion. It would seem that he can be mistaken both about the nature of the emotion, and about its object; such mistakes, Collingwood would argue, arise only from incomplete effort, which amounts to self-deception, for one would know that one felt something, even if one misidentified it. It may be doubted, however, whether Collingwood is right to use the accompanying characteristic of alleviation as the first-person inner criterion of expression; actual experience needs no other experience, *a fortiori* no sensation, as a criterion of its occurrence. Further, he has to hold that we all know what an uncorrupt consciousness is like, for he holds that a man cannot fail to know that he has expressed or failed to express (*PA*, 283); expression of emotion becomes incorrigible, like sincere avowals; but if the criterion of alleviation were allowed, then an inference would be possible of the form 'I feel better, so I must have expressed', which now resembles 'I have been behaving in such and such a way, so I must have been afraid of X', and such an inference breaks the link between expression and self-consciousness.

6. The Practice and Criticism of Art

Collingwood always agreed with Croce that the proper way to approach the problems of aesthetics was via a theory of language, not, as traditionally, via a theory of perception: 'the aesthetic object can be identified with language, i.e., with objects created by us for the purpose of expressing our feeling'.[1] Similarly the notion, although not the term, of 'expression' remained central throughout his writings—the term belongs to the later period (e.g. *EPM*, 212). One concept, earlier prominent, was later dismissed altogether: beauty. In the early work, beauty, defined as imaginative coherence, was the aim of art and posed the central problem for the philosophy of art (*OPA*, 48, 70; *EPM*, 200); later, however, the term merely denoted an attitude of admiration (*PA*, 38, 41), which suggests

[1] Collingwood, review of L. A. Reid, *A Study in Aesthetics* (London, 1931), in *Philosophy*, vii (1932), 325–7.

that perhaps Collingwood had taken more notice of I. A. Richards than he was wont to admit.

The most conspicuous aspect of Collingwood's philosophy of art so far omitted from this selective summary of his views is his discussion of the relations between art and its craft or techniques; these views will provide a convenient bridge to his comments on the task of critics. It should be observed that Collingwood's use of the term 'art' undergoes considerable strain during his discussion of these topics, being used in a colloquial way in addition to the technical sense of something primarily mental, namely, in the early work, the activity of imagining, and in the later, the activity of expressing. Collingwood always stressed that technique was necessary to art, where technique is understood as the control which enables an artist to create exactly what he wants (*OPA*, 117); skill is a necessary, although not a sufficient, condition of art (*PA*, 27) and it is acquired by copying other works of art (*OPA*, 118). But although a strong emotion or a profound interest in something is the germ of the artistic process, once the work has begun 'the problems occupying your mind are the technical problems of your craft' (*E*, 229, 225-6), which cannot be tackled if one is under the dominance of the inspiring emotion; one's work will be accompanied by emotions, of course, but these are in no sense the subject-matter of the art. The 'subject' is distinct from the work, and the artist attempts to give outward form to the way in which he has been impressed by it (*E*, 219, 227; cf. *OPA*, 127 where the 'subject' is the author's experience). In this same essay, dating from 1929, Collingwood argued that two conditions are necessary for art, conviction and technique, a sense of having something to say, together with a mastery of one's craft; the former he called the romantic requirement, the latter, the classical. The obscure emotional perturbations which constitute the conviction do not take the shape of a message until the artist has learnt to speak (*E*, 231), for the work of art is the creature of his technical proficiency (*E*, 226). It is of great interest that artists at any one time confine themselves to a minute number of stylistic procedures, which they modify only gradually; a consequence of this fact is that a work 'cannot be understood or appreciated except by reference to the medium and the stylistic tradition' (*OPA*, 120–1). The critic's task is precisely that of explaining the processes by which an artist reached his particular point of view (*OPA*, 67, 152), for the tradition to which he belongs circumscribes the content and the form in so far as they are intimately related (*PA*, 318–20). In his later work, Collingwood stresses that the emotional subject-matter of works of art is usually drawn from emotions at the intellectual level; but, on the premiss that works uniquely express an artist's emotions, the status and permissibility remain unclear of his claim that 'what emotions it expresses' are those of 'thinking in a certain way and then expressing how it feels to think in that way' (*PA*, 292–6). This is especially so since his concept of expression entails a denial of any standard form–content distinction. He admits that artists begin their work with very mixed motives, and also that some emotions are more worthwhile than others, but it is never clear whether an artist is allowed to choose from the galaxy of emotions he may be experiencing which to express (*PA*, 302–3; *SM*, 70; cf. *E*, 214).

Collingwood would justify his use of the phrase 'work of art' to cover both physical artifacts, where they exist, and mental experiences, on the ground that the production of, say, physical paintings is 'necessarily connected with the aesthetic activity, that is, with the creation of the imaginative experience which is the work of art' (*PA*, 305). It is in virtue of this necessary connection that an audience can retrace the steps, as it were, back to the work of art proper; it is an assumption that, even in the absence of a theory, most people have no difficulty in discriminating art from other things (*PA*, 3). Recognition of instances, however, is quite different from understanding, and for the latter the audience has to engage in a re-creative activity, as we have seen. A number of recent historians of art and also psycho-analysts have given a similar account of the audience's role as re-creation, including Panofsky, Gombrich, and Ernst Kris.[1] The problem-solving

[1] e.g. E. Panofsky, *Meaning in the Visual Arts* (New York, 1955), p. 15n; E. Kris, *Philosophy and Phenomenological Research*, vol. vii (1947–8), reprinted in *Psychoanalytic Explorations in Art* (London, 1953), p. 254; E. H. Gombrich, *Art and Illusion* (London, 1960), *passim*.

element of the artist's activities has been stressed both by historians and philosophers,[1] and among the latter Stuart Hampshire follows not only Collingwood's analysis of expression, but also his distinction between the aesthetic and technical aspects of art.[2] Karl Popper[3] also subscribes to Collingwood's view of the development of language from primitive signs, via expression and description, to the higher levels; to his view that the problem solved by expression is only recognized in its solution (*PA*, 315); and to his view that problem-solving always proceeds by trial and error—a view which Collingwood perhaps insufficiently emphasized before *NL*, 11.37, although it is implicit in most of what he says. Collingwood's assertion that art is embedded in the full social life of the community to which it belongs should also be stressed (*OPA*, 151). But does the mere conformity of his views with those of such artists and critics as Proust and Roger Fry[4] justify renewed attention to his attempts to synthesize commonly fragmented issues?

7. *Conclusion*

Collingwood insisted that every work of art possessed non-aesthetic qualities;[5] but he was concerned primarily with the aesthetic essence of art. In seeking to define that essence he also tried to do justice to the large number of questions that arise in connection with art, such as its relations to emotions, imagination, understanding, self-deception, knowledge, morality; these questions, in his view, were prior to those concerning the language of criticism, to which his successors addressed themselves. To the extent that his theory of art depends on, and is integral to, his theory of mind, it must be judged unsatisfactory; for his theory of mind often repeats traditional muddles. I have criticized above

[1] Cf. B. Croce, *Aesthetic as Science of Expression and General Linguistic*, trans. Douglas Ainslie (2nd ed., New York, 1922), ch. 17.

[2] S. Hampshire, 'Logic and Appreciation' (1952), in *Aesthetics and Language*, ed. W. Elton (Oxford, 1954); and general arguments in *Thought and Action* (London, 1959), *Freedom of the Individual* (London, 1965).

[3] K. R. Popper, *Of Clouds and Clocks* (Missouri, 1966).

[4] e.g. R. Fry, *Vision and Design* (London, 1920), *passim*. For Proust, see my 'Knowledge and Illusion in *À La Recherche du temps perdu*', *Forum for Modern Language Studies*, vol. v (1969).

[5] Collingwood, in *The Mind*, ed. R. J. S. McDowall (London, 1927).

the logical coherence of some of the central tenets, as well as Collingwood's conflation of importantly different concepts.

Although it remains possible that expressing might be a sufficient means to knowledge, Collingwood failed to establish that it is a necessary means. On Collingwood's assumption that art is the discovery of whatever the agent himself feels, whether or not those feelings have reference to the external world, it can be with only a sub-class of feelings that art is concerned; namely, those to which we can actively attend, not those which catch our passive attention. I argued that the existence of these latter feelings shows how we can attain knowledge without expression; and, in any case, it is not clear how the doctrine of expressing explains those occasions on which a man achieves recognition of his past states. Objections were also urged against the two necessary conditions of successful expressing, namely, trying and the possession of an uncorrupt consciousness; and against the two accompanying characteristics used as criteria of success, namely, the artist's inner alleviation and his acclaim by an audience. It was unclear how an audience, by definition unable to express, could judge an artist's success, even on the further obscure assumption that their emotions were shared. And if, in spite of these objections, they were able to judge an artist better than he himself, his self-knowledge could not be a necessary condition of another's knowledge of him; it then becomes hard to see how his mere attempt at expressing remains a necessary condition of knowledge. It was not obvious how an audience could check either themselves or the artist for corruption of consciousness; and if they could understand his expression only by re-creating from its traces, they would need clear rules for this operation, in which case their engagement would belong to the level of intellect, not imagination. In parenthesis, it should be noted that Collingwood's notion of craft denotes an activity subsequent to expression, since it belongs to the level of conceptual thought. I argued that alleviation seemed to be possible without expression or clarification of one's feelings. On Collingwood's premiss that the majority of a man's feelings remain beyond the focus of his attention, many perturbations will disappear without their nature being known; the cessation of perturbation could not therefore be an unambiguous criterion of knowledge through expression. Further, inferences would be possible from the recognition of the alleviation to the recognition of the expression, in which case the intimate link between expression and self-consciousness would be broken. Above all, no experience requires another as a criterion of its occurrence.

Collingwood did not himself satisfactorily fuse his theory of mind with his theory of language, nor either of these theories with his knowledge derived from the practical experience of art. Most that is fruitful, illuminating or true in his writings derive from the latter two sources; indeed, the tension between the sources became most apparent whenever, all too infrequently, he sought to test his philosophical theory against particular works of art. It should not be inferred from the criticisms made above, and others that can be made of his arguments, that Collingwood's work in this field is no longer worthy of attention; space alone has precluded an attempt to modify, where possible, his central positions in order to retain their insights but avoid the objections. Before the next comprehensive account of art is attempted, we shall need not only wide and detailed experience of particular works of art against which to measure our theories, but also careful analysis of all the complexities of the central concepts used in, and presupposed by, our account. Collingwood at least has the merit of having showed us what most of those concepts are.

IV

ON AN ALLEGED INCONSISTENCY IN COLLINGWOOD'S AESTHETIC

RICHARD WOLLHEIM

1. In Book I of *The Principles of Art* Collingwood asserts that the work of art is something imaginary: it exists in, and only in, the artist's head or mind. In Book III he denies that the relation of the audience to the work of art is non-existent or inessential. Collingwood goes on to say that these two views—one an assertion, the other a denial—which conjointly constitute his aesthetic, are not inconsistent: though superficially they might seem so. The inconsistency that Collingwood concedes that some might allege, but that he would dispute, provides the theme of this paper.

However, two preliminary points.

2. First, it might be objected that the first of the two views that I have attributed to Collingwood is in fact not his. For the view that he actually holds is considerably weaker. So we find him writing, 'A work of art need not be what we should call a real thing' (*PA*, 130); or 'It may be what we call an imaginary thing' (loc. cit.); or, again, 'A work of art may be completely created when it has been created as a thing whose only place is in the artist's mind' (loc. cit.). In other words, the objection would run, the sense in which the work of art is asserted by Collingwood to be imaginary is perfectly compatible with its being, or its also being, in the real world.

Now, there clearly is such a sense. Moreover, it is a sense that would appear to be recognized by Collingwood: as, for instance, when he writes of the plan for a bridge, which can, at different times, be in the engineer's head, and on his drawing-board (*PA*, 134), or indeed, of the bridge itself which can, at different times, be in the engineer's head, on his drawing board, and thrown across the river (*PA*, 132). I maintain, however, that it is not in this sense that the work of art is asserted by Collingwood to be imaginary. The point is not easy to establish. With so carelessly written a work as *The Principles of Art*, appeals to the text are vain, if not perilous. So a more fundamental form of argument is called for.

If we start by asking what sort of claim Collingwood thought he was making in asserting that the work of art is imaginary, the answer is that he thought that he was making a claim about the nature of the work of art. Now, to assert that something is imaginary in the sense in which this is compatible with its being, or its also being, in the real world, is to assert that it is being imagined: and to assert that something is being imagined is not to make a claim about its nature. For we can, in principle at least, imagine anything. However, to assert that something is imaginary in the sense in which this is incompatible with its being, or its also being, in the real world, is to make a claim about its nature—as we do, for instance, when we assert this of gods, or the heroes of mythology, or fictitious characters. So, I would maintain, there is at least a *prima facie* case for holding that Collingwood's view that a work of art is something imaginary requires a strong interpretation, or, at any rate, a stronger interpretation than his 'need not be real' or 'may be imaginary', in the formulation of his view, would naturally suggest. Though in this sense, I shall maintain, the claim is certainly false.

3. I have expressed the second of the two views that I have attributed to Collingwood by saying that he is concerned to deny that the relation of the audience to the work of art is non-existent or inessential. And this way of expressing it may suggest that Collingwood is equally concerned to deny the claim either way round. However, it must be pointed out that Collingwood's primary concern is to deny that the relation is non-existent, i.e. that the audience has no knowledge of, or acquaintance with, the work of art. And, indeed, it is not hard to see how the first of Collingwood's two views might be thought to commit him to the non-existence of a relation of knowledge or acquaintance between the audience and the work of art.

The view that the relation of the audience to the work of art is inessential comes about only in a roundabout way. It comes about only if, to the view that the work of art is imaginary is appended a subsidiary premiss designed, in the first instance, to obviate the conclusion that the relation of the audience to the work of art is non-existent. The subsidiary premiss would achieve this design by maintaining that the artist always could, though he never did, externalize the work of art by making an object which, though not itself a work of art, yet stood in such a relation to the work of art that the audience could, through knowledge of, or acquaintance with, it, have indirect knowledge of, or oblique acquaintance with, the work of art. Collingwood, however, argues that any such subsidiary premiss could be objected to—quite apart, that is, from the conclusion to which it leads, which is, in Collingwood's eyes, no better than the conclusion it is designed to obviate. The subsidiary premiss could, according to him, be objected to because it belongs to what he thinks of as the technical theory of art; and this makes it for him both objectionable in itself and inconsistent with the view about the imaginary nature of the work of art to which it is appended, and, which, in some sense, it is designed to protect.

4. Collingwood argues for the view that the work of art is imaginary by considering the way in which the work of art comes into being; more specifically, the fact that it is made, or made up, or created, in the artist's mind or head.

Now, clearly, everything that is imaginary is made or made up in the mind or head: it could not be made or made up in the real world. But, does the converse hold? And the answer seems to be, No. For if we accept that the engineer can make, or make up, a plan in his head, the plan that he makes up could also be in the real world—if, for instance, it were drawn. In other words, the engineer's plan would be imaginary only in what we have seen to be the weak sense of the notion: that is, the plan may be imagined, and, indeed, is imagined by the engineer.

I conclude, therefore, that Collingwood is wrong to argue that the work of art is imaginary, where this touches on its nature, by considering the way in which it comes into being. For such considerations do not provide conclusive evidence as to its nature.

But, at this stage, I might be rounded on in the following way: I argued, in section 2, that Collingwood's view that the work of art is imaginary must be taken in the strong sense, since, in asserting it, he thought that he was making a claim about the nature of the work of art. But now we are considering Collingwood's argument for his view that the work of art is imaginary, and I am arguing that this argument is insufficient to establish that the work of art is imaginary, where this touches on its nature. Why do I not rather argue the other way round, and say that, since Collingwood clearly regards his argument as sufficient, this shows that, in arguing for the view that the work of art is imaginary, or in asserting that the work of art is imaginary, he is not concerned to make a claim about its nature?

To this I would have two retorts. First, Collingwood clearly regarded his argument not merely as sufficient to establish that the work of art is imaginary but as sufficient to establish this where this touches on its nature. Secondly, his argument is sufficient to establish something about the nature of the work of art—though not that it is imaginary. I shall now take up this last point.

5. The example by means of which Collingwood argues for his view that the work of art is imaginary is that of a man making or making up a tune in his head. And there are three features of this case on which he concentrates.

The first is that the tune is complete before the man endeavours to set it down on paper. 'This tune is already complete and perfect when it exists merely as a tune in his head' (PA, 139). The second is that, when the man endeavours to set down the tune on paper, what he sets down is not the tune. 'The musician's tune is not there on the paper at all. What is on the paper is not music, it is only musical notation' (PA, 135). And the third feature is that, when we listen to music, the music is not just the sounds that we hear. 'What we get out of the concert is something other than the noises made by the performers . . . [W]hat we get out of it is something which we have to reconstruct in our own minds, and by our own efforts; something which remains for ever inaccessible to a person who cannot or will not make efforts of the right kind, however completely he hears the sounds that fill the room in which he is sitting' (*PA*, 140–1).

This last feature is one of considerable generality; for the premiss it takes is simply the fact that a tune is something to which meaning or sense can be assigned. An argument that runs from the fact that something has meaning or sense to the conclusion that it is in (and not just made, or made up, in) someone's head or mind not merely lacks any evident plausibility but raises issues larger than can be dealt with in the present context. Accordingly, I shall pass over this feature of the example, and it is with the other two that I shall be largely concerned.

6. Collingwood, I want to maintain, is right to see the first two features as linked, though wrong in the link that he sees.

Roughly, Collingwood thinks that the fact that what the man sets down is musical notation is a consequence of the fact that the tune is complete in the man's head, and, furthermore, it shows that the view that the tune is imaginary is properly taken in a strong sense, such that the tune could only be in the man's head. By contrast, I maintain that the fact that what the man sets down is musical notation is a precondition of the fact that the tune is complete in the man's head, and, furthermore, it shows that the view that the tune is imaginary is properly taken in a weak sense, such that the tune need not be in the man's head.

7. Let us consider the following activities:

> writing a (short) poem
> composing a tune
> painting a picture
> making a sculpture

I shall call these art-activities.

And now let us in each case postulate an internalized version of that activity so that e.g. a man writes a poem in his head.

It will be evident that, as we go down the list, an increasing discrepancy asserts itself between the original activity and the internalized version of it. The difference between making a sculpture and making a sculpture in one's head seems greater than that between writing a (short) poem and writing a (short) poem in one's head. And, significantly—though I shall not make much of this—a natural way of thinking about making a sculpture in one's head, or, for that matter, painting a picture in one's head, is as imagining making a sculpture or imagining painting a picture: whereas to talk of imagining writing a (short) poem is in no sense a natural way of talking about writing a (short) poem in one's head, for it is to talk of something quite different.

There are, perhaps, various ways in which the discrepancy to which I refer can be characterized. One way is that, when I write a poem in my head, I can write a complete poem, whereas, when I paint a picture in my head, I cannot paint a complete picture. Another way is that when I write a poem in my head, there is (or may be) a poem that I have thereby written, whereas, when I paint a picture in my head, there is not (or cannot be) a painting that I have thereby painted. For the moment, I want to bear in mind the first way in which the discrepancy can be characterized, and to put to one side the second way: for, clearly, to take it up straightaway would be to beg the issue at stake.

And now we have a choice. For it would be possible to regard the discrepancy as something not further explicable. On this view, it would be an irreducible fact of nature, or of our inner life, or both, that certain art-activities lend themselves readily to internalization whereas others only do so awkwardly or incompletely. Now, there certainly are some broad facts about the various art-activities and, behind them, about the different media of art that bear upon the issue, but to leave the whole problem resting on them, and to leave them quite unspecified, seems highly unsatisfactory. Furthermore, it will be appreciated that the discrepancy itself comes into focus only when we move beyond contrasting, say, writing and writing in one's head with painting and painting in one's head, and take as the terms of the contrast writing a poem and writing a poem in one's head, on the one hand, and painting a picture and painting a picture in one's head, on the other hand. In other words, the discrepancy becomes evident when we take into consideration not just the art-processes or the media of art but also the resultant works of art. Perhaps we have here a suggestion or an intimation which will enable us to pursue the discrepancy a little further and not leave it as an unexamined brute fact.

8. Works of art fall into two very different categories. Some, like poems or pieces of music, are types: others, like paintings, are particulars. This distinction is not explicitly recognized by Collingwood, and I should like to suggest that his indifference to it is responsible for some of the ultimate difficulties of his aesthetic, as well as for some of the unjustified plausibility that attaches to it on a cursory reading. I think that we can come to see this by considering the following three facts, all of which are grounded in this important logical distinction within works of art: between what I shall from now on call work of art-particulars and work of art-types.

(i) that it is a sufficient condition of the making of a work of art-type that one should internally produce (e.g. say to oneself, play to oneself) a token of that type

(ii) that it is a sufficient condition of a work of art's being a work of art-type that it should be expressible in a notation

(iii) that the discrepancy between an art-activity and the internalized version of it arises acutely, or, more acutely, with work of art-particulars.

These three facts are interrelated in a number of interesting and complex ways. I shall take up just a few of these ways as they are relevant to our theme.

9. Let us begin with (i).

This in part rests upon certain empirical differences between the art-activities or the various media of art to which I have already made reference in general terms (section 7). Nevertheless, it would be quite wrong to think that (i) can be explained entirely in terms of, say, the peculiar adaptability of music to internalization, or a peculiar power that we happen to have for internally producing music. For what is germane here is not simply that we can internally produce music, nor even that we can internally produce a tune, but that we can internally produce a token of a tune-type. And this depends partly (it is true) on certain empirical differentiae of music, but partly on the fact that tunes are types, or, more generally, that pieces of music are work of art-types. And this last fact is, of course, not an empirical but a logical fact.

However, just as there are empirical considerations that bear upon internalization, so there also are empirical considerations that bear upon the question whether the works of a given art are work of art-types or work of art-particulars. If we turn to (ii), we see that one empirical consideration that bears on this question is whether a notation for the expression of a given art, or of works in that art, is available. For where such a notation is available, then there is a clear and determinate way of individuating particulars as tokens of a given type, and hence of identifying the work of art with a type.[1]

Thus there is clearly a relation between (i) and (ii), in that the existence of a notation enables a certain way in which work of art-types may be made, i.e. through the internal production of a token of these types. The question now arises whether the relation is stronger, in that a notation is required if works of art are to be made in this way. Now, clearly there can be an art whose works are work of art-types and yet there be no available notation for the expression of these works: consider prints. But the further question is whether in such an art the work of art-types can be made in the relevant way: that is, by the internal production of a token. (Clearly prints aren't). And the answer seems to be, No. It is only where a notation is available that this method of making works of art can be employed—even though, of course, in the making of these works of art, there need not be employment of, or resort to, the notation. If a man composes a piece of music, and does so by playing it to himself, he does not, in the course of this, write out the score to himself. Nevertheless, the existence of a notation in which such a score could be inscribed does seem to be a precondition of the way in which he composes the music.

Now, for the relations between (iii), on the one hand, and (i) or (ii), on the other. It must already be evident that the case where

[1] See on these issues Nelson Goodman, *Languages of Art* (London, 1969).

the minimum discrepancy arises between art-activity and its internalization is where the work of art can be made through an exercise of the internalized activity. And this, as we have seen, presupposes that the work of art is a work of art-type, not a work of art-particular. Conversely, the discrepancy will be at its greatest where the art-activity is exercised in production of work of art-particulars. And we can see this to be so in virtue of two closely related logical features of the situation—apart, that is, from any empirical considerations that bear upon the issue. In the first place, in, say, painting a picture to oneself (or imagining painting a picture), one is not engaged in internally producing a token of a type which, in turn, is a work of art. And this might even suggest that, in painting a picture to oneself, one is not making a picture: though it is possible that one might later make the picture that one previously painted to oneself (or imagined painting). However—and this is the second feature—the identity of a painting that one paints to oneself and some painting that, at a later moment in time, one actually paints is notoriously difficult to determine. These two features, taken together, account for the somewhat tenuous relation, or discrepancy as I have called it, between painting a picture and painting a picture to oneself.

10. Collingwood, as we have seen, argues for his view that the work of art is imaginary, by means of the example of the man who makes or makes up a tune in his head. The preceding discussion will have shown on how complex and delicately poised a set of factors this case rests. What is true of it cannot, without grave risk of error, be generalized over the other arts. It cannot, without certainty of error, be applied to those arts where the two conditions structural to Collingwood's example do not conjointly hold: that is to say, to those arts of which it is not true that their works are both work of art-types and expressible in a notation. For, unless these two conditions hold, though one may be able to engage in the internalized version of the relevant art-activity, this will not necessarily result in the making of a work of art.

Furthermore, in Collingwood's example and in any other case for which what is true of it holds true, the resultant work of art will be imaginary only in a weak sense. Indeed, in a sense weaker than any we have conceived. For, if a man makes up a tune and does so by playing the tune in his head, it does not seem correct to say that the tune is in his head, though it need not be—which is, it will be recalled, what it is for something to be imaginary in the weak sense. That is to say, it does not seem correct to say this so long as reference is intended to the tune-type. What is true is that there is a tune-token that is in the man's head i.e. the tune-token that he plays in his head in the course of composing the tune, and there could be, probably will be, other tune-tokens not in his head i.e. those that are actually played, if his tune receives that degree of attention in the real world. But it is unclear that this justifies us in saying that the tune, if this means the tune-type, is, or ever was, in the man's head: or, for that matter, out of it.

11. With the first of the two views that constitute Collingwood's aesthetic so evidently in ruins, it is hard to know what is to be made of the second view.

Collingwood himself, as we have seen, was anxious to claim their consistency. And perhaps the most promising interpretation that can be put on this claim is that the second view deals with those arts to which the first is, though not recognized by Collingwood to be, inadequate. In other words, the second view might be taken as giving the aesthetic of those arts whose works are work of art-particulars. However, it is difficult to proceed far with this suggestion, precisely because the view that Collingwood advances in Book III of *The Principles of Art* is so very fragmentary. It seems that, instead of an internalized art-activity, we are, rather, to think of an activity that is compounded partly of an art-activity and partly of an internal activity. However, the suggestion seems to be at once that these two activities can be independently identified and that they are inextricably connected. For instance, apropos painting. 'There are two experiences, an inward or imaginative one called seeing and an outward or bodily one called painting, which in the painter's life are inseparable, and form one single indivisible experience, an experience which may be described as painting imaginatively' (*PA*, 304–5). Too little indication is given how these activities combine. A similar uncertainty attaches to the characterization of the work of art that issues from this dual activity, and how it is to be categorized: what principles of identity and individuation apply to it.

Collingwood's aesthetic, for all its audacity and its richness of suggestion, for all the concern it most evidently expresses for art and the arts, suffers irreparably from the failure to harmonize the demands of mental philosophy and those of philosophical logic. It was the fault of the times, as much as the failure of the man, that these demands seemed so irreconcilable, the products of an ultimate conflict of interests.

V

RELIGION AND THE RAPPROCHEMENT BETWEEN THOUGHT AND ACTION

LIONEL RUBINOFF

IN 1934 R. G. Collingwood was asked by the editor of *Philosophy* to define the role of philosophy in the modern world. He replied that 'philosophy ought in some way to help our generation in its moral, social, and political troubles'. But, he continued, as currently practised it is far from contributing to that end (PNP, 262). Some years later he repeated this charge complaining that philosophers of today have no sense of the philosopher's calling. They neither hear, nor even listen for, the voice of Delphi at whose beckoning Western philosphy, through the agency of Socrates, became a genuine *Geisteswissenschaft* (FML, 62 ff.).

The important thing about Socrates, the first not only to have *answered* the call but to have become *aware* of what it *meant* to have done so, was that in becoming a philosopher he ceased to act solely in his private capacity. He had become, at Apollo's bidding, the organ by which the corporate consciousness of the Greeks examined and criticized itself, and in so doing, according to Collingwood, Socrates defined for all times the calling of philosophers, which is, to re-affirm the covenant first made by Socrates, and to bear witness thereafter. The philosopher sets out to redeem himself by contributing toward the redemption of his fellows. In more secular terms, the philosopher is one who criticizes his generation's ideas of itself, and what it is doing, in order thereby to criticize his own idea of what he is and what he is doing—thereby amending his idea of himself in order to amend further his neighbours' ideas of themselves.

As the organ of his own society's self-criticism the philosopher finds himself called to follow Socrates in the calling that led Socrates to condemnation and death. That call came from Delphi; and the philosopher who makes his pilgrimage to Delphi sees there not merely the place where long ago an event happened which was important in its time and may still interest the historian, but the place whence issued the call he still hears a call which, to one who can hear it, is still being uttered among the fallen stones of the temple and is still echoing from the pathless peaks of the daughters of Parnassus (*FML*, 68.)

But, Collingwood warns, in answering this call there is a temptation which philosophers must resist. They must resist descending like a *deus ex machina* upon the stage of practical life and out of their superior insight into the nature of things, dictate the correct solutions for this or that problem in morals, economics, and politics. The Delphic call proposes not that professional philosophers be dragged, blinking from their studies and forcibly seated on thrones; it suggests, rather, 'that expert knowledge of political life and its practical difficulties should be illuminated by philosophical reflection on its ultimate end'. This again is not to be confused with mere moralizing and rhetorical exhortation. For, as Hegel so ably pointed out, in the Preface to his *Phenomenology of Mind*, philosophy must beware the temptation to be edifying. Philosophy, he argued, seeks not edification but insight.[1] Were Collingwood and Hegel to be writing today, they might well have been tempted to add that philosophy must also beware the temptation to be 'relevant'. It is through the labour of the notion and not mere rhetoric that philosophy illuminates the problems of its time.

But if philosophy must beware the temptation to be edifying (the mark of romanticism) it must equally be wary of falling under the spell of mere formalism, the attempt to reduce the flow of concrete existence to mere abstraction. This latter tendency is exemplified by 'logicism' and 'positivism'.[2] The message of 'logicism' and 'positivism' is the view that, with the possible exception of mathematics and natural science, philosophy has

[1] *The Phenomenology of Mind*, transl. J. B. Baillie (London, 1955), p. 72.
[2] 'Logicism' is discussed in 'Ruskin's Philosophy', in Alan Donagan, ed., *Essays in the Philosophy of Art* by R. G. Collingwood (Bloomington, Ind., 1964), pp. 9 ff., while 'Positivism' is discussed in *EM*, 143 ff.

little of interest to contribute. And whether or not philosophy is dealing with science or with the life-world, the results of philosophic thinking make no difference to the actual conduct of its subject-matter, and philosophy, therefore, is no more able to influence the processes which it describes than astronomy can influence the movement of the stars. It thus follows, that the only motive to pursue it is a pure disinterested curiosity, the only good to be gained from it, pure theoretical knowledge, and that Plato, Spinoza, and all others who have thought this knowledge some-how serviceable to our well-being were victims of a gigantic and inexplicable illusion (*PNP*, 263).

The truth, according to Collingwood, lies somewhere between these extremes, and the task of philosophy is to achieve a rapproche-ment between theory and practice. This means that the philosopher is neither the pilot shouting orders from the bridge nor a mere spectator watching the ship from his study's window. He is rather one of the crew and must bear a responsibility commensurate with that position. Philosophy so defined aims at what Bernard Lonergan calls 'Insight'.[1] Insight or understanding (*Verstehen*), as opposed to mere theoretical knowledge (*erklaren*), is itself a *praxis*. As *praxis* insight transforms thought into action in such a way as to give rise to further insights, which in turn lead to better policies and more effective courses of action. Insight is thus dialectical. If it occurs at all, it continues to recur, leading not simply to the accumulation of knowledge, but to a deepen-ing of it. At each recurrence, in other words, knowledge itself undergoes substantial change, so that the distance between thought and action steadily decreases. Collingwood, for example, likens the process of knowledge to the flow of a river 'always rising at its source, always flowing over each part its course, and always discharging itself into the sea' whose unity is 'the unity of an infinitely increasing spiral rather than the unity of a rotating circle' (*OPA*, 94–5). Knowledge makes a difference not only to the knower but to the object known (A, 44 ff.). The world of action becomes a more and more adequate home for reason and consciousness, while reason and consciousness become more and more adequate to

---

[1] *Insight* (New York, 1900).

the task of giving rise to actions in accordance with justice. The philosopher's 'knowledge is therefore explicitly action; he is creating himself by knowing himself, and so creating for himself an intelligible world, the world of spirit in general' (*OPA*, 94).

It was Collingwood's view, however, that the flight from understanding which characterized his time, blocks insights and dams up the flow of knowledge. The result is a succession of unintelligent policies and inept courses of action. But the process of corruption is also dialectical. For as situations continue to deteriorate, the demand for intelligence increases, and as this in turn is blocked, policies become even *more* unintelligent and actions even *more* inept. What is worse, the deteriorating situation seems to encourage a reliance on emotional substitutes for actions which should otherwise have been informed by reason. So in ever increasing measure, intelligence and reason come to be replaced by emotion and rhetoric. Human activity settles down to a decadent routine and initiative becomes the privilege of violence. As the poet W. B. Yeats put it, in his remarkable poem, "The Second Coming":

> Turning and turning in the widening gyre
> The falcon cannot hear the falconer;
> Things fall apart; the centre cannot hold;
> Mere anarchy is loosed upon the World,
> The blood-dimmed tide is loosed, and everywhere
> The ceremony of innocence is drowned;
> The best lack all conviction, while the worst
> Are full of passionate intensity.[1]

Thus are born the conditions which, according to Collingwood, lead to the process of 'barbarization', the mark of the 'New Leviathan', as manifested throughout the 1930's in the phenomena of Fascism and Nazism.

In such a world, the inference which any young person can draw for himself—when told that philosophy is a mere exercise in logic, producing only *theories* of action without making any difference to the *performance* of such action—is, 'that for guidance in the problems of life, since one must not seek it from philosophers or

[1] *Collected Poems* (London, 1952), pp. 210–11.

from philosophizing, nor from philosophies and principles, one must look for guidance to people who were *not* thinkers (but fools and Sophists), to processes that were not specimens of thinking (but passion) to aims that were not ideals (but caprices), and to rules that were not principles (but rules of expediency)'. If, then, philosophers and educators desire to train up a generation of young persons as 'the potential dupes of every adventurer in morals or politics, commerce or religion, who should appeal to their emotions and promise them private gains which he neither can procure then nor even *means* to procure them', no better way of accomplishing this can be recommended than by preaching the dogma that knowing makes no difference to the object known, and philosophy is, therefore, indifferent to the quality of action (*A*, 49).

The flight from understanding, which we have been discussing, contributes to conditions which give rise to what Collingwood has aptly described as 'The Propaganda of Irrationalism' (*EM*, 133 ff.). Irrationalism is an epidemic withering of belief in the obligation to think and to act in a systematic and orderly way. The epidemic, as Collingwood has pointed out, will express itself in every aspect of life. In education, for example, it manifests itself as the practice of favouring technical and vocational training and pretending that it is education; in religion it appears as a cult of emotion which in our own time has replaced the anguished and disciplined search for God. Infecting politics, it is the substitution of order for virtue, of emotional communion with a leader's thought for intelligent agreement with him, of conformity by terror for conformity by persuasion, of unpatriotic and treasonous activities for criticism and dissent.

But let us suppose next that the tissues of the civilization invaded by this irrationalist disease are resisting it. The infection can thus progress only by concealing its true character behind a mask of conformity to the spirit of the civilization it is attacking. The attack will not succeed if the victim's suspicions are aroused. If you explicitly propose to abandon the ideals of justice and morality, you will lose your reputation with the persons you are trying to infect. But so long as nothing like a panic sets in, liberties can be taken which otherwise would not have any hope of succeeding.

In short, 'let a sufficient number of men, whose intellectual respectability is vouched for by their reputations, pay sufficient lip service to the ideals of justice and morality, and they will be allowed to teach by example whatever kind of injustice and anti-morality they like, even if this involves a hardly disguised breach with the accepted canons of scientific method'.

The ease with which this can be done will be much greater if it is done in a society dominated by a cult of abstract specialism, a cult whose distinguished lineage can be traced as far back as the Renaissance. By abstract specialism Collingwood means, both the idea that the study of any single subject can be carried out in isolation from every other subject, and the dogma that the scientific, philosophical, or intellectual pursuit of truth must be conducted in total indifference to its ethical implications.

The most damaging consequence of specialism is the reluctance of others to criticize the work of a specialist or to test his results and ideas by applying them to the actual practice of living. In that case, the agents of irrationalism can ensure immunity by putting forward their propaganda under the pretence that it is itself a special science which other specialists will understand that they must neither criticize nor subject to the test of lived experience. Irrationalism thus avails itself of the privileges accorded by a *rationalist* civilization in order to undermine the fabric of that civilization. Eventually, this kind of irrationalism will produce a total inversion of the moral order. In the beginning, at the time of Socrates' covenant with Delphi, *praxis* was regarded as the servant of truth and morality. Gradually, however, the two were allowed to separate: morality and the pursuit of truth became indifferent to the practical needs of political action. And finally, the battle won, irrationalism celebrated in its victory by rejoining morality and action—but this time morality was placed in the service of action. This is the source of the special problem of modern times, the disease of modern man, which Collingwood identifies as 'the co-existence of overproduction on the one side with unsatisfied demand on the other' (*SM*, 21).

On the one hand, there is an unsatisfied demand for art, religion, and philosophy. On the other, there is a crowd of artists, philosophers, and ministers of religion who can find no market for their wares. Every street and every village in the country contains people who are hungering for beauty, for faith, for knowledge, and cannot find these things. And those who have them are starving for mere bread, because no one will buy. The producers and consumers of spiritual wealth are out of touch; the bridge between them is broken and only a daring spirit here and there can leap the gulf (*SM*, 20).

II

It was Collingwood's lifelong belief that philosophy selects its subject-matter from the special problems of the generation or age in which the philosopher lives. For most of modern history, and in particular during the seventeenth century, the most pressing philosophical problems were posed by the attempt to develop the natural sciences. The primary task of philosophy was to provide a reasoned vindication of the possibility of science. In the end the possibility of science is grounded in the belief that nature is a single system of things, controlled by a single system of laws. In adopting this idea, 'civilized man was setting aside his immemorial belief in demonic agencies, magical influences, and the inscrutable caprices of individual things, and accepting a new view of the world, not received on faith, and not arrived at by scientific induction, but thought out and stated in a systematic form by the philosophers of the sixteenth century. This philosophical conception of nature has played the part, in relation to scientific research, of a constant stimulant to effort, a reasoned refutation of defeatism, a promise that all scientific problems are in principle soluble' (*PNP*, 264).

As the seventeenth century needed a reasoned conviction that nature is intelligible and the problems of science in principle soluble, so the twentieth needs a reasoned conviction that human progress is possible and that the problems of moral and political life are in principle soluble. In both cases the need is one which only philosophy can supply. What is needed today is a philosophical reconsideration of the whole idea of progress or development, and especially its two main forms, 'evolution' in the world of nature and 'history' in the world of human affairs. What would correspond to the Renaissance conception of nature as a single intelligible system would be a philosophy showing that the human will is of a piece with nature in being genuinely creative, a *vera causa*, though singular in being consciously creative; that social and political institutions are creations of the human will, conserved by the same power which created them, and essentially plastic to its hand; and that therefore whatever evils they contain are in principle remediable. In short, the help which philosophy might give to our 'dissatisfied, anxious, apprehensive generation' would lie in a reasoned statement of the principle that there can be no evils in any human institution which human will cannot cure (*PNP*, 265).

The two most pressing problems of modern times, then, according to Collingwood, are first of all the problem of the co-existence of overproduction and unsatisfied demand, and secondly the loss of confidence in the efficacy of reason. Overproduction is driven by the propaganda of irrationalism which feeds what Lewis Mumford has called 'the forces of anti-life now swarming through our inner world, proclaiming that mechanical automation is superior to personal autonomy, that empty confusion is authentic design, that garbage is nourishing food, that bestiality and hate are the only honest expressions of the human spirit'.[1] Meanwhile the loss of confidence in the efficacy of reason is a direct result of the academic dogma, that knowing makes no difference to the object known. This too is a consequence of the propaganda of irrationalism, which, as we have already noted, is itself to be traced to the Renaissance cult of abstract specialism. It is this dogma, according to Collingwood, more than any other one, which has contributed to the spiritual crisis of the modern world.

In the first flush of that dawn, when art, religion, and thought, strengthened by their long medieval discipline of intimacy with each other, broke apart and suddenly began to work miracles, men might be excused for thinking that in their mutual separation lay the secret of their well-being. But the contrary soon appeared. Each, cut off from the others, tended more and more to lead its followers into some desert where the world of human life was lost, and the very motive for going on disappeared. Each tended to become a specialized activity pursued by specialists for the applause of specialists, useless to the rest of mankind and unsatisfying even to the specialist when he turned upon himself and asked why he was pursuing it. This is the point to which we have come today . . .

[1] Cited in L. Rubinoff, *The Pornography of Power*, New York: Ballantine, 1969 p. 42.

This is the fruit of the Renaissance. . . . In the middle ages the artist was perhaps not much of an artist, the philosopher was by our standards only mildly philosophical, and the religious man not extremely religious; but they were all men, whole of heart and secure in their grasp on life. Today we can be as artistic, we can be as philosophical, we can be as religious as we please, but we cannot ever be men at all; we are wrecks and fragments of men, and we do not know where to take hold of life and how to begin looking for the happiness which we know we do not possess (*SM*, 34–5).

If, as Collingwood suggests, what is wrong with us is precisely the detachment of the forms of experience—art, religion, and the rest—from one another—then our cure can only be their reunion in a complete and undivided life. The task of philosophy, then, in the modern age, is to 'seek for that life, to build up the conception of an activity which is at once art, and religion, and science, and the rest' (*SM*, 36). But this, as Collingwood himself insists, is the fundamental principle of Christianity, 'that the only life worth living is the life of the whole man, every faculty of body and soul unified into a single organic system. Incarnation, redemption, resurrection of the body, only repeat this cardinal idea from different angles' (*SM*, 27).

This principle, implicit in the doctrines of Christian ethics, teaches that the individual man is nothing without his fellow men—and this not *in spite of* but *because of* the absolute worth of the individual; that the holy spirit lives not in this man or that but in the church as the unity of all faithful people. It was thus in their institutionalism and their insistence on the unity of the mind that the middle ages were distinctively Christian. And it was for this reason that Collingwood regarded the Renaissance version of individualism as a revolt against Christianity and a return to paganism.

For the separatist principle is the principle embodied in the pagan world and idealized in the pagan philosophies; whether it takes the form of slavery or the doctrine of the immortality of the soul, whether it appears as a practice of religion in which divine worship is a duty to be discharged and done with, or as a theory of art in which piety and fear are emotions to be got rid of, when they become troublesome, by attending a tragedy (*SM*, 37).

7

For the Christian, as never for any pagan, religion becomes an influence dominating the whole of life, and this unity of life, once achieved can never be forfeited again. The permanent effect of Christianity is that consciousness is compelled toward some form of unity; either the positive concrete unity achieved by bringing every activity into harmony, or the negative abstract unity achieved by suppressing all but one or else bringing everything into conformity with one. The pursuit of concrete unity was the goal of the middle ages. The achievement of negative unity was the consequence of the Renaissance. The Renaissance idea of unity is thus not a genuine alternative to the medieval synthesis, but rather a pathological corruption of the rationality of life, or as Collingwood himself put it, 'a kind of desperate Christianity, the Christianity of the plucked-out eye and the lopped-off limb' (*SM*, 38).

The solution, then, if it is to be a genuinely Christian one—and it is clear for Collingwood that only a *Christian* solution can be a *genuine* one—must lie in a recovery of the concrete unity which once pervaded the middle ages, or to use philosopher's language, in a restoration of the concrete universal. The hope of the world's future lies, then, in some kind of revived medievalism, some new interpretation of Christianity. And the only philosophical tradition adequate to that task of interpretation is, as we shall see, the tradition of Hegelian idealism. For Collingwood the growth of spiritual unity, indeed the growth of culture itself, is synonymous with the return of Christianity and its philosophical counterpart, absolute idealism, the idealism of the concrete universal.

According to Collingwood, then, not only is the unity of thought and action to be achieved according to the model of Christianity, but Christianity itself must be expected to contribute to this achievement. It is thus evident that religion occupies an importance equal to that of any of the other basic forms of life and knowledge. Indeed, a careful reading of the development of Collingwood's thought from the publication of *Religion and Philosophy* in 1916 to *The New Leviathan* in 1942 suggests that religion (in the form of Christianity) is the *sine qua non* of the very possibility of the self-realization of the other forms. Against the then fashionable claim that since knowing makes no difference to the object known, the aim of philosophy of religion is to inquire into the structure, meaning, and essence of religion in abstraction from any commitment to religious truth as such. Collingwood argues, as we have already noted, that in any encounter between philosophy and religion there must be mutual self-disclosure and self-making, and no inquiry into the structure of religious experience can be separated from a commitment to that experience.

Now the only one who can be expected to judge an experience, is he who has lived it (*SM*, 44). What is more, to embrace a particular form of religion and to believe in its validity are one and the same thing (*SM*, 43). In other words, for Collingwood, philosophy is not simply methodology but is a systematic attempt to render explicit what is already implicit (*EPM*, 11). It therefore follows that to be a philosopher of religion is to be the archaeologist of one's religiosity. The philosopher of religion is *qua* philosopher a religious man committed to a religious truth. And since in every case of knowledge we are committed not *cogitare* simply but *de hac re cogitare* (*RP*, 100), the philosopher's religiosity is not just a general attitude toward reality but a specific set of commitments. For Collingwood that set of commitments is to Christianity.

III

In addition to the importance which Collingwood attaches to religion throughout much of his writings, however, it is also the case that he places religion at the lower end of the developing scale of forms which characterize the growth of knowledge. In *Speculum Mentis*, for example, Collingwood introduces the metaphor of the natural growth of human beings as a model for understanding the natural order of the forms of life (*SM*, 50–7). The life of individuals he suggests, falls into periods of predominantly aesthetic, predominantly religious or predominantly intellectual activity. Art is the natural food of the very young. Religion comes next. But both religion and art are assigned to the pre-puberty stage of development while scientific and intellectual activities are assigned to the post-puberty period of development. Finally, Collingwood argues, 'the same general tendency towards a series of phases

beginning with art seems to be at work in the history of mankind'
(*SM*, 51).

Now the fact that Collingwood places religion at the pre-puberty
stage of development, and hence at the lower end of the scale of
forms, has misled some of his critics into concluding that religion
therefore enjoys a lower order of priority than do the higher forms
(science, history, and philosophy). It is also claimed that in the
course of time religion has been superseded by the higher forms
and has therefore been rendered obsolete. Thus, for example,
Louis Mink argues that by 1928 Collingwood had adjudicated the
conflict between reason and faith in favour of philosophy, leaving
religion with nothing in particular to say or have said for it.[1]
Mink thus argues that since Collingwood had virtually nothing to
say about religion after 1928, it is reasonable to suppose that 'once
Collingwood explicitly elaborated his notion of the scale of forms,
he came to believe that religion survives only as the unarguable,
absolute presupposition of science (that the universe is knowable),
of action (that life is worth living), and of art (that the world is
our home or is not) . . . But all the questions, all the struggle, and
all the fun, are in science, action and art'.[2]

Mink bases this judgement in part on the fact that 'Collingwood
had virtually nothing to say about religion after 1928' and in part
on Collingwood's declaration in 'Reason is Faith Cultivating
Itself' (1927) that while 'reason cannot generate faith . . . reason
alone can reveal faith to itself, can display to it its own nature'.[3]

Similar conclusions have been reached by T. M. Knox and Alan
Donagan. Donagan supports Knox's claim that 'the sceptical strain
in Collingwood's thought appears in his attitude to Christian
doctrine, while it is the claims of philosophy which tend to be
dogmatic.'[4]

---

[1] Review of L. Rubinoff, ed., *Faith and Reason, Collingwood's Papers in the
Philosophy of Religion, Journal of the American Academy of Religion*, vol. xxxviii,
No. 1 (March 1970), pp. 119–20.

[2] Ibid., p, 119.

[3] Ibid., p. 120. Passage from Collingwood cited in Rubinoff, op. cit., p. 119.

[4] T. M. Knox, Preface to the *Idea of History*, p. xv; A. Donagan, Review of
L. Rubinoff, ed., *Faith and Reason, Collingwood's Papers in the Philosophy of
Religion, Dialogue: The Canadian Philosophical Review*, vol. vii (March 1969), pp.
678–81.

According to Knox, Collingwood's view on religion underwent change in the direction of paying less and less emphasis on religion as a contributing factor to the life of reason. In *Speculum Mentis*, for example, Collingwood explicitly withdrew from his earlier identification of religion with theology and philosophy and adopted instead a view of religion, according to which, religion mistakes imagining for thinking, and asserts the reality of what is only a symbol. Christianity solves the religious problem of reconciling God with man and thus prepares the way for its supersession by philosophy. If the Christian religion continues in existence, it is 'only because it is the sole means of escaping the superstition which is a constant pitfall for the human mind'.[1]

In 1928, however, Knox continues, Collingwood put forward a new view. In 'Faith and Reason' (1928) religion and philosophy are shown to be mutually implied and indispensable to each other. Taken together, they produce a truth which is universal and valid for all thought.[2] The shoals of scepticism and the billows of dogmatism have been safely passed and the ship is at anchor in the calm sea of that philosophical serenity which produced the *Essay on Philosophical Method* and the (unpublished) philosophical theology which in 1933 closed his lectures on ethics.

Finally, according to Knox, all this was washed away by the publication of the *Essay on Metaphysics* in which absolute presuppositions (the content of religious faith) are no longer said to be knowledge. They are no longer universal characteristics of all thought but are rather historically conditioned. With the *Essay on Metaphysics* the attitude of reason toward absolute presuppositions becomes one of unquestioning acceptance, the basis of which is more irrational than rational.[3]

Against Mink's interpretation, I would argue that to define reason and philosophy as the dialectical presupposition of the possibility of the self-understanding of religion does not necessarily imply that the only role left for religion *per se* is to supply the unarguable absolute presuppositions of science, action, and art.

---

[1] Knox, op. cit., p. xv.
[2] Ibid., p. xvi.
[3] Ibid., p. xvi.

Primitive as religion may be with respect to philosophy, religion is and will forever remain the *sine qua non* of philosophy. Thus, while it is true, as Mink points out, that *qua* religion or *qua* faith, consciousness is unable to give an account of itself to itself, it is only because there is already a truth implicit in faith that reason is able to render that truth explicit.

As for Knox's claim that with the possible exception of 'Faith and Reason', Collingwood's attitude toward religion wavers between scepticism and irrationalism, one can only appeal to the systematic role assigned to religion throughout the whole of Collingwood's thought as evidence to the contrary. Knox's observation that in *Speculum Mentis* religion is imagining mistaking itself for thinking, must be evaluated in the context of Collingwood's theory of dialectic underlying the scale of forms, a doctrine to which Knox pays insufficient attention. One must distinguish in *Speculum Mentis* between religion as a category or habit of mind and religion as a specialized discipline or form of knowledge.[1] As a general category of mind, religion is metaphor mistaking itself for literal assertion. As a specialized form of knowledge, religion undergoes a dialectical development which exhibits the influence of the other forms of knowledge. There is thus an aesthetic, a scientific, an historical and a philosophical form of religion. The latter is founded on a rapprochement between faith and reason which assimilates all of the other forms. In philosophical religion, all of the other forms, the aesthetic, the scientific, the historical, are accounted for. Rather than being a source of scepticism, religion is recognized as the source of knowledge. The relationship between religion and philosophy parallels the relationship between intuition and concepts. Faith without reason is blind, being nothing more than metaphor mistaking itself for literal assertion. But reason without faith is empty, being a mere habit without 'punch'.

We must also take into account that, according to the theory of the scale of forms, the forms undergo development both vertically and horizontally, so that the process which stretches horizontally over a given period of time repeats itself vertically at each stage of

---

[1] On this distinction see L. Rubinoff, *Collingwood and the Reform of Metaphysics* (Toronto, 1970), pp. 113 ff.

horizontal development. Thus Collingwood declares, in the very same passage in which he assigns religion to the pre-puberty stage of child development, 'a little later, beginning at puberty, the same process seems to repeat itself on, as it were, a higher level' (*SM*, 50). Thus Collingwood declares with respect to the logic of individual development:

Childhood, adolescence, and maturity seem thus to correspond with art, religion, and science as their proper spiritual antitypes; and each phase splits up into the art, religion, and science of childhood, all tinged with the fancifulness of art, the art, religion, and science of adolescence, all affected by the passionate and devotional character of religion, and the art, religion, and science of maturity, all consolidated by the reflectiveness and stability of thought (*SM*, 51).

And this means, in so far as the logic of the scale of forms is con-concerned:

that our five forms of experience are not five abstractly self-identical types of event which, by their recurrence in a fixed or changing order, constitute human experience; but types whose recurrence perpetually modifies them, so that they shade off into one another and give rise to new determinations and therefore new types at every turn (*SM*, 56).[1]

IV

The relationship between religion and philosophy which is implied by the logic of the scale of forms is two-fold. On the one hand, as we shall see, religion supplies the emotions from which the habits of reason, the various political and ethical beliefs, derive their 'punch'. At the same time, religion, in the shape of Christianity, contains the implicit structure of philosophy, and the clue to the solution of certain pressing philosophical problems. Thus, Collingwood declares, the Christian creed is to be treated, not as a dogma, but as a critical solution of a philosophical problem (*RP*, xiii). In *Religion and Philosophy*, the problem is identified as the classical problem of permanence and change, monism and pluralism, transcendence and immanence, while in *Speculum Mentis*, as we have already noted, the special problem of modern

[1] For a further amplification of Collingwood's doctrine of the scale of forms see L. Rubinoff, *Collingwood and the Reform of Metaphysics*, ch. III, v.

life is identified as 'the co-existence of overproduction on the one side with unsatisfied demand on the other' (SM, 24).

In Religion and Philosophy, the philosophical problem is posed as follows. 'Is every part an independent and entirely individual mind or is there one mind, of which every separate thing in the universe is a fragment and no more?' (RP, 96). Upon the resolution of this problem depends the possibility of a genuine human community, which for Collingwood means an intersubjective community of individuals.

Collingwood characterizes the issue between monism and pluralism as follows. Pluralism, like realism, aims at the preservation of the freedom and reality of the individual without, however, defining the structure of the relationship among individuals. Pluralism conveys the false impression that the individuality of the individual can be conceived independently of every other individual. Nor does it account for the fact that the single individual is itself a product of a plurality of experiences, such as, for example, in the case of the individual person with respect to the many acts which make up the history of his mind and character.

Monism, like nominalism, asserts the abstract reality of the whole at the expense of the parts. Neither monism nor pluralism, however, are satisfactory. Each is one-sided and dogmatic. Neither succeeds in dealing with the problems at hand. Neither provides a proper model for comprehending either the nature of personality or the nature of community. Collingwood inquires into the self-identity of the person and the self-identity of society at one and the same time. The person is 'the unity of a single consciousnesses', while a society is 'the unity of different and co-operating consciousnesses' (RP, 97). Communication between two or more persons presupposes that two or more persons can actually share the same knowledge—the two pieces of knowledge being identical, not merely resembling each other. The important thing about knowledge is that it can be communicated, which means that knowledge is not a state or property of mind, in the sense in which weight, for example, is a property of body.

Collingwood's definition of 'mind' as a being whose essence (knowledge) is to share itself with another, serves as a differentia from nature proper and begs comparison with the distinction between mind and nature drawn in the *Idea of History*. In that work, mind is defined as the product of a self-making process. It is now clear that this is in turn derived from the Christian view of 'person'.

For Collingwood, since two people may be conscious of the same object, the question arises, 'Do they thereby share the same consciousness?' 'Is my mind different from your mind?' Collingwood's response draws attention to the presupposition underlying the difficulty that minds are objects, possessing the property of knowledge, as table possesses the property of holding things (*RP*, 100). But mind is pure act. The mind seems to be not so much that which thinks as the thinking itself; not so much an active *thing* as an *activity*. Its *esse* is *cogitare*.

Collingwood's definition of mind is one which today would be regarded as phenomenological. Mind is intentional. To speak of consciousness at all is to speak of consciousness of something definite, of an object intended. 'There is no thought in general but only particular thoughts about particular things.' To repeat: 'The *esse* of mind is not *cogitare* simply, but *de hac re cogitare*.'

The identity of minds, which forms the basis of the inter-subjective community, is explained by arguing that two minds are identical to the extent that they have knowledge of the same object. Collingwood anticipates two sorts of objections which might be raised against this doctrine and deals with them accordingly.

The first sort of objection may be stated as follows. Granted A's mind is nothing but his consciousness of X, and B's mind nothing but his, yet A's mind and B's remain absolutely different. Each knows the same thing, but it is now argued that each knows it by having a 'thought about it' which is peculiar to himself. Against this, Collingwood contends that it is based on an instance of the confusion between thinking in the sense of knowing and imagining. My imagination of the table is certainly a different thing from the table itself, but my knowledge of the table is simply the table *quod nos*. My thought of the table is not something like the table but *is* the table as I know it. Similarly, your thought of the table is what you know of the table, the table as shown to you;

and if we both have knowledge of the same table, it seems to follow that our thoughts are the same, not merely similar. Further, if the mind is its thoughts, we seem to have, for this moment at least, actually one mind; we share between us that unity of consciousness which was said to be the mark of the individual (*RP*, 101; *FR*, 173).

This distinction between imagination and knowledge closely resembles the distinction of *Speculum Mentis* between pure imagination, defined as sheer supposal, 'the attitude which neither asserts reality, truly or falsely, nor denies it, but merely imagines' (*SM*, 76) and thought defined as the assertion of reality. The imagination, so defined, can never be the basis of society. Each person lives in his own imagination; taken together, a world of imaginations is lived by the imagination alone, a world of windowless monads. 'This is because they are acts of imagination, from which it necessarily follows that they are careless of mutual consistency and interested only in their internal coherence' (*SM*, 71). This monadic withdrawing into itself of the aesthetic consciousness, this ignoring of everything factual, even of its own historical nature and situation, is the necessary consequence of its imaginative character (*SM*, 72).

Community is made possible only when consciousness shares the common objective of the pursuit of reality. It is only because the intention of mind is to know reality that such knowledge is possible and that two minds, through knowledge of that reality, become one. But the attitude which makes this possible is religion. Religion is the attitude which not only intends reality but which makes possible the pursuit of reality by minds which do not yet possess it. For the mind cannot know whether it has possession of reality until it has made the effort to know it, and that effort is fraught with error. It is therefore only on the faith that reality is a possible object of knowledge, that such an act is bearable. Hence, Collingwood declares in *Speculum Mentis*:

Religion is social, as art can never be ... the sociability of religion is part of its fundamental nature ... religion ... is assertion, and in its higher forms knows that it is assertion ... Now assertion ... is the recognition of reality as such, and reality is that which is real for all minds. If a number of minds are engaged in 'imagining', they have no common ground, for each man's imaginations are his own. But if they are engaged in asserting, they at once become a society, for each asserts what he believes to be not his own but a common property, objective reality. And even when their assertions are different, they are not merely different like different works of art, but contradictory; and contradiction, even in its extreme forms of persecution and war, is a function of sociability (*SM*, 116).

A second possible objection rests on a distinction between two elements in knowledge, namely, the object, and the act of knowing itself. Knowledge, as possession, may be common to different minds, but knowledge as activity is peculiar to the individual mind. Collingwood's reply anticipates the doctrine of mind as pure act, as stated in *Speculum Mentis* and in his 1923 essay 'Can the New Idealism Dispense with Mysticism?' According to this doctrine, there is no act of mind which is not, to use more contemporary language, 'intentional'. To repeat once again: the *esse* of mind is not *cogitare* simply, but *de hac re cogitare*. There is therefore no difference between thinking and willing to think, and willing is willing some particular goal. Thus, if two minds are identical in thinking the same thing, they are equally and for the same reason identical in willing to think the same thing. To know and to will to know are one and the same.

The account given above of the conditions which account for the possibility of communication leads to the conclusion that, as knowledge becomes common property, the minds concerned come to share the same content. And because to know X is equivalent to willing to know X (i.e. willing to act in such a manner as brings knowledge of X about), to share a common body of knowledge is to share the will to action whereby that knowledge is made possible. Thus, to share the knowledge of what constitutes 'justice', 'good', and 'duty', for example, is to share the intention of realizing through action the 'ideals' upon which such knowledge is based.

If there is a co-operation of will and action, what is the consequence? Since willing, like knowing, is always the will to do some particular thing, the distinction between the will and its specific actions, like the distinction between mind and its objects, is quite abstract. My will is nothing more nor less than the things I do.

It thus follows that in so far as the relationship between individual wills is concerned: 'If two people will the same thing, the personal distinction between them has given way to an identity, in virtue of which the two can be described as one mind' (*RP*, 104).

But how is the communion of different minds to be saved from being converted into a mere blank identity which is indistinguishable from a blank nothingness? Given that the structure of thinking and knowing is the basis of identity, how do we account for differences?

Collingwood locates the source of differentiation both on the the side of the subject and on the side of the object. On the side of the subject, identity consists in the fact that each wills the same thing; it is an identity not existing as a fixed unchangeable fact but depending for its existence on the continued harmony of the two persons. It does not unite them inspite of themselves but because they choose to be united (*RP*, 105). Will is not only the power of acting but the power of choosing how to act (*RP*, 103).

It is thus the freedom of the will to dissolve the communion, which is the source of individuality. But, Collingwood warns, if, because of its freedom, a mind may forfeit the unity, whether with itself or another, to which it has attained, that does not mean that it never attained it. 'For all the conquests of mind are made and held by its own freedom, held no longer than it has the strength to hold them; and it can only lose its strength by its own self-betrayal' (*RP*, 105).

Collingwood's argument on the side of the object is to define the object as a concrete rather than an abstract universal.

Any truth or ideal of conduct expresses itself under infinitely various aspects. A single truth never means quite the same thing to different minds; each person invests it with an emphasis, an application peculiar to himself. This does not mean that it is not the same truth; the difference does not destroy the identity any more than it destroys the differences. It is only in the identity that the difference arises (*RP*, 106).

The truth is the object of my will-to-action. But since the truth is a concrete universal, it does not appear *qua* truth like the absolute shot out of a pistol. It appears rather as one perspective, whose content is affected by the situation in which it appears. Yet the whole of 'being itself' or 'truth' is communicated through that 'moment'. To know one moment of truth is to caress (but not to consume) the body of the whole. And thus to will my aims (given that these aims are experiences of truth) is to will the whole, including the aims and perspectives of others.

The community of aims consists in the fact that what I want is something which I cannot have, except with your help and that of everyone else. The object of my desire is one part of a whole which can only exist if the other parts exist. . . . I desire the existence of a whole to which I can only contribute one among many parts. The other parts must be contributed by other people: and thereby in willing my part, I will theirs also (RP, 106).

The unity, whose possibility Collingwood seeks to prove is the fully concrete identification, by their own free activity, of two or more personalities. The individual members of a society are related to the whole in such a way that the generic unity of the whole may be said to be identical with its individual members. This means that the question 'What is X?' leads to questions concerning the relations of X to Y, Z etc. A definition of X can only take the form of a definition of the whole system, X, Y, Z. Thus Collingwood declares:

To explain the nature of the part we have to explain the nature of the whole; there seems to be no distinction between the part and the whole except that the part is the whole under one particular aspect, seen as it were from one point of view. In the same way and in the same sense, Y and Z are identical, each with the whole and with each other and X. Each part is the whole, and each part is all the other parts (RP, 111).

The character or self of a thing, what it is, cannot be separated from its relations (RP, 112).

In the *Essay on Philosophical Method* (1933) the formal and logical relations between the whole and the part are more clearly worked out. In the language of this work the person is 'a scale of over-lapping forms' and a society likewise is a scale of overlapping forms. The structure of society thus reflects the integrity of the person, and what self-knowledge is to the person so 'communism' is to society. According to the logic of the scale of forms, the actions of the individual person do not stand to his self-hood or self-identity as the species of a genus to the genus. For, according to the logic of species and genus, the species are co-ordinate and mutually exclusive, and the generic essence transcends the variable element. There is thus no sense in which the appearance or discovery or even behaviour of a new species makes any difference to the essence of the genus. Whether the genus is interpreted as 'society', 'being', or 'God', then, the behaviour of persons—whether that behaviour be social, ontological (i.e. directed toward knowledge of being), or devotional—makes no real difference to the essence of reality (whether that reality be social, ontological, or religious). The actions of persons must be interpreted as expressive of a reality which pre-exists to the acting out of man's intentions, rather than productive of that reality which is created through the acting out of man's intentions. The latter is provided for only by the logic of the scale of forms, according to which, the generic essence rather than transcending the variable element, is identical with it, so that, as the latter undergoes change, so does the former.

The implications of the logic of species and genus are expressed in the dogma that 'knowing makes no difference to the object known' or 'acting makes no difference to the reality or nature expressed through that action'. In the act of knowing, mind conforms to the object known, and in acting, man conforms to the pre-existing laws of action. The philosophical guardians of these dogmas are realism and positivism. The implications of the logic of the scale of forms, however, are expressed in the doctrine that knowing makes a difference both to the knower as well as to the object known, and acting, whether it be political, scientific, aesthetic or religious, is not only the product but the source of reality. And all action, of whatever form, is historical.

V

This doctrine, that all action is historical, and all historical action is a form of self-making, which readers of Collingwood will recognize as central to his entire philosophy, is explicated by

Collingwood in terms of the Christian image of the incarnation. In one of the most important passages in all of his writings, Collingwood declares, with respect to the relationship between philosophy and religion:

Religious imagery cannot prove the truth of any philosophy, because the interpretation put upon such imagery is already the work of philosophy; but it will illustrate, if it does not help to demonstrate, our conception of the absolute mind to point out the way in which one religion at least has expressed itself, when dealing with the ultimate questions which here concern us.

God is conceived as the absolute spirit, alpha and omega, the beginning and the end. Behind him, beyond him, apart from him, there is nothing: neither matter nor law, neither earth nor heaven, neither space nor time. In the beginning, by an absolute act which was not itself subject to any determination of time or space, God created the heavens and the earth: the visible world, with all its order and furniture, even the very space in which it floats and the time in which it endures and changes, is the work of this absolute act. But this world is no mere toy shaped by God and thrown off from himself in contemptuous alienation. His spirit moves upon the face of the waters, even the waters of chaos, and this same breath becomes the soul of life in the man whom he creates in his own image. Man is one with God, no mere part of a whole, but informed by the indwelling of the divine spirit. Now man, by his misguided thirst for knowledge, partakes of that knowledge which is forbidden, namely error, or the human wisdom which negates God's wisdom. This error deforms his own true, that is divine, nature, and the deformation takes the shape of banishment from the presence of God into the wilderness of the visible world. Having thus lost even the sight of God, the knowledge of what he himself ought to be, he cannot recover his lost perfection until he comes to know himself as he actually is. But not knowing himself as he ought to be, he cannot know himself as he is. His error is implicit just because it is complete. It can only become explicit if God reveals himself afresh, if the true ideal breaks in upon the soul clouded by error. This, in the fullness of time, is granted. Human nature sunk in error is confronted by the confutation of its own error, and thus, through a fresh dialectical process, redeemed.

Now in this imagery there is one flaw, namely the transcendence of God. God standing aloof from the drama of human sin and redemption, a mere stage manager, is no true symbol of the absolute mind in its concreteness. But this is exactly where the truth of our religious imagery shines most brilliantly. It is God who accepts the burden of error, takes upon himself the moral responsibility for the fall, and so redeems not his creature but himself.

The absolute mind, if our account of it is true, can never be more profoundly or impressively pictured than in this drama of the fall and redemption of man (*SM*, 302–3).

This relationship between man and God, as expressed in Christian doctrine, is the basis, not only of the theory of reality expounded in *Speculum Mentis*, it is also the basis of social ethics and hence of community, the community of the *New Leviathan* as well as of *Religion and Philosophy* (*SM*, 304–5).

The contingent unity of the mere habit of tolerance and co-operation thus gives way to the concrete unity of the interacting scale of forms, the unity of intersubjectivity. Just as philosophy builds its absolute out of the differences of the world as it finds them, dealing individually with all contradictions and preserving every detail that can lend character to the whole, so theology finds its God in the same system of differences, in a world of man. 'Here, as elsewhere, the instinct of religion is the deliberate procedure of philosophy at its best' (*RP*, 115). Indeed, as *Speculum Mentis* makes clear, it is only out of the implicit structure of religion that philosophy grows.

In *Religion and Philosophy* Collingwood asserts the doctrine of God as immanent-transcendent, a doctrine which can be understood only in terms of the metaphysics of concrete universality. To begin with, we must distinguish carefully between the various kinds of abstract identity, on the one hand, and the identity of the concrete universal on the other. The relation between man and God, for example (which coincides with what in *Speculum Mentis* is identified as the relation between the forms of knowledge or types of experience and the prize of truth (41 ff.)) can be represented in a variety of different ways. In the first place, there is the position of 'absolute transcendent theism', according to which only one man is truly divine (*RP*, 149, 163). Secondly, there is the doctrine of 'immanent pantheism', according to which all men are *equally* divine (*RP*, 148–9, 162). Another version of this same view is 'materialism', which represents God as a whole composed of separate and mutually exclusive parts (*RP*, 152).

In *Religion and Philosophy*, Collingwood advances various criticisms of these two views, In the first place, he points out that they both proceed from the same logical error of postulating an abstract separation between God as universal and man as particular. 'These two tendencies of false logic,' he writes, 'the tendency to elevate one particular into the standard and only real instance of a universal' (*RP*, 163), and the tendency to regard every man as 'equally an instance of that nature and a manifestation of the essence of God' (*RP*, 164), both assume that 'God is the universal of which man is the particular'. This assumption is part of the logic of the abstract universal, or the logic of genus and co-ordinate species. But, Collingwood declares, the logical conception of the universal, or, the logic of genus and species, 'is in fact inapplicable to the relation between God and other minds'. 'And therefore we cannot argue that any particular mind shows the nature of God as well as any other. The question to be asked about mind is not what it is, but what it does; a question with which the logic of things does not deal' (*RP*, 165). Against these false views of the relation between the universal and the particular Collingwood advances an alternative interpretation which introduces the concept of a 'concrete identity in difference' (*RP*, 151 ff.). The latter is essentially an 'identity of intention' (*RP*, 158): a concept which is only imperfectly worked out in *Religion and Philosophy* but which is given a more definitive expression in *Speculum Mentis* and *An Essay on Philosophical Method*.

At the centre of the doctrine of immanence–transcendence is a concept which appears throughout the whole of Collingwood's thought. In *An Essay on Philosophical Method*, for example, Collingwood argues that there are three types of universal judgement which, however appropriate they may be in science, are inappropriate to philosophical analysis. The first type of judgement is the generalization in which the content of the universal is determined by the act of generalizing from instances. Thus, for example, it might be noticed that many individual right acts promote happiness—from which it is presumed that their being

8

right is either identical or in some way especially connected with
their 'felecific' property. This judgement corresponds to the
position of 'absolute transcendent theism', which embodies the
dogmatic tendency to define the whole of the genus in terms of
only one of its species (*EPM*, 112–13). The second type of judgement 'treats the concept or universal as a genus, distinguishes its
various species, and looks for the generic essence in the shape of
something common to these species and indifferently present in
all of them' (*EPM*, 113 and 37 ff.). This corresponds to the doctrine
of 'immanent pantheism'. Finally, there is the third type of judgement. But this differs from the second only in the sense that the
universal element which binds the species together, rather than
deriving from an empirical survey of the species themselves, follows
by definition from the *a priori* nature of the universal. In effect,
however, the consequences are the same—namely, the species are
mutually exclusive and are univocally related to the generic concept whose essence transcends the specific variables. Perhaps this
type of judgement can be compared with the dogma of materialism.

Against these false interpretations of the relation between the
universal and the particular, Collingwood proposes, in *An Essay on
Philosophical Method*, a 'fourth' way of arranging the elements
of judgement. This 'fourth' way, which is really a synthesis of the
first three, proceeds by 'arranging the species in a scale and showing
that the features of the generic essence shine out more clearly as
the scale reaches its culmination' (*EPM*, 115–16). This is clearly to
be compared with the doctrine of immanence–transcendence or
'concrete identity in difference' which Collingwood advances in
Religion and Philosophy as the proper Christian interpretation of the
relationship between man and God.

Both the doctrine of immanence–transcendence, which characterizes the relationship between God and man, and the doctrine of
judgement, which characterizes the relationship between the
universal and the particular, may be compared with the doctrine
in *Speculum Mentis* concerning the relationship between truth and
the various forms of experience which seek to express it. Collingwood likens that relationship to a competition for the prize of truth.
Now a prize may be dealt with in one of three ways. It can be given

to one competitor and denied to the others; it can be divided between two or more of the competitors; or, it can simply not be awarded at all. The first way corresponds to both the doctrine of 'absolute transcendent theism' and the first type of judgement while the second way corresponds both to the doctrines of 'immanent pantheism' and materialism and the second and third types of judgement. But the third way of awarding the truth, however, is the moment of scepticism and negativity which constitutes the turning-point in the dialectical recovery of truth. It leads to the insight which Collingwood characterizes as a new beginning (*SM*, 50). For implicit in the third way is the recognition that the argument for the separation of forms is illusory. And this is only the negative moment of a total process for which the positive moment is the systematic organization of these claims into a scale of forms. As Collingwood himself puts it:

. . . we are asking for a type of experience capable of giving true knowledge. Now to say that there is no such type is to imply that one *knows* both what knowledge would be if it existed, and that it does not exist. But this is to claim for oneself the possession of that very knowledge whose existence one is explicitly denying. That form of experience, therefore, which denies truth to all the five recognized forms claims to be itself a sixth form which is the rightful claimant to truth. Hence the refusal to allot the prize stultifies itself (*SM*, 42).

If criticism is to survive this paradox, then, it must clearly make a new beginning (*SM*, 50). This new beginning, however, is not just a fourth alternative but is more like a Hegelian *Aufhebung*, a synthesis which both rejects and preserves what has gone before. The characteristics of this new beginning derive from the insight that the recognition of the illusory nature of each form's claim, to exist independently of all the others, must be accompanied by the realization that the truth has, after all, been implicit from the start, and that the five types of experience constitute an overlapping scale of forms, each exemplifying the truth to a degree by embodying it more adequately than the one below (*SM*, 50, 55, 56).[1]

The new beginning announced in *Speculum Mentis* thus bears a positive resemblance both to the doctrine of 'concrete identity in

---

[1] Cf. Rubinoff, op. cit., ch. III.

difference' announced in *Religion and Philosophy* and the fourth
type of judgement announced in *An Essay on Philosophical Method.*
All three solutions to their respective sets of problems are recog-
nizably expressions of the 'Christian solution' (*SM*, 38).

Collingwood's attempt to restore the unity of life by restoring
the rapprochement between the forms of experience is, then, by
his own declaration, conceived as an essentially Christian response.
The fundamental principle of Christianity, according to Collingwood, is that 'the only life worth living is the life of the whole man,
every faculty of body and soul unified into a single organic system
(*SM*, 36). Christianity teaches that the individual is nothing without his fellow-men, that the Holy Spirit lives, not in this man or
that, but in the church as the unity of all faithful people' (*SM*, 37).
Such a doctrine is the basis of the philosophical doctrine that truth
resides not in any particular form of reason but in all forms united
together in a single dynamic unity, which Collingwood calls the
concrete universal (*SM*, 196, 221, 229–31; *IH*, 234). It is also the
basis of the political doctrine that power lies neither in the single
individual nor in the majority will but in the general will.

Thus philosophy finds in Christianity the touchstone by which
to test the power of explanation (*RP*, xiii). Religion can both
illustrate and demonstrate the philosopher's conception of finite
as well as of absolute mind, and of the relationship between them.
In *Religion and Philosophy*, as we have seen, Christian doctrine is
brought to bear on the solution of the problem of intersubjectivity
and community. In *Speculum Mentis* the doctrine of absolute
mind is explicated in terms of the religious drama of the fall and
redemption of man (*SM*, 303). The Christian solution to the problems of philosophy is to destroy the illusion that each form of
knowledge exists independently of every other form and that
truth resides exclusively in one or the other of these forms. Collingwood's theory of rapprochement, which in the *Autobiography* he
identifies as his lifelong mission, together with its corollary, the
doctrine of the scale of forms and the overlap of classes, is explicitly
presented as an application of Christian doctrine.

According to the doctrine of the scale of forms, the forms
constitute an overlapping scale such that each partakes of the others

in varying degrees. The overlap, moreover, is one of dynamic interaction. It is not only that each individual form bears traces of every other in its very structure but the structure itself is in a state of permanent dynamic alteration, reflecting the influence of the other forms. There is thus a religious dimension to politics, history, art, science, and philosophy, as well as an aesthetic, scientific, dimension to religion. But the interaction is historical. The understanding of any one form is mediated by an understanding of all other forms (*A*, 148-9). All existence is inter-existential; all understanding is inter-cognitive or interdisciplinary. Thus *Religion and Philosophy* sets out to view religion not as the activity of one faculty alone, but as a combined activity of all elements in the mind (*RP*, xvi), while *Speculum Mentis* places religion on a dialectically developing scale of forms.

VI

In *An Essay on Philosophical Method*, Collingwood advances a theory of philosophy as categorical thinking which has serious implications with respect to philosophy of religion. Although philosophy of religion is not specifically mentioned, what Collingwood does say about moral philosophy and logic provides a basis for drawing inferrences concerning the logic of philosophy of religion. In particular the doctrine of *An Essay on Philosophical Method* may shed some light on the nature of the commitment from which philosophy of religion grows.

Collingwood's views are drawn from reflections on the ontological argument. The ontological argument demonstrates, according to Collingwood, that in the 'special case of metaphysical thinking, the distinction between conceiving something and thinking it to exist is a distinction without a difference' (*EPM*, 125). At the same time, Collingwood declares: 'Every philosophical science partakes of the nature of metaphysics which is not a separate philosophical science but a special study of the existential aspect of that same subject matter whose aspect as truth is studied by logic, and its aspect as goodness by ethics' (*EPM*, 127). With respect to the point at hand, Collingwood might well have added—'and its aspect as "holy" by philosophy of religion' (*RP*, Preface).

Logic stands committed to the principle of the ontological proof in the sense that its subject-matter, namely thought, affords an instance of something which cannot be conceived except as actual, something whose essence involves existence (*EPM*, 131). Logic not only discusses, it also contains reasoning (*EPM*, 130).

Moral philosophy, by a different path, reaches the same goal (*EPM*, 131). Like logic, it cannot be either merely descriptive or merely normative. As merely descriptive, it would content itself with giving an account of the various ways in which people actually behave, which is psychology or anthropology of conduct. As merely normative, it would set aside how people actually behave and consider only the question, how they ought to behave. But for this, people do not need guidance from moral theorists. To decide how we ought to behave is the task of the agent himself.

Moral philosophy, as opposed to anthropology and moralizing, can be defined as giving 'an account of how people think they ought to behave' (*EPM*, 131-2)—which is precisely what the *Essay on Metaphysics* defines metaphysics as doing. Here the facts and the ideals of conduct alike are included in the subject-matter. But the question of how people think is not in any philosophical science separable from the question of whether they think rightly or wrongly, in which case, moral philosophy must face the responsibility *either* of holding that people are *always* right when they think they ought to do some act, or judge an action, *or* of instituting some kind of comparison and criticism of moral judgement. In the first alternative, the view is taken that the moral ideal already exists as an ideal in the minds of all moral agents; in the second that it partially so exists, and more completely as they try to think out more clearly what they believe their duties to be. In either case, the science is both normative and descriptive; it describes, not action as opposed to ideas about action, but the moral consciousness; and this it is forced to describe as already being in some sense what it ought to be. This in turn will affect the account which it gives of action; for no theory of moral ideals is conceivable which does not admit that to some extent moral ideas affect action (*EPM*, 132). To believe that 'X is what is to be done' is equivalent to willing or intending to so act.

Collingwood writes: 'Without considering cases drawn from other philosophical sciences, I may now venture to state generally, that the body of any philosophical science consists of categorical propositions and not merely, as in the case of exact and empirical science, of hypothetical' (*EPM*, 133). If, then, philosophy of religion too consists of categorical judgements, then it should not be too difficult to infer the implications of this with respect to the relationship between philosophy of religion and religious commitment.

The ontological argument, according to Collingwood, thus contains a clue to the understanding of the relation between faith and reason. This is especially evident in the correspondence between Anselm and Gaunilo, in which Anselm admits that the ontological proof of the existence of God proves something only to a person who already believes it. Thus Anselm declares: 'I believe in order that I may understand; for this I know that unless I first believe I shall never understand' (*FR*, 135).

Collingwood interprets this as meaning that, unless we already believed on faith in the existence of God, we could never receive a rational account of it. This is really a variation of the principle, *nihil est intellectu quod no fuerit in sensu*. If we read for intellect 'scientific thought' and for sense 'religious intuition', we may say with substantial truth 'that the intellect discovers nothing that faith has not already known'. Indeed, Collingwood concludes, we may view the whole of life as *fides quaerens intellectum* (*RFCI*, 120).

In this notion lies a clue to the understanding of all other rapprochements, including that between 'essence' and 'existence'. *Nihil est in intellectu quod non feurit in sensu*. Let us read for '*intellectu*', essence (or whatever is the object of philosophical thought), and for '*sensu*', experience or existence. Then nothing can be an object of philosophy which does not exist in experience. Philosophy renders explicit what is already implicit in experience. Philosophy is autobiography—revealing the presuppositions of experience, which are unconscious and which, to the extent to which they are implicit, may be said to be held on faith; and to be so acted on. It is thus not inappropriate for Collingwood in 1938–9 to define metaphysics as the act of translating beliefs into reasons. Metaphysics is the science of absolute presuppositions.

Not only reason, but culture itself is emptied by the loss of faith which accompanies the corruption of religion. Indeed, it was Collingwood's lifelong conviction that it is only in a culture in which religion flourishes that there can be any integrity to the pursuit of art, science, history and philosophy. Any society which has lost its religious integrity, lives in bad faith if it deceives itself into believing that it can still remain faithful to the requirements of reason and science. Writing in 1916, at the very outset of his career, Collingwood declares:

Every man has his own duties, and every class of men has duties proper to itself as a class; but just as the 'man of action' is not freed from the obligation to truth nor the 'man of contemplation' from the obligation to morality, so the layman is as much bound as the priest by the ideals of religion which in some form or other he cannot help professing (RP, 36).

And in 1942, at the very end of his career, Collingwood declares in 'Fascism and Nazism' that the principles of liberal democratic society are derived from Christianity 'and the emotional force, the "drive" or "punch" that once made them victorious was due to Christianity itself as a system of religious practice rich in superstitious or magical elements which, in Christianity as in every other religion, generate the emotion that gives men the power to obey a set of rules and thus bring into existence a specific form of life' (FN, 174). But, Collingwood complains, the rationalization of contemporary society has purged democracy of this emotional force and reduced it to a mere matter of habit. And, as we have already noted, a mere habit has no 'punch'. What is more, its capacity to withold stress is inversely proportional to the emotional strength of the destructive forces operating upon it. It is for this reason that fascism and nazism have so easily taken root in certain countries in Europe. They satisfy the appetite for emotional experience denied by an overly rationalized society.

Fascism and nazism are functions of pre-Christian paganism which has survived, according to what Collingwood calls elsewhere 'the principle of incapsulation', by the failure of Christianity and secular society to give adequate expressions to the emotions which in the *New Leviathan* Collingwood identifies as lying at the centre of consciousness. The 'punch' of fascism and nazism is derived from the pagan emotions which have become substitutes for the more genuine emotions of Christianity. By repressing the emotional side of religion in the favour of the so-called rational elements, modern society has succeeded only in keeping alive the emotions of paganism and of ensuring the success of any political movement which derives its 'punch' from these emotions. Thus Collingwood concludes:

The time has long gone by when anyone who claims the title of philosopher can think of religion as a superfluity for the educated and an 'opiate for the masses'. It is the only known explosive in the economy of that delicate internal combustion engine, the human mind. Peoples rich in religious energy can overcome all obstacles and attain any height in the scale of civilization. Peoples that have reached the top of the hill by the wise use of religious energy may then decide to do without it; they can still move, but they can only move downhill, and when they come to the bottom of the hill they stop (*FN*, 176).

The charge of paganism which in 1942 Collingwood lays against the modern world, and which he blames on the secularization of society, resembles closely the charge of paganism which he laid at the feet of society in 1923, and which he then blamed on the Renaissance revolt against Christianity. We thus come full circle. The disease of modern man, which characterized the society of the 1920s is even more virulent in the 1940s. And the solution in 1942 is the same as it was in 1923. It is the Christian solution, not only in the sense of bearing witness to the implicit principles of Christianity, but in the sense also of arising directly from within the religious form of life which provides, to repeat, 'the only known explosive in the economy of that delicate internal combustion engine, the human mind' (*FN*, 176).

In conclusion, then, it would seem difficult to reconcile the doctrines of 'Fascism and Nazism' and the *New Leviathan*, not to speak of *An Essay on Philosophical Method* and the *Essay on Meta-*

physics, with any claim to the effect that Collingwood had virtually nothing to say about religion after 1928 because he recognized that in the modern world religion had been superseded by philosophy.

VI

COLLINGWOOD'S TREATMENT OF THE ONTOLOGICAL ARGUMENT AND THE CATEGORICAL UNIVERSAL

ERROL E. HARRIS

'WITH HEGEL's rejection of subjective idealism, the Ontological Proof took its place once more among the accepted principles of modern philosophy, and it has never again been seriously criticized.' This Collingwood wrote in *An Essay on Philosophical Method* (*EPM*, 126), in 1933, and the statement moved Gilbert Ryle (later to become his successor as Wayneflete Professor) almost to tears, because it dismissed as backsliding what Ryle believed to be 'one of the biggest advances in logic that has been made since Aristotle, namely Hume's and Kant's discovery that particular matters of fact cannot be the implicates of general propositions.'[1]

In some sense this controversy expresses what has been the central issue of contemporary philosophy between then and now. As Ryle put it a few pages before the passage quoted, 'if Mr. Collingwood is right, constructive metaphysics is the proper business of philosophy' whereas he himself held (at the time, at least) that no such business was proper, if at all possible—for he says in the correspondence with Collingwood that arose out of his published criticism: 'I have to give a different sort of account of what constitutes the object (in the sense of subject-matter) of philosophic thought and an account which is overtly non-metaphysical.' Collingwood, on the other hand, had declared that what the Ontological Argument does prove is

[1] 'Mr. Collingwood and the Ontological Argument', *Mind*, xliv, No. 174 (1935), 142.

that essence involves existence, not always, but in one special case, the case of God in the metaphysical sense: the *Deus sive Natura* of Spinoza, the Good of Plato, the Being of Aristotle: the object of metaphysical thought. But this means the object of philosophical thought in general; for . . . all philosophical thought is of the same kind, and every philosophical science partakes of the nature of metaphysics . . . (*EPM*, 127).

Ryle represents, in this confrontation, the whole subsequent movement in philosophy (already, as he points out, launched by such writers as Russell, Moore, Wittgenstein, Carnap, and Schlick), which declared that 'particular matters of fact' could be established only empirically and must therefore be relegated to empirical (natural) science; while metaphysics, posing as a science which could establish *a priori* matters of fact such as the existence of 'a designated entity',[1] God, the infinity in extent, the contingency or otherwise, of the world, must be bogus.

More recently this rejection of metaphysics has been less absolute, for the followers of the movement thus represented have since discovered that certain explicitly stated fundamental principles of their creed were untenable, and metaphysics has come to be tolerated, first as a means to seeing what we already know on empirical (or other) grounds in a new way (it may be remembered that Collingwood maintained a not dissimilar doctrine, cf. *EPM*, 11), then as a way, possibly with the help of linguistic analysis, of describing the nature of things ('descriptive metaphysics'), and, finally, as a set of proposals for modifying our ways of speaking about the world in order to clarify our concepts or render them mutually consistent ('revisionary metaphysics'). This loosening of the strictures and lifting of the ban has latterly produced a revival of interest in metaphysics; and in this new and more tolerant atmosphere some profit may be had from a re-examination of the position that declared, in stark opposition to the positivists, that all philosophy is ultimately metaphysics.

Ryle was protesting against the apparent disregard in Collingwood's statement of the implicit critique of the Ontological Proof in what he (Ryle) describes as the Russellian developments in logic. Collingwood, however, was fully aware of these de-

[1] Cf. Ryle, op. cit., p. 140.

velopments (as his unpublished letter in reply to Ryle gives evidence) but considered them either false or irrelevant to his main thesis, which was not to defend the Ontological Argument as a piece of formal reasoning, but to demonstrate a fundamental characteristic of philosophical method and at the same time (for they are only different aspects of the same fact) a fundamental metaphysical truth. Indeed the Russellian developments were not devoid of metaphysical implications. The doctrines to which Ryle drew attention were (i) the alleged discovery that all universal propositions are hypothetical: All S is $P \equiv$ If x is S, it is P (a view put forward by Bradley prior to and independently of Russell and opposed by Collingwood—as he asserts in the correspondence) and (ii) the consequent 'discovery' that existence-propositions (which are categorical) cannot be deduced from non-empirical premisses. The metaphysical presuppositions of this doctrine are that only particulars can exist, and that hypothetical statements assert no more than connections (or conjunctions?) between attributes of particular things the existence of which may or may not be a fact. It follows that no categorical proposition can be necessary, for the existence of particulars is always contingent, and as Ryle contends in his *Mind* article, particular matters of fact cannot be established by *a priori* arguments—that is, cannot be entailed by purely hypothetical premisses. It follows likewise that only hypothetical propositions can be necessary (paradoxical as that may sound), because necessity is a modal characteristic implying logical entailment, and that can obtain only between propositions attributing properties to subjects. The connection expressed is only between the properties and cannot be between the existences of the subjects or the facts that they possess those properties. This, again, rests on the metaphysical presupposition that existences are connected, if at all, only causally, and on the Humean doctrine that the causal relation is never more than constant conjunction in a contingent succession of experiences.

Long before the debate between Ryle and Collingwood, or before Russell had made his 'discoveries', Bernard Bosanquet had written a book, *Knowledge and Reality*, in which he criticized

Bradley's doctine that all universal and necessary judgements were hypothetical. He pointed out that the connection asserted in a hypothetical proposition was asserted categorically and, to be true, must be based upon an affirmation tacitly presupposed of an actually pertaining state of affairs which constitutes the ground of the connection. That any triangle has internal angles the sum of which is 180° is a necessary proposition on the condition and ground that space is Euclidean. 'If anything is a triangle' is the protasis of the implied hypothetical and it need not be true for the necessary connection to hold. But the entire implication depends on the prior condition that space is Euclidean. That again need not be the case, but then the more comprehensive hypothetical rests upon certain more general characteristics of manifolds and numerical series ultimately founded upon the series of natural numbers. Here we seem to have reached something to deny the existence of which would be nonsense, or at best would involve the impossibility of mathematics as a whole. This statement of the argument is mine rather than Bosanquet's, who would have said that the connection is rooted in the nature of reality, and would presumably have made the same claim for the series of natural numbers, so that his doctrine is ultimately in agreement with Bradley's in so far as both maintain that every judgement affirms of reality, which is the universal subject. The point of Bosanquet's criticism is that Bradley is inconsistent to hold at the same time that necessary and universal judgements are always only hypothetical; and, in pointing out this inconsistency in Bradley, Bosanquet was correct. Russell, however, had repudiated Bradley's metaphysical position and had opted for a logical (and metaphysical) atomism, on the basis of which one might (at least *prima facie*) consistently hold the kind of logical theory that Ryle defends against Collingwood. Oddly enough, in the correspondence which followed the publication of his attack, Ryle rejects the logical atomism of Russell: 'If that is what logical atomism is', he writes, referring to Russell's article of that name in the *Monist*, which he says he has not seen, 'I don't hold it.'

Collingwood, on the other hand, clearly understood the metaphysical implications of the Russellian developments, and it was his aim to combat them, not by direct criticism and attack but by developing the alternative position, in essence the same as that which Bosanquet sought to propound. If this position is what is properly called 'Idealism', Ryle's remark was justified that 'Mr. Collingwood is presumably to be classified, for what such labels are worth, as an Idealist'[1] and Collingwood's resentment against the label, expressed both in this correspondence and in his *Autobiography*, is perhaps as odd as Ryle's rejection of Logical Atomism (though each undoubtedly had other and special reasons for his attitude).

The position Collingwood was defending is, as we shall presently see, diametrically opposed to the atomistic pluralism of Hume, Russell, and their successors; but how far does one refute or dispose of a doctrine simply by asserting its opposite? The answer is to be found in the very theory that Collingwood propounded in the *Essay on Philosophical Method*,[2] a central feature of which was the categorical force of philosophical propositions—the point attacked by Ryle—which, Collingwood thought, was the true significance of the Ontological Proof. The gist of the doctrine is that the categorical (one might even say the apodeictic) claim of philosophical insight absorbs into itself and sublates the hypothetical and contingent claims of less adequate phases in the development of knowledge through which philosophy itself is generated. To this I shall return in due course; first let us examine in detail the position as Collingwood set it out.

II

In his letter to Ryle he explains his view that no affirmation, of whatever form, in the actual operation of thinking, is independent of, or devoid of entailment with, propositions of other forms. When one says 'It is not yet noon' one enunciates a negative proposition but this does not exhaust what one is thinking. That in all probability includes (and if one is thinking soundly implies) something like 'It is about 11:30 a.m.' (an affirmative proposition).

[1] Ryle, op. cit., p. 137.
[2] Cf. especially ch. IX, sect. 3.

Similarly it implies 'If it had been noon the clock hands would have stood at 12.' In short, to affirm a proposition seriously is to affirm a context—an entire complex of known fact. He maintains of this context first that it is a logical context, not merely psychological (not just everything one may happen to be thinking at the time), secondly that it is a necessary and not just a fortuitous context. The mutual implications involved are not haphazard but depend on the actual structure of the facts about which affirmation is being made. We cannot say (or think) simply 'it is not yet noon and the sun is shining' as a substitute for 'it is not yet noon and it is half-past eleven'. Unless we think the context in its logical interconnections we cannot think what in fact we are thinking (about the time of day). Thus the context has a definite logical structure including affirmative and negative, hypothetical and categorical, propositional and inferential elements, all of which are present, though not all expressed in words, or all at (or even near) the focus of attention.

This logical structure, Collingwood says in his letter, constitutes a whole of element-types, and clearly from what he has said, it is based upon a system of fact as known or conceived, which, though never complete or exhaustive, shades off into a factual totality throughout which factors are linked by necessary logical ties. A whole of this nature is what other philosphers had called a concrete universal, a totality at once universal, in that it determines the character of all its members by the principle of structure or order that constitutes them a whole, and also individual in being constituted by its particular components and the way they are interrelated. It is thus both universal and concretely real, and while statements about its elements may be hypothetical, statements about the whole—universal statements—would be categorical.

The science of logic, we may presume, would be the attempt to analyse and characterize this whole and to classify the element-types involved in thinking about it—a theory of the way we think when we think validly and truly. No such science could be successfully pursued unless the pursuit of it were itself an attempt to think validly and truly. Each and all of its propositions would involve just such a complex of element-types as it strives to characterize, and so far as it succeeds it must exemplify the theory which, *qua* logic, it elaborates. It cannot, therefore, postulate the existence of its subject-matter merely hypothetically, for it is itself an instantiation of what it studies. It must exist in virtue of its very nature as a self-reflective science. This, Collingwood argues, is the nature of every philosophical science, and, in consequence, hypothetical and categorical elements merge in all philosophical assertions because the very essence of its subject-matter implies existence.

What, then, is this subject-matter? It is surely that total context, in its necessary systematic articulation, implicit in every assertion so far as it is part of a genuine effort to think truly about the world: It is the concrete universal, the systematic structure of which gives cogency to any theory and to any reasoning. This is what Hegel called the Absolute, what Spinoza called *Deus sive Natura*, what Aristotle called Being and what Plato called The Good, and it is this (and this alone) the existence of which is involved in its essence —the existence proved by the Ontological Argument. So Collingwood contends (*EPM*, 127).

But Collingwood is not here defending the Ontological Proof as a formal argument. He is defending it as a statement of the impossibility of denying existence to, or even of merely hypothesizing the existence of, that ultimate ground of validity of all formal argument and all legitimate hypotheses. To attack any particular formulation of the proof as formally invalid is, accordingly, to miss the point; while to deny the metaphysical theory to which it gives expression is to assert, by implication, an alternative metaphysic which demands support.

The opponents of the doctrine (and of Collingwood) seldom attempt to substantiate the metaphysical alternative their own position involves, sometimes taking refuge behind subtle logical refutations, sometimes affecting to repudiate all metaphysics as a bogus science. Collingwood, in his correspondence with Ryle, complains that he refrains from expressing any positive ideas of his own, and Ryle in reply disclaims all metaphysics. But the metaphysic is there all the same and has been subjected from many quarters to criticism, to which it succumbs as a rule by default, for the criticism is never answered.[1]

Meanwhile, to convict the Ontological Argument of formal invalidity is no criticism of Hegel, who agreed that existence was an inappropriate category, and one under which the Absolute could not be brought. An attempt to prove that God exists, as if He were a finite entity like Kant's hundred dollars, would necessarily be invalid. It would be like trying to prove syllogistically the truth of the law of non-contradiction. The exposure of formal invalidity applies only to inept forms of the argument, a fact recognized and understood by its chief proponents, but the true significance of the doctrine was finally established by Hegel who elaborated in detail the kind of metaphysic on which the proof was grounded—that which conceived the real as a self-maintaining, self-developing totality immanent in every detail, determining and making every particular matter of fact to be what it is. Assertions about this ultimate totality would have to be universal, but concretely universal and therefore categorical. They could not be purely hypothetical, for any logical nexus on which the hypothetical connection could rest, must be rooted in the system which is the subject of the assertion.

This is Collingwood's thesis and this is why his statement is fully vindicated that Hegel's re-establishment of the Ontological Proof has not since been seriously challenged. Challenged in some sort it may have been, but as its critics have argued beside the main point at issue, the challenge has not been serious. More recent evidence of this fact is the reaffirmation of the Ontological Proof by Norman Malcolm, a philosopher who accepts all the strictures imposed by Kant, Russell, and Ryle on subject–predicate logic and the masquerade of existence as a predicate, as well as the need for empirical premisses to establish particular matters of fact.

---

[1] Cf. B. Blanshard, 'The Philosophy of Analysis' in *Clarity is not Enough* (London, 1963); idem, *Reason and Analysis* (London, 1962); J. O. Urmson, *The Philosophy of Analysis* (Oxford, 1958); G. J. Warnock, *English Philosophy since 1900* (Oxford, 1958); J. Weinberg, *An Examination of Logical Positivism* (London, 1936); G. R. G. Mure, *Retreat from Truth*, (Oxford, 1958); and my own *Nature, Mind and Modern Science* (London, 1954), 'Scientific Philosophy', *Philosophical Quarterly*, II (1952), and 'The End of a Phase', *Dialectica*, vol. xvii, No. 1 (1963).

III

The strength of Collingwood's position and its relation to Hegel, whom he invokes, can be more fully displayed by considering his doctrine of the scale of forms (to which, so far as it involves overlap of classes, Ryle makes one oblique and derisive allusion,[1] revealing, if anything, only lack of understanding). Though Collingwood does not use the phrase 'concrete universal' in the *Essay on Philosophical Method* his doctrine of the scale of forms is his version of what Bosanquet called by that name. For the concrete universal was characterized as system and the account which Collingwood gives of system in the *Essay* is that it is a scale such as in chapter III he describes. Moreover the scale reveals the nature of the philosophical universal, which is precisely the concrete universal of Bradley and Bosanquet, but more appropriately still of Hegel.

In the second chapter of the *Essay*, Collingwood says that when a concept, as used by common sense or natural science, is raised to the philosophical level its generic character, which at the lower level was specified in mutually exclusive classes, comes to be displayed in specific forms which overlap. He then goes on to explain the overlap by developing the doctrine of the scale. The first point to notice is that universality is itself just such a concept; and at the scientific level it is abstract and has a character (e.g. in the nature of its specification), which at the philosophical level, where it becomes concrete, is transformed. It is entirely consistent with this doctrine to maintain that the scientific universal is merely hypothetical (as Russell and Ryle would agree), but that at the philosophical level, the universal is no longer merely hypothetical but is essentially categorical, and that those adjectives themselves do not denote mutually exclusive classes. It is also consistent with the doctrine that science and philosophy, as species of knowledge (which is a philosophical concept), overlap and are forms in a scale constituted by philosophical species within such a universal. But let us examine the nature of the scale itself.

[1] Op. cit., p. 141.

The philosophical universal, or generic concept, is specified, not as a collection of mutually exclusive *distincta*, but as a series of forms each of which is related to the next as a degree or gradation in a scale, yet is at the same time a distinct species of the generic essence. Equally, the species relate to one another as opposites. Being gradations they overlap and merge each into the next, but what they are gradations of is the generic essence, thus they are more and less adequate exemplifications of the universal. As such they stand in mutual opposition for what exemplifies the universal less adequately, is, from the point of view of the more adequate, to that extent not what the universal is.

Examples of this kind of specification are numerous. Plato's divided line is an obvious one. Each division is a species of knowledge distinct from every other, yet each is also a degree of knowledge. ἐικασία is less adequate than πίστις, δόξα is less adequate than ἐποτήμη. Again from the point of view of scientific and philosophical knowledge, opinion is not properly knowledge at all and ranks as its opposite, just as sense is opposed to thought. Another Platonic example is the specification of virtue into temperance, courage, wisdom, and justice. Each is a distinct virtue, yet each is related to the next as a less adequate and complete virtuousness, and, as we see in the *Phaedo*, temperance and courage abstracted from wisdom are virtually the opposite of what they should be (hence the opposite of wisdom). Still another example is the specification of goodness into kinds of good such as pleasure, expediency, rightness, and devotion. Each is a good, yet each is only good in a certain degree and from the point of view of the higher good, the lower may be regarded as positively bad. The pursuit of pleasure for its own sake is opposed to prudence, the merely expedient is opposed to duty for duty's sake, and the stern voice of duty assumes an appearance of hypocrisy in contrast with loving devotion to the welfare of one's fellow-men.

In every such scale the highest form is the most complete and adequate realization of the generic essence, and, in spite of the element of opposition to which attention has been drawn, the higher forms presuppose and incorporate in themselves the lower, they fulfil the unrealized potentialities of those which precede them in the scale. Collingwood maintains that the variable element in the scale (that of which there is more or less in each form) is identical with the generic essence; so the deficiency of the lower forms is not a quantitative deficiency but a purely qualitative one. The varying 'amounts' of the generic essence realized in different forms cannot be summed—just as one cannot sum the pleasures of eating, dancing and the aesthetic enjoyment of a performance of *Hamlet*, or the value of a succession of virtuous acts. Each form, as a specific form, is a particular realization of the universal; but as one ascends the scale each form is more fully what the universal essence connotes. The final form in the scale is thus the exemplification of the universal *par excellence*. But scale and end overlap, for in the final realization all the prior forms are included as well as transcended and the universal is actualized at once in and as the whole scale and the final specific form. Another way of saying this is to state, what is after all an obvious truth, that the universal essence is immanent in every specific form and is progressively more adequately realized as the scale ascends.

Collingwood demonstrates how this scale of forms is exemplified in every philosophical system, in the system of each individual philosopher, in the system of philosophy current at a particular time, and in the systematic development of philosophical systems over an historical period.[1] In fact, a philosophical system is a scale of forms. I have tried to show, in *The Foundations of Metaphysics in Science*, and in *Hypothesis and Perception*, that system of every kind, natural and theoretical, has this typical scalar character. What Bradley and Bosanquet called the concrete universal was a system, and Hegel's Absolute Idea was 'the truth of', and the ultimate realization of, the whole dialectical series of categories in the logic. The universal so conceived is never abstract, it cannot be expressed in merely hypothetical propositions. It is essentially concrete and self-specifying, so that propositions that assert its essence in its most adequate realization are both categorical and necessary. Let us examine this position in more detail.

[1] Hence different cotemporary theories rank in relation to each other both as species of a universal theory and as opposing theories. Thus Collingwood's statement and defence of a position opposed to logical atomism is implicit criticism and correction.

The universal is self-specifying. While I should be prepared to argue for this thesis in general, for my present purpose it is necessary only to maintain that the philosophical universal is self-specifying, for it is on this contention that Collingwood rests his case. Philosophy is a self-reflective pursuit, what Collingwood called science of the second degree. Each of its branches is reflection upon a realm of experience, itself a degree of self-reflection. Morality is the fruit of reflection upon deliberate action in a social context and ethics is the theory which results from reflection upon that reflection. It arises directly out of moral experience, out of the conflicts of duties with which the moral agent is almost inevitably faced, at some stage (if not at every stage) of his conduct; out of the conflict of demands and judgements that result from the application in different societies, and in different groups within one society, of conflicting standards. What ethics reflects upon is the moral concept (or system of concepts) operative in practiced morality. It is through this reflection that these concepts come to be specified, as the various types of good listed above, and as the various forms of virtue. The reflection is itself stimulated and triggered by the conflicts in moral practice which is the actualization, in the specific, factual occurrence of examples, of the moral universal. In the continued course of this reflection this universal is further specified—i.e. it specifies itself as a scale of forms—in the manner already described. In short, in the pursuit of ethics, philosophical reflection is neither more nor less than the self-specification of the ethical universal (which is continuous with actual moral practice). The final fully elaborated ethical theory is the most adequate specification, and itself the most complete and typical example attainable by the philosopher of what that universal is—the ethical system; and the ethical system is, in actuality or *in posse*, what is practised as a matter of fact. So, again, in the final ethical theory the universal is self-specified.

This is but one example, and the same character of the philosophical universal could have been illustrated by knowledge and epistemology or art and aesthetics, or science and religion and metaphysics. In every case the exposition of the generic essence of the appropriate universal is its self-specification—its exemplification, *as a matter of fact*, in and as the philosophical system, which is always continuous with the subject-matter on which it reflects. But specification of a universal (its 'instantiation') is existential. In its specific forms it exists, and in the ultimate form of a scale, in which the philosophical universal specifies itself, essence and existence coalesce. This, according to Collingwood, is what the Ontological Argument proves, namely the necessary existence of the subject-matter of philosophy, an existence which is necessarily involved in its essence because philosophy is self-reflective.

IV

The position maintained by Hegel is essentially the same and in as much as it had not been effectively refuted by any philosopher, who fully understood it and directed his argument against the relevant issue, Collingwood was justified in declaring that it had not been seriously threatened.

Hegel calls philosophy 'the thinking study of things' (*Enc.*, sects, 1–2). It is the mind's reflection upon itself and its experience, for the Hegelian definition of thought or reason, is reflection-into-self which is much the same as *Fürsichsein* (being for self); or, alternatively, absolute negativity (the negation of the negative). Philosophy is the culmination of the mind's reflective thinking activity, it is that activity in which absolute spirit realizes its potentiality, and as such is the climax of the whole dialectical process. Mind (*Der Geist*) is actualized in and through human intelligence as it develops out of nature, in which spirit is implicit (*an sich*) or potential. It is, therefore, the truth of nature, what nature essentially is in itself, now (as spirit or conscious mind) become for itself. Nature, in short, comes to consciousness of itself as mind by means of a development through living forms which issues in human personality,[1]

Self-consciousness is thus the essential nature of all reality. It is the truth of nature and issues from it first as sentience and then as consciousness (in animals and in man); subsequently it develops through man's intelligent activity, practical (morality) and theo-

---

[1] Cf. *Phänomenologie des Geistes*, C(AA) V, A, x, (2) and *Enc.*, sects. 388–482.

retical (science and philosophy). The essential reality of the world is subject, not mere substance. And this is actual in man's thinking. That, moreover, is aware of itself, and so its existence is self-guaranteed. *Cogito ergo sum* cannot, without self-refutation, be denied. Consequently, self-conscious thought, the generic essence of all reality, by its very nature, involves existence. Hegel expresses this by insisting that the Idea must exist, it must be real, it cannot be purely abstract or hypothetical, for it is the truth of everything to which reality can belong and the meaning of 'reality' itself. In its intuitive immediacy it is identical with nature—'the external world is implicitly the truth; for the truth is actual and must exist.' [1]

This, he says, is the essential significance of the Ontological Proof.[2] The metaphysical conception of God is that in which the pure concept is by virtue of its own self (*durch sich selbst*) real. God is characterized as absolute idea, that is, as spirit. 'The essential character of revealed religion', he writes, 'is the form in which substance is spirit.' But this revelation contains within it, what he calls 'the moment of difference', the opposition as well as the atonement between the finite spirit of man and the infinite spirit or absolute idea that is called God. 'Spirit is thus the living process in which the implicit unity of the divine and the human nature becomes explicit and self-conscious (*für sich*).'[3] Finite spirit knows itself as finite in its awareness of an other which limits it, be this another finite object or an infinite beyond. But this opposition reduces the other equally to a finite, and the very consciousness of it is already a transcendence of the limitation; so the infinity implicit in self-reflection and self-awareness forces the finite to sublate the opposition. In short, man's awareness of his own finiteness and deficiency is, *ipso facto*, his awareness of the infinity and perfection by reference to which he finds himself wanting. It is that consciousness of God the possession of which gives him title to the claim that he is created in God's image.

[1] *Enc.*, sect. 38, *Zusatz*. Cf. sect. 244.
[2] Cf. *Philosophie der Religion, Dritte Teil*, B, *Gesammelte Werke*, Band 16 (Jubiläumsausgabe, 1959), pp. 209–18.
[3] Ibid., p. 210.

But this consciousness of the infinite cannot be merely subjective (mere *Vorstellung*) for it is essential to consciousness as such, which by its very nature is self-transcendent. Its own existence is thus the existence or reality of the transcendent infinite—the idea (or essence) involves existence. This is what the Anselmic proof asserts—the mere subjective idea (*Vorstellung*) is incomplete, whereas God is absolute completeness. It cannot therefore be that than which a greater is inconceivable. The concept of such absolute completeness is, therefore, no mere *Vorstellung*, it is *Begriff*, 'which is at the same time also real, existent being.'[1]

The traditional Ontological Proof, however, falls short, in Hegel's view, because it states only the affirmative identity of idea and being and overlooks the equally (if not more) important negative aspect of difference and opposition between being and thought, ideality and reality, an opposition which demands abolition and sublation ('dieser Gegensatz soll aufgehoben werden'). The true unity of thought and being can be demonstrated only through the dialectic of the logical movement which carries the finite (through nature and finite spirit) to absolute self-awareness. In a sense, therefore, though Anselm's insight is in one way sound, the form of his proof is inadequate and invalid, and it does fail to show how the pure thought of God can involve existence. Hegel makes this clear in no uncertain terms and he was as fully aware as any neo-Kantian or neo-empiricist of the formal shortcomings of the argument. But he declares the Kantian insistence on the mere subjectivity of the idea to be equally one-sided. It limits its view purely to the empirical and regards that as concrete, whereas the truly concrete is the identity of concept and reality.

But this identity works itself out and becomes aware of itself only in that dialectical process which raises nature to spirit; in which human personality realizes itself and aspires to an infinite completeness. The aspiration is the essence of religion and its object is that which philosophy strives to bring to clear self-consciousness. But the mind becomes aware of this object only through awareness of, and reflection upon, itself and its experience of the world (its other), which it discovers to be identical with itself as its own source

[1] Ibid., p. 214.

and origin. This final identity of subject and object is the Absolute, and the whole dialectical progression gives evidence of its immanence in finite consciousness. As Hegel says, it is (and all along has been) this immanence of the infinite that forces the finite to transcend its own limits and sublate the opposition between self and other so engendered. Man's idea of God, or of Infinite Spirit, therefore, is only possible as the very product of the immanence in man of that infinite spirit. The idea, therefore, cannot lack reality or being, for it is implicit (*an sich*) in the very thought which generates it and whose activity is a perpetual effort to bring it to explicit (*für sich*) self-consciousness. The existence cannot be denied of the actual thinking of the self-reflective subject, and the infinity implicit in such self-reflection is the object (or if one prefers 'subject') of the Absolute Idea, the essence of which involves and for that reason must involve existence.

This again is why the propositions of philosophy—what philosophy essentially propounds—cannot be merely hypothetical. To pretend that its subject is only contingent and might possibly not exist would be self-stultifying, for the subject is what is thinking the propositions. It is *die Sache selbst*.

The dialectical process, moreover, is the paradigm case of a scale of forms. Its phases and categories are mutually opposed yet each is a provisional form (or definition) of the Absolute. Each is therefore a specific case of the universal which ultimately transpires to be spirit, but it is so only in a degree characteristic of the level of development to which it belongs. So Hegel can represent the series as a continuous development of consciousness (e.g. in the *Phäno-menologie*), or as a continuous evolution from the self-external forms of nature through organism to mind (as in the *Natuur-philosophie* and *Philosophie des Geistes*), or as a continuous differentiation of the universal idea into categories (as in the *Logik*). The identity (or overlap) of universal and particular, despite, or even because, of their opposition, is explicitly established in the logic and is exemplified throughout the hierarchy of phases. Thus the universal is manifestly concrete. It exists in virtue of its immanence in all its provisional forms and is real as the individual actualization of what is potential in them. In this logic, therefore (the logic of the notion, *des Begriffs*), universal propositions are both categorical and necessary; and they are never merely verbal or symbolic forms, but always genuine acts of thinking, actual judgements. Logic, which is the prime example of thinking that is its subject-matter, cannot therefore propound about that subject-matter, *merely* hypothetical judgements.

V

The self-transcendent subject, as absolute being in and for itself, is thus the presupposition, the necessary ground and condition, in fact the inner reality, of all existents and of all valid thinking. Consequently, it is that of which it would be mere foolishness to attempt to deny existence. And this position is either implicit, or is explicitly stated, in every treatment of the ontological argument that we find in Collingwood's writings. In his early work, *Religion and Philosophy*, he says little about the Ontological Proof, as such, but he does say that the proper business of theology is to define and characterize its subject-matter—that is, God—and that to do so is *ipso facto* to prove its existence.

In *Speculum Mentis* Collingwood identifies the Ontological Argument as one form of dogmatic philosophy, and the opposite dogmatism as Rationalism. This corresponds quite closely to Hegel's argument that the Anselmic proof is one-sided and that the opposing one-sidedness is empiricism. The Rationalism to which Collingwood refers, and which he criticizes as 'a peculiarly futile and unintelligent form of sophistry' (*SM*, 265), shares with the religious philosophy, which uses the Ontological Argument, the fault of taking religious language literally, whereas it is and should be understood as only figurative. Thus the argument asserts that as the conception of God is indispensable to the existence of religious consciousness, it must be a true concept—God must exist. On the other side, the rationalist contends that as the idea is clearly a figment of mythological fancy, religion must be an illusion. The rationalist, here, is the empirically-minded rationalist and the parallel with Hegel's antithesis is obvious.

But the sustained argument of *Speculum Mentis* is an exemplification in the forms of experience of a scale the theoretical exposition of which is given only in the *Essay on Philosophical Method*. The scale is constituted by Art, Religion, Science, History, and Philosophy in dialectical succession, and it is in philosophy that the metaphorical assertions of religion finally find their literal meaning. The description of philosophy as 'the mind's knowledge of itself' is correct, but (Collingwood tells us here) is 'only a formal and abstract description' likely to mislead, for the mind's self-knowledge is its knowledge of beauty, holiness, the world, and man. It is the explicit and self-conscious knowledge of all these that is absolute knowledge. The mind's self-knowledge is its knowledge of everything else, and absolute mind is the whole, aware of itself. But this is precisely what the imagery of religion represents as God—the alpha and omega. So we may conclude that the Ontological Proof is sound by implication, for the existence of the whole implicit in 'the self-knowledge of mind' cannot, without self-contradiction, be denied.

In his essay on 'Faith and Reason'[1] Collingwood points out that the objection brought against Anselm, that his proof was acceptable only to those who already believed in God, was accepted by Anselm himself, who replied: 'I believe in order that I may understand; for this I know, that unless I first believe I shall never understand.' In short, the Ontological Argument is less an argument than a confession of faith. But it is not merely that, for the faith is asserted as the condition of understanding; and it turns out, as Collingwood goes on to demonstrate, to be the condition of all understanding (and so of all proof).

In this essay he argues that the spheres of reason and faith are not external to one another but coincide, only the sphere of faith is the infinite or whole, while that of reason is the detail which makes up the whole. But the whole is prior to the parts. It is (as he had said in *Speculum Mentis*), 'totum in toto et totum in qualibet parte'. Hence faith is the presupposition and (as Anselm maintained) the prior condition of reason.

---

[1] Originally published as a pamphlet by Ernest Benn (London, 1928); reprinted in *God and the Modern World*, ed. A. A. David (New York, 1929), and more recently, under the original title in, *Faith and Reason: Essays in the Philosophy of Religion*, ed. Lionel Rubinoff (Chicago, 1968).

Collingwood, in this essay, traces with great skill and genius the historical connection between Descartes' *cogito ergo sum* and Kant's affirmation of God, Freedom, and Immortality as the objects of faith. *Cogito ergo sum* is a certainty obvious at once to intuition and to reason (for to deny it is to contradict that denial by implication). Here, then, is a meeting-point of faith and reason. But faith in God seems less secure. Kant, however, saw that the transcendental unity of subjective experience (the undeniable fact that my experience, as a whole, is all mine), the necessity of which Descartes has discovered, corresponds to an objective unity. Whatever we may discover the details of the world to be, one truth holds of them universally—that they belong to a single whole within which all distinctions fall. This cannot be discovered scientifically because unless it is assumed prior to investigation no discovery whatever is even possible. This belief (or faith) in the wholeness of nature is the same as the belief in its intelligibility or rationality—the possibility of reducing its details to system—the belief that they are throughout subject to laws. But the truth of this belief cannot be scientifically demonstrated, because it is presupposed in any such demonstration. It cannot be 'a mere assumption' for that implies that it might intelligibly be denied and we might entertain some contrary belief and rationally develop its consequences. We could no more assume in science that there are no laws of nature than we can assume in logic that false conclusions can follow validly from true premisses. Nor is it simply that our minds are so constituted that we must assume that nature is one. For to believe this would be tantamount to disbelieving the rationality of nature, or to rejecting science, as a mere subjective invention. Finally, we may not legitimately say that we learn by experience that natural events are subject to law, for the very evidence which we might seek for that conclusion must depend, if it is to rank as evidence, on belief in the conclusion to be proved.

The existence of the whole, or the infinite, therefore, cannot be proved. Kant, Hegel, Russell, Ryle, are all vindicated. It is an article of faith—but not of *blind* faith. The faith is rational, for the belief, which cannot be proved, is indubitable. To doubt or deny it would be like doubting or denying my own existence. The belief is the ground and condition of all proof and must therefore be true, if anything at all is to be believed. So the Ontological Argument is vindicated also. *Credo ut intelligam.*

This position is elaborated further by Collingwood in the Third Part of the *Essay on Metaphysics.* In that work he argues that the task of metaphysics is to discover the absolute presuppositions of science. These presuppositions, though stated in propositional form are not, he maintains, propositions, because they cannot be judged true or false. A proposition—what may be either true or false—is the answer to a question and its truth or falsity depends in large measure on what question it seeks to answer. But questions do not arise *in vacuo.* They presuppose some prior beliefs, which may in their turn be answers to questions. As the regress cannot be infinite, there are certain beliefs which are not answers to questions, but are adopted solely because of their fruitfulness in giving rise to questions—what he calls their 'logical efficacy'. These presuppositions are absolute and are the necessary prerequisite of questions arising and so of answers being given. To ask of an absolute presupposition whether it is true or false, therefore, is senseless. To attempt to prove it would be futile, to demand for such proof premisses of this or that kind would be to misunderstand the nature of a metaphysical statement, which is always an historical statement of the form that *P* is presupposed by science at a particular time.

The first example of metaphysical thinking which Collingwood analyses in the light of this thesis is Anselm's proof of the existence of God. This, he says, must be read with the 'metaphysical rubric'. It must not be taken as a proposition stating what Ryle wished to call a particular matter of fact, but as an historical statement to the effect that the belief in God's existence is a necessary presupposition of science. That God exists cannot be proved, for it is not a proposition, and what Anselm sought to prove was only the historical proposition that our idea of God as *id quo maius cogitari nequit* committed us to believe in God's existence. That is why Anselm's withers were not wrung by Gaunilo's objection that the proof would be accepted only by a person who already believed.

Belief in a monotheistic God, Collingwood argues, is the same as belief in a unitary world (or whole) and this *is* the fundamental belief of science and has been since the twelfth century. It is the belief that nature is a single intelligible system ordered according to systematic laws in the light of which particular events and existences can be explained rationally. Such a complete and unitary system is the absolute whole or what even Kant recognized as the Ideal of Reason and admitted to be a theoretical condition of all coherent science—the ultimate presupposition of all experience conditioned by the categories of the understanding. As Collingwood had said earlier, it is the metaphysical conception of God, Spinoza's *Substantia sive Natura*, and Hegel's Absolute. The existence of such a God is no matter of fact and of course it cannot be empirically demonstrated; but it must be presupposed, for otherwise nothing could be empirically demonstrated at all. The presupposition is an act of faith upon which all scientific understanding rests.

Taken by itself, this argument is neither as far-reaching nor as convincing as the doctrine of the *Essay on Philosophical Method* or of 'Faith and Reason'. But in conjunction with what Collingwood has written in those treatises, the position of the *Essay on Metaphysics* can be seen as simply another version of the same view and by no means incompatible with what he had written elsewhere. The other versions are needed to supplement this one and render it plausible. It is only if we see the absolute presupposition of science as 'the whole' that the view holds firm, and it is only if we realize that the whole is absolute mind, or the self-reflective subject of *Speculum Mentis* that we are committed to its undeniability. In the *Essay on Metaphysics* Collingwood keeps these ultimate truths in the background and at least appears to be advocating a relativistic type of historicism which is not typical of his philosophy at its best. That this is, however, only an appearance, his theory of history, as he expounded it in detail in other works, gives evidence. For that theory presents history itself as a dialectical process, if not quite as Hegel presented it, yet as a progressive self-discovery and self-knowledge of mind.

VII

COLLINGWOOD AND
METAPHYSICAL NEUTRALISM

W. H. WALSH

COLLINGWOOD WAS always reluctant to admit that he had a metaphysical position. *Speculum Mentis*, his first major philosophical work, may appear to the external eye to contain an outline account of a metaphysical system, but that is not how its author saw it. He offered it rather as a series of studies of different forms of consciousness or 'types of experience' (*SM*, 42)—artistic, religious, scientific, historical, philosophical—arranged in an order of cognitive adequacy; each member of the series except the last was supposed to develop naturally into its successor, and to that extent to be taken up into and superseded by the latter. Collingwood's ultimate model in writing the book may have been Hegel's *Phenomenology of Spirit*, which Hegel presented as a way of getting into his system rather than as an exposition of his systematic views. *Speculum Mentis* can be seen as a latter-day version of the *Phenomenology*, smoother, tidier, easier to follow; it preserves, under its surface clarity, much of the arbitrary character of Hegelian thought but not so much of its insight and penetration. In arguing that man could rest content only when he attained to the philosophical attitude Collingwood was certainly suggesting a distinct view of the world: he was implying that what exists is penetrated and indeed constituted by mind, and hence that any attempt to characterize it in, for example, merely natural terms is bound to prove inadequate. But it must equally be allowed that Collingwood does not put his position in quite this way. Despite what contemporaries said or believed about his offering a new statement of idealist metaphysics, he nowhere claims that this is what he was attempting.

Speculum Mentis was written at a time when Collingwood was deeply influenced by Croce as well as Hegel: its nervousness in avowing a metaphysical position no doubt connects with Croce's general suspicion of abstract thought. By the time he came to publish his next main philosophical work, *An Essay on Philosophical Method*, in 1933, Collingwood had developed a more independent line. But despite the fact that this work contains a vigorous if somewhat oblique defence of the Ontological Argument, we look in it in vain for a statement of general metaphysical doctrine. It is, in fact, not so much a first-order as a second-order study: it aspires to take philosophical thinking as Collingwood understood and practised it and to make clear its peculiar character. There are important differences, Collingwood argued, between philosophical and scientific concepts: the latter are mutually exclusive species of a genus, the former overlap and, in a sense, include one another. A philosopher may describe an action as good without implying thereby that it cannot be useful or pleasant; pleasant, useful, and good in a philosophical classification are not so much strict alternatives as successive members of the same scale of forms, the higher members of which preserve the virtues of their predecessors whilst avoiding their vices. If we ask ourselves what all this amounts to one answer would be to say that it is an attempt to explicate the Hegelian doctrine of the concrete universal: Collingwood's philosophical concepts are supple and concrete, in contrast to the rigid abstractions of science. Another way to put it, suggested by Professor Louis O. Mink in his recent study of Collingwood, *Mind, History and Dialectic*,[1] is that the book makes explicit the principles on which Collingwood had proceeded in *Speculum Mentis*: it does not supersede the latter but presupposes it. And it is certainly true that in this work Collingwood was trying to write down the theory of a certain way of thinking philosophically, a way which was practised by, for example, H. H. Joachim among his contemporaries but not by G. E. Moore. Since one thesis urged by those who philosophized in this manner was that there can be no such thing as a wholly neutral logic, whose principles are valid regardless

---

[1] Bloomington, Ind., 1969.

of the subject-matter to which they are applied, it must be admitted that here too Collingwood was assuming the truth of a certain view of the world, without directly advocating it. What made the concrete universal and everything that went with it the proper vehicle for the expression of philosophical truth was that the world was, properly understood, a special sort of unity in diversity; it had the structure and properties of a self-developing mind. To anyone who refused to proceed on this assumption Collingwood's main contentions in the essay must have seemed wholly arbitrary; as indeed they did.

In his *Essay on Metaphysics*, published seven years after the *Essay on Philosophical Method*, Collingwood announced that metaphysics could only be a special kind of history. Aristotle, he said, had offered a double characterization of metaphysics: as the science of being as such, the 'science of pure being', and as a study of the presuppositions involved in 'ordinary science' (*EM*, 11). A science of pure being was an impossibility, since it would have no determinate subject-matter; you could arrive at 'pure being' only when abstraction was pushed to the limiting case, and then you would have nothing left on which to focus attention. Collingwood invoked Kant's dictum that 'being is not a predicate' and Hegel's contention that pure being is the same as nothing, in support of this view. But though Aristotle was wrong in believing in the possibility of metaphysics as ontology, he was not wrong in his whole analysis of the nature of metaphysics. That subject was indeed a study of presuppositions, in fact of absolute presuppositions, presuppositions which were ultimate and unquestioned. But the task of the metaphysician, current opinion notwithstanding, was only to find out what was or had been absolutely presupposed, or to investigate changes in such presuppositions; it was in no sense to justify the latter. Nor indeed could it be, for principles of the type in question were simply supposed, not propounded, and accordingly could not be properly considered either true or false. Collingwood added blandly that the account he gave of metaphysics corresponded to metaphysical practice through the ages, though he admitted that some confusion had been caused by omission in works of metaphysics of what he called 'the metaphysical rubric'

(*EM*, 55), the formula whose presence made clear that their authors were reporting on absolute presuppositions, not advocating their use.

The preface to *An Essay on Metaphysics* begins with these words:

This is not so much a book of metaphysics as a book about metaphysics. What I have chiefly tried to do in it is neither to expound my own metaphysical ideas, nor to criticise the metaphysical ideas of other people; but to explain what metaphysics is, why it is necessary to the well-being and advancement of knowledge, and how it is to be pursued.

What in the context of the book could Collingwood mean by expounding his own metaphysical ideas, or criticizing those of others? Clearly exposition and criticism alike would have to refer here to what was in fact the case. To expound a metaphysical idea would be to offer a statement of the absolute presuppositions which underly or underlay some first-order activity; to criticize a metaphysical idea would be to argue that some such statement was factually incorrect. In Part III of the *Essay* Collingwood put forward three examples of what might be called New Style metaphysical thinking, 'in order to show how metaphysical inquiry will be conducted if the principles laid down in the opening chapters are taken as sound' (*EM*, vii). One concerned the idea of God and its relevance to modern science, a second the metaphysics of Kant, the third the problem of causation. The section on Kant is peculiar in that it deals not with a topic in metaphysics but with a writer on the subject: its aim is to show that Kant was doing a good job if we read him as a proto-Collingwoodian, concerned to make explicit the absolute presuppositions of his time, but a poor one if we take him at his word and see him as trying to set out the *a priori* principles of objective thinking generally. Whatever the merits of this way of looking at Kant, the statement that this is the truth about him is clearly not an historical statement. Historians, according to Collingwood, have it as their business to rethink the thoughts of the agents with whom they deal. But it was never part of Kant's thought that he was uncovering the absolute presuppositions, or even the synthetic *a priori* principles, peculiar to his time, and accordingly the proposition that this was what he was doing cannot be historically established. In fact, Collingwood's acceptance of this proposition depended on two things: taking as correct his own analysis of the logic of question and answer, which ruled out Kant's own account of his enterprise, and being determined to find some interpretation of the work of a major philosopher which would allow it to have real merit. The historical fact, if it is an historical fact, that scientists today have a different attitude to the causal principle from that of their predecessors in the eighteenth century is certainly relevant to whether or not we feel sympathy with the rewritten version of Kant which Collingwood offers. But it is relevant to it as a *re-reading*, not as a piece of simple history.

Collingwood's first example, about the existence of God, might seem to illustrate his theory more exactly. His pages on this subject are sketchy in argument and sometimes bombastic in expression, but they put forward what certainly looks like an historical thesis: that the development of the scientific attitude as we know it went along with the development of mono-theistic religious belief. Collingwood attempts to set out the articles of this scientific/religious creed as they were successively held by the Greeks and the Christian Fathers; reversing the normal order of expectation he argues impishly that the latter were in fact sounder metaphysicians than the former, since they recognized that what the Greeks had taken to be propositions resting on the authority of experience were in fact principles presupposed absolutely. Yet there are difficulties in taking Collingwood at his word even here. It is not only that the historical evidence he adduces in support of his thesis is thin; that might be excused in circumstances where what is being offered is an example, rather than a full-scale study. The trouble lies elsewhere, in Collingwood's conviction that religious belief and belief in the existence of an orderly world of nature are logically bound up together. That they in fact were held together at a certain stage of human history can, one supposes, be historically demonstrated; that decline in religious belief might carry with it inhibition of the investigation of nature is something which could be the subject of historical investigation. But that it is logically improper to abandon belief in God and stick to belief in nature as the scientist sees it has surely nothing to do with the historian. He can tell us only what men in fact have thought, not what they should have thought.

'The metaphysical problems connected with the idea of causation,' writes Collingwood (*EM*, 321), 'are historical problems, not to be solved except by historical treatment.' And it is certainly true that he makes intriguing historical remarks in the course of his lively and penetrating discussion of this subject. It is true again that, especially as the discussion proceeds, he becomes more and more concerned to refute what he takes to be a metaphysical error in his own sense of the term, a view about causality held by what he calls (*EM*, 341) 'a group of reactionary thinkers, wedded to the errors of the past . . . obstructors of all progress whether in metaphysics or in science, natural or historical'. These thinkers have taken over from Kant the mutually incompatible assumptions that there is a tight one-to-one relationship between cause and effect, and that a cause precedes its effect in time; by clinging to this outmoded view, which was, it appears, a mistake from the first, they constitute a threat to civilization itself. But we do not need to share these forebodings to see that this part of his book constitutes a philosophical essay of unusual significance. It is, however, as a piece of philosophical analysis that it is most naturally read. What Collingwood does in these chapters is distinguish and comment on three different though historically connected senses which we give to the word 'cause': one which it bears in history, according to which a cause is, roughly, a motive; one which it bears in practical sciences of nature such as medicine, where a cause is 'an event or state of things which it is in our power to produce or prevent, and by producing or preventing which we can produce or prevent that whose cause it is said to be' (*EM*, 196–7); finally the sense given to the term in theoretical natural science, according to which the cause of a phenomenon is (again roughly) the sum of those antecedent conditions which are necessary and sufficient to produce it. Now Collingwood's attitude to the first two senses is very different from what it is to the third, for whilst he accepts the historical and practical notions of causality as being evidently in order, he criticizes the pure scientific notion as ultimately quite incoherent.

His point about it is that it retains uncritically elements which properly belong to one or other of the earlier senses: the idea of force or power which goes naturally with the historical sense (we show our power over other people in affording them motives to act in certain ways), the idea of a time-gap between cause and effect which makes sense when we speak of practical causes, which can come into effect only with the co-operation of further conditions whose presence is assumed. Thus the scientific notion of causality is in the end ill-thought out. Collingwood tries to turn this result to his own advantage in a number of ways. He argues in some places that we have to do here with a case in which a constellation of absolute presuppositions exhibits 'strain'; he had said in an earlier chapter that one task for the metaphysician was to point out such strains and explain their genesis. Again, he quotes Russell with approval as saying that 'physics has ceased to look for causes'; the implication of this is presumably that the term strictly has no sense in theoretical natural science and should now be abandoned altogether. Finally, he attacks his fellow-philosophers, past and present, for failing to do the job which he thinks they should be doing, namely that of reporting accurately on what is in fact presupposed absolutely in this area. Their horror of metaphysics, which they confuse with pseudo-metaphysics, keeps them from this task, and in default of it they are content to repeat dogmas which they do not understand and for which they have no warrant.

It hardly seems possible to run all these lines at once. We may grant that Collingwood had interesting things to say about the historical connections of his various senses of the word 'cause'; we may grant again that he was percipient, if not quite alone, in discerning the difficulties into which those who use the term in pure science are led. But on his own theory the most he could hope to do about such difficulties was to explain in what historical circumstances they arose; it was not for him to try to resolve them. To resolve a strain in a cluster of absolute presuppositions you need on Collingwood's account to engage in first-order thinking; you need to be a creative scientist. A metaphysician of the Collingwoodian kind can help in this work only to the extent of getting the record straight: he can set out the facts as he sees them, somewhat as a civil servant can set out facts for his minister, but he cannot go beyond that point. Should other subsidiaries appear on the scene with their own accounts of the matter, accounts which he sees to be confused and ill-informed, he can make sure that they are roundly abused and so carry little weight. In this way he can do something to ensure the progress of science, if only in a negative way. But these are modest achievements at best.

The question is whether Collingwood's practice kept him within these modest bounds. I am inclined to think that it did not. Collingwood professes to be doing no more than his job as a reformed metaphysician when he reports Russell as saying that the word 'cause' is no longer part of the vocabulary of the advanced sciences (*EM*, 269, 322); he adduces this fact as a piece of historical evidence. But the general tone of his discussion of the topic of causation in natural science is such as to preclude us from thinking that he was wanting to make a purely historical point. It is clear enough on the contrary that Collingwood's interests here were as much philosophical as historical; that he wanted to expose muddled thinking and not just inaccurate or outdated history. It was his conviction that the pure scientific concept of cause tries to combine elements which cannot be combined; it is incoherent and in consequence cannot figure in anyone's thought. Once we are assured of this we need no evidence about whether physicists acknowledge the idea or not, for we know that they cannot work with it whatever they say.

Collingwood claims that 'unexceptionable metaphysical grounds' exist for denying the principle of Kant's Second Analogy; they consist in the historical fact, reported by Russell, that 'in advanced sciences such as gravitational astronomy the word "cause" never occurs' (*EM*, 269). But at least one object of his chapter on 'Causation in Kantian Philosophy' in *An Essay on Metaphysics* is to show that 'the two suppositions that constitute Kant's definition of the term "cause" are not consupponible,' i.e. that they cannot be logically combined. Collingwood adds lamely that the fact that two suppositions are logically incompatible

does not prove that they were not concurrently made; it only proves that, if they were concurrently made, the structure of the constellation that included them both was subject to severe strain, and that the entire fabric of the science based upon them was in a dangerously unstable condition (*EM*, 332).

But, once more, we can scarcely be expected to take much interest in this when the incompatibility has been made clear. Nor can we resist the conclusion that Collingwood is as eager to prove Kant's philosophical incompetence on the subject of causality as he is to make historical points. And philosophical incompetence in this context means inability to think clearly, not being careless or misinformed about what other people are in fact presupposing.

I have tried to show that, despite Collingwood's claim in his later writings to have dissolved metaphysics in history, the re-formed metaphysics he describes and illustrates in fact has a good deal of philosophy about it. Putting off the old Adam proved a more difficult task than Collingwood was willing to admit. But even if this point is granted, it does not follow that Collingwood was at this stage committed to metaphysics in the old sense of the term. I take metaphysics in the traditional sense to be either a doctrine of what there is or a reasoned account of the principles by which we are to understand what there is. Collingwood would have nothing to do with the former; does anything we have said so far show that he should in logic have recognized his commitment to the latter? I do not think it does. For though I have argued that being a metaphysician in Collingwood's revised sense sometimes involves philosophical as well as historical thinking, the object of the philosophizing is essentially negative. The reformed metaphysician is not confined to saying what first-order inquirers are in fact presupposing; he can go on to ask if their presuppositions are logically coherent. But when he comes up with the news that what is supposed to be a key concept in some important branch of learning is in fact confused, he is not in a position to remedy the defect himself. Straightening out such a concept is work for someone who is actively engaged in scientific inquiry, not for the mere commentator which is all that Collingwood's metaphysician can aspire to be. As a commentator he possesses no first principles of his own, though he is skilled in detecting the first principles which others use and has a good eye for any internal discrepancies they may involve. And thus he cannot advocate or argue for any set of first principles; he can argue only that some such sets are impossible.

It is interesting to observe that, as Mink has pointed out, the doctrine of absolute presuppositions has a certain continuity with a view about philosophy which Collingwood expressed at a much earlier stage, in *Speculum Mentis*. The main object of that work is to explore and comment on a number of first-order activities: art, religion, science, history. In it Collingwood tries to set out what is essential to the artistic, religious, scientific and historical mind, and so to make explicit the principles by which each proposes to understand the world. But he holds at this stage that none of these forms of consciousness is fully coherent; for a true understanding of experience we must pass beyond them to philosophy. Yet when we ask what philosophy has which they have not, the answer is surprisingly thin. It turns out, if Collingwood is to be believed, that 'art, religion, science, history, and whatever other forms of thought may be distinguished, are not autonomous forms of experience but philosophical errors' (*SM*, 252). But philosophy itself seems to consist in little more than a repetition of this claim, as is shown by the fact that Collingwood's discussion of it includes sections on Aesthetic Philosophy, Religious Philosophy, Scientific Philosophy, and Historical Philosophy. True, there is a later section entitled 'Philosophy as Absolute Knowledge', together with others on 'The Absolute Mind' and 'Absolute Ethics' (Collingwood was anxious in this book to say that each of his forms of consciousness involved a distinctive ethical position). But these sections are remarkably uninformative. Philosophy is 'the mind's knowledge of itself' (*SM*, 291); it is also 'the self-liberation of thought from uncriticized assumptions' (*SM*, 247). The philosopher knows, as the scientist and even the historian do not, that there is no real separation between the subject and object of knowledge. But apart from this he seems to know very little on his own account. Confronted by the objection that to describe philosophy as the self-knowledge of mind is abstract, Collingwood comments:

If the mind feels cold without an object other than itself, nothing is simpler for it than to create a palace of art, a world of mythology, a cosmos of abstract conceptual machinery, and so forth. In fact that is precisely what it does when it cannot achieve what it really wants—self-knowledge—without the help of these things. But it is not these things that it wants: it is self-knowledge. For when it has its works of art, what it values in them is not themselves but the glimpses they give of hidden and mysterious beauty. What it worships in the figures of the gods is not these figures themselves in their externality to itself but the revelation through them of something really divine; and so on (*SM*, 291–2).

In other words, if you want philosophical truth, you must immerse yourself in something which is not philosophy; philosophy is a a spirit rather than an autonomous doctrine. And this result is borne out by Collingwood's two pages on 'Absolute Ethics'. The state of mind here commended is one in which an agent does his duty but not for duty's sake; in which he operates a system of moral rules, but freely adapts these on each occasion of acting to a unique situation. If we ask where we are to find a real content for such an ethics, it is hard to see to what else we can be referred than the ethics of utility and mere duty which Absolute Ethics is alleged to supersede.

Despite all this, it seems clear that when he wrote *Speculum Mentis* Collingwood held officially that there is a philosophical view of the world as well as an artistic, a religious, a scientific, and an historical view; except on this supposition he could not have aspired to arrange his different forms of experience in an order of cognitive adequacy, which means in effect an order of metaphysical truth. Philosophy at this stage is not just an analytic but also a critical activity; it possesses standards to which it insists that other types of thinking shall conform. Collingwood is vague about the source of its standards, but that it has them is certainly implicit in his whole procedure in this book. Hence *Speculum Mentis*, despite what was said at the beginning of this paper, can properly be treated as a metaphysics in at least one recognized sense of the term: it reviews different sets of first principles and recommends one such set as alone fully adequate to reality. And if it is correct to see Collingwood's *Essay on Philosophical Method* as writing out the theory of which *Speculum Mentis* was the practice, it would seem that Collingwood retained this metaphysical outlook for at least another ten years. Admittedly, a certain difficulty arises here from the fact that the essay is ostensibly more of a contribution to logic than to metaphysics; had Collingwood had the courage of his convictions he might have been expected to enlarge on 'Philosophy as Absolute Knowledge' instead of treating the more general subject of the differences between philosophical and scientific thinking. But as has been pointed out already, his account of thinking is such that he rejects the idea of any neutral, topic-indifferent logic: to commend a certain way of thinking is for him to say that this is how the world is. Hence in arguing for the overlap of classes and the notion of a scale of forms as characteristics of philosophical thought Collingwood was implicitly continuing with his old view of the nature of things. And this conclusion derives support from the reflection that, in the *Essay* as in *Speculum Mentis*, there is ample evidence of Collingwood's continuing hostility to science and above all the scientific attitude. Philosophical knowledge, according to the argument of the essay, is expressed in propositions which are both universal and categorical; scientific propositions are universal but also hypothetical. There can be no doubt which of these Collingwood believes to be superior. And indeed in the whole book he is not just idly describing differences, but advancing a point of view as well. The fact that he wrote on 'logic' may be evidence of the existence of a certain strain in his philosophical position, but it is not enough to prove that his views had changed in any radical way.

What now about his later position? Collingwood's publishers labelled his books in a way which suggests that *The Principles of Art* and *An Essay on Metaphysics* continue a series which was begun by *An Essay on Philosophical Method;* and perhaps that is how Collingwood himself liked to think of the matter. But if it was, the suggestion was very misleading. For with the appearance of *An Essay on Metaphysics* at least Collingwood took a step which marked a decisive break with his earlier thought. He now asserted, in effect, that philosophy cannot judge but only record. And though as we have seen this statement does only partial justice to his practice, the fact remains that his theory and practice alike leave no room for any independent philosophical principles. Philosophy on Collingwood's new account of the matter becomes wholly and solely a second-order study; it presupposes the existence of first-order activities like art, religion and science, but it can no longer claim ability to judge of their adequacy as forms of experience. Each of them must be taken by the philosopher as being in order as it is.

Collingwood held a chair of metaphysics and was anxious to find a proper role for metaphysics; throughout his essay on the subject he insisted that current hostility to metaphysics was having or would have dire practical results. But the metaphysics for whose legitimacy he argued in 1940 (and a year earlier in his *Autobiography*) was not the sort of metaphysics he had himself practised in the earlier part of his philosophical career. In *Speculum Mentis* Collingwood had proceeded on the assumption that every form of experience is or involves a philosophy; his whole effort was directed to putting four such philosophies in order and to indicating how their shortcomings might be supplemented to arrive at a truly adequate view. According to the argument he developed later this project was impossible in principle. To insist that a certain set of first principles is true, which according to *Speculum Mentis* is what artists, religious men, scientists, and historians alike do, is to make a gross philosophical mistake; it is to engage not in metaphysics, but in pseudo-metaphysics. For first principles or absolute presuppositions are not true or false; they are not propositions but presuppositions. And that being the case the philosopher can only say what they are; he is in no position to argue either for or against them. He is unable to commend or to condemn, but must leave everything as it is.

I do not propose to inquire how far, if at all, Collingwood's defence of metaphysics could be expected to give comfort to someone who was seriously troubled by positivist attacks on the subject, except to say that a positivist could take Collingwood *au pied de la lettre* and argue that accepting his views was entirely compatible with his own contentions. According to the positivists, metaphysical propositions (or pseudo-propositions) are meaningless because they are neither analytic nor empirically verifiable; according to the later Collingwood, metaphysical propositions are historical and can be pronounced true or false by reference to historical evidence. But what Collingwood means by a metaphysical proposition is different in a vital way from what the positivist means by a metaphysical proposition: the difference lies in the presence or absence of the metaphysical rubric. The proper form of a metaphysical statement, in Collingwood's own words, is: 'In such and such a phase of scientific thought it is (or was) absolutely presupposed that . . .' (*EM*, 55). The positivist would obviously have no difficulty in accepting the existence of meaningful metaphysical propositions of this kind, though he would of course have to maintain that in some cases (e.g. when it was a question of God's existence) what was presupposed did not make sense, or made sense only if the words were taken in a peculiar way. Collingwood's interpretation of some metaphysical beliefs might surprise him, as in the case quoted, but it need not constitute any radical challenge to the position he was attempting to establish.

It is perhaps more interesting to explore certain continuities and contrasts in Collingwood's earlier and later thought about the subjects we have been considering. One topic to which he gives continuous attention is that of self-knowledge. In *Speculum Mentis*, as we have already seen, it is philosophy that provides self-knowledge: one definition of philosophy is the mind's consciousness of itself, and though this is misleading when taken alone, suggesting as it does that the mind is one thing among others, it is nevertheless fundamentally correct (*SM*, 247). What distinguishes the philosopher from the artist, the scientist, and even the historian is that he is fully aware of what he is doing in so far as he philosophizes; he knows his own mind as they do not. Collingwood was still laying great emphasis on the importance of self-knowledge when he came to write his British Academy lecture 'Human Nature and Human History' in 1936: self-knowledge, he says there, 'is desirable and important to man, not only for its own sake, but as a condition without which no other knowledge can be critically justified and securely based' (*IH*, 205). However, he went on to claim that it is history, not philosophy, which provides self-knowledge; history is the science of human nature for which earlier philosophers had looked in vain. The two positions are to some extent reconciled in the *Essay on Metaphysics*, where it emerges that metaphysical philosophy, which is of course a form of history, provides self-knowledge in its most fundamental and valuable form. Metaphysical analysis, presumably in contrast to ordinary history, makes us aware of the absolute presuppositions which underlie our first-order investigations and so facilitates the carrying on of these investigations. Scientists, it appears, can operate without benefit of metaphysical knowledge, but not for long or at a very high level. And bad metaphysics, i.e. false beliefs about what is being presupposed absolutely, menaces scientific advance gravely, which was one reason why Collingwood thought it so important that metaphysics should be done properly and with full knowledge of what it was.

On self-knowledge Collingwood contrived to maintain some appearance of self-consistency, though it is clear enough that he shifted his position at a vital point. On other matters his change of view was too great to allow of concealment. Thus while he held throughout his philosophical life that mind is what it does, his conception of the different spheres in which it is active changed radically. In *Speculum Mentis* art, religion, science, and history are rivals to each other as well as to philosophy; they are each thought of as making assertions, implicit or explicit, about the nature of things. Collingwood is not content to treat art or religion exclusively at its own level, as if it were self-contained, for he sees it and the other departmental forms of consciousness as constantly breaking out of its own narrow bounds and making a claim to possess the whole world. In his later writings Collingwood nowhere to my knowledge formally repudiates this view; he just silently drops it. His three books *The Principles of Art*, *The Idea of Nature*, and *The Idea of History* may be seen in one way as revised versions of what he wrote about art, science, and history in *Speculum Mentis*. But they really constitute fresh treatments of their subject-matter from a completely different point of view. They proceed on the assumption that art and science and history are distinct areas of experience, each complete in itself and none threatening the others. Collingwood argues explicitly for the 'autonomy' of history, but the truth is that at this later stage of his thought he believed equally in the autonomy of science, the autonomy of art, and so on. In fact, he had arrived at something like the Wittgenstinian conception of autonomous language-games, each of which serves its particular purpose and none of which need be seen as a rival to any other. He differed from Wittgenstein in thinking that individual games were constantly changing their rules, and in assigning to the metaphysical philosopher the task of saying what the rules are and have been. But his position in other respects was surprisingly similar to the one Wittgenstein was developing at the same time.[1]

If these arguments are correct it would appear that Collingwood in his later years was not entitled to any metaphysical position, in the sense of a view of the world as a whole. Despite his claim to be a defender of metaphysics, the standpoint to which his essay on the subject committed him is that which I have called elsewhere Metaphysical Neutralism, the denial that it is necessary or even possible to take up any overall metaphysical attitude. Like Wittgenstein, the later Collingwood thought that philosophy cannot judge or explain; at bottom it can only describe. But we may well wonder if Collingwood lived up to his own professions in this matter. In one respect it seems to be evident that he did not. Although the full-blooded idealism of his Crocean–Hegelian period is absent from his later writings, something of the anti-naturalism which went along with it survives. Collingwood's attitude to natural science grew more sympathetic as he progressed: his remarks about science in the *Essay on Metaphysics* are altogether better informed and more appreciative than what he has to say on the subject in *Speculum Mentis*, which is arbitrary and abstract, or in the *Essay on Philosophical Method*, which leaves no doubt of his general hostility to scientific claims. But though Collingwood

[1] In one respect Collingwood's position fell short of Wittgenstein's, since he held that 'natural science as a form of thought exists and always has existed in a context of history, and depends on historical thought for its existence' (*IN*, 177). For criticism and interpretation of this obscure dictum see Mink, *Mind, History and Dialectic*, pp. 40–1. If all Collingwood meant by it is that scientific concepts have a history, the same is true, of course, of the concepts of art and religion, to say nothing of history itself. But this can be admitted without turning art, religion, and science into history.

became more reasonable or at least more orthodox in his estimate of natural science, he remained a severe and unrelenting critic of the social sciences. In his British Academy lecture he argued that the project for a generalizing science of human nature, outlined by Hume and strongly supported by his English and Scottish successors, had not only turned out to be unsuccessful, but would be of no value even if it were feasible. We already possess a non-generalizing science of human nature in the shape of history, which involves a special form of understanding of its own. Natural phenomena have to be dealt with by the method of observation and induction, for we stand outside of them and can comprehend them only externally. But in the sphere of human affairs, which Collingwood identifies with the sphere of history, we have to do with events which have both outsides and insides, the former being mere movements in the physical world, the latter the thoughts which the agents expressed in those movements. Historians describe what was going on in terms of thoughts or purposes; their central concept is the concept of action. And just because of this there is no gap in their thinking, as there necessarily is in the thinking of natural scientists, between description and explanation: once they know what was occurring they know why it was occurring. Accordingly they have no need to appeal to any generalizing science of human affairs, nor would their understanding be improved in any way if they could make such an appeal. It follows that the social sciences are either impossible or otiose. Collingwood does not say that they are downright impossible (see *IH*, 222). But he does emphasize that if such sciences existed they would be of no use, for 'if, by historical thinking, we already understand how and why Napoleon established his ascendancy in revolutionary France, nothing is added to our understanding of that process by the statement (however true) that similar things have happened elsewhere' (*IH*, 223). And he argues that since 'social orders are historical facts . . . subject to inevitable changes, fast or slow', a 'positive science of mind' can at most record uniformities of behaviour which hold over a period of time, and so can be no more than a generalized form of history. The decline of classical economics is supposed to illustrate this; orthodox political theory, which professedly dealt with the problem of the state, but in fact dealt with a series of separate if not unconnected problems, is given as another example. Collingwood is prepared to allow that psychology is, or could be, a genuine science, but only if it is recognized that it concerns not mind proper but the natural basis of mind—'the blind forces and activities in us which are part of human life as it consciously experiences itself, but are not parts of the historical process: sensation as distinct from thought, feelings as distinct from conceptions, appetite as distinct from will' (*IH*, 231). But it is obvious that psychology as so explained is a natural, not a social, science.

If we ask what lies behind this, the answer must be that Collingwood is urging a certain view of man as what might be called the correct and proper view of man; he is saying, in effect, that man is essentially a free agent or a rational being. That he is free and rational, despite the fact that he acts in a natural setting from which he can never escape and of which he must take account in all he does, is the most important thing about him. It goes along with the fact that man is a being who thinks. To say that man thinks is to say that he thinks freely; thinking is an activity, not a mere passivity, something that happens to us whether we like it or not. To speak of action or thought as being determined in the strict sense of the term is to be involved in a contradiction in terms. It was Collingwood's view that those who try to explain history by reference to the operation of economic, social, or psychological forces are blind to these obvious facts; their attempt to import what is really the scientific mode of explanation into history involves in effect the devaluing of human beings from persons to automata. I do not say that Collingwood was mistaken to subscribe to this opinion. But it seems to me obvious that in voicing it he was doing more than simply recording facts.

To reinforce this point let me conclude by suggesting a way in which Collingwood could have taken a more sympathetic view of the possibilities of social science without sacrificing his main position. To do this it is necessary to begin by making an amendment in his formal account of historical thinking. In his discussion of historical causation in the *Essay on Metaphysics* Collingwood explained that an historical cause had two components, which he called the *causa quod* and the *causa ut*. The *causa quod* was, roughly, what the agent made of the situation, his reading or assessment of it the *causa ut* was his aim or purpose, framed and pursued in the light of that assessment. In saying that to cause someone to do something in this sense of the term is to afford him a motive for doing it Collingwood was thinking that you can change a man's mind by showing him that the situation in which he has to act is other than he thought it to be. But concrete thought involves more than premisses which state what is the case and declarations about what is being aimed at; it involves principles of action as well. As Professor Dray has made clear, we both characterize the situations in which we find ourselves under general descriptions and have rules for dealing with situations of this or that type. Nor can these principles of action be deduced analytically from knowledge of how a man saw his situation and what he was trying to achieve: we do not always know the best means to attain our ends, and in any case many of our activities are not undertaken in direct pursuit of a goal. In reconstituting any piece of historical thinking we must accordingly state both what the agent thought the facts were and what principles governed his action. We have to recognize (and it is in fact recognized by historians in practice) that men can not only see facts in a peculiar light, but further can embrace principles for dealing with them which diverge in all sorts of important ways from the principles which govern our own conduct. For obvious instances of this we have only to reflect on the diversity of morals and manners, though it is by no means confined to these: it extends to styles of life generally.

Now when Collingwood claims that history is the true science of human nature he is arguing that to reconstitute an agent's thought is already to understand what he did. In one sense this is quite correct. I understand your action when I succeed in reconstructing in my own mind the practical syllogism which lay behind it. But I may do this without seeing, or without seeing fully, why you thought as you did; what it was that gave those particular premisses their special appeal for you. And this difficulty may become acute if it happens that you are a person whose principles of action diverge very markedly from my own. How can it be reduced? One way is of course to realize that a man's outlook and principles of action are not adopted in isolation but tend to go together; further historical investigation will often make clear their interconnections. But explanation of this sort can at most be partial: it can lead us to see why somebody who accepted p came also to accept q, but not why he accepted p in the first place. To put the point in different terms, there must always be in these conditions some feature of the situation which is acquiesced in as given fact. And that being so it is natural that we should look for further enlightenment at a different level, by inquiring whether there was anything about that type of man in that type of situation which made it natural for him to think in that way. To do this is not to abandon the idea that man is a rational being, for the object of the whole exercise is to supplement explanation in rational terms, not to set it aside. It seems to me clear that we appeal to generalizations of the type mentioned, formal and informal, both in our everyday lives and in reading and writing history. That Collingwood gave no consideration to this aspect of historical thought, and indeed was dogmatically opposed to any recourse by the historian to explanations of the social science kind, argues that there was more to his attitude than a Wittgenstinian respect for the autonomy of history. A well-defined and persistently held metaphysical outlook of an antinaturalist kind came into it as well.

VIII

COLLINGWOOD'S HISTORICISM:
A DIALECTIC OF PROCESS

LOUIS O. MINK

Plato's discovery was *how the intellect could find its way about in a Heraclitean world.* The answer is: *think dialectically.*

The New Leviathan, 24.63

I

VIRTUALLY ALL of the growing critical literature on Collingwood's philosophy of history has taken its proof texts from *The Idea of History*—the posthumous collection of two previously published lectures and five excerpts from his unpublished manuscripts, collectively entitled 'Epilegomena'. No doubt it is a tribute of a sort that both his influence and an entire corpus of critical animadversions are based on a mere 130 pages, largely unrevised and never conceived by their author as a whole. But it serves as well to call attention to remarkable lacunae both in the understanding of Collingwood's views on history and in the criticism of them. For one thing, critics have made few attempts to range Collingwood's theoretical reflections against his own actual practice as a working historian of Roman Britain—despite his repeated claim that the philosophy of a subject, such as the philosophy of history, consists of second-order reflection on the actual practice of working at that subject. A second lacuna is even more surprising. Few supporters or critics of Collingwood, to judge by their citations and conclusions, have even bothered to read the 'Epilegomena' in the light of the history of the idea of history which occupies the first four sections of *The Idea of History*. Yet most of the main points of the Epilegomena appear in these historical sections, often in clarified form because they appear in criticism of classical positions. It would in fact be possible, if the 'Epilegomena' and other published essays on the philosophy of history did not exist, to reconstruct from the first four sections of *The Idea of History* most of the views which have attracted to Collingwood the sympathetic loyalty of so many admirers and the darts of so many critics.

Yet this 'Collingwood' is largely a fiction, invented, however unwittingly, by a process of selective interpretation calculated to minimize anomalies for the reassurance of supporters or to convert passing remarks into theses as targets of critics. The third lacuna in the interpretation and criticism of Collingwood is the gravest of all. It is the failure to see *The Idea of History* as a part of a more comprehensive philosophy the understanding of which greatly illuminates and partially modifies it but which cannot be reconconstructed from the text of *The Idea of History* itself. In *The Idea of History* certain doctrines are dominant, others recessive. The 'recessive' doctrines have virtually escaped notice, while the 'dominant' doctrines are those from which the fictional Collingwood has been put together and sent abroad. By 'fictional', of course, I mean the sense in which Shakespeare's or Shaw's Julius Caesar is fictional, not that in which Mr. Pickwick is fictional. The fictional Collingwood is not an invention but an interpretation. But if one sees *The Idea of History* from the standpoint of Collingwood's larger philosophy, the apparently dominant doctrines are diminished in importance or modified in meaning, while the recessive doctrines are revealed as centres of unsuspected conceptual connections. There are two keys to achieving such an altered angle of vision in the interpretation of Collingwood: the first is to see that the main questions of *The Idea of History* belong to the philosophy of mind rather than to what is *ordinarily* called the 'philosophy of history'; the second, and harder, is to see that the conceptual system which informs Collingwood's answers is *dialectical*, in a complex and original way. I shall try first to call attention to several 'recessive' doctrines as a way of calling the received interpretation of Collingwood into question, and then to give a summary account of his idea of dialectic in order to suggest how it can resolve that question. To do more than suggest this, of course, is the task of a much more extended reconsideration of all of Collingwood's philosophical doctrines and arguments than can be essayed here.

II

The fictional Collingwood is something like this: as an 'idealist', he believes that reality is mental. History is therefore a form of knowledge superior to natural science, because the subject matter of history is human actions, and actions are caused by thoughts in the heads of their agents (natural events do not, like actions, have 'insides' made up of intelligible and repeatable acts of thought). By exercising a kind of empathy, the historian can succeed in rethinking exactly the sequences of thought hidden behind the actions which he is investigating; and to the extent that he succeeds, he knows those thoughts and therefore those actions in the strong sense that his re-enactment of a past act of thought is identical with the thought re-enacted. For this to be possible, however, that thought must be conscious, purposive, and rational, as in such cases as proving a mathematical theorem or making a tactical plan, for only such intellectual acts can be identical in the mind of the agent and in the mind of the historian; identity is the criterion of re-enactment. Early historians merely stitched together a patchwork of testimony and documents, however unreliable; later historians learned to criticize their sources for accuracy and veracity; but only by consciously adopting the method of mental re-enactment can history become truly scientific, achieve certainty, and be immune to the kinds of criticism and constant correction to which the natural sciences are condemned because there is nothing in the course of natural events for them to 're-enact'.

Although few of Collingwood's critics have promulgated this myth in all of its details, anyone who has read much of the Collingwood literature of the last two decades will recognize it as a composite of views attributed to Collingwood more often than not. And texts—sentences, at least—supporting each point *can* be found in *The Idea of History*. The fiction shows how easily the dominant views can be caricatured. As a beginning toward correcting the fiction, there are in particular three doctrines of Collingwood's which cannot be understood without invoking his idea of dialectic; all of them are 'recessive' in *The Idea of History* in the sense that their visibility there is very low, although they are of major importance in the process of thought by which Collingwood reached his more obvious conclusions.

The first doctrine is that the 'history' which Collingwood says is the true science of mind which psychology fails to be (*IH*, 205–9), is not uniquely nor even characteristically exemplified in what we ordinarily regard as the activity of historians; it refers rather to a form of consciousness which bears the same relation to working history as does 'religion' in 'Money in his religion' 'to 'religious' in 'He has joined a religious order'. The second doctrine is that the subject-matter on which this form of consciousness reflects comprises not only rational and deliberate individual action (re-enacted in the 'mind of the historian' as exactly as possible as it was enacted and *known to be* enacted by the agent), but also processes of change of which no participant *could* have given the account which historical inquiry *can* give. And the third doctrine is that the 'thought' which historical inquiry seeks to re-enact does not exclude but includes emotions, desires, motives, attitudes, and acts of will—all those non-rational aspects of human life which Collingwood has been thought by critics of his 'idealism' to have forcibly expelled from the field of historical knowledge. These three theses are not easy to discern or to understand. But they are like the hidden faces in the clouds and trees in a child's picture-puzzle: first they cannot be seen at all, and then, when they are seen, it is they which seem to determine the outlines of the clouds and trees.

What 'history' means. Because *The Idea of History* devotes so much attention to such questions as the differences among 'scissors-and-paste', 'critical', and 'scientific' histories, the analogy between the historian and the detective, and the relation between the historian and his evidence, it is easy to regard Collingwood as engaged primarily in the philosophical analysis of historical methodology. This is reinforced by his review of the successes and failures of historians from Herodotus to Bury and Toynbee—all paradigmatic examples of 'historians'. It thus seems that while history has a history, it yet comprises a more or less clearly defined class of activities and products. Whatever conceptual problems there may be in deciding in borderline cases whether a writer is an 'historian' or his book a 'history' are peripheral.

But the concepts of 'history' and 'historian' so employed are what Collingwood throughout his career called 'empirical', 'scientific', or 'classificatory' concepts (or uses of concepts); and he fundamentally distinguished these from what he called 'philosophical' concepts or uses of concepts. The distinction was first made explicitly by Collingwood in his 1925 article 'Economics as a Philosophical Science',[1] where he treated empirical concepts (e.g., money and credit) as applying to specific classes of facts, but philosophical concepts (e.g., labour and utility) as tending to expand to apply to all rational actions; such concepts become, in fact, 'universal and necessary characteristics of rational action as such'. The distinction between empirical and philosophical concepts was developed throughout the (unpublished) lectures on moral philosophy which Collingwood gave annually, and finally appeared a decade later as a major theme in the *Essay on Philosophical Method*. A non-philosophical (i.e., scientific) concept, or a concept in its non-philosophical significance, according to the latter book,

qualifies a limited part of reality, whereas in its philosophical phase it leaks or escapes out of these limits and invades the neighbouring regions, tending at last to colour our thought of reality as a whole. As a non-philosophical concept it observes the rules of classification, its instances forming a class separate from other classes; as a philosophical concept it breaks those rules and the class of its instances overlaps those of its coordinate species (*EPM*, 35).

As examples of concepts which have both kinds of use Collingwood mentions the concept of mind, the concept of evolution, and the concept of art. In *The Principles of Art* (written *after* most of the

---

[1] *International Journal of Ethics* (now *Ethics*), xxxv (1925), 162–5. The basis for the distinction is in *SM*, esp. the section on 'Science as the assertion of the Abstract Concept' (158–66). In the Hegelian language which Collingwood abandoned soon after *SM*, the 'abstract concept' of 'Science' is there contrasted with the 'concrete universal' of 'Philosophy'.

'Epilegomena' of *The Idea of History*) the distinction is fundamental: the book begins with the problem of defining 'work of art' in the ordinary sense (i.e., the empirical concept of art) but the argument leads to and ends with a characterization of art as an aspect of all human activity: 'every utterance and every gesture that each one of us makes is a work of art' (*PA*, 285). Here the concept of art has 'leaked or escaped' (with much assistance from Collingwood) from its empirical application to a specific class of objects and performances to reveal the expressiveness of all human activities.

Now my suggestion is that in *The Idea of History* (and elsewhere), Collingwood often uses the term 'history' empirically to refer to the specific class of activities and products ordinarily called by that name, but also often *philosophically* to refer to a form of consciousness, characterized by ideas and beliefs which have come into existence in connection with the development of historical studies but which now escape any attempt to restrict them to historical inquiry as practised by 'historians'. His discussion ceases at this point to be methodology and becomes a philosophy of mind of potentially unrestricted application.

A major purpose of the historical sections of *The Idea of History* is to show the emergence and development of the ideas and beliefs which contribute to the historical consciousness in its unrestricted sense. Some of these are very new, as for example the conception that there can be rational knowledge of individuals as individuals, which before the turn of the twentieth century 'the whole tradition of European philosophy had declared with one voice' to be an impossibility (*IH*, 167). Others are more traditional ideas which have found new applications or different conceptual connections. For example, Collingwood credits the revolutionary effect of Christian thought in the fourth and fifth centuries A.D. for the 'recognition that what happens in history need not happen through anyone's wishing it to happen', a recognition which is 'an indispensable precondition of understanding any historical process' (*IH*, 48). The Christian basis for this belief, of course, is in the doctrines of original sin and of providential grace, but the 'new attitude to history' derived from those doctrines has survived the secularization of history. Or again, Herder's great innovation as 'the first thinker to recognize in a systematic way that there are differences between different kinds of men, and that human nature is not uniform but diversified' (*IH*, 90–1) remains a central conception in Collingwood's idea of history, although for Herder it was still connected with the unhistorical view that human differences are themselves not historical products but represent the fixed and unchanging psychological attributes of racial stocks.

Now it is easy to suppose that when Collingwood says that history is 'the science of human nature' he is awarding kudos to professional historians and their discipline. But it puts his aim and his achievement in truer perspective to say that this statement belongs to his philosophy of human nature rather than to his philosophy of history; for in it, 'history', as a philosophical concept, has 'leaked or escaped' from its ordinary application to the historical craft and its subject-matter and has become the description of a kind of existence and thought which may be found in any enterprise, and equally well may not be found in an example of what is ordinarily called 'history'. To understand Collingwood—or at least not to misunderstand him gratuitously—it is therefore necessary to be clear when he is speaking of 'history' as an *empirical* concept and when he is speaking of it as a *philosophical* concept. It is the empirical concept of history as a specific form of inquiry which is at issue when he asks 'What kind of things does history find out? I answer, *res gestae*: actions of human beings that have been done in the past' (*IH*, 9). It is the philosophical concept of history which is at issue when he says of the Roman constitution and its Augustan modification, 'The peculiarity which makes it historical is not the fact of its happening in time, but the fact of its becoming known to us by our re-thinking the same thought which created the situation . . .' (*IH*, 218). The empirical concept of history applies to what historians most characteristically do; the philosophical concept of history applies to what anyone does when he comes to understand an action, his own or another's, by reflecting on the thought exhibited in it. Collingwood is perfectly explicit about this:

All knowledge of mind is historical . . . If I want to know whether I am as good a man as I hope, or as bad as I fear, I must examine acts that I have done, and understand what they really were: or else go and do some fresh acts and then examine those. All these inquiries are historical . . .. The same historical method is the only one by which I can know the mind of another, or the corporate mind (whatever exactly that phrase means) of a community or an age (*IH*, 219).

According to the philosophical concept of history as knowledge of mind by re-enactment on the evidence of action, therefore, much 'ordinary' thinking is historical, as well as the characteristic methods of disciplines not usually regarded as 'historical' in the empirical phase of the concept: some literary criticism or field-work in anthropology, for example. So it comes as no surprise when Erik Erikson says that as a clinical psychotherapist he places himself 'next to the historian' and quotes Collingwood in support.[1] But this, if Collingwood were right, is only one of innumerable possible confirmations, since in its 'philosophical' significance the concept of history is no longer restricted to the special preoccupations of historians however much it finds their activities exemplary and worthy of analysis.

Actions and processes. Yet *The Idea of History* is also about the empirical concept of history, and one might therefore wish to focus only what it has to say about how historians come to understand '*res gestae*: actions of human beings that have been done in the past'. This definition of 'what history is about' seems straightforward, and it is reinforced by the well-known discussions of historical inquiry as the 're-enactment of past thought in the mind of the historian' and of thought as the 'inside' of action, action as the 'outside' of thought. Yet it too is not the whole story. To this received version of Collingwood's view of the 'object' of history (or what by the cunning dialectic of language is the same thing, its 'subject-matter'), there must be added another and different view: the object of history is *also* those processes by which things in the human world have *come to be*. The constituents of processes of coming-to-be are actions, but not all processes are actions (although some may be), and not all actions are constituents of such processes.

---

[1] Erik Erikson, 'The Nature of Clinical Evidence', *Daedalus*, lxxxvii (1958), 68. Erikson is referring to his methods as a clinician, not to his work in 'psycho-history'.

It is by revealing turns of phrase that Collingwood discloses this recessive but important view of the object of history. The very first question of Part I clearly presupposes it: 'By what steps and stages did the modern European idea of history *come into existence*?' (*IH*, 14; italics added.) But it appears *passim* throughout the historical sections of *The Idea of History*. Although a modern historian regards a history of Rome as a 'history of how Rome *came to be* what it is, a history of the *process* which *brought into existence* the characteristic Roman institutions and moulded the typical Roman character' (*IH*, 43; italics added), Livy is said to have had no such conception of history. Livy regarded 'Rome' as a substance, changeless and eternal, revealing itself in a succession of events but undergoing no 'spiritual change'. In general, because the concept of *development* is lacking in Greco-Roman historiography, the latter 'can therefore never show how anything *comes into existence*' (*IH*, 44–5; italics added). Or again, in Vico's conception of history as 'the history of the genesis and development of human societies and their institutions, . . . we reach for the first time a completely modern view of what the subject-matter of history is' (*IH*, 65). Or again, Kant's programme for a universal history is applauded for its idea of showing human rationality 'coming into existence' (*IH*, 104); and Schelling's doctrine of history as a manifestation of the Absolute is interpreted and approved as meaning that 'History is a temporal process in which both knowledge and the knowable are progressively coming into existence' (*IH*, 113). Or again, Toynbee's conception of historical method has the consequence that 'We are not allowed to say that Hellenic civilization has *turned into* Western Christendom by a process of *development* involving the accentuation of some of its elements, the fading away of others, and the emergence of certain new elements within itself and the borrowing of others from external sources . . . Toynbee's principle is that if a civilization changes it ceases to be itself and a new civilization comes into being' (*IH*, 162; italics added). Finally, and most generally, 'the historical fact, as it actually exists and as the historian knows it, is always a process in which something is changing into something else. This element of process is the life of history' (*IH*, 163). But how all of these 'processes' are

related to 'actions of human beings that have been done in the past'
is at best not clear.

The emphasis on 'process', on 'coming into existence', on
'turning into', and the like is in no way a late or incidental idea of
Collingwood's. As early as 1927 it had been clearly expressed in
his devastating critique of Spengler's thesis that cultures are closed
or self-contained systems: 'It is bad history and bad philosophy
alike to argue that because the Pantheon is Magian it is not classical.
. . . the Pantheon is *both* Magian *and* classical; it is classical in the
act of *turning into* Magian. And this conception of "turning into",
the conception of becoming, is (as Spengler himself industriously
asserts, and industriously forgets) the fundamental idea of all
history.'[1] As early as 1920, Collingwood tells us in his *Autobiography*,
he was occupied with analyzing the concept of process as a way of
understanding how the past can be a living past: '"processes" are
things which do not begin and end but turn into one another'
(*A*, 97–8).[2]

It is generally taken for granted (and parodied in the fictional
account of Collingwood) that he was 'a methodological indivi-
dualist in the strongest sense of that disputable term'.[3] This
description seems simply to acknowledge his plain statements about
res gestae and the re-enactment of individual acts of thought. It is
also taken to be Collingwood's view that an action can be known
to the historian only as it was *known* to the agent, since only conscious and rational thought can be re-enacted. One must therefore
raise an eyebrow at his repeated claims that actions can be known
in ways different from those in which they were understood by
their agents. Collingwood in fact criticizes Greco-Roman historiography for the very over-intellectualism attributed to him. Ancient
historians, he says, supposed that everything happened as the result

[1] 'Oswald Spengler and the Theory of Historical Cycles, I', *Antiquity*, i
(1927), 311–25; reprinted in R. G. Collingwood, *Essays in the Philosophy of
History*, ed. W. Debbins (Austin, Tex., 1965), p. 74. Italics in original.

[2] The 'essay of short book-length' on 'the nature and implications of process or
becoming' which in this passage Collingwood says he wrote in 1920 was never
published and the manuscript has been lost; but by Collingwood's account it
was his first study in the logic of dialectical processes.

[3] Alan Donagan, *The Later Philosophy of R. G. Collingwood* (Oxford, 1962),
p. 206.

of deliberate human purposes; but this was naïve, for 'to a great extent people do not know what they are doing until they have done it . . . something has taken shape as their actions went on which was certainly not present to any mind when the actions which brought it into existence began' (*IH*, 42). In a different context, as we have seen, Collingwood credits the Christian idea of providence with introducing an idea which survives in the modern concept of history: the 'recognition that what happens in history need not happen through anyone's deliberately wishing it to happen is an indispensable precondition of understanding any historical process' (*IH*, 48). Finally, that what Collingwood means by 'thought' is not necessarily known by or even accessible to introspection is made perfectly explicit when he generalizes the *philosophical* concept of history as a form of consciousness: 'It is only by historical thinking that I can discover . . . what I thought five minutes ago, by reflecting on an action that I then did, *which surprised me when I realized what I had done*' (*IH*, 219; italics added).

By this point Collingwood's dominant principles begin to appear unstable indeed. Against the principles that history is about individual human actions and that actions are brought about by conscious thought, we have Collingwood himself insisting that history is about processes of change which are not necessarily actions, and that actions themselves may not be known to their own agents even from the 'inside' as they can be known to later historical thinking. What are we to do with these apparent contradictions? We might suppose that the recessive principles are slips to be ignored, or else that they are grudging admissions that the dominant principles are indefensible exaggerations. But we might also come to suspect that the meanings of 'process', 'action', and 'thought' which give rise to the difficulties are not Collingwood's but are unwittingly imposed on his statements.

What 'thought' means. Confronted with a document, Collingwood says, the historian's task is to discover the writer's thought 'in the widest sense of that word' (*IH*, 282). But elsewhere he says that an act of thought can be subject-matter for history only if it is 'an act not only of thought but of reflective thought, that is, one which is performed in the consciousness that it is being performed, and is constituted by that consciousness' (*IH*, 308). If this is the 'widest' sense of 'thought', it seems remarkably narrow; and it reinforces the contradiction noted above. Yet it is precisely at this point that a recessive principle is most important and least visible. That principle, which cannot be stated with any precision until we consider Collingwood's conception of dialectic, is that thought does not exclude what we ordinarily refer to as emotions, motives, acts of will and the like, but is intimately connected with them and *includes* them in the sense in which a dialectical product includes and transforms the stages of the process leading to it. 'Thought', in fact, is a quasi-technical term in the theory of mind which Collingwood first developed in his lectures on moral philosophy as early as the 1920s but published in outline form only in his last book, *The New Leviathan*. It forms the conceptual background of both *The Principles of Art* (1938) and *The Idea of History* (the relevant sections of which were written as lectures in 1936) although in both books he *uses* bits and pieces of the theory only as they become relevant to asking and answering specific questions about art and history.

According to Collingwood's theory of mind, mind is not an entity but a set of activities or functions effective at different levels of consciousness, each of which is constituted by awareness of acts at a prior and lower level of consciousness. The lowest level of consciousness is the sensuous-emotional flux which is our primitive awareness of the states and processes of our bodies. Awareness of this first level appears both as 'appetite'—practical consciousness of hunger or need which has no clear conception of an object which would satisfy it—and as 'imagination'—theoretical or cognitive consciousness which expresses in language and action the emotional charge of first-level consciousness. In turn, consciousness *of* appetite is a third-level act of practical consciousness called 'desire', and consciousness *of* imagination is a third-level act of theoretical consciousness, or 'perception'. Finally, awareness of desire constitutes fourth-level 'will' and consciousness of perception constitutes fourth-level 'intellect'. In passing to higher levels, consciousness preserves the prior level in its consciousness of it (as its matter, so to speak) but also introduces something new (as form, or transformation); thus desire has an object, as appetite has not, while will introduces *choice* because it can contrast an object with other possible objects, as desire can not. Now the relevant point is that both in *The New Leviathan* and in *The Principles of Art* Collingwood called *every* level above the first a form of 'thinking' or 'thought'; although the lower levels are rudimentary and primitive compared with the upper, nevertheless they have the characteristics which survive in and are developed in the upper. Imagination—which for Collingwood is primitive and ubiquitous rather than exalted and rare—even at the second level is a kind of thought, although 'it is the kind of thought which stands closest to sensation or mere feeling' (*PA*, 223). On the practical side of second-level consciousness, 'appetite is what thought makes out of feeling when thought develops by its own activity from mere consciousness to conceptual thinking' (*NL*, 7.6). In *The New Leviathan*, the second level of consciousness is called 'conceptual thinking', the third 'propositional thinking', and the fourth 'rational thinking', thus making clear the principle that thinking in the generic sense has specific forms at every level, although only at the fourth level is it the explicit and self-conscious activity which is ordinarily called 'thinking'.

This briefest of sketches cannot have made Collingwood's theory of mind clear or plausible; but it does call attention to the fact that the 'widest' sense of the term 'thought' was for him really very wide indeed; the term refers to every level of consciousness except the most primitive level of undifferentiated and transitory sensations and feelings. Now it is significant that in *The Idea of History*, 'thought' is always contrasted with 'sensations and feelings' (*IH*, 294, 297–8, 302, 306). It is clear, therefore, that when we are told that 'the peculiarity of thought . . . is that it is not mere consciousness but self-consciousness' (*IH*, 306), we can understand 'self-consciousness' as characterizing *all* mental activity beyond 'those elements in experience whose being is just their immediacy (sensations, feelings, &c. as such)' (*IH*, 297). 'Reflection' does not for Collingwood mean an act of purely intellectual ratiocination; rather it is the relation of an act at *any* level to the experience of a lower level in becoming conscious of the latter; the formation of desire, for example, comes about through becoming conscious of—i.e., 'reflecting'—the experience of appetite. To put it all shortly, human desires *as* consciousness of appetites *can* be 're-enacted' although appetites which recede or pass without being converted into desires by consciousness cannot; they cannot, in fact, even be revived in memory. But in turn, consciousness of desire is will, expressed in choice and action, and therefore it is only through the fourth-level 'reflection' on desire that desires (ambitions, etc.) leave traces in the world from which they can be re-enacted. Thus it is mental activities of the fourth level which are primarily recoverable and intelligible; but they preserve and carry with them the whole range of activities at lower levels just so far as those activities have become objects of consciousness. Critics of Collingwood who have, understandably enough, argued that historical knowledge includes far more than 're-enactments of acts of reflective thought' have simply not understood that in Colling-wood's sense one is performing an 'act of reflective thought' when one orders from a menu, punishes a child, argues about politics, or climbs a mountain. Although his terminology trans-forms ordinary meanings, this is the best way Collingwood knew to call attention to complex and pervasive characteristics of all human experience. And it exemplifies his own view that 'philo-sophical' concepts begin with but indefinitely expand the range of application of 'empirical' concepts.

III

A fundamental characteristic of Collingwood's philosophical thought is expressed in his conception of levels of consciousness: the key concepts of philosophical argument are regarded as referring to different levels in different contexts. For example, far from asserting or assuming that thought and emotion are mutually exclusive, Collingwood identifies different acts of thought and different expressions of emotion as belonging to different levels of consciousness and beyond this regards acts of thought at one level as transformations of expressions of emotion at a lower level. To use a not entirely misleading analogy, Collingwood's model of consciousness is three-dimensional. But since our ordinary and uncritical model of consciousness is two-dimensional (perceptions, thoughts, feelings, memories, and the like regarded as a sort of mosaic of shifting forms and causal relations), critics generally interpret Collingwood's statements as referring to activities and processes all at the same level, where they exclude each other, while he is thinking of them at different levels related so that one includes but transforms the other. A relation of this sort is *dialectical*; and the key to understanding Collingwood's thought is an appreciation of how fundamentally and pervasively dialectical it is.

I shall try to give a general description of Collingwood's concept of dialectic, although this is for at least two reasons very difficult. For one thing, it is not captured by any simple and abstract schema, like the textbook triad of thesis–antithesis–synthesis. The standard expositions of Hegel and of Marxism–Leninism must be ignored if one is to avoid ludicrous misinterpretations of Collingwood (or, for that matter, of Hegel and Marx). For another thing, his conception of dialectic had its own history of development over all but the earliest years of his career[1] and is exemplified in almost all of his works although summarized in none. How it changed is therefore as important to understanding it as how it was applied at any given time. However, its development can be roughly divided into three stages—the first coincident with *Speculum Mentis* (1924), the second with the *Essay on Philosophical Method* (1933), and the third with the theory of mind which is revealed piecemeal in his later books.

Speculum Mentis is a phenomenology of forms of experience which attempts to show how each (except the last) tends to break down from the internal tensions generated by its own activity and to turn into the next form. The forms of experience, in significant order, are called Art, Religion, Science, History, and Philosophy,

---

[1] Collingwood's first book, *Religion and Philosophy* (1916), neither mentions nor exemplifies dialectic. *Speculum Mentis* (1924) is dialectical and repeatedly refers to itself as such; in general, it sounds like a not quite successful attempt to teach Hegel to speak the language of Locke. All of the later books presuppose and develop the idea of dialectical process, although Collingwood hardly ever again used the term 'dialectic' (except as an historically descriptive term in discussions of Plato, Hegel, and Marx) until his final book, where it surfaces at last.

although these names bear relatively little connection with the ordinary descriptions they suggest. 'Science', for example, is the form of experience which consciously distinguishes between thought and language, between words and what they mean and which therefore is capable of abstraction and analytical thinking. Theology, therefore, belongs to 'Science', but so do industrial management and some literary criticism. As in Hegel's *Phenomenology of Mind*, the order of the five forms of experience simultaneously models, although vaguely, the history of the series of dominant ideas in the development of Western civilization and the ontogeny of individual development; in both, for example, the free play of imagination ('Art') precedes the distinction between appearance and reality ('Religion'), which in turn precedes the habit of abstraction and the capacity for analytical thought ('Science'), and so on. Now the forms of experience are explicitly ordered as a dialectical series, in the following sense: each form of experience undergoes its own typical development in the course of which it generates tensions which it cannot resolve within its own form. At the same time it has developed in an implicit and rudimentary way the elements of the next form of experience. 'Religion', for example, which essentially is imagination uncritically asserting the reality of its object, depends on the distinction between symbol and reality but cannot acknowledge this distinction without abandoning the immediacy of belief which is essential to it. At the crucial point it must either remain blind to the distinction and resort to defensive dogmatism, or else recognize it, create theology to mediate the immediacy of uncritical belief, and thereby willy-nilly pass over into 'Science'.[1]

This is a grossly oversimplified sketch of the formal relations of complex forms of experience, each of which gives rise among other things to an ethics, to its own type of dogmatic philosophy, and in fact to an entire cultural *Weltanschauung*. The forms of experience are in fact too rich in detail for Collingwood to make

[1] Collingwood believed that the rise of Western science was possible only because Christianity had provided the necessary 'absolute presuppositions' of empirical science, e.g., that the universe is one system—because created by one rational deity. Cf. *EM*, Pt. IIIa, esp. pp. 201–27.

plausible the idea of a single pattern of development. But in the course of his attempt he formulated in a metaphorical way the idea of a dialectical series which is developed and applied in all of his subsequent thought. The differences between one form of experience and its successor, he said, is 'a dialectical distinction in which one tries to be what the other is, one implies what the other expresses, one questions where the other answers, one overlooks what the other recognizes; and of which therefore the more primitive is absorbed without residue in the more advanced' (*SM*, 200).

Almost ten years later, in the *Essay on Philosophical Method*, Collingwood undertook to work out in detail a 'logic' of dialectic.[1] Where *Speculum Mentis* tended to wander through the complexity of 'experience', the argument of the *Essay on Philosophical Method* focuses on the dialectic of *concepts*, and tries to explain why 'philosophical' concepts 'leak or escape' from their restricted application to definite classes. Scientific concepts, Collingwood points out, classify a subject-matter into mutually exclusive sub-classes such that a set of sub-classes also exhausts their superordinate class; equilateral, scalene, and isosceles are mutually exclusive and exhaustive species of the genus triangle. Philosophical concepts, on the contrary, determine classes which 'overlap'; pleasure, expediency, and rightness as subclasses of goodness do not exclude each other, since an action may be both pleasurable and expedient, or expedient and right. A generic philosophical concept, in fact, determines an order among its species, each of which not only instances the generic concept but also embodies a variable

---

[1] That *EPM* is about the 'logic' of dialectic has often gone unrecognized, perhaps because Collingwood never said that it is. The unstated premiss of the book is that philosophical thinking is dialectical; hence Collingwood throughout speaks of 'philosophical' rather than of 'dialectical' concepts, distinctions, relations and theories. To be clear about this, compare with the passage on 'dialectical distinctions' quoted just above the following description in *EPM* of the relation of terms in a 'philosophical scale of forms': 'This relation may be described ... by the metaphor of promising and performing; or it may be described by saying that the higher is the reality of which the lower is an approximation, or the truth of which the lower is a perversion. These are not so much metaphors as descriptions of something simpler and therefore more truly intelligible in terms of something more complex and, to us, more familiar' (*EPM*, 87).

attribute in a specific degree. It is at certain critical points in the variation of this attribute (cf. the freezing-point and boiling-point of a liquid) that one species is distinguished from adjacent species. A conceptual system of this sort Collingwood calls a 'scale of forms'. There may be non-philosophical scales of forms, such as a system of progressive taxation. What distinguishes a philosophical scale of forms is that the relation which determines it as a 'scale' uniquely 'fuses' four different kinds of relation, each of which may apply individually to non-philosophical concepts but which jointly characterize only philosophical concepts: difference of degree, difference of kind, relation of opposition, and relation of difference (*EPM*, ch. III). Different temperatures vary in degree; water differs from ice and steam in kind; physical cold differs from physical heat by 'opposition' (i.e., the relation between a term and its own negation or absence); perceived red differs from perceived blue by 'difference' (both are positive terms); felt cold differs from felt heat by both opposition and difference (and also in degree, but not in kind). All this is complicated by self-reference: difference in degree and difference in kind are clearly mutually exclusive only in the *non*-philosophical concepts of these differences. As *philosophical* concepts they must themselves overlap, and so also for the relations of opposition and distinction. Hence the conclusion that in a philosophical scale of forms the four relations 'fuse' rather than merely forming an aggregate of four elements. A scale of forms is not 'triadic'; it may have any number of stages or levels. The kind of example Collingwood has in mind as exemplifying a philosophical scale of forms is the series of types of knowledge represented in Plato's Divided Line; in other cases a pair of concepts may constitute a scale, as in the classic relation of understanding (*Verstand*) and reason (*Vernunft*) (cf. *SM*, 195–200).

Toward the end of the *Essay on Philosophical Method* the model of a dialectical scale of forms finds a new and significant application: now, not concepts but philosophical *theories* are regarded as forming a scale, such that

from the point of view of a philosopher whose thought has reached a given form, each subordinate form, considered as a self-contained and distinct philosophy, presents two aspects. As a philosophy distinct from his own, it is a discussion by a method which he does not use of a problem with which he is not concerned; as a philosophy opposed to his own it is a concrete example of how philosophizing should not be done. But this same form, when considered as subordinate to his own, appears as an error whose refutation he has already achieved; and as something reabsorbed into his own, it constitutes an element within his own system (*EPM*, 190).

In effect Collingwood has historicized the idea of a philosophical system: systematic philosophies are seen as stages in a real process of development within which they are related to each other *something* like the series of forms of experience or the scale of forms which specify a philosophical concept. In this application, a scale of forms has become something which develops in time rather than a timeless set of conceptual relations.

The way in which the seminal idea of a scale of forms provides the background of all of Collingwood's later thought can only be suggested. His unfinished and posthumous books on the idea of nature and the idea of history both apply the notion to the history of theories centring on those concepts. In his theory of absolute presuppositions, 'constellations' of absolute presuppositions represent stages on a scale of forms, and the shifts from one constellation to another (rare but fundamental conceptual revolutions in the history of a whole civilization) are dialectical relations.[1] Perhaps most significantly, the theory of mind which was sketched above also represents levels of practical and theoretical consciousness as constituting a scale of forms.

Undeveloped as these suggestions are—they summarize without argument, in fact, a comprehensive interpretation of the development and systematic connections of Collingwood's mature

---

[1] The theory of absolute presuppositions also confirms the extent to which Collingwood's conception of history is 'philosophical' rather than 'empirical' and the degree to which he regards the subject-matter of history as including more than individual human actions. After arguing that 'metaphysics' is an historical inquiry—'all metaphysical questions are historical questions' (*EM*, 49) —he says that 'the metaphysician's business, when he has identified several different constellations of absolute presuppositions, is not only to study their likenesses and unlikenesses but also to find out on what occasions and by what processes one of them has turned into another' (*EM*, 73).

philosophy—it is now possible to attempt a general description of Collingwood's conception of dialectic without arousing the suspicion that there is nothing to which it applies.

The thesis which Collingwood often seems to be defending in the *Essay on Philosophical Method*, that dialectic is an alternative to formal logic, is subject to fundamental criticisms, not least that his own arguments appeal to the canons of formal logic and could hardly do otherwise. It is unnecessary to canvass these objections, however, since Collingwood made no later use of this thesis. It becomes clear that dialectic is not a kind of inference but a set of characteristics common to the description and understanding of certain kinds of processes. In Collingwood's view, there are no dialectical laws, no dialectical forces, no dialectical truths, or proofs, or necessities. The only proper use of the term is to refer to dialectical *series*, and to the *relations* among the members of such a series. Other uses are at best derivative (a process may be dialectical insofar as it forms a dialectical series; a distinction may be dialectical insofar as it distinguishes the members of such a series), and at worst metonymical (as in calling a style of writing or of debate 'dialectical'). A properly dialectical series has four main properties. (1) A dialectical series is *connective*; all of its terms fall under the same general description although each is particularized differently, and each is related to other terms in the series in ways determined by the general description. In the *Essay on Philosophical Method* this was expressed by saying that the terms in a scale of forms 'embody the same generic essence' (*EPM*, 54–61). This property does not of course distinguish dialectical series from many non-dialectical series (such as the natural numbers), but it does exclude arbitrarily constructed series. A series of actions may be dialectical if they carry out a single (although changing and developing) policy; a series of events such as the random selection of specimens for investigation is not. (2) A dialectical series is *cumulative* in the sense that earlier or 'lower' members are not merely replaced by later or 'higher' members but are preserved although modified in the later ones; elements of the earlier may even survive unmodified (*NL*, 9.51). Thus in the transition of one architectural style to another the former is not (usually) entirely abandoned; the *kind* of series differs from that of the letters of an alphabet or of the series of chemical elements in order of atomic weight. It is in virtue of this property that revolutions never seem in retrospect to have been the sharp and complete break with the past which they seemed to be in their own time. (3) A dialectical series is *asymmetrical*; and this is because the relation of any term or stage to its predecessor is that it makes explicit what was only implicit in the predecessor (cf. *SM*, 108, 164). What is implicit in it will in turn become explicit in its successor, if it has one, although *how* it may become explicit is, as we shall see, indeterminate. The illustrations from Collingwood given in preceding sections are all examples of series which have this property. Theology, for instance, makes explicit the distinction between symbol and meaning which is only implicit in 'Religion'. To say that the distinction is explicit is to say that theology can *describe itself* as making the distinction, as 'Religion' cannot do without losing its essential immediacy of uncritical belief. Or again, 'appetite' as the second-level form of practical consciousness implicitly contains the distinction between self and object, but since it is a kind of hunger or need without awareness of a specific object, it is only in 'desire' as the consciousness *of* appetite that the distinction becomes explicit. The vague sense of *something* becomes in the passage to desire directed on some *thing*. In Collingwood's theory of mind generally, what is implicit at one level of consciousness becomes explicit at a higher level. It is by virtue of this that the latter can be called both a different level (that is, different in kind) and a higher one (that is, different in degree). Moreover, that something is implicit at a given level can be known only retrospectively by an act of a higher level, as formal logic (a fourth-level activity) analyzes and makes explicit the forms of statement and inference which are only implicit in their use in ordinary or third-level discourse. (4) Finally, a dialectical series is *non-deterministic*; terms do not determine their successors either logically or causally (*SM*, 56; *NL*, 9.48). On the other hand, later terms absolutely presuppose the earlier. This is the most original and difficult of Collingwood's contributions to the conception of dialectic. It is tempting to interpret him as meaning that earlier terms are necessary but not sufficient for the generation of the later. But his view,

I think, is rather that earlier terms are *retrospectively and only retrospectively* both necessary and sufficient. From their *own* standpoint (since what is implicit in them has not yet become explicit, and in any case may become so in different ways), there is nothing either necessary or sufficient for the coming into existence of their successors. And this is due not to the contingent lack of a basis for prediction but to the real nature of the unfinished series or development of which they are the latest stage. For Collingwood's conception of dialectical development, not only are there no 'dialectical predictions' but the very phrase is a contradiction in terms. Now none of this will seem very plausible if one supposes that a dialectical series can be analysed and described from a vantage-point outside that series; from that vantage, it is true, if the development up to a certain point is correctly seen to have been a necessary development, then it was also at earlier stages a necessary development even though it could not have been known to be so. But the character of a dialectical series is not just that earlier ignorance may be succeeded by later knowledge. The element of necessity in such a series itself *comes into existence* and hence can in principle be known only retrospectively. The oddity of such a claim is partially removed if one sees that such a series is intelligible only from the standpoint of a stage in the series itself. To identify it as a series at all one must place oneself at the latest stage, while not forgetting that the very act of doing so belongs to the development of the series as it will appear in retrospect to yet later stages. One might think of the moving asymmetry of indeterminacy and necessity as a track-laying machine which men guide across a wilderness without features, constantly debating about which way to go next and navigating accordingly. Looking ahead, there are indefinitely many ways one may go (although in all of them only *from* where one has arrived); looking back, the gleaming tracks stretch to the horizon as a permanent record explaining the unique path one has traversed.

Now what counts as an instance of a dialectical series with these properties? I think that Collingwood's answer is: anything which is an object of historical knowledge (understanding 'historical' as a philosophical, not an empirical concept). In stating the properties of a dialectical series, that is, we have at once given the formal characteristics of a developmental process and the formal structure of the historical consciousness. Collingwood's special form of historicism rests on his analysis of processes which, so to speak, historicize themselves. Every example of such a process essentially involves consciousness directed on—or 'reflecting' on—the process up to its own vantage-point (at least on its immediate predecessors). This is why the understanding of a dialectical series cannot occupy a vantage-point outside the series: by reviewing the stages of such a process one becomes part of its unfinished story. In effect, Collingwood has adopted as his own the dictum which he praised as Hegel's insight into the nature of history: history ends not in the future but in the present (*IH*, 119), or '*Bis hierher ist das Bewusstsein gekommen*' (*IN*, 174). The revolution of the planets, the evolution of species, the erosion of land and the deterioration of machines, the formation of a volcano and the respiration of animals—all are processes but not dialectical ones. But the history of concepts and of theories,[1] of politics, warfare, economic activity, morals, and religion, of social institutions as shared ways of life, and of artistic styles, genres, and schools—all of these are processes of development which may satisfy the criteria of a dialectical series.[2] This is more or less Collingwood's list of forms of activity of which there can be historical knowledge

[1] In his classic essay 'What is Dialectic?" (reprinted in *Conjectures and Refutations* (New York, 1968), 312–35), Sir Karl Popper made a devastating critique of 'dialectic' as an alternative to formal logic and scientific method; but he admitted that 'a dialectical interpretation of the history of thought may sometimes be quite satisfactory' (p. 315). But he regards such a dialectical interpretation as an empirical descriptive theory which is not 'fundamental', like formal logic which is the theory of *all* sorts of inferences. Popper limited his discussion to the 'dialectic triad' and its alleged rejection of the 'law of contradiction'. We might say that Collingwood's conception of dialectic has just those features which Popper accepted, but expanded in the direction of being 'fundamental' in a way which escapes Popper's criticism. Popper accepted dialectic as appropriate to the understanding of the 'history of thought', by which he meant intellectual history. Collingwood makes all human history the 'history of thought' by making the concept of thought both more complex and more comprehensive.

[2] There may even be a history of clothes. 'Paris dressmakers could not tell you why they alter a certain fashion in a certain way this autumn, or if they did the reason would be a wrong one; but there is a reason, and it can be traced if the problem is approached from an historical point of view' (*SM*, 227).

(*IH*, 309–15; cf. *OPA*, 99–100). The criterion of selection which he states in giving his list seems to be quite different: there can be a history of *purposive* actions and only of those. But given what we have already seen as his recessive but not casual view that actions can be known retrospectively in ways which even their agents could not have known *explicitly* while they were being enacted, we can infer that 'purposive action' is itself an example of a dialectical series. At least some purposive actions undergo development such that later stages make explicit what was only implicit in earlier stages, and even a complete action may contain implicit elements (such as its incompatibility with other purposes or principles of the agent) which become explicit only in retrospect. Although Collingwood never attempted a classification of types of action, it is clear that he meant by 'action' not merely activities of short duration and unitary in quality, like striking a blow or voting for a candidate, but also enduring and even interrupted activities, like building a house or campaigning for office. An 'aesthetic act'—i.e., the creation of a work of art—he said, 'may last for five years at a time' (*SM*, 70). Of such an action it is clear *a fortiori* that the correct description of it differs from the description which the agent would give at any stage before its completion; but the correct description would also 're-enact' the agent's *changing* understanding of what he regarded himself as doing.

Despite the many details omitted from this account of a dialectical series and the kinds of development which it models, and despite the many questions which it leaves unanswered, it should be possible to see why Collingwood's theory of history has been so subject to misinterpretation. What were called above the recessive doctrines in *The Idea of History* are in fact among his most general principles. Their meaning is dependent on his conception of dialectic as a presupposition, and it is they which most systematically relate his 'principles of history' to his larger philosophy. In illustrating these principles, however, he regularly chose especially clear and limited cases as paradigms. Caesar's crossing of the Rubicon is easier to discuss than the process by which the Roman Republic gave way to the monarchy, as a syllogism is easier to analyse than a judicial decision. The dominant doctrines, however, are generalizations of what makes these cases clear and limited rather than of what makes them paradigms. In some places Collingwood is alone responsible for this, but in most it results from the systematic illusion of interpreting in an ordinary sense what for Collingwood had a special sense which is clear once the implicit dialectic of his thought is made explicit. As I have tried to show, what he means by 'history', 'action', and 'thought' are all internally more complex and wider in denotation than the ordinary senses of those terms which one brings to the reading of *The Idea of History* and may not be shocked into reconsidering. And it is Collingwood's dialectical philosophy which awaits the unsparing criticism which is its due and which it has not yet received.

IX

METAPHYSICS AND HISTORICISM

NATHAN ROTENSTREICH

I

IN COLLINGWOOD'S conception, metaphysics is a body of 'absolute presuppositions' assumed for the sake of formulating scientific propositions:

Metaphysics is the attempt to find out what absolute presuppositions have been made by this or that person or group of persons, on this or that occasion or group of occasions, in the course of this or that piece of thinking (*EM*, 47).

This formulation refers to metaphysics as investigating the process of thought of an individual or of a plurality of individuals and not of one's own thinking; it suggests that metaphysics is a reflection about somebody else's reflections. Being an attempt to find out what absolute presuppositions have been made, metaphysics is related to the body of knowledge which takes advantage of these presuppositions without spelling them out. Metaphysics thus becomes related to science,[1] by articulating the presuppositions of science.

Metaphysics, in spelling out the presuppositions of a certain piece of thinking, changes together with the changes occurring on the level of that thinking:

Aristotle describes us the absolute presuppositions of Greek science in the fourth century B.C.; St. Thomas those of European science in the central Middle Ages; Spinoza those of European science in the seventeenth century, or rather those of them which he thinks relevant to his special purpose (*EM*, 71).

Two points should be stressed here: (1) Collingwood refers to the *description* provided by metaphysics; he does not refer to the

[1] In the Greek sense of the term, as well as in the sense of Newton and Einstein; *EM*, 54–5.

justification which might be assumed to be one of the functions of metaphysics, as metaphysics understood itself. (2) Collingwood speaks of Spinoza's 'special purpose' in his description of the presuppositions of seventeenth-century European science. What is this special purpose? Does it go beyond the task of describing the presuppositions? From where does Spinoza derive his special purpose of going beyond the description of the presuppositions of science in his era?

The function of describing the presuppositions without justifying them is but the opposite aspect of the logical status of these presuppositions: 'The logical efficacy of a supposition does not depend upon the truth of what is supposed, or even on its being thought true, but only on its being supposed' (*EM*, 28). The position of the presupposition is beyond the distinction between true and false, and justification relates to the assessment of truth or it results in the rejection of a statement because it failed to exhibit its truth: 'Absolute presuppositions are not verifiable. This does not mean that we should like to verify them but are not able to; it means that the idea of verification is an idea which does not apply to them . . .' (*EM*, 32). One may ask here whether Collingwood eventually conducts a description only of the alleged presuppositions or whether the fact that he brings forward the aspect of efficacy does not imply that he is drifted to point out an aspect of a relative justification of the presuppositions in terms of their function for the sake of a body of knowledge and science which is based implicitly on these presuppositions. This would be a pragmatic justification of sorts—an *Annahme,* in Meinong's sense: a proposition lacking conviction, a proposition without a presupposition as to the former's validity. It could be understood as a presupposition laid down on the basis of 'as if'. Yet Collingwood did not take this notion of absolute presuppositions as a point of departure for a theory of entertaining meanings, without assuming their validity, or for a general theory of a manifold as Husserl, for instance, suggested.

Collingwood went on to emphasize the historical character of these presuppositions and satisfied himself with a very brief outline of their efficacy. The metaphysician is a special kind of historian;

(*EM*, 62); Collingwood does not realize at this point the difference between the historian of metaphysics, who might be a special kind of historian, and the metaphysician proper, who lays down or articulates the presuppositions. The historian of metaphysics might state that metaphysics is about a certain class of historical facts; the metaphysician himself is not concerned with a historical fact but with a body of knowledge or a scientific world-outlook articulating the presuppositions implied in it.

II

After this brief summary of Collingwood's position, let us proceed now to a critical examination of it. The concern of this examination will not be the soundness of Collingwood's view of the presuppositions in terms of their logic or efficacy, but his interpretation of traditional metaphysics which he turned into a subject-matter of historical interest, as well as with the problems involved in this shift of interest from a metaphysical to a historical level.[1]

There are many instances in the writings of Collingwood where he changes his own views and refutes arguments which he had presented elsewhere. This change applies also to metaphysics. Once metaphysics is placed as the understanding of the historical character of the presuppositions of changing scientific outlooks, it ceases to be the science of pure being. Understood in this way, metaphysics is metaphysics without ontology (*EM*, 17 ff.).

Collingwood tried to avoid a kind of philosophical utopianism, to keep in touch with facts, and to inquire about the methods used by the philosophers of the past (*EPM*, 4).

III

In *Speculum Mentis* Collingwood attributes to philosophy and to the scientific philosopher the function of justifying the activity

[1] On this aspect consult John F. Post, 'A Defense of Collingwood's Theory of Presuppositions', *Inquiry*, viii (1965), 332–54, and A. Donagan, *The Later Philosophy of R. G. Collingwood* (Oxford, 1962), pp. 551 ff. See also the polemic essay of D. Rynin, 'Donagan on Collingwood: Absolute Presuppositions, Truth and Metaphysics', *The Review of Metaphysics*, xviii (1964), 301–33.

of science: 'The scientist thinks abstractly: the scientific philoso-pher justifies him in so doing' (SM, 271). But there, Collingwood's central concern—from the point of view of our topic—was the interdependence of logic and metaphysics:

Logic and metaphysics are necessary to each other. Without metaphysics, logic can only show that thought has principles and abides by them; but these principles might be such as to falsify, instead of verifying, the thought which obeys them. Without logic, metaphysics can only show what the real world is like; but it may be such a world as, to our thinking, must remain unknown and unknowable (SM, 271).

The interrelation between logic and metaphysics is stated here as a need and not as a fact, a need grounded in the possibility that the principles of thinking might be void, that is to say without onto-logical relevance or without being warranted by things as they really are. On the other hand, the need of metaphysics for logic is warranted in that the real world might be real but unknown, and if it is to be known it has to comply with principles of knowledge, the latter being eventually principles of thought articulated by logic: '. . . we must demonstrate that what we have hitherto called logic or the theory of thought is really metaphysics or the theory of reality, and that what we have called the laws of thought are the laws of being' (SM, 273-4). The argument seems to be that the correlative relationship between logic and reality which we started off with turns out eventually to be an identity between logic and metaphysics. Since this identity is established we reach the conclusion that the investigation into reality or being is impossible, precisely because of the fact that it does not appear within the horizon of thinking or knowing:

. . . the theory of being as distinct from thinking (metaphysics) will only be the theory of thinking as distinct from being (logic);. . . just as logic can never analyse real thinking . . . so metaphysics can never analyse real being, being as it is in itself untainted by thought (SM, 274).

Collingwood is aware of the mutual dependence between logic and metaphysics, but he does not draw the Hegelian conclusion that logic coincides with metaphysics as the science of things comprehended in thought.[1] His conclusion is that metaphysics is impossible because access to pure being is impossible or implies a contradiction in terms. In this he seems to follow those trends of neo-Kantian philosophy which presented this argument as the law of immanence or the law of phenomenality, or as "the law of consciousness":[2] whatever exists is subject to the universal condition—it is a fact of consciousness. In the neo-Kantian school this argument was formulated against realism; Collingwood directed it against metaphysics. In spite of this difference in direction, the two formulations of the argument are very close. In *Speculum Mentis* Collingwood grants the programme of metaphysics as the knowledge of being but he seems to conclude that this programme cannot be materialized philosophically. In *An Essay on Philosophical Method* he retains the view as to the trend of metaphysics or philosophy in general, without, however, doubting the possibility of a systematic expression of this view, by avoiding the pitfalls implied in the 'law of consciousness'.

IV

In *An Essay on Philosophical Method* the direction of the investigation is already indicated by Collingwood's conscious attachment to the philosophical tradition. To spell out that which is concealed in the mind does not amount to spelling out the presuppositions of that which is concealed in the mind. This spelling out is an attempt towards knowledge of a metaphysical first principle called God. Metaphysics and philosophical knowledge in general comprise here both the epistemic and the ethical principles, while in the *Essay on Metaphysics* the concern is with the epistemic aspect only. This difference in interest is by no means fortuitous.

In terms of the character of philosophic thinking the main point made by Collingwood is that philosophy is a categorical thinking (*EPM*, 117). From this point of view philosophical thinking is fundamentally different from that character of mathematical thinking, mathematics consisting exclusively of hypothetical propositions. Again Collingwood follows here the Platonic view,

---

[1] Hegel, *Encyklopädie der philosophischen Wissenschaften im Grundrisse*, sect. 24.
[2] *Satz des Bewusstseins.*

13

except that he replaces the *unhypotheton* in Plato with the categorical statement in his own terminology. This exchange is made possible by the character of the system: for Plato there is a climbing of the ladder from the hypothetical to the unhypothetical; for Collingwood the two approaches or the two characters of statements are placed one beside the other. Collingwood envisages the continuity from Plato to Aristotle to the extent that that which for Plato is *unhypotheton* is for Aristotle reality or being, the latter placed as the subject-matter of the science of metaphysics. Collingwood quotes here specifically *Metaphysics* 1003 A 20: 'There is a science which investigates being as being and the attributes which belong to this in virtue of its own nature' (*EPM*, 123). (The second part of the sentence is not quoted there by Collingwood.) In metaphysics the distinction between conceiving something and thinking it to exist is a distinction without a difference. Hence the subject-matter of philosophy is no mere hypothesis, but something actually existing (*EPM*, 125–7).

It would be appropriate to insert at this juncture an observation on the difference in the views on the character of philosophical thinking as presented in *Speculum Mentis* and in the *Essay on Philosophical Method*. *Speculum Mentis* points out the dilemma of metaphysics in trying to reach being or reality but remaining confined to thinking. In *An Essay on Philosophical Method* this dilemma seems to be overcome because conceiving and thinking are eventually reaching reality, or else there is no difference between the aspect of thinking and the aspect of existing. Here Collingwood seems to remedy his own perplexity in a Hegelian way. This character of philosophical thinking does not pertain only to what might be called the theoretical branch of philosophy. Collingwood deliberately uses the language employed in the Ontological Argument for the existence of God in order to point to the nature of ethical thought: 'the subject-matter of ethical thought must be conceived as something whose essence involves existence' (*EPM*, 133). The categorical way of thinking characteristic of philosophy in general and of metaphysics in particular amounts to the assumption of the existence of the subject-matters which are the concern of philosophy proper. Since Collingwood takes advantage of the

Ontological Proof we may say that for him metaphysics is ontological. In *Speculum Mentis* metaphysics tried to be ontological and
failed because of the dilemma inherent in the 'law of consciousness'.
In the *Essay on Philosophical Method* metaphysics succeeds to be
ontological because essence involves existence.

V

Metaphysical thinking, as presented in the *Essay on Philosophical
Method*, is the Ontological Proof written large; essence involves
existence not only in terms of God but also in terms of other subject-
matters of philosophical thinking like the Good. The Ontological
Proof can thus serve as an axis for the next step of our presentation.

Speculum Mentis refers to the Ontological Proof in the context of
an analysis of Religious Philosophy; this context is relevant in the
evaluation of the significance of the Ontological Proof:

For though religion expresses itself in terms which, taken literally,
imply the objective existence of God, its meaning is only apprehended
when we make up our mind to regard these expressions as metaphorical
statements of something else, something which is never by religion
actually stated in literal terms, though it is capable of being so stated
(*SM*, 264).

This means that what is stated in religion metaphorically can be
stated outside religion, i.e., in philosophy, in literal terms. As long
as we preserve the *raison d'être* of religion we have to preserve the
metaphorical character of religious statements. This applies
directly to the Ontological Proof:

... God must exist or religion could not exist. And this argument is
incontrovertible in the sense that, since religion certainly exists, that
which it means by the term God must also exist; but what it means by
God is not what it says, and hence the recurring objection to the Ontological Proof that what it proves is indeed the existence of something,
but not of the religious man's God (the literal God, God as an image),
rather of the philosopher's absolute (the concept which the image of God
metaphorically means) (*SM*, 264-5).

In a certain sense, the *Essay on Metaphysics* continues this presentation. This essay is not concerned with the religious outlook, but

with the absolute—if we may apply here the term used in *Speculum Mentis*, although Collingwood does not use it in his *Essay on Philosophical Method*. But that which in *Speculum Mentis* has been a deficiency in terms of religion, becomes here an advantage in terms of philosophy:

Clearly it does not prove the existence of whatever God happens to be believed in by the person who appeals to it. Between it and the articles of a particular positive creed there is no connection, unless these articles can be deduced *a priori* from the idea of an *ens realissimum*. What it does prove is that essence involves existence, not always, but in one special case, the case of God in the metaphysical sense: the *Deus sive natura* of Spinoza, the Good of Plato, the Being of Aristotle: the object of metaphysical thought (*EPM*, 127).

The difference in the evaluation of the importance of the Ontological Proof (*Speculum Mentis* has it in small characters) is due to the difference of the frame of reference: the shortcomings in religion as a metaphoric speech are not present in philosophy as a non-metaphoric, categorical speech.

The point made by Collingwood that the Proof does not prove that essence involves existence, *not always* (our emphasis) seems to be parallel to the point made by Hegel against Kant's criticism of the Ontological Proof. Hegel argued that Kant assumed that existence is not a predicate and cannot, therefore, be used as a predicate as it is used in the Ontological Proof, and that he projected its character of a finite existing thing unto infinite existence. In the realm of infinity thinking and being coincide and thus the predication of being to the idea is not only warranted by dialectically essential.

An Essay on Metaphysics comes back to the Ontological Proof or to Anselm's proof. Compared with *Speculum Mentis* the exposition of the *Essay* might be summed up as follows: In *Speculum Mentis* the Ontological Proof did not fit the character of religion. In *An Essay on Metaphysics* Collingwood argues that Anselm himself agreed to the point made against him by Gaunilo, namely that the proof proves the existence of God only to a person who already believed it: 'What it proves is not that because our idea of God is an idea of *id quo maius cogitari nequit* therefore God exists, but that because our idea of God is an idea of *id quo maius cogitari nequit* we stand committed to belief in God's existence' (*EM*, 190). According to Collingwood's interpretation, the existence of God is not a proposition but an absolute presupposition. As such it can be neither true nor false. If 'God exists' means that 'somebody believes that God exists' (which it must mean if it is a metaphysical proposition) then it is capable of proof. The proof must of course be an historical one, and the evidence on which it is based will be the ways in which this 'somebody' thinks (*EM*, 188). Collingwood's presentation is not too clear here. What he seems to say is that the belief in God as *ens realissimum* is the presupposition of the onto- logical argument. The ontological argument is an articulation of that which is implied in one's belief in God, or in one's belief that God as *ens realissimum* exists, or that God as *ens realissimum* is by the same token an existing God. Here the ontological proof does not carry religion beyond its own realm as in *Speculum Mentis*; neither is it a paradigmatic argument for metaphysical thinking, *qua* thinking where essence involves existence, as in the *Essay on Philosophical Method*. Here the ontological proof presupposes a belief. The scholastic argument is a presupposition and has no independent validity. Instead of being a paradigm of the character of philosophical thinking, the Ontological Proof becomes an illustration of the dependence of thinking on changing presuppo- sitions. This change occurs in history.

VI

In the preceding pages, Collingwood's views have been presen- ted independently, without any indication of a relation between them. In those views, Collingwood seems to defeat Collingwood, as it were; the position of the *Essay on Philosophical Method* could be taken as an argument against that of the *Essay on Metaphysics*, for instance. Let us raise, however, another question: having in mind the variety of Collingwood's views, did he do justice to metaphysics by placing metaphysics without ontology as his own ultimate presentation of metaphysics? It seems that by putting forward this last view of metaphysics Collingwood made an endeavour toward 'saving the phenomenon of metaphysics'. Did he succeed?

In the *Essay on Metaphysics* Collingwood posits metaphysics as the sum total of the absolute presuppositions of the changing outlook of science. He devotes a great part of his presentation to an interpretation of Kant in the light of his own position.

Collingwood may not have been fully aware of the extent to which his views were influenced by Kant. His conception is indebted even terminologically to Kant's *Metaphysische Anfangs-gründe der Naturwissenschaften*. His absolute presuppositions correspond to Kant's *Anfangsgründe*, and they are metaphysical in the sense given by Kant, namely as concerned with reason, its elements and highest maxims, which must underly the possibility of some of the sciences and the application of all of them.[1] There is, however, an obvious difference between Kant and Collingwood in terms of the truth-value attributed by them to the *Anfangsgründe* and to the absolute presuppositions respectively: Kant assigned to them *a priori* position as synthetic judgements, while Colling-wood placed them beyond the distinction between true and false as assumptions only. In speaking about the efficacy of these pre-suppositions Collingwood is close to the pragmatic considerations underlying C. I. Lewis's conception of the flexible *a priori*: 'The names of our categories may be very old and stable, but the con-cepts, the modes of classifying and interpreting which they represent, undergo progressive alteration with the advance of thought.'[2] Whitehead, in turn, referred to the faith in the order of nature which has a logical and an aesthetic ingredient and cannot be justified by any inductive rationalization. Hence Whitehead assumed that there are certain ideas taken for granted in science and by science, and that they form what he called 'the climate of opinion'.[3]

In spite of this difference with regard to the epistemological position of the presuppositions, Kant was for Collingwood a classic example of metaphysics 'without ontology'. An additional example of the same trend can be found in the neo-Kantian

[1] *Critique of Pure Reason*, transl. N. Kemp Smith, B25.
[2] Clarence I. Lewis, *Mind and the World Order* (New York, 1956), p. 235.
[3] A. N. Whitehead, *Science and the Modern World* (New York, 1954), ch. I.

interpretation of Platonic ideas, which are understood not as entities but as hypotheses—hypotheses being here the plural of *Hypothesis* which differs from the German rendering of the same root, *Hypothese*: 'Sie (sc. *Hypothesis*) ist die Grundlage, vielmehr die *Grundlegung*, welche der Instruktion einer exakten Untersuchung vorausgehen muss.'[1]

Each *Hypothese* calls for another *Hypothese*, but this infinite regress reaches its end at the thinking of the *Hypothesis* which amounts to the thinking of the idea. The idea is the *Hypothesis* and the *Hypothesis* is the idea. The *unhypotheton* becomes a *Hypothesis* in terms of the chain of hypotheses. In spite of the difference in terminology there is a close affinity between Collingwood's position and the Kantian and neo-Kantian tradition.

Collingwood himself presents his theory of metaphysics by way of a critical analysis of Aristotle's metaphysics which he divides into two components: the science of pure being and the science which deals with the presuppositions underlying ordinary science (*EM*, 11 ff.). Collingwood rejects the first component and tries to preserve in his own way the second one.

Why does Collingwood think that metaphysics as the science of pure being is impossible?

To push abstraction to the limiting case is to take out everything; and when everything is taken out there is nothing for science to investigate. You may call this nothing by what name you like—pure being, or God, or anything else—but it remains nothing, and contains no peculiarities for science to examine . . . .. But the science of pure being would have a subject-matter entirely devoid of peculiarities; a subject-matter, therefore, containing nothing to differentiate it from anything else, or from nothing at all (*EM*, 14).

The formulation of this view is similar, to some extent, to Hegel's formulation of the relation between being and nothing. The trend of Collingwood's argument differs, however, from that of Hegel. Collingwood tries to show that the subject-matter of metaphysics as the metaphysics of being is void and thus inconceivable. He does not argue, like Kant, that this subject-matter lies

---

[1] H. Cohen, *Logik der reinen Erkenntnis*[2] (Berlin, 1914), p. 7; *idem, Der Begriff der Religion im System der Philosophie* (Giessen, 1915), p. 29.

beyond experience, but that it is not capable of being conceptually articulated because it is entirely devoid of peculiarities, and a conception of peculiarities is the prerequisite of any conception whatever.

It should be noted here that Aristotle does not use the term 'pure' being. The description 'pure' appears in *De Anima* in connection with Anaxagoras' *nous* in the sense of being simple and unmixed. Being as such has certain properties, and the philosopher has to investigate them. The whole Book Z of the *Metaphysics* is dedicated to the different senses in which a thing may be said to 'be', and the explication of the peculiarities of being runs parallel to the comparison between its different meanings. Aristotle does not refer to *pure* being but to being *qua* being, i.e., to the full realization of the peculiarities of being; thus, where there is only *energeia* and not potentiality, there is full being in its full realization. In Aristotle, the argument centres around a classification of the different meanings of 'being' and their ranging in the order of actuality's priority over potentiality, whereas in Collingwood the peculiarities are removed altogether. Aristotle retains the correlation and places the various meanings and levels of being within this correlation.

A case in point is the relation between being and substance, which is obvious and needs no further elaboration, although Collingwood did not take cognizance of it. But let us take an example from Collingwood himself, namely from his presentation of Aristotle's *Metaphysics* in the *Idea of Nature*. Collingwood gives there a most adequate formulation of the Aristotelian meaning of matter: 'Matter is thus unrealizedness of unrealized potentiality' (*IN*, 92). Being as being only (that being which Collingwood seems to refer to as *pure* being, thus superimposing a Kantian term on Aristotle's system) is the full reality or the realization of the to be realized potentiality. From the point of view of its conception being as being only is a correlate of the unrealizedness of the unrealized potentiality. Being is actuality only, as matter is the correlate of actuality precisely in the way Collingwood interpreted its meaning and its position in the system.

Collingwood goes a step further: he splits the Aristotelian system into two halves, rejecting the ontological aspect and retaining the aspect of principles of science. But in terms of the principles of science he looks at Aristotle as describing the absolute presuppositions of Greek science in the fourth century B.C. (*EM*, 71). In *The Idea of Nature* Collingwood sums up the 'Greek concept of nature' (*IN*, 82–3), though one may wonder whether the position of the Greek concept of nature was independent from Aristotle's system or whether Collingwood looks at the Greek concept of nature through Aristotelian glasses. Assuming that there is an overall Greek view of nature, does the philosopher only articulate that underlying view or can the philosopher, precisely because he is a systematic and a deliberate thinker, offer different interpretations of the alleged underlying anonymous view? Collingwood himself mentions two interpretations of the common view of nature:

Plato in the *Timaeus* represents God, in virtue of his creative act of will, as the efficient cause of nature, and the forms, in virtue of their static perfection, as its final cause; Aristotle, identifying God with the forms, conceives one single unmoved mover with a self-contained activity of its own, namely self-knowledge ... inspiring the whole nature with the desire for it and a nisus towards reproducing it ... (*IN*, 87).

Two points have to be made here:

(a) Collingwood sees the characteristic features attributed to being *qua* being both in terms of its position as a cause, and in terms of its self-contained activity of self-knowledge.

(b) Plato's interpretation of the position of an efficient cause differs from that of Aristotle. There is no clear determination of Greek science by a climate of opinion which would impose on the philosopher to interpret this world-view and to state univocally its presuppositions.

A philosophic system has a logic of its own and even when the philosopher addresses himself to a common world-view his interpretation of this common ground is determined, at least to some degree, by the logic of his own system. In his critical interpretation of Aristotle's view of metaphysics Collingwood failed to show the methodical infeasibility of Aristotle's subject-matter of metaphysics as being *qua* being related to the analysis of the different senses of being. He also failed to show the exclusive historicity of Aristotle's system. If we are to keep in touch with facts, as Collingwood reminds us, we may never lose sight of the question of what methods have actually been used by philosophers of the past. This principle will guide us now in our analysis of two additional views discussed by Collingwood: the view of Spinoza, which is considered only briefly, and that of Kant, which is dealt with more extensively.

In his discussion of Spinoza, Collingwood shows that he describes the absolute presuppositions of seventeenth century European science (*EM*, 71) and that, like the historian Tacitus, he is bound to a certain climate of opinion (*EM*, 69). Elsewhere he states that 'the great feat of Spinoza is to bring together two conceptions which in Bruno are not yet distinguished, the conception of a world of mechanical matter and the conception of a world of mind, as these were worked out separately by Descartes' (*IN*, 100). Spinoza overcomes the main philosophical paradox of Galileo's physics inherent in the separateness of material nature from the perceiving mind on the one hand and from its divine creator on the other, by insisting upon its inseparable unity with mind and giving to this unity the name of God (*IN*, 106). The statement made in *The Idea of Nature* seems to be more adequate than that made in *An Essay on Metaphysics*, where Spinoza is viewed as spelling out the presupposition of science as it was conceived in the seventeenth century. In *The Idea of Nature* Collingwood seems to allude to problems inherent in the philosophical tradition as such—like the problem of unity of mind and matter—thus assuming an immanent philosophical determination which in turn is not fully submerged in the set-up of science in the limited sense of the term. Furthermore, Collingwood seems to imply the inner philosophical motivation towards a systematic unity or totality, that same motivation of which he was oblivious when he dealt with Aristotle's metaphysics.

The relation between a philosopher's system and the background of knowledge—including science—on which he formulates his system is unquestionable. However, one should not overestimate this relation—and precisely Spinoza is a case in point. Although he lived in the seventeenth century, Spinoza's philosophy is close to the classical tradition. This feature of his philosophy is apparent in several central issues of his system.

(a) We find in Spinoza a double causality: an eternal causality and a finite causality. The eternal, divine causality exhibits itself in the intellectual love for God, while the finite, mechanistic causality comes to the fore in the different affects of man. Hence the mechanistic view is rather limited compared with the broad perspective of the system.

(b) A central aspect of the scientific interpretation of facts and nature, i.e., time, is not included in Spinoza's system: '. . . it is clearly to be seen that measure, time, and number are merely modes of thinking, or rather, of imagining'.[1] Actually Spinoza disposes not only of time but also of measuring and numbering— that is to say, the mathematical tools of modern science. Hence it would be rather difficult to classify Spinoza taking this view as a philosopher of modern science, in spite of the affinity with what might be considered as the deterministic view of modern science. Spinoza's determinism is a deductive and not a causal one.

(c) Spinoza adheres to the classical view of degrees of knowledge among which the *scientia intuitiva* is the highest. Along with this theory of the degrees of knowledge goes his identification of the highest degree of knowledge with the ethical ideal. This again is a Platonic or Aristotelian idea which is outside the scope and trend of modern science. What we are aiming at here is not a detailed analysis of a certain philosophical system, nor a denial of a system's affinity with a given exterior set of concepts. Our aim is to disclose, through a close reading of the text, those inner problems of philosophy created by its own logic and exhibited in the course of a philosophic tradition. A philosopher does not invent problems, nor does he pick them up from a given approach to nature. Even when he is a child of his time, a philosopher is not only a child of his time. An interpretation of the texts removes the ground for an analogy between Spinoza and Tacitus—with all due deference to the latter.

[1] *The Chief Works of Spinoza*, transl. R. H. M. Elwes (New York, 1951), ii, 320 (Letter XII).

VII

We said before that Collingwood's view of the status of metaphysics or metaphysical presuppositions was strongly influenced by Kant. Collingwood interprets Kant in accordance with his own view of metaphysics:

I suggest that the relation between the Transcendental Analytics and his own metaphysical system was, after all, not one of analogy but one of identity (*EM*, 241).

The truth is that the Transcendental Analytics is an historical study of the absolute presuppositions generally recognized by natural scientists in Kant's own time and as a matter of fact for some time afterwards (*EM*, 245).

Along these lines Collingwood presents an interpretation of Kant's Analytic. Some parts of this interpretation are, no doubt, ingenious. Let us take but one example:

'Axioms of Intuition' are absolute presuppositions of science . . . depending on the principle that mathematics can be applied to the world of nature; in other words, that natural science is essentially an applied mathematics (*EM*, 249–50).

As to Kant's Anticipations of Perception Collingwood writes:

He has moved from Galileo and the general principle that a science of nature must be an applied mathematics, to Leibnitz and Newton and the special principle that a science of nature must consist of differential equations (*EM*, 259).

Collingwood is correct in his rendering of Kant's view, as far as his rendering goes. For Kant the principle of the Anticipations of Perception states that in all phenomena the real which is the object of feeling (*Empfindung*), has an intensive magnitude, i.e., a degree.[1] Collingwood is right in interpreting this principle as enabling the application of differential equations to the data of experience. In stressing this positive aspect implied in the principle of the Anticipation of Perception Collingwood omits its negative or its

---

[1] *Critique of Pure Reason*, B207.

critical aspect; anticipation applies only to the concept of the degree of feeling but one cannot anticipate the feeling as such.[1] This distinction between the degree and the feeling is by no means a minor one: it points to the limitation of rationality including the limitation of the application of the differential equations to the data of experience. *Nature* is not a book written in mathematical characters; only the *form* of nature can be rendered mathematically. This is an issue which cannot be looked at as taken over from Galileo and placed simply as a statement of the presuppositions of modern science; this is a problem of the meaning and scope of rationality. Again it is a philosophical problem which gains its reformulation by being addressed to modern science, but it does not coincide with the problematic situation of modern science proper.

The example of the Anticipations of Perception is significant from an additional point if view: in as much as the theory of the Anticipations of Perception is a theory about the applicability of a mathematical order on experience it is also a theory of the nature of consciousness. Perception, as Kant says, is the empirical consciousness, that is to say, a consciousness in which there is also feeling. There is no void perception; hence we cannot draw from experience a proof for an empty space and an empty time.[2] The theory of Anticipations is by the same token a theory of the state of consciousness.[3] For Kant who is looking for a given material to which the mathematical order could be applied, the aspect of the differential calculus and the aspect of the character of consciousness coincide. His is both a theory of application of rational tools to experience as well as a theory or a phenomenology of the empirical consciousness. The second aspect might be subsidiary in terms of the presuppositions of modern science, but it is essential in terms of the character of Kant's system. Here again Collingwood's interpretation of a system as a sum total of presuppositions, of a body of knowledge outside the system is, to say the least, a partial interpretation. The partiality is due to the assumption of an

[1] Ibid., B208.
[2] Ibid., B214, 208.
[3] *Prolegomena zu einer jeden künftigen Metaphysik, die als Wissenschaft wird auftreten können*, sect. 20.

exclusive determination of the system by science or by knowledge, which as such is non-philosophical or extra-philosophical.

We are not concerned here with the logical status of the presuppositions. The point which we are trying to make is that the concept of presuppositions, even when granting its validity, does not do full justice to the interpretation of a philosophical system, to the inner logic and to the variety of aspects embraced by a philosophical system. It is not clear from Collingwood's theory what the driving force of a system actually is or why a laying down of presuppositions is called for altogether. Unless we assume that there is a *nisus* towards reflection we cannot assume that tacit presuppositions, which cannot be verified, need an explication in the first place. Granting the activity of reflection we can assume that reflection turns towards available bodies of knowledge; it states or spells out the reflection implied in these bodies of knowledge and proceeds according to the direction set up by reflection. Proceeding along this line, reflection is its own judge and standard and cannot limit its function to the articulation of the extant presuppositions of science. It is for this reason that Collingwood's interpretation falls short. He takes issue, for instance, with Mill's theory of induction, but his criticism is questionable because Mill does not state the limited presupposition of induction or the axiom of it, as he calls it. Mill shows that the axiom is broader than what is implied here and now in the procedure of induction, because this presupposition is an extrapolation of actual experience rather than an articulation of the body of knowledge attained at here and now. The circle is there as Collingwood has it, but the circle is part of the game and deliberately so and is not a pitfall. We are engaged in a systematic thinking and in a systematic justification, and justification and systematization go beyond articulation—the task to which Collingwood confines philosophical or metaphysical thinking.

The ethical aspect was included in the discussion of the categorical character of ethical thinking as presented in *An Essay on Philosophical Method*. *The Essay on Metaphysics* fails to apply the concept of presupposition to the sphere of ethics, and confines it to the sphere of knowledge or science. The Kantian logic of presupposition in the domain of ethics does not appear in the context of the statement of the relation of knowledge and presuppositions. It would be indeed a difficult enterprise to include this aspect on the changing background of world outlooks. 'Freedom', says Kant,

is the condition of the moral law; the moral law is the only condition under which freedom can be known; though freedom is certainly the *ratio essendi* of the moral law, the latter is not the *ratio cognoscendi* of freedom. For had not the moral law already been distinctly thought in our reason we would never have been justified in assuming anything like freedom, even though it is not self contradictory. But if there were no freedom, the moral law would never have been encountered in us[1].

The logic of synthetic propositions *a priori* can lend itself to a historicist interpretation, that is to say, these propositions are but absolute presuppositions. But freedom as the *ratio essendi* of the moral law is not a proposition but an ultimate datum—ultimate on the level of reason. This datum cannot possibly be interpreted in the relativist mode as Collingwood interprets science. Collingwood tried to replace the notion of ultimate data, even in the realm of consciousness, by the notion of absolute presuppositions. Not only to the philosopher's intention can he do no justice—although he may try to understand Plato better than Plato understood himself—but even to the points of departure in the phenomenological sense of a philosopher. A case in point is Kant's view of the relation between freedom and the moral law.

VIII

We tried to show in the previous pages the deficiencies of Collingwood's view of the historical character of metaphysics. We saw that he looked at metaphysics as an historicist and assumed that a metaphysical system is determined by the state of science in a particular era. He combined the historicistic aspect with the relativistic one: theoretically he could argue that no metaphysical system has an established validity. This absence of validity was not bound to be related to its historical determinateness but to the very attempt to articulate that which totality is. Yet for Collingwood

[1] *Critique of Practical Reason*, transl. Lewis White Beck (New York, 1956), p. 4n.

the adequate awareness is the historical one and Kant could be saved from his illusion 'if he had known more history' (*EM*, 249).

We have tried to show that a historicistic explanation of a metaphysical system does not offer a balanced account of that which is contained in it.[1] This alone was already a criticism of the historicistic trend in Collingwood. In *The Idea of Nature* Collingwood himself, though still pointing to the position of philosophy *vis-à-vis* natural science (*IN*, 2), assumed that these are indispensable presuppositions of any 'natural science' (*IN*, 30). These presuppositions are: (1) there are 'natural things', and they are to be distinguished from 'artificial things'; (2) 'natural things' constitute a single 'world of nature' (*IN*, 29–30). These two presuppositions are not related to any particular way of operation put forward by a particular mode of natural science. They refer to the delineation of natural things from things which do not fall into the orbit dealt with by natural science—the distinction between natural and artificial is an illustration of such a delineation. This second presupposition makes a totalistic assumption as to the realm of nature, an assumption already implied in the distinction between things natural and things artificial. We encounter here not only a concession in terms of presuppositions as not confined to the changing historical pattern of natural sciences; we encounter here a presupposition which is related to the category of the whole which differs from a category like causality, the latter being the main illustration of Collingwood's analysis and his view as propounded in *An Essay on Metaphysics*.

This difference in the status of the presuppositions is not a matter of technicality, since the presuppositions delineating the domain of natural science in general are related to the very trend of this science. Collingwood does not raise the question of why natural sciences in their changing patterns and outlooks need absolute presupposition at all. In one of his comments he says:

[1] On Collingwood's view of historicism consult the present author's essays, 'Historicism and Philosophy', *Revue Internationale de Philosophie*, xi (1957), 401–19; 'From Facts to Thoughts', *Philosophy*, xxxv (1960), 122–37; and 'History and Time', *Scripta Hierosolymitana*, vi (1960), 41–103.

It is because absolute presuppositions are not 'derived from experience', but are catalytic agents which the mind must being out of its own resources to the manipulation of what is called 'experience' . . . that there must be institutions for perpetuating them (*EM*, 197).

We know clearly that absolute presuppositions are not derived from experience. We know also that were it not for the specific character of Greek science or Newtonian science, philosophy would not put forward the absolute presuppositions of these very sciences. In a way, these sciences in their pattern are the experience which philosophy addresses itself to and formulates the absolute presuppositions which are the subject-matter of metaphysics. Experience should not be taken in its impressionistic sense but in its cultural connotation as that pattern of culture which is the concern of the anthropologist. Further still: Collingwood speaks here about mind and its resources. What is mind? Is it a presupposition? Is it an absolute presupposition above the absolute presuppositions formulated in different philosophical systems according to the changing scientific outlooks? It seems that Collingwood was compelled to assume here a constant agent with its own resources, an agent maintaining the constant position of manipulating experience. Here the spontaneity of mind is assumed, possibly *malgré soi*. Once Collingwood supposes the constant agent of mind, he should and could ask himself about additional constant patterns in the changing systems, as for instance time and space understood differently in magic and in quantum physics but still having some possible common phenomenological features. Had he gone in this direction, he might have come close to a sort of Philosophy of Symbolic Forms.

What actually emerges from Collingwood's *Essay on Metaphysics* is a kind of cultural anthropology of metaphysics, a study of different world views entertained in the course of history by individuals and by groups of individuals. Collingwood speaks about metaphysics as a historical science and does not distinguish between the intention and intentionality of a metaphysical system which attempts to be categorical. His own attempt to unmask systems is to show that systems are historically determined by changing outlooks on nature. When, in answer to his question,

14

'Where do we go from here?' (Collingwood concludes 'We go from the idea of nature to the idea of history' (*IN*, 177)), he seems to include in this statement not only the results of his historical observation but also his convictions and his approval of those results. His view is formulated both from the level of his own intentionality and from the level of a historical or cultural anthropologist referring to views and revealing their disguised historicity. He is caught in the dilemma similar to that of the sociologists of knowledge who look at the mind as a function of a social reality and still assume the independence of mind by way of attributing to it the capacity of detachment for the sake of analysis of the phenomena dealt with in the sociology of knowledge. This is not only a biographical dilemma. It exhibits the intrinsic difficulty of Collingwood's own confessed historicism.

X

CONCEPTUAL CHANGE AND THE PROBLEM OF RELATIVITY

STEPHEN TOULMIN

I

THE RELATIVITY of concepts and attitudes has been a persistent scandal of twentieth-century philosophy. 'What makes the fundamental ideas of one culture or epoch better than those of another? Or are the men of each period and group all of them equally entitled to employ their own basic modes of thought?' Faced with this question, many philosophers have taken up inconsistent positions, conceding over ethical issues a relativism they deny over intellectual matters. Each social group (on their view) is at liberty to frame its own moral rules and concepts; but the ideas and principles of natural science, say, can somehow be shown—perhaps, by extending Frege's 'objective' methods of analysis—to impose themselves on the men of all cultures alike.

It was one of R. G. Collingwood's greatest virtues as a philosopher that he declined this easy way out. Once we abandon Kant's claims about the unique intellectual authority of Euclidean geometry and Newtonian mechanics (he saw) the same arguments that drive one towards relativism with regard to ethical concepts can be extended to concepts of other kinds also. In science as in ethics, each group and period acknowledges the authority of its own fundamental concepts, and the problem of explaining how the ideas and methods of different cultures and epochs are to be rationally compared is equally pressing in all fields of thought and action. Instead of trying to fence this problem off, as applying only to the special class of 'value judgements', Collingwood had the vision and courage to confront it in all its generality. Though, in the last resort, he succumbed to the charms of an historical relativism that his successors have not found convincing, his *Essay on Metaphysics* nevertheless presents the most careful account yet available of the arguments which may lead a man to that extremity; and they are arguments that still have to be taken seriously, and answered on their own level of clarity, if we are ever to see our way beyond them. So I shall devote this essay to discussing Collingwood's argument for historical relativism, and I shall use the discussion to throw light on the broader significance that he attached to the idea of 'presuppositions', which is dealt with from another point of view in Michael Krausz's essay in this volume.[1]

The significance of Collingwood's *Essay on Metaphysics* has recently been underrated. There are several reasons for this, some personal and historical, others concerned with matters of substance. To begin with, his exposition made use of very bad examples. For instance, he presented the argument as applicable to the natural sciences, including physics: unfortunately, having little first-hand knowledge of science, he picked his illustrations less from authentic scientific texts than from the meta-scientific writings of philosophical colleagues like Alfred North Whitehead. If Collingwood had been really familiar with physics himself and so had furnished it with more apt and telling examples, his exposition of the relativist position would probably have carried wider conviction, as T. S. Kuhn's later presentation has done. As they stand the illustrations Collingwood used, both in the *Metaphysics* and in his later *Idea of Nature*, were less than convincing; and this is a great pity, since—in itself—his central argument has great weight.

Again, Collingwood's position at Oxford during the late 1930s was that of a lone wolf. His philosophical colleagues, especially the brighter young men, were in growing revolt against idealism in all its forms. They were no more ready to sign on at Magdalen College, as subscribers to a revised version of Vico and Croce, than they were to join G. R. G. Mure in his Hegelian bastion at Merton. Other things were more immediately exciting and

[1] Essay XI.

interesting: Russell's mathematical logic, Ayer's positivist trumpet-blasts, stirrings from Gilbert Ryle at Christ Church, rumours from Cambridge about G. E. Moore and Ludwig Wittgenstein.

Finally, with the approach of the Second World War, Collingwood was under great personal strain—he had only four more years to live—while the grave political developments of the thirties had left him in a querulous mood. Seeing himself as the only Oxford philosopher to have grasped the historical significance of Fascism and of Nazism, he carped at his colleagues for fiddling while Central Europe burned, and he was too easily upset by the supposed ideological 'tendencies' and 'implications' of their views. This irritation came to a head in the years 1938-9, when he was writing the *Essay on Metaphysics*, and the results are evident in the text of the book itself. His positive arguments are interlarded with polemical attacks and rhetorical caricatures, some of which unfortunately boomeranged. For by the time the book appeared in print, in 1940, many of the colleagues he had pilloried were already soldiers in uniform. So, for transitory reasons quite beyond his control, the book provoked at Oxford reactions of resentful hostility, and his argument was ignored.

If we re-read Collingwood's book from thirty years on, we do so in an entirely new situation. Looked at afresh, it strikes one very differently. His central idea, that the task of analysing systems of concepts may involve us (among other things) in studying their history, nowadays sound much less strange: we are, for instance, becoming more open today to the programme for philosophy of science stated a century ago by William Whewell, and adopted around 1900 by Ernst Mach—that of expounding the philosophy of the natural sciences in the light of, and in parallel with, their history. So we may here ignore the polemical sections of the *Essay on Metaphysics*, and pick out for examination, rather, the substantive arguments in the course of which Collingwood posed some crucial questions about conceptual change and evaluation.

II

The foundation of Collingwood's arguments is his account of the formal relations holding within a conceptual system—i.e. the logical connections between the different terms, questions and propositions of a scientific theory. This account is unorthodox in one significant respect. In any such theory or system (Collingwood tells us) the general, comprehensive principles stand at the summit of a logical hierarchy or structure, with successively lower levels occupied by the narrower and more specific propositions dependent on them; and, up to this point, there is nothing unusual about his account. But, as Collingwood describes them, the relations holding *within* this hierarchy are very different from those commonly set out in books on logic and scientific method. For it is a mistake (Collingwood argues) to treat the most general and comprehensive principles of a system as 'major premisses', or 'universal propositions' *from which* more specific and particular statements are *inferred deductively*. An axiomatic structure of this formalized kind is at home only in those parts of pure mathematics whose basic concepts have been settled definitively: most typically, in a system that is intellectually fossilized, like Euclidean geometry. Instead (he declares) the more specific statements and questions in a conceptual system *rely for their meaning and relevance* on the more general doctrines. Specific questions either 'arise' or 'do not arise', depending on what more general principles are assumed; and the more comprehensive doctrines are related to the narrower ones, not as 'axioms' are related to 'theorems', but rather as 'presuppositions' to 'consequential questions'.

In Collingwood's language, the 'logical efficacy' of narrower, specific concepts is referred to—and made contingent on—the 'logical efficacy' of broader, general concepts. Or, to put the point in more familiar terms: the narrower, specific concepts and questions are *operative*, only for so long as the broader, general concepts and principles are *relevant and applicable*. This kind of structure—on Collingwood's account—characterizes conceptual systems in all their parts, and at every level; so that, ultimately, whether any specific element in a system is operative depends on whether its most general principles are relevant and applicable. In a natural science (physics, for example) the most general presuppositions will then determine what basic patterns of thought are employed in interpreting 'physical phenomena'; and, in doing so, they will determine also the forms of question by which inquiries in that area are led forward.

From an historian's point of view, such an account of the structure of conceptual systems makes better sense than the more orthodox 'axiomatic' account. Classical nineteenth-century physics, for instance, relied on a whole string of a very general, but tacit assumptions: e.g., that the movements of inanimate bodies can be explained in abstraction from their colours and smells, or that determinate 'actions' or 'forces' can be identified to explain all changes in linear momentum. Assumptions like these—if my reading of Collingwood is correct—are among the classical physicist's most general and fundamental 'presuppositions', or among his most basic 'hypotheses', if we prefer the Greek term: it is on these presuppositions or hypotheses that the specific concepts and questions of classical physics *depend for their meaning*. Certainly—to come to the heart of the matter—this account applies well enough to Newtonian mechanics. For consider what would be the effect, if the general axioms and presuppositions of Newton's dynamics were entirely abandoned. This would not merely *falsify* a large number of statements about 'forces' and their effects on the 'momentum' of bodies that were previously supposed to be true: much more drastically, it would strip these terms of meaning, so that the statements in which those terms were employed would cease any longer to arise, or even to *make sense*.

At this stage, Collingwood sharpened up the central point of his argument, by introducing a convenient and attractive pair of technical terms. Within the main body of a conceptual system (he claimed) concepts and questions on any one level are related to those on adjacent levels in both directions; and, in each case, the 'logical efficacy' of concepts and questions on one level will depend on the 'logical efficacy' of those on the next level up. We can again give an authentic illustration from physics. Questions about 'optical dispersion' arise—that is, have a determinate meaning —only within the scope of the broader concepts 'refractive index'; for, by the 'dispersion' of a transparent substance, we just *mean* the manner in which its refractive index varies with the wavelength of the refracted light. So any use of the narrower term, 'optical dispersion', presupposes the applicability of the broader terms, 'refraction' and 'refractive index'. Yet such assumptions are, in Collingwood's terminology, only *relative* presuppositions: the concepts of 'refraction' and 'refractive index', for instance, presuppose in their turn the applicability of other, still broader terms, such as 'light-ray'. (Only in cases where optical phenomena can be described in terms of 'light-rays' do questions about 'refraction' have a straightforward meaning). Thus, the concepts presupposed on one level are normally dependent on yet broader presuppositions one level up—and this is what, in Collingwood's terminology, makes their applicability a 'relative' presupposition.

When we reach the summit of any conceptual hierarchy, however, we arrive at a set of entirely general presuppositions. At this level, our concepts and principles are no longer dependent on others of a still more general kind: here at last (as Collingwood puts it) we are faced with *absolute* presuppositions, on whose applicability a whole mode of thought depends. Whereas 'relative' presuppositions have logical relations in both directions—being presupposed by some concepts, while presupposing others— 'absolute' presuppositions must stand on their own feet. Once an argument gets to this level, no more basic assumptions remain to be brought to light. Abandoning a set of absolute presuppositions means giving up the corresponding pattern of thought and explanation *as an entirety*. This distinction between 'relative' and 'absolute' presuppositions is essential (Collingwood argues) for a proper understanding both of philosophy and of the history of thought. In each field, the beginning of wisdom lies in recognizing how the logical structure of conceptual systems is reflected in the patterns of conceptual change: that is to say, how an intellectual discipline develops through a succession of distinct historical phases, and how each phase operates with a characteristic set of concepts, questions and propositions, forming a self-contained hierarchy governed by its own 'absolute presuppositions'.

In general terms, this picture of conceptual history can be made attractive and plausible. Broadly speaking, for instance, one can see how a term like 'light-ray' serves as a fundamental conception of all geometrical optics, and how the abandonment of that notion would involve giving up entirely the branch of physics we know as 'geometrical optics'. Even so, there are difficulties about matching Collingwood's account against specific examples in detail. He leaves it unclear at what exact level, in practice, our presuppositions finally cease to be 'relative'—i.e. dependent in turn on other, broader principles—and become 'absolute' or self-sustaining. Granted that his argument is cogent if stated in broad enough terms, what exactly (we must ask) does he regard as a specific example of an 'absolute' presupposition?

At this point, Collingwood's lack of first-hand scientific experience had unhappy effects, and his own illustrations leave the matter as obscure as before. Though he was a distinguished historian of Roman Britain, his grasp of the history of science was limited. For instance, he gave a highly personal account of the development of physics from 1680 to 1930. This development could, he thought, be divided into three successive stages—governed, respectively, by a 'Newtonian presupposition' to the effect that 'Some events have causes', a 'Kantian presupposition' to the effect that 'All events have causes' and an 'Einsteinian pre-supposition' to the effect that 'No events have causes'. (This characterization is in his own words.) Yet how far can one in fact fit the actual history of physics into such a scheme? Certainly the concept of 'cause' has played a continually changing part in the physics of the last three hundred years, but Collingwood's three-stage formula scarcely does justice to the complexities of the story; and, in general, if we try to apply his account of conceptual change to the natural sciences, we shall get little help from his own illustrations.

All the same, bad illustrations should not distract us from worthwhile points. Instead, we should look for better illustrations of our own. For—as an historian—Collingwood was, surely, right to insist that the physical theories of Newton (or Maxwell, or Einstein) do depend on certain characteristic and extremely general assumptions, for which no yet more general justification can be given without going beyond the scope of the science in question. All the specific dynamical explanations of classical physics, for instance, involve the Newtonian concept of 'inertia'; the

Newtonian concept of 'inertia' presupposes, in turn, the idea of an inertial principle of some kind; and, beyond that, where can we turn? An idea such as that of 'inertia-in-general' is, one might say, *constitutive* of dynamics: essential to the very existence of dynamics as a science, since without some conception of 'inertia' the intellectual enterprise we know as 'dynamics' would be at-an-end. (Other sciences might, of course, step in and take over the phenomena involved, as the heirs or successors of dynamics; but that is another matter.)

We can go further. For Collingwood was surely right also in his next philosophical claim—namely, that the crucial intellectual choices within a science involve *changes* in its deepest presuppositions; that we can understand these crucial choices only by studying them against their historical backgrounds; and that this can be done only by scrutinizing the processes, or procedures, by which entire conceptual systems—absolute presuppositions and all—displace one another in the historical development of a discipline. The effect of Collingwood's *Essay on Metaphysics* was thus to confront philosophers directly with the problem of *conceptual change*. The virtue of his exposition was that it presented the problem in an entirely general form: the same problem arises (as he showed) about any conceptual system characterized by a coherent structure of concepts and presuppositions.

In Collingwood's eyes, then, the role of concepts in human thought was a matter, not for psychology, but for the history of ideas—or rather, in his own idiosyncratic usage, for 'metaphysics'. In a long polemical digression, he argued that psychology was a misbegotten and presumptuous pseudo-science: that the question *how* we think is inseparable from the question *in what terms* we think, which is a matter for 'conceptual history' rather than for 'behavioural science'. And the understanding of conceptual change required a three-stage inquiry into the history of ideas, which represented the only legitimate task left to metaphysics. The three stages are as follows:

(i) First, we must 'identify different constellations of absolute presuppositions' in the area of our concern;

(ii) Next, we must 'study their likenesses and unlikenesses', so as to discover which features do (or do not) change in the transition from one historical phase to the next;

(iii) Finally, we must go on 'to find out *on what occasions and by what processes* one such constellation has turned into another'.

III

Thus Collingwood posed the central—and still unanswered—question about the 'dynamics' of conceptual change and conceptual choice:

On what occasions, and by what processes, do conceptual systems (or constellations of presuppositions) succeed one another?

We read on with excitement, to see how he will answer the questions; but we are in for a disappointment. Having formulated this crucial problem, he stops. The remainder of the *Essay on Metaphysics* describes a number of static sections across the historical development of scientific and philosophical thought, but it leaves the problem of conceptual dynamics entirely without a solution. About the general *occasions* on which 'constellations of presuppositions' succeed one another he says a little, though not nearly enough. About the general *processes and procedures* by which one constellation 'turns into another', he says nothing at all.

This gap in Collingwood's draft manuscript was so glaring that a colleague advised him to explain just how he conceived of such changes:

I have hinted . . . that absolute presuppositions change. A friend thinks readers may credit me with the opinion that such changes are merely 'changes of fashion', and asks me to explain what, otherwise, I believe them to be.

In response, Collingwood added to his text a substantial footnote, which is probably the most significant thing in the whole book, and it is worth quoting in full:

A 'change of fashion' is a superficial change, symptomatic perhaps of deeper and more important changes, but not itself deep or important. A man adopts it merely because other men do so, or because advertisers, salesmen, etc., suggest it to him. My friend's formula "if we like to start new dodges, we may" describes very well the somewhat frivolous type of consciousness with which we adopt or originate these superficial changes. But an absolute presupposition is not a 'dodge' and people who 'start' a new one do not start it because they 'like' to start it. People are not ordinarily aware of their absolute presuppositions, and are not, therefore, thus aware of changes in them: such a change, therefore, cannot be a matter of choice. Nor is there anything superficial or frivolous about it. It is the most radical change a man can undergo, and entails the abandonment of all his most firmly established habits and standards for thought and action. Why, asks my friend, do such changes happen? Briefly, because the absolute presuppositions of any given society, at any given phase of its history, form a structure which is subject to 'strains' of greater or less intensity, which are 'taken up' in various ways, but never annihilated. If the strains are too great, the structure collapses and is replaced by another, which will be a modification of the old with the destructive strain removed; a modification not consciously devised but created by a process of unconscious thought.

This reply tells us a lot about Collingwood's own view; yet at the same time it forces us to move beyond it. For it sidesteps the crucial issue. We may speak metaphorically, of a 'structure' of presuppositions being subjected to 'strains', if we please; provided only that we explain *through what effects* these 'strains' reveal themselves, and *by what criteria* one can recognize when their 'destructive' effects have been 'removed'. However, when such questions are pressed, Collingwood fudges. He hovers uneasily, half-way between two possible answers; and he is unable in good conscience to answer all these questions consistently in either of the two ways. Can we change from one constellation of absolute presuppositions to another, because we have *reasons* for doing so; or only because certain *causes* compel us to? Are questions about such 'modifications' to be answered by appeal to reasons, considerations, arguments, and justifications—that is, in terms of 'rational' categories? Or are they to be answered in terms of forces, causes, compulsions, and explanations—that is, by appeal to 'causal' categories? Given Collingwood's previous argument, neither kind of argument can entirely satisfy him.

He cannot answer these questions in consistently *rational* terms, because his own analysis will not permit it. If we advance 'reasons' to 'justify' replacing one constellation of absolute presuppositions by another, the validity of this further argument will have to be judged in terms of some yet 'higher' principle—and this will imply that neither constellation of presuppositions was fully 'absolute and self-sustaining' in the first place. In this way, we shall implicitly invoke a 'super-absolute' presupposition, for deciding when the step from one set of presuppositions to another is 'rationally justified'; and the two initial sets of presupposition—though initially supposed to be 'absolute'—will turn out to be 'relative' to this 'super-absolute' presupposition. If looked at in these terms, the elimination of 'strains' from a conceptual system will then revert to being a standard intellectual operation within a basically-unchanging framework of theory. To give an account of conceptual change in terms that he himself can accept as strictly 'rational' will therefore be inconsistent with the whole doctrine of 'absolute presuppositions', and so will involve him in abandoning his own most distinctive contribution to the philosophical argument.

Yet what alternative is there? Under pressure, Collingwood hints—though without explicitly asserting it—that the attempt to describe 'the removal of strains' in rational terms must be given up finally. But he is clearly unhappy about this prospect. For, if no possibility remains of justifying such transitions rationally, all we have left to do is to explain them causally; and then, how will any 'thought' come into the process? Notice how Collingwood tries to dodge this conclusion in his footnote. There, he argues that people are 'not ordinarily aware' of changes in their absolute presuppositions, so that these changes 'cannot be a matter of (rational) choice'; but he still credits the 'modification' of a 'structure of absolute presuppositions'—in quasi-rational language—to a 'process of *unconscious thought*'.

Elsewhere in the *Essay on Metaphysics*, Collingwood goes still further in the causal direction. For instance, he likens the 'strains' in conceptual systems to the 'social strains' that arise within a culture, society or civilization: and he suggests that intellectual 'strains' within systems of ideas may be associated with—may even be epiphenomena of—broader socio-historical crises. Thus he describes 'the history of the steam-engine' from James Watt up to Daimler and Parsons 'as a parable of the time', and he finds a direct parallel in 'the history of the English Parliamentary System, as worked out by John Locke before the end of the seventeenth century':

That theory, with certain modifications introduced in the eighteenth century, became the official doctrine of European politics in the nineteenth century, when parliamentary constitutions on Locke's model were manufactured with as much regularity and as much self-satisfaction as steam-engines on the model of Watt.

Yet Collingwood never took the final step, of replacing 'reasons' by 'causes' completely. At the highest level, conceptual change may come about through 'unconscious' thought; but it remains a matter for 'thought', not for entirely anonymous 'forces' or 'compulsions'. What then—are we left asking—is the exact nature of this 'unconscious thought'? And how does it operate on us? (Does Collingwood have Freud's ideas in mind? That seems unlikely, given his general scorn for psychology; yet what alternative interpretation are we to put on this phrase?) How far is the 'thought' that goes on at this level analogous to rational argument, and how far does it operate like a causal agency? . . .

Collingwood lapses into final silence at a particularly tantalizing and ambiguous moment. Still, for our purposes, his hesitation between a rational and a causal account of conceptual change is the essential clue we need, if we are to recognize the weak point in his whole position. For this is the price he pays for keeping his 'absolute' presuppositions entirely independent and self-sufficient; and, once that step is taken, he landed in an historical relativism from which he cannot retreat.

To set the position out concisely, his argument runs as follows:

(i) At any given stage of development, the intellectual content of a discipline can be presented as a system of concepts and principles that operate on different levels of generality;

(ii) Our reasons for accepting concepts and propositions on the lower levels of generality are 'relative to'—and must be explained in terms of—those on the higher levels, and such lower-level concepts and propositions are presupposed only 'relatively' to those on the higher levels;

(iii) Our reasons for accepting concepts and principles on the highest level of all cannot be explained in this way, and these upper-level concepts and propositions are accordingly presupposed—at that stage in the development of the discipline—not relatively, but 'absolutely'.

(iv) We can make rational comparisons between propositions and concepts current at any one stage in the development of a discipline, to the extent that they are both operative 'relative to' the same constellations of absolute presuppositions;

(v) On the other hand, if we attempt to compare propositions or concepts which are 'relative to' different constellations of absolute presuppositions, or if we attempt to compare different constellations of absolute presuppositions as wholes, we shall find no common, agreed set of rational principles or procedures for judging them;

(vi) So a proposition can be rationally appraised only 'relative to' a given constellation of absolute presuppositions and, once we leave this particular framework, we leave also the scope of rational comparison and judgement.

By this argument, the undoubted fact that our rational standards are in part *dependent on* the historical context of judgements—what we called the 'relativity' of concepts and attitudes—is taken as a reason for *confining* rational comparisons and relations within one particular historical context. Historical relativity (in a phrase) is taken as entailing historical relativism; the need to bear differences of context in mind, when making comparisons between contexts, is made a ground for limiting rational judgement to relations holding within a single context.

IV

At this point, we have to part company with Collingwood. Yet he leaves us with one deep insight and a correspondingly profound problem. When we reach the most general level of all within a conceptual system, as he shows, it becomes uncommonly difficult to distinguish 'explanations'—to be given in terms of 'causal processes'—from 'justifications'—to be given in terms of 'rational procedures'. At this final level, most of the tests by which we would normally draw such a distinction fail us, and we must develop fresh criteria. Yet how can we retain what is sound in Collingwood's account, without being driven all the way down the road to historical relativism? In order to do so, we shall have *either* to weaken the distinction between 'absolute' and 'relative' presuppositions, *or* to find some alternative way of matching it against the historical process of conceptual change. The one thing we cannot agree to do is pay the full price that his argument exacts—i.e. to give up entirely all references to 'reasons', 'procedures', and 'justifications' at the final, 'absolute' level, and restrict ourselves to 'causes', 'processes', and 'explanations' alone.

There is room here to indicate only very briefly how Collingwood's difficulties might be circumvented. We can, in fact, do justice to the historical and cultural relativity of our concepts without being stampeded into philosophical relativism, only by drawing some further distinctions which both Collingwood and his successor, T. S. Kuhn, leave obscure—e.g., the distinction between considerations of *theory* and considerations of *disciplinary aim*, and that between two correspondingly different kinds of 'fundamental principles'.

We may happily grant that, at the level of substantive theory, the content of scientific thought has frequently changed in a discontinuous manner; so that, within any particular intellectual discipline, one conceptual system may well come to be displaced by another system based on contrary, and even on incongruous, *theoretical* principles. Yet, however serious the discontinuities, misunderstandings, and cross-purposes may be on the theoretical level, the natural sciences have displayed a far greater continuity on the level of aims, methods and programmes. The intellectual content of a science may change radically, but the scientific argument after each theoretical revolution goes on—methodologically speaking—in very much the same manner as before. So even though, at the most fundamental level, the replacement of one complete theory by another may no longer be justifiable by appeal to yet broader 'theoretical' principles, it does not follow that the step cannot be justified by appeal to *any* reasons, properly so-called. For the parties to such a debate—both those who cling to the older constellation of presuppositions, and those who advocate the newer one—may still share all the common ground they require: not, perhaps, any common body of theoretical axioms, but rather a shared body of intellectual ambitions and rational methods, manifested in common *disciplinary* principles, selection-procedures, and criteria of adequacy. Both parties to such a debate will (in a word) be composed alike of 'physicists' working as physicists, or 'astronomers' working as astronomers, or of 'neurophysiologists' working as neurophysiologists.

The shared considerations uniting the physicists, astronomers or neurophysiologists of an age are, accordingly, not so much theoretical principles that are *operative within* the science concerned, as disciplinary principles that are *constitutive of* that science. The Copernican debate, for instance, was eventually resolved in rational terms, not because agreed 'absolute presuppositions' were invoked at the theoretical level, but because the forerunners and successors of Copernicus shared enough in the way of disciplinary or method-ological conceptions: i.e., were sufficiently agreed about the intellectual achievement at which the whole enterprise of 'physical astronomy' should aim. Likewise, with the transition from Newtonian to Einsteinian physics: once again, the indispensable thing in this case was the common body of disciplinary ambitions and demands by which physicists—both classical and relativistic alike—could appraise Einstein's innovations *as physics*.

Two brief qualifications will clarify the exact meaning of this further distinction.

(1) In the first place: even though we may deny Collingwood's claim that successive constellations of absolute presuppositions represent separate intellectual systems—so that scientists committed to different constellations cannot debate their disagreements rationally—this does not mean that such absolute incomprehension

never *in fact* occurs. Rather, our further distinction suggests that communication breaks down inescapably, only when there are cross-purposes *both* at the theoretical *and* at the disciplinary level. The nearest thing to a real-life example is, perhaps, the story of Goethe's *Farbenlehre*. In his writings on colour, Goethe denounced Newton's optical theories, arguing that they grossly misrepresented facts about colour of a kind that are evident in our direct experience. Newton's whole approach to optics must therefore be set aside, with a sigh of regret that so talented a man should have been seduced by his passion for mathematics into starting off in so manifestly wrong-headed a direction. In place of Newtonian optics, Goethe set out to reconstruct the theory of colour from the ground up, around different theoretical principles and different fundamental concepts; and he was content to see the Newtonian theories thrown into the waste-basket, as a temporary aberration of the human intellect.

At a quick glance, Goethe's argument might seem to be just one more attempt at a scientific take-over, on a par with those of Copernicus and Einstein, except that it aborted. On closer inspection, it turns out that the cases are not genuinely parallel. For Goethe's ambition was to explain not physical phenomena, but psychological ones. The theory he dreamed of was not a physical theory of light-rays or light-waves, regarded as the 'material bearers' of colours, but a psychological theory of visible light, regarded as the 'immediate object of colour-perception'. Goethe rejected Newton's theory (that is) not because it gave bad answers to the questions he himself was asking, but because for his purposes its answers were irrelevant.

Goethe's difference with Newton was thus not a disagreement within a common discipline, since the two men were not working in the same discipline at all. Between the electromagnetic theories of (say) Maxwell and Heisenberg there is a genuine intellectual difference: one cannot consistently accept both. Between the colour-theories of Goethe and Newton, by contrast, there was a flat cross-purpose. Newton was concerned with the physics of light, Goethe with the psychology of perception, so they could never hope to agree about what a 'theory of colour' should be, or should aim at achieving. The true successors of Goethe have in fact been, not physicists like Maxwell and Heisenberg, but sensory physiologists and psychologists like Helmholtz and Lettvin.

(2) The second qualification is this. Having distinguished between 'theoretical' principles and 'disciplinary' ones, we may be tempted to use in this distinction as a short way of countering the challenge of relativism. For historical relativity might be tolerated on the theoretical level, provided only that the relevant disciplinary considerations were historically invariant. Let the theories and ideas of (say) dynamics vary, if need be, provided the central goals and methods of the discipline remain fixed: if this much could be assumed, we could then apparently breath easy. Yet even that much invariance may be more than we can properly demand, and we must keep an open mind about it. Given enough *continuity* in the disciplinary principles/assumptions/conceptions of a science, outright *invariance* may not be indispensable: to take it for granted that physicists (say) have had the identical ambitions in all epochs is too easy a way out of Collingwood's difficulty. How far in practice such disciplinary principles are *in fact* historical invariants is a question to which I shall be returning elsewhere, but a substantial degree of continuity can safely be assumed. As with Newton, Kant, and Einstein, so with Bradwardine and Heisenberg: they might not share any theoretical vocabulary at the outset, but, given patience, they should eventually succeed in establishing communication, given only a sufficient overlap in their respective disciplinary aims.

To sum up: when two systems of presuppositions are the products of sufficiently similar intellectual aims, and so fall within the scope of a common discipline, the historical transition between them can—at any rate, in principle—be discussed in rational terms. Radical incomprehension is inescapable, only when the parties to a dispute have nothing in common even in their disciplinary ambitions. If we keep this further distinction in mind, one can hope to justify a middle-ground position: acknowledging the historical and cultural diversity and relativity of intellectual concepts and judgements, without being compelled to accept historical or cultural relativism as the inescapable consequences of this diversity. For of course (we can concede) any concept or doctrine must be considered and judged in relation to the intellectual situation within which it is was originally operative. Of course (that is to say) the merits of any lower-level concept depend on the particular 'paradigm' or 'constellation of presuppositions' by reference to which its original 'niche' was defined. But this does not destroy all rational basis for comparing concepts or doctrines that are operative in different contexts. Comparisons may be impossible in a few exceptional cases, as with Goethe and Newton, where the parties concerned did not even share any disciplinary common ground. But in general, given a minimum community of disciplinary aims and methods, scientists whose fundamental ideas are quite incongruous will still have a basis for comparing the merits of their theoretical systems. Given this minimum basis, rival paradigms or presuppositions—even those which are incompatible on the *theoretical* level—may nevertheless remain rationally commensurable, as alternative approaches to a common set of *disciplinary* tasks.

V

In fairness to Collingwood, we should make one last concession. The explicit argument of his *Essay on Metaphysics* left it uncertain whether he intended his term, 'absolute presuppositions', to apply to the most fundamental theoretical principles within a science, or to the disciplinary principles constitutive of it. If he had really been clear in his own mind about the significance of this distinction, he might in fact have ended up in far less damaging kind of relativism; so we may be tempted to interpret his argument charitably, by treating his 'absolute' presuppositions as defining the intellectual boundaries between distinct disciplines. Unfortunately, his own examples rule this interpretation out. To recall his favourite illustration, viz. the contrast between the physics of the 1680s, the 1770s, and the 1900s: however different the *theoretical* principles by which Newton, Kant, and Einstein organized their respective concepts and explanations, physics as a subject displayed enough *disciplinary* continuity from 1680 to

1910 for us to treat all three men as participating in a single, continuing rational debate. The three men might be divided by incompatible theoretical presuppositions, but their disciplinary presuppositions were not—as Collingwood appears to have believed—separated by the same unbridgeable gulfs.

Taken in their own terms, of course, Collingwood's final conclusions should not surprise us. When the *Essay on Metaphysics* originally appeared, his associates did not know what to make of it. His last years were a time not only of war, but also of personal crisis; before he died, dark rumours had begun to circulate that he had been converted to Marxism, perhaps even to Communism; and the *Essay* itself contains plenty of circumstantial evidence to support such rumours—declarations about the 'dynamics of history', sideswipes at capitalists, and truculent comparisons between political power and steam-power. These hints only confirmed the suspicion of Collingwood's opponents that psychological stress had thrown him intellectually off-balance, while they were a source of pained alarm to his remaining friends and supporters. By now we can take a calmer view. For the argument of the *Essay on Metaphysics* was, of course, quite consistent with certain broad Marxian positions; and a liberal form of historical materialism was in some ways a natural sequel to Collingwood's earlier idealism.

The reasons for saying this go to the heart of Collingwood's position. Faced with the transition from the principles of eighteenth century epistemology to a full-scale nineteenth-century historicism, Collingwood—like his immediate predecessor at Oxford, F. H. Bradley—baulked at the final hurdle. Classical German idealists like Hegel had been entirely happy to blur the difference between *logical* relationships (holding *within* the conceptual systems current in a given era) and *dialectical* relationships (holding *between* successive stages in the historical development of these systems) or, as anthropologists would put it, that between the 'synchronic' and 'diachronic' aspects of our intellectual systems. Indeed, before they could talk of History having a Logic of its own, this blurring was indispensable. Despite all Collingwood's sensitivity and acumen as an historian, however, he recoiled—as a philosopher—from running together 'logic' and 'history' into a unified 'historical dialectic'. Rather than follow Hegel into the Logic of History, he agreed with his empiricist predecessors that the scope of 'logic' must be confined to the *internal* structure of conceptual systems.

The resulting contrast between logic and dialectic was reinforced by his rigid distinction between 'absolute' and 'relative' presuppositions. For that distinction implied that 'logical' or 'rational' relationships hold good only *synchronically*, within the theories of a given epoch and 'relative to' a given constellation of presuppositions. This made it impossible for Collingwood to consider the diachronic relationships between complete conceptual systems (i.e. to discuss conceptual change) in terms of 'reasons' and 'reasoning'—still less, in the quasi-logical terms associated with idealist jargon about Inner Rationality of History. Under the circumstances, it was a natural next step for him to adopt instead of some kind of historical materialism, in which conceptual change was discussed, instead, in terms of quasi-causal factors—whether 'processes of unconscious thought', socio-cultural 'strains', or analogies between intellectual change and technological invention. Collingwood's long exposure to the British empiricists had had its effect:

> In spite of all temptations
> To belong to other Nations,
> He remained an Englishman.

Still, even in the act of rejecting Collingwood's ultimate relativism, we must give him credit for facing us with some highly important arguments and questions. In particular, it was he who stated explicitly and clearly the central, and still unanswered question about conceptual change in natural science and elsewhere:

How—on what occasions, and by what processes—do our constellations of fundamental concepts succeed/displace/turn into one another as they do? . . .

And, in order to end up with a satisfactory answer to this question, we ourselves must now add a further gloss of our own—a gloss which the principles of Collingwood's historical relativism did not permit him to ask—namely—

. . . And to what sort of reasons, principles and procedures can we appeal, in order to justify the intellectual step involved in abandoning one constellation of fundamental concepts for another?

It is perhaps the best tribute to Collingwood's originality and foresight that philosophers of science who recognize no explicit debt to him, such as Paul Feyerabend and the late Russ Hanson, should have come around to discussing these questions for their own independent reasons in the 1960s, some twenty-five years after the *Essay on Metaphysics* first posed them.

[NOTE: The argument of this essay overlaps substantially with that of a paper on 'Conceptual Revolutions in Science', given before the Boston Colloquium for Philosophy of Science and printed in R. S. Cohen and M. Wartofsky (eds.) *Boston Studies in Philosophy of Science*, vol. 3 (1967), pp. 331–47. It will be treated more fully, and in a broader philosophical context, in section 1.2 of *Human Understanding*, vol. I, 'The Collective Use and Evolution of Concepts' (Clarendon Press, Oxford, and Princeton University Press, 1972).]

XI

THE LOGIC OF
ABSOLUTE PRESUPPOSITIONS[1]

MICHAEL KRAUSZ

COLLINGWOOD'S THEORY of absolute presuppositions is an attempt to articulate the logical character of presuppositions fundamental to systematic inquiries. Such fundamental presuppositions are constitutive of systematic inquiries in so far as they render certain questions appropriate and others inappropriate to the given inquiry, and in so far as they encourage certain modes of research and discourage others.

When taken together with his theory of meaning, Collingwood's theory of absolute presuppositions implies an extreme relativism which rules out the possibility that an inquirer might offer objective reasons for abandoning one inquiry in favour of another. Consequently, the historian of ideas could account for such change only in non-rational terms (e.g. economical and sociological).

I shall argue that Collingwood's theory of meaning is false, and that the remaining theory of absolute presuppositions bears at least two interpretations. The first interpretation makes possible a rational historiography of ideas; the second interpretation does not.

In *An Essay on Metaphysics* Collingwood characterizes systematic inquiries as hierarchies of well-ordered questions and answers. In such hierarchies the presupposition(s) of any question is (are) an acceptable answer to a logically prior question. Collingwood designates the relation from presupposition to question as *logical*

[1] For their helpful suggestions the author thanks E. Benton, W. H. Dray, and R. Keat.

efficacy: logical efficacy is the power of a presupposition to *give rise* to a question (*EM*, 39). *Presupposing* is the relation from question to presupposition.

At the base of the hierarchy of questions and answers are *absolute presuppositions*, presuppositions which answer no questions and which Collingwood views as having no truth value. *Relative presuppositions* are presuppositions which answer prior questions. Collingwood views relative presuppositions as having truth value. According to Collingwood, the logical efficacy of a presupposition does not depend upon the truth or falsity of the presupposition; for otherwise absolute presuppositions could not be logically efficacious and not have truth value. As examples of absolute presuppositions Collingwood cites the Newtonian principle of continuity, the Kantian principle of universal causation, the Kantian principle that natural science is essentially an applied mathematics, the principle of indestructibility of substance, the principle of reciprocal action, and 'God exists.'

There are two possible positions consonant with Collingwood's view that an absolute presupposition can answer no question.

Position I. If P is an absolute presupposition, then in the *given* systematic inquiry P cannot be an answer to a question.

Position II. If P is an absolute presupposition, then in *any* systematic inquiry P cannot be an answer to a question.

Both Position I and Position II imply that if P is an absolute presupposition, then P in the given systematic inquiry is not an answer to a question. While P, in Position I, can be only an absolute presupposition in a given systematic inquiry, P could be a relative presupposition within another systematic inquiry. In Position II, P cannot be an answer in any systematic inquiry, and therefore cannot be a relative presupposition in any systematic inquiry.

In so far as Collingwood adduces examples of presuppositions which may be relative in one systematic inquiry and absolute in another, he seems to embrace Position I. He suggests that the principle of the conservation of energy was a relative presupposition of the scientists of Kant's time, for example. (It was an 'assistant' to the principle of conservation of matter). In the nineteenth century the principle of conservation of energy superseded the principle of conservation of matter as an absolute presupposition (*EM*, 264–8).[1]

Since a consequence of Collingwood's theory of meaning is, however, that an absolute presupposition in one systematic inquiry cannot be or mean the same as a relative presupposition in another systematic inquiry, Collingwood is committed to Position II. According to this position no *given* presupposition may be, in turn, relative then absolute.

Collingwood's fusion of his view of absolute presuppositions and his theory of meaning is unfortunate. Unlike Position II, Position I is defensible, independently of Collingwood's theory of meaning. In setting out Position I, I draw a distinction, implicit in Collingwood's treatment, between *objective* relations (inquirer independent) and *phenomenological* relations (inquirer dependent). Collingwood's failure to make this distinction explicit invites objections which can be avoided. I use P. F. Strawson's theory of presupposing to support Collingwood's view that one can suppose certain statements which have no truth value. Some important modifications of Collingwood's notion of absolute presuppositions result. The modified version of absolute presuppositions will be seen to account more adequately for Collingwood's examples of absolute presuppositions than does his original account of such presuppositions. It is to Collingwood's theory of meaning that I now turn.

II

Collingwood states: 'Whether a given proposition is true or false, significant or meaningless, depends upon what question it was meant to answer; and anyone who wishes to know whether a given proposition is true or false, significant or meaningless, must find out what question it was meant to answer' (*A*, 39). Collingwood holds to a dual thesis of meaning in which (a) the meaning and truth of a proposition depend upon the question which the

---

[1] For another example of this kind see Collingwood's discussion of Locke's system of politics (*EM*, 97–9).

proposition answers, and (b) the meaning and truth of a proposition cannot be known without recourse to the question which the proposition answers (*A*, 30, 33). If one successfully disambiguates, in Collingwood's view, one must make overt or covert reference to appropriate questions. Collingwood's thesis is a logical one. To refute his claim it is not sufficient to show that some people do not (or think they do not) in fact refer to appropriate questions when disambiguating, for Collingwood might insist that all disambiguation without overt question-reference is *logically reducible* to disambiguation by question-reference.

According to Collingwood, propositions *P* and not-*P* are contradictory only if they answer the same question (*A*, 41). If *P* and not-*P* answer different questions, '*P*' would not be univocal and no contradiction would obtain. If Collingwood means that for any contradiction there exists *some* question answerable by each of the terms of the contradiction, then his position is trivially true. Both '*P*' and 'not-*P*' answer 'Is it the case that *P*?' But if Collingwood's position is the non-trivial view that for any contradiction all questions answerable by one term of the contradiction are answerable by the other term, then Collingwood's position is false. Surely the statements 'Thomas Hobbes wrote *Leviathan*', and 'Thomas Hobbes did not write *Leviathan*' are contradictory. While the first statement answers the question, 'Who wrote *Leviathan*?' the second statement answers the question, 'What did Thomas Hobbes not write?' The questions are non-identical, yet the statements are contradictory. To make good his theory of meaning, Collingwood would have to provide criteria for sameness of questions, according to which the above questions could be shown to be identical after all. Collingwood has failed to do so. Furthermore, to establish the claim that the terms of a contradiction *necessarily* answer a given question, it is not sufficient to show that, for every contradiction, there is some such question. That for every contradiction, there might be some such question, could be a gratuitous rather than a necessary condition. Collingwood has not shown this condition to be necessary.

Collingwood contends that no two presuppositions have the same meaning unless they have identical presuppositions. In order to establish sameness of meaning of two relative presuppositions, he would have to provide an account of how the meaning of absolute presuppositions is to be identified. Such an account must differ from that according to which the meaning of relative presuppositions is identified, for the identification of meaning of absolute presuppositions cannot be by question-reference.[1] Collingwood fails to provide such an account. He offers no account of how absolute presuppositions derive meaning. Nor does he provide criteria for sameness of absolute presuppositions, criteria necessary for establishing sameness of meaning of two relative presuppositions.

Since in Collingwood's theory of meaning sameness of meaning of two presuppositions depends upon both answering the same question, no relative presupposition could mean the same as an absolute presupposition. Collingwood provides no account of how absolute presuppositions derive meaning independent of how relative presuppositions derive meaning. He therefore has no grounds for asserting that a given presupposition P may be in turn absolute then relative.

For an apparently contradictory pair of statements, where the respective sets of presuppositions are thought to be identical, an uninvestigated level of presuppositions may exist. Without satisfactory criteria for identifying absolute presuppositions and sameness of absolute presuppositions, one cannot know that all levels of presuppositions of a given statement have been exhausted. Thus, in Collingwood's account, one never has assurance that a pair of statements is contradictory. Correspondingly, since the meaning of a question depends upon the meaning of its presuppositions, one never has assurance that a pair of questions has the same meaning.

[1] In *IH* Collingwood says that the historian discerns the thoughts of historical agents by rethinking those thoughts in his own mind. Yet, according to Collingwood's theory of meaning one could have the same thoughts as another person only if the first person presupposed all the second person's relevant presuppositions, including the second person's absolute presuppositions. Lacking adequate criteria for identification of absolute presuppositions, one could not know that an historian had successfully rethought the thoughts of an historical agent. Collingwood compounds the problem by maintaining that no person can be aware of his own absolute presuppositions.

Since, for Collingwood, relative presuppositions have truth-value and absolute presuppositions have not, questions of verification and truth can be asked intelligibly only about relative presuppositions. To pose questions about verification or truth of absolute presuppositions is to mistake absolute presuppositions for relative presuppositions; it is to engage in what Collingwood calls 'pseudo-metaphysics' (EM, 162–3). Whereas questions of verification and truth of relative presuppositions admit of alternative answers, questions of verification and truth of absolute presuppositions do not (A, 37–40; EM, 31–2).

One might be tempted to identify a presupposition as absolute by asking an evidential or a truth question about it. If the presupposition were absolute, such questions would be 'bogus'. If such questions were non-bogus, one presumably would have a relative presupposition. While Collingwood does term bogus those questions of evidence or truth which do not admit of alternative answers, he fails to outline what it is for a question to admit of alternative answers. He neither shows that some questions of evidence or truth do not admit of alternative answers, nor does he clearly indicate what is bogus about 'bogus' questions. Collingwood has not given a sufficient criterion for identifying bogus questions. Absolute presuppositions also would not be the only entities about which questions of evidence or truth are inappropriately asked, and Collingwood does not distinguish absolute presuppositions from those other entities.

Collingwood holds that one cannot be aware of one's own absolute presuppositions. 'If people became aware that in certain contexts they were in the habit of treating this or that presupposition as an absolute one, they would be unable to go on doing it.' (EM, 96). He also maintains (without satisfactory argument) that awareness of presuppositions is necessary for rational choice between them. Thus rational choice between absolute presuppositions is impossible.

Since absolute presuppositions are culturally inherited and not acquired through argument, in Collingwood's view, to argue the acceptability of absolute presuppositions is to engage in 'pseudo-metaphysics.'[1] Actually, he seems to have been of two minds regarding justification of absolute presuppositions. Eschewing justification as to truth, he does admit 'pragmatic' justification. He states:

... The principle that natural science is essentially an applied mathematics is ... by no means an indispensable presupposition for any science of nature. A presupposition it certainly is, and an absolute presupposition. It could not possibly be learnt from experience or justified by research. The only sense in which it can be justified by research is the pragmatic sense. You can say, and rightly, 'see what noble results have come from its being accepted for the last three hundred years!' One must surely admit that it works; and that is sufficient justification ...(*EM*, 254).

The 'pragmatic justification' is inconsistent with Collingwood's explicit thesis. It is consistent, however, with Position I.

According to Collingwood, the metaphysician's job is to uncover the absolute presuppositions of previous thinkers; the metaphysician's job is historical. A metaphysical claim should be read as introduced by the 'metaphysical rubric,' namely, 'so and so absolutely presupposed such and such'. A 'metaphysical' statement not introduced by this rubric is a piece of 'pseudo-metaphysics'.

By requiring the metaphysical rubric for *all* metaphysical statements, stated and unstated, Collingwood eliminates the possibility of non-historical metaphysical statements; no 'pseudo-metaphysics' would exist. Yet if no 'pseudo-metaphysical' statements existed there would be no person of whom it would be true that he absolutely presupposed such and such. Thus, not only would 'pseudo-metaphysics' be bankrupt, Collingwoodian historical-metaphysics would be bankrupt as well.

I have indicated why Collingwood's theory of meaning fails. Let us examine what in his theory of presupposing survives.

III

Question Q, 'Have you stopped beating your wife?' presupposes P 'You used to beat your wife.' Collingwood suggests that while

[1] Curiously, Collingwood's non-awareness condition exempts one from the need to produce criteria for *identifying* absolute presuppositions. If one consciously produced a presupposition which was itself absolute (rather than an historical report of someone else's absolute presuppositions—which would be a relative presupposition), one would violate the non-awareness condition.

one may mouth the sounds or write the inscriptions of a question without supposing the presupposition(s) of the question, one cannot ask a *real* question unless one supposes the presupposition(s) of the question. Collingwood views the supposing condition as necessary (though not sufficient) for a question to arise.[1]

If a question does not presuppose a particular presupposition, it does not arise from that presupposition. Thus, if a question arises uniquely from a particular set of presuppositions, any further presuppositions would be irrelevant, or non-essential, with respect to the question's arising, and would not be a presupposition of that question.

Collingwood states:

... the logical efficacy of a supposition does not depend upon the truth of what is supposed, or even upon its being thought true, but only on its being supposed ... the process from question to question does not depend on each question's being answered truly, but only on its being answered: and not upon the questioner's thinking the answer true, but only on his accepting the answers given him, or 'assuming them for the sake of the argument' (*EM*, 39).

For a question to arise it makes no difference, according to Collingwood, whether its presupposition(s) is true. For the question 'Have you stopped beating your wife?' to arise, the inquirer is committed only to supposing an affirmative answer to the question 'Used you to beat your wife?' One might argue, in opposition to Collingwood's view, that the logical efficacy of a presupposition depends upon the truth of the presupposition and that presuppositions are deducible (hence, have truth value) from statements which assert that a given question arises. 'Question Q arises' implies, however, not the presupposition(s) of Q but rather 'the presupposition(s) of Q is supposed'. Collingwood could maintain, consistently, that the truth of a presupposition is non-essential with respect to the logical efficacy of the presupposition.

[1] While the supposing condition is a necessary but not sufficient condition for a question to arise, in the following discussion a question will be said to 'arise' if the supposing condition is fulfilled. It will be assumed that the other conditions required jointly to form a class of sufficient conditions are fulfilled. Those further conditions are not of central concern in this discussion.

Collingwood holds absolute presuppositions to be logically efficacious but not truth-valued. Consequently, he is committed to the claim, stronger even than the claim cited above, that the logical efficacy of a presupposition does not depend upon the presupposition's having any truth value. One should be able, in this view, to suppose something having no truth value. Now Collingwood suggests that when one supposes something he supposes it to be true (*EM*, 165–7; CRC,[1] Letter I, p. 6). Yet, if 'suppose' is elliptical for 'suppose to be true', one wonders how absolute presuppositions can be supposed at all. One cannot suppose to be true something to which truth-value predicates cannot attach.

If the distinction between absolute and relative presuppositions outlined under Postion II at the outset of this essay is to be retained, and if absolute presuppositions can be supposed, then either (1) one must introduce a sense of 'suppose' not elliptical for 'suppose to be true', or (2) one must agree that one may suppose to be true an absolute presupposition which can have no truth value. I have set out Collingwood's grounds for rejecting (1) along with my objections to (1). Regarding (2), recall Collingwood's argument in support of the claim that no questions of evidence or truth can appropriately be asked of absolute presuppositions. He argued that, since absolute presuppositions are neither true nor false, it is nonsensical to ask whether an absolute presupposition is true or false, or whether there is evidence for or against the truth of an absolute presupposition. The claim that one cannot suppose absolute presuppositions to be true does not necessarily follow, however, from the claim that questions of evidence or of truth are inappropriately put of absolute presupposition.[2] It remains that

---

[1] R. G. Collingwood—Gilbert Ryle Correspondence, unpublished typescript. Bodleian Library, Oxford.

[2] Collingwood gives the general impression of subscribing to the view that absolute presuppositions are not truth-valued or verifiable *in order* to ensure his claim that questions of evidence or of truth are inappropriately put of absolute presuppositions. By adopting this posture the fruitful question did not arise for Collingwood, 'What conditions make questions of evidence or of truth inappropriately put of some possibly truth-valued entities?' Collingwood did see that there are statements fundamental in systematic inquiries of which questions of evidence or of truth are inappropriately put in certain contexts. He pursued a mistaken path of analysis, however.

one cannot suppose to be true something to which truth-value predicates cannot attach.

If, as Collingwood seems to hold, the logical efficacy relation is the same both for absolute and relative presuppositions and for their respective questions, and if logical efficacy depends upon one's supposal of presuppositions, Collingwood must alter his view that one cannot suppose an absolute presupposition to be true. Since (1) and (2) are unacceptable, we may modify the contention that absolute presuppositions can have no truth value. Such a modification is captured by Position I outlined at the outset of this essay. According to Position I as expanded in the following discussion, the logical efficacy relation is the same for both absolute and relative presuppositions and their respective questions; the logical efficacy relation depends upon the supposal of truth of such presuppositions. Position I withstands the rejection of Collingwood's theory of meaning.

IV

Collingwood states: 'The answer to any question presupposes whatever the question presupposes' (*EM*, 63). For response *R* to be an answer to question *Q*, it is necessary that (i) *Q* be not presuppositionless, (ii) *R* be not presuppositionless, and (iii) *R* presuppose what *Q* presupposes. Accordingly, no response which contests the presupposition(s) of a question can be an answer to that question. An answer to *Q* implies the presupposition(s) of *Q*, but the presupposition(s) does not imply the answer.

The presupposition 'That line was put up for some purpose' gives rise to the question 'For what purpose was that line put up?' (*EM*, 21). To give an answer such as '. . . to hang clothes on' is to accept the question as one which arises. A questioner or respondent for whom the question is appropriate, that is, for whom the question arises, is committed to supposing the presupposition(s) of the question.

A distinction implicit in Collingwood's treatment should be made between a question's arising from presuppositions which are true regardless of an inquirer's attitudes, and a question's arising from presuppositions as supposed to be true by an inquirer regardless of the truth-value of the presuppositions. We may designate the first case as 'objective' logical efficacy (or 'O-efficacy') and the second case as 'phenomenological' logical efficacy (or 'P-efficacy').

Collingwood's view of logical efficacy is phenomenological in the sense that the logical efficacy of a presupposition depends not upon the presupposition's being true, but upon its being supposed. In this sense questions arise *for* inquirers. One must distinguish objective from phenomenological relations in order to make Collingwood's theory of presupposing arguable, for that theory is not articulable exclusively in terms of objective relations.

A revised account may be offered in accordance with the objective–phenomenological distinction. A given question may O-arise (or its presupposition(s) is O-efficacious), (i) if its presupposition(s) is (are) truth-valued, and (ii) if its presupposition(s) is(are) true. A given question may P-arise (or its presupposition(s) is(are) P-efficacious), (i) if its presupposition(s) is(are) either truth-valued or contingently non-truth-valued, and (ii) if Inquirer I supposes the presupposition(s) of the question to be true.[1] If the presupposition(s) of a given question is(are) true and is supposed by Inquirer I to be true, the question may P-arise and O-arise. If the presupposition(s) of the question is(are) supposed by Inquirer I to be true but is(are) not true, i.e. false or contingently non-truth-valued (a notion developed later in this section), the question may P-arise but not O-arise. If the presupposition(s) of the question is(are) true but is not supposed by Inquirer I to be true, the question may O-arise but not P-arise. And, if the presupposition(s) of the question is(are) neither true nor supposed by Inquirer I to be true, the question neither O-arises nor P-arises.

Let us distinguish between conditions necessary for a response R to be an objective answer (or 'O-answer'), and conditions necessary for response R to be a phenomenological answer (or 'P-answer'). For R to be an O-answer, (i) question Q must not be presuppositionless, (ii) R must not be presuppositionless, (iii)

[1] As mentioned previously, I am concerned with conditions necessary for P-efficacy and O-efficacy. No attempt is made to specify the further conditions which form a class of jointly sufficient conditions for a question to P-arise and for a question to O-arise. It is assumed in this essay that such further conditions obtain.

R must presuppose what Q presupposes, and (iv) the presuppositions of Q and R must be true. For R to be a P-answer, (i) Q must not be presuppositionless, (ii) R must not be presuppositionless, (iii) R must presuppose what Q presupposes, and (iv) Inquirer I must suppose to be true the presuppositions common to Q and R.[1] Whereas an O-answer entails the presupposition(s) of the question it answers, the presupposition(s) of the question does not entail the answers. The fact that R is a P-answer entails one's supposal of the presupposition(s) of the question which R P-answers. Of course, that one supposes the presupposition(s) of a question does not entail an answer.

One might wish to argue that P-relations are reducible to conditional statements about O-relations. In that view, to say that a presupposition P-gives rise to Q but does not O-give rise to Q is to say nothing more than that the presupposition, if true, would O-give rise to Q. However, the truth of the presupposition(s) does not bear upon whether Q P-arises. Conditions fulfilled in a given case may be sufficient for P-relations to obtain, but they might not be sufficient for O-relations to obtain. Thus, P-relations are not reducible to O-relations.

According to our revised account, one can suppose only true presuppositions, false presuppositions, or contingently non-truth-valued presuppositions. A statement is contingently non-truth-valued if its presupposition(s) is false and if logically realizable conditions are specifiable which would render its presupposition(s) true. Certain features of P. F. Strawson's view of presupposing are useful for developing the notion of 'contingently non-truth-valued statement' and for furnishing a basis for making a Collingwoodian position arguable.

---

[1] One might object that these conditions do not hold for all questions and responses, and one might cite as an example, Q: 'Does something exist?' R: 'Something exists.' While Q appears to be presuppositionless, one is inclined to regard R as an answer. It should be kept in mind, however, that in offering an account of questions and answers as they function in systematic inquiries, Collingwood is not offering a completely general theory of questions and answers. The above sort of question and response might be regarded by Collingwood as 'extra-systematic' or 'pre-systematic' rather than as constitutive of a systematic inquiry.

Strawson maintains that a statement S presupposes S^1 if 'the truth of S^1 is a precondition of the truth-or-falsity of S.'[1] If it is true that Jones was in the habit of beating his wife, then 'Jones stopped beating his wife' is truth-valued. If Jones was not in the habit of beating his wife, then 'Jones stopped beating his wife' would not be truth-valued. The truth-valuedness of an ostensible statement depends not upon the suppositions or beliefs of the inquirer but upon the truth of the presupposition(s) of the ostensible statement.

If one of the presuppositions of a statement is contingently false, the statement is contingently non-truth-valued. Where 'Jones has been in the habit of beating his wife' is false 'Jones stopped beating his wife' is contingently non-truth-valued. A statement also is contingently non-truth-valued where one of its presuppositions is contingently non-truth-valued. In such a case, one presupposition of the presupposition would be contingently false. For example, if 'Jones is married' is false, then the presupposition 'Jones has been in the habit of beating his wife' is non-truth-valued, and 'Jones stopped beating his wife' is contingently non-truth valued.

While an inquirer would be mistaken in believing that a particular statement which presupposed a false presupposition is truth-valued, the statement nonetheless might be sensible for him. Strawson remarks, as follows, about the case where John has no children:

> Of course, the sentence 'All John's children are asleep' is not meaningless. [Rather] it is perfectly significant . . . to say that the man who uses the sentence in our imagined case fails to say anything either true or false, is not to say that the sentence he pronounces is meaningless. Nor is it to deny that he makes a mistake. Of course, it is incorrect (or deceitful) for him to use this sentence unless (a) he thinks he is referring to some children whom he thinks to be asleep; (b) he thinks that John has children; (c) he thinks that the children he is referring to are John's. We might say that in using the sentence he *commits himself* to the existence of children of John's.[2]

[1] P. F. Strawson, *Introduction to Logical Theory* (London, 1952), p. 175. My concern in this essay is to render the Collingwoodian position arguable, not to argue the relative merits of Strawson's and Russell's views on presupposing.

[2] Strawson, op. cit., pp. 174–5.

'Are John's children still watching television?' presupposes 'John's children were watching television.' Although that presupposition may be either false (John's children were not watching television) or not truth-valued (John has no children at all), an inquirer still might suppose the presupposition. Thus, the question would *P*-arise for the inquirer who supposes 'John's children were watching television.' Strawson's observations about commitment to presuppositions by virtue of using certain sentences parallels commitment to presuppositions by virtue of counting certain questions as appropriate. It is irrelevant to that to which the inquirer is committed whether or not his sentence really is truth-valued, or whether or not his question really is appropriate.

Position I now may be stated in its modified form:

(i) *Q O*-arises only if presupposition *P* is true;
(ii) response *R* is an *O*-answer of *Q* only if *R* presupposes *P*, *Q* presupposes *P*, and *P* is true;
(iii) all *O*-answers are truth-valued;
(iv) *Q P*-arises for Inquirer *I* only if Inquirer *I* supposes presupposition *P* to be true, and *Q* presupposes *P*;
(v) for Inquirer *I* to suppose *P*, *P* must be truth-valued or contingently non-truth-valued;
(vi) response *R* is a *P*-answer of *Q* for Inquirer *I* only if *R* presupposes *P*, *Q* presupposes *P*, and Inquirer *I* supposes *P* to be true;
(vii) all *P*-answers are either truth-valued or contingently non-truth-valued;
(viii) where *P* is false, any answer of *Q* is non-truth-valued;
(ix) not all *P* answers are *O*-answers;
(x) not all *O*-answers are *P*-answers.

In Position II absolute presuppositions are neither true nor false nor can they be contingently non-truth valued, for absolute presuppositions are presuppositionless in this position. Thus, in Position II absolute presuppositions can be neither *O*-efficacious (for they cannot be true) nor *P*-efficacious (for they cannot be supposed). Modified Position I allows that absolute presuppositions be both non-truth-valued and capable of being supposed; modified Position I allows that absolute presuppositions be *P*-

efficacious. Furthermore, modified Position I allows that a *given* presupposition under certain circumstances could have truth-value and under other circumstances not.

Modified Position I, while side-stepping many difficulties in Position II, might appear to be un-Collingwoodian. Yet, modified Position I in fact accounts more adequately than Position II for Collingwood's own examples of absolute presuppositions.

V

Collingwood holds that an answer to a question presupposes what the question presupposes. Thus, an answer must presuppose something. If a presupposition presupposed something, there would be no reason that it could not be truth-valued and answer a question. Absolute presuppositions themselves must be pre-suppositionless; otherwise they could answer questions. Most of Collingwood's examples of absolute presuppositions are not presuppositionless, however.

As an example of an absolute presupposition Collingwood cites the Newtonian principle of continuity, the principle that 'between any two terms in a series, however close they are, there is always a third term' (*EM*, 258). This principle presupposes, at least, 'There are series of two terms', in the same way that 'All John's children are asleep' presupposes 'John has children.'[1] If the presupposition were false, the question would not *O*-arise as to whether all series of two terms always have a third term. If the presupposition were not made, the question would not *P*-arise. The important point is that the principle of continuity is not presuppositionless and may be an answer to some question. To be sure, one may begin his inquiry by supposing the principle of continuity and one may treat the principle as a fundamental presupposition of the inquiry. But such a procedure does not render the principle an absolute presupposition as characterized by Position II.

[1] Put in its conditional form, the principle itself does not imply the existential statement. To offer the principle in a systematic inquiry without affirming the existential statement would be pointless, however. It is in this Collingwoodian sense of presupposing that this and the following examples are said not to be presuppositionless.

Indeed the principle of continuity, considered fundamental to the Newtonian inquiry, has been challenged partly by the eigenvalue consequences of Schrödinger's wave equation, according to which some two-termed series have no third term; that is, some series are discontinuous. If Collingwood maintained that the principle of continuity could not be truth-valued, he would have to deny logical inconsistency between the principle and the consequence of the wave-equation, a position which clearly is untenable.

As another example of an absolute presupposition Collingwood cites the 'Kantian' principle of the indestructibility of substance (or the 'conservation of matter'). According to that principle, for any change in substance there is a corresponding change in substance; substance cannot be destroyed. As was the case in the preceding example, the principle is not presuppositionless; it presupposes that there is such a thing as substance, or that there are substantial things. Without such a presupposition, question concerning the consequences of changes in substance would not arise. Thus, the principle may be truth-valued.[1]

Collingwood cites the principle of reciprocity, expressed in Newton's theory of gravitation, as the principle that 'every body attracts every other body with a force varying directly as the product of their masses and inversely as the square of their distance' (*EM*, 270). He identifies the principle of reciprocity as one of Kant's list of absolute presuppositions of natural science. That principle presupposes, however, that there are entities which function in the way specified by the principle. Only if one supposes that there are bodies can a question arise about the relation between them. The principle of reciprocity is an answer to the

---

[1] One might ask whether the principle of conservation of energy implies the old principle of the indestructibility of substance where substance is definable in terms of energy. When 'substance' is defined in terms of 'energy', the meaning of the original concept of substance is shifted. Thus, the 'substance' accounted for by the principle of the conservation of energy is not the same as that mentioned in the original principle of indestructibility of substance. We are left with the vexing problem of whether theories employing different sets of concepts justifiably can purport to be about the same phenomena. Are such theories commensurable? If they are not, we are faced with a hopeless (though fascinating) relativism.

question about the sort of relation obtaining between such bodies. Collingwood himself suggests that the principle presupposes that the relation between two bodies is expressible in terms of *force*. Deferring to Sir Arthur Eddington, Collingwood points out that the concept of *force* now is obsolete. The presupposition of the principle is held not to be true and so the principle has been abandoned. Collingwood thus accounts historically for the rejection of a presupposition of the principle which, according to Position II, ought not to be there at all.

As a further absolute presupposition of Kant, Collingwood points to the principle that the language of natural science is (non-statistical) mathematics. This principle, with roots in the Pythagorean–Platonist tradition, clearly presupposes that there is such a thing as a world of nature which is expressible in a certain (non-statistical) 'language'. The question, 'In what (non-statistical) language is the world of nature expressible?', arises once one affirms the presupposition; the principle is a possible answer to that question. Collingwood acknowledges the presence of the presupposition, and even offers a partial historical account for the rejection of the principle in terms of rejection of the presuppositions of the principle. He concludes that the principle is doomed by the view that the laws of nature are statistical laws obeyed by the average of numbers of bodies rather than by single bodies. Thus, the principle fails to meet the requirement of Position II that absolute presuppositions be presuppositionless.[1]

Collingwood holds the 'Kantian' idea of causation to be only a historical report by Kant about what scientists of his time absolutely presupposed. They presupposed a 'constellation' of absolute presuppositions, 'that a cause and its effect are related by a necessary

---

[1] Collingwood maintains that 'God exists' and 'Nature is monomorphic' are absolute presuppositions of modern science (*EM*, 232, 206). He is unclear about both the exact meaning of these presuppositions and the relation between them. His discussion of polytheistic and monotheistic science leads one to interpret Collingwood's 'God exists' as 'Nature exists.' In that interpretation the relation between 'God exists' and 'Nature is monomorphic' is that the second presupposes the first. In such a case, 'Nature is monomorphic' presupposes 'God exists' (or 'Nature exists') and hence the former cannot be an absolute presupposition. (See *EM*, ch. XX, and 187 ff.)

connexion, and that a cause and its effect are related by way of temporal sequence' (*EM*, 332). Clearly, neither part of the above conjunctive statement is presuppositionless; both presuppose that there is such a thing as a causal nexus with distinctly characterizable relations.[1] Thus the 'Kantian' absolute presupposition may answer the question, 'What sort of relation obtains between cause and effect?' Collingwood maintains that the two 'elements' of the constellation are subject to 'strain' because they are mutually incompatible. His reasons for believing in the incompatibility of the two elements are not compelling. Still, in view of Position II, Collingwood is confronted with the problem of characterizing the nature of the incompatibility. Such incompatibility cannot be characterized as a relation between possibly truth-valued entities. Collingwood's solution is to suggest that incompatible absolute presuppositions are 'non-consupponible', but he fails to indicate precisely in what this relation consists. If Collingwood were to abandon Position II for Position I, the appeal to such a mysterious relation would be unnecessary. If the presuppositions of the elements were true, one then could analyse strain as a logical relation between truth-valued entities. For those cases where the presuppositions are false, the elements might be treated in the following way, as Strawson suggests:

Sentence S_1 is the contradictory of sentence S_2 if and only if, necessarily, in any context in which S_1 expressed a true proposition S_2 would express a false proposition, and conversely. This relation would then hold between *sentences* irrespective of whether, in a given context, either sentence expressed a proposition or not. Of course as it stands, for familiar reasons, the definition is only satisfactory for sentences capable of expressing *contingent* propositions.[2]

Collingwood adduces no presuppositionless example of an absolute presupposition. Moreover, no example fulfils the characterization of absolute presuppositions required by Position II.

---

[1] This point also holds good for the 'Newtonian' absolute presupposition, 'Some events have causes.' The 'Einsteinian' absolute presupposition, 'No events have causes', presupposes the existence of events. Collingwood reports that in the Einsteinian view it is laws rather than causes which account for change in such events.

[2] P. F. Strawson, in a letter to me of 3 July 1970.

All Collingwood's examples presuppose existential statements. This might suggest that, ultimately, Collingwoodian absolute presuppositions are ontological commitments, and that one's systematic inquiries vary with one's ontology.

For what reasons are certain presuppositions regarded as fundamental? Why do changes in absolute presuppositions occur? Those tantalizing questions may admit of rational answers only if—as the proposed modifications suggest—the logical character of a given presupposition does not vary as the presupposition appears 'absolutely' or 'relatively' in different systematic inquiries. Any position which decries answering those questions by reference to objective reasons is an embarrassment to the rationalist historian of ideas.

XII

COLLINGWOOD ON THE CONSTITUTION OF THE HISTORICAL PAST

LEON J. GOLDSTEIN

I

ONE OF the pervasive features of Collingwood scholarship, particularly as concerns the interpretation of his philosophy of history, is the virtually unanimous refusal of his critics and commentators to approach his view on his own terms. Thus, almost no effort is made to place *The Idea of History* in its own proper context, the two main elements of which are Collingwood's work as historian and his philosophical preoccupation with what he had been doing as historian. The overwhelming interest of present-day philosophy of history, at least in the English-speaking philosophical world, is with the nature of historical explanation, and it is clear enough that most writers who discuss Collingwood on history purport to present, modify, or criticize his conception of that. Almost no one, I am sure, doubts for a moment that the well-known dictum about the historian rethinking or re-enacting past thought is intended as a contribution to a theory of historical explanation. Unfortunate for this interpretation—shared both by hostile and friendly critics alike—is that there are two sorts of evidence that may be cited against it: the actual language of *The Idea of History* and the actual practice of 'Roman Britain'.[1] In addition, the usual view would be entirely inconsistent with Collingwood's conception of human action. Thus, he says: 'Since history proper is the history of thought there are no mere "events"

[1] Collingwood, 'Roman Britain', in R. G. Collingwood and J. N. L. Myers, *Roman Britain and the English Settlements*, 2nd ed. (Oxford, 1937).

in history: what is miscalled an "event" is really an action, and expresses some thought (intention, purpose) of its agent' (*A*, 127 f.). In *The Idea of History* he says: 'By the outside of the event I mean everything belonging to it which can be described in terms of bodies and their movements.. ... By the inside of the event I mean that in it which can only be described in terms of thought. . . . The historian is *never* concerned with either of these to the exclusion of the other. He is investigating . . . actions, *and an action is the unity of the outside and inside of an event*' (*IH*, 213).[1] But if the usual understanding of Collingwood is correct, he must hold that the two are frequently separated in the historian's work, and that the historian reconstructs outsides of events—understood in a way at which no behaviourist could cavil—which he must then explain by appeal to an inside. In principle, it should be possible for historians to agree about the outside and disagree about which inside explains it adequately. But all this clearly flies in the face of Collingwood's plainly expressed intention. In his view, the two sides of the action are inseparable aspects of it and are not to be treated as different things.

To understand what a philosopher of history who was himself an historian means by his central notions, it seems most reasonable to look for guidance to his own historical writings. There are quite a number of passages in 'Roman Britain' which clearly exemplify the re-enactment of past thought, and I shall be presenting a number of them further along in my discussion. But it will be most instructive, I think, to attend to the character of something Collingwood actually offers as an explanation. I think that some will find it rather surprising. The problem is set by evidence of the decline of villas all over Britain late in the fourth century. There is very little directly to go on, but we do have an account, by a writer named Salvian, of similar difficulties in Gaul, and these are related to a series of peasant revolts. Collingwood thinks that the Gaulish situation is relevant to the problem which confronts him. Thus, he writes:

The underlying cause of these recurring peasant revolts, as expounded by Salvian, was the contrast, not in wealth alone but in security, between

---

[1] Italics added.

rich and poor. The great landowners were favoured by the incidence of taxation, and could pass on their burdens to the poor. The legal and administrative system of the late empire favoured economic tyranny. It was in the power of a rich man to deprive a poor man of all he possessed; and Salvian gives examples where the power was exercised without pity and without appeal. Hence, to the poor, 'the enemy is kinder than the tax-collector'; it needed only the occasion of a barbarian inroad to convert exasperated peasants into Bacaudae[1] and bring into existence wandering bands of broken men, escaped slaves, and despairing debtors.[2]

Thus the situation in Gaul. But what has that to do with Britain? Collingwood proceeds to make the connection:

The same legal and administrative system, the same distinction between rich men in great villas and poor men in village huts, and the same barbarian invasions, were present towards the end of the fourth century in Britain. Causes being identical, it is hardly to be doubted that effects were identical too; and that the wandering bands which Theodosius saw in Britain included large numbers of Bacaudae. But every man who became a Bacauda ceased to be a productive labourer. Consequently the rich estates, in addition to suffering actual plunder and the deprivation of trade, suffered a diminution in their own productive powers.[3]

Here, surely, is an explanation to warm the soul of the most tough-minded covering-law theorist. There is no obvious way in which this explanation rests upon re-thinking thought. Instead, we find reference to social and economic causes of social and political disorganization with particular emphasis upon the explanation of recurrent effects by appeal to recurrent causes. It would, of course, be a mistake to claim Collingwood for nomothetic social science and naturalism. There are too many other things he has said that would preclude that. But here we do have a perfectly tenable historical explanation which is quite clearly unlike what we have been led to expect that such an explanation offered by Collingwood would be like. And I think it provides still another reason to doubt the general view that for him historical explanation is accomplished by rethinking.

[1] The Gaulish term for the peasant rebels.
[2] 'Roman Britain', p. 304.
[3] Ibid., p. 304.

I I

If one turns directly to that part of *The Idea of History* in which the doctrine of rethinking gets its most systematic exposition and reads it without expectations built upon our own interests—particularly our interests in explanation—that anyone should think that it is intended by its proponent as a theory of explanation becomes more surprising still. The section in question, called 'History as Re-enactment of Past Experience', opens with the question: 'How, or on what conditions, can the historian know the past?' And the beginning paragraph ends with the question: 'If then the historian has no direct or empirical knowledge of his facts, and no transmitted or testimoniary knowledge of them, what kind of knowledge has he: in other words, what must the historian do in order that he may know them?' He immediately tells us that his 'historical review of the idea of history has resulted in the emergence of an answer to this question: namely, that the historian must re-enact the past in his own mind'. And he thinks what he has been saying may be easily understood in the following way: 'When a man thinks historically, he has before him certain documents or relics of the past. His business was to discover what the past was which has left these relics behind it . . . . This means discovering the thought . . . expressed by them' (*IH*, 282 f.). It is hard to see how Collingwood could have made his intentions any plainer. Re-enactment of past thought is part—indeed a cental part—of his conception of how the historical past is known or constituted in historical research. It has nothing to do with explanation at all. The point to be kept in mind is that historical events are human actions. Thought, the inside of the action, is an inseparable part of it, and in order to know at all what the action was—a determinate piece of military strategy or the attempt to solve a specific mathematical or philosophical problem—you have to know the thought in terms of which some bit of overt behaviour may be recognized as action.[1] I shall not insist upon this any more at this point other

[1] I venture to predict that any attempt to save the peasant-slave revolt example from exploitation by covering-law theorists by showing that it may be conceived in terms of re-enactment, would, in effect, prove to be dealing with the event being explained and not the explanation. And that would only reinforce my

than to reiterate that what I have quoted makes it clear that Collingwood's own intention was to use the idea of re-enactment in his account of how the historical past is known, not explained. Instead, I shall turn directly to the presentation of some actual examples of re-enactment from Collingwood's 'Roman Britain' in order to show that the purpose he said re-enactment serves is precisely the purpose he tried to make it serve in his own historical writing.

We shall begin by considering what Collingwood has to say about the activity in Britain of the emperor Severus early in the third century. We are told about the restoration of fortifications, campaigns in Scotland which the emperor came to Britain to lead in person, heavy casualties as a result of the successful use of guerilla tactics by the enemy, and so on. After that, we know 'that Severus died, worn out by his labours, at York in 211, and that his sons forthwith broke off the Caledonian war and returned to Rome'.[1] Collingwood now turns to a final summary account of the situation he has been talking about, and it will be helpful simply to quote a bit at length:

It looks like the story of a misguided and wholly unsuccessful war. Yet after its conclusion the British frontier enjoyed unbroken peace for nearly a hundred years. If the war ended in complete failure for Rome, why did the Scottish tribes do nothing to follow up their victory? . . . But it is difficult to say that the second phase of his frontier policy was a failure unless we are first sure what it was meant to achieve. Certainly not the complete conquest of Caledonia; if that had been its aim the elaborate reconstruction of Hadrian's Wall would have been sheer waste. Certainly not the restoration of the Antonine Wall, or he would have got to work on that . . . as soon as he had possession of the ground on which it stood . . . It seems that he did not intend a permanent occupation of any part of Scotland . . . The evidence . . . suggests that his campaigns were meant as wars of devastation, . . . punitive ex-

---

belief that there is nothing about the covering-law thesis that weds it necessarily to behaviourism. Because most covering-law theorists are behaviourists, it is assumed, without argument, that they have to be; cf. A. R. Louch, *Explanation and Human Action* (Berkeley and Los Angeles, 1966), pp, 64, 65, 68, 69, 70, 71, 83, 90 ff., 101. At very least, this ought to be discussed and not settled by tacit agreement.

[1] 'Roman Britain', p. 159.

peditions, visiting the wrath of Rome on enemies outside her grasp but not outside her reach . . .[1]

To some it might appear that having presented an account of what Severus had done, Collingwood was now attempting to explain it by eking out the thought behind it. But this is not the case. The earlier remarks which may seem to describe what Severus did are, in fact, only limited to the event—in the sense we have seen that Collingwood gives to this word—the external husk which is only one aspect of the action in which he was engaged. To be told that Severus sent troops to Britain, had some fortifications restored, and came, finally, to lead the troops himself, is still not to know what Severus did. That, surely, is the point of his saying that 'it is difficult to say that the second phase of his frontier policy was a failure unless we are first sure what it was meant to achieve.' Knowing only the sorts of thing mentioned two sentences ago is not knowing yet what the action upon which Severus was engaged actually was. What Collingwood tries to do in the paragraph from which the above is excerpted is to examine several possibilities in order to determine which of a number of seemingly plausible alternatives could be the right one. In other words, Collingwood is not attempting to explain what Severus did as much as he is seeking to determine what the policy he was pursuing actually was. It is only once that has been established, once, that is, we know what the action we are concerned with happened to be, that we can raise the two obvious subsequent questions: (1) 'Was it successful?' and (2) 'Why was such a policy adopted at all?' The second of these is the explanation stage, and while we may expect that Collingwood would disagree with a good bit that has been said about explanation in history in the last decades, it is clear from the peasant-slave-revolt example discussed earlier that he was open to a wider variety of possible explanations than those believe who think re-enactment of past thought is his conception of explanation. It is, in any event, at the stage of inquiry during which what the historical action was is being determined that re-enactment takes place. What Collingwood does in the material

[1] Ibid., pp. 159 f.

just presented in the long excerpt is attempt to re-enact Severus's thought, to try to see his problems from the vantage-point of his situation and in terms of the alternatives of policy which were open to him, thus to determine what in fact he did. This, of course, requires that Collingwood make use of everything he knows about Roman colonial and military administration at the period in question. Rethinking requires a good deal of preparation,[1] and one cannot expect to rethink the thought of any historical actor without knowing a good bit of what he must have known before determining his own course. To re-enact Severus's thought is to determine what he set out to do; it is not to explain why he set out to do it. The only way to avoid this conclusion, it seems to me, is to take what he did as something to be characterized in behaviouristic terms: a course of behaviour to be explained in terms of its rationale.[2] That is, only if the historical event[3] has already been fully described before we reach the paragraph from which the excerpt was made can the excerpt be taken to explain it. But if the event is fully described before the excerpt, it is fully describable without reference to thought. Whatever merit that view may be thought by some to have, it is not Collingwood's view.

The next instance of re-enactment which we shall consider has to do with the Antonine Wall. It is perhaps worth noting in passing that much of Collingwood's 'Roman Britain' is taken up with such things as walls and fortifications, not because this is particularly to be wondered at in a book about a period so much of our knowledge of which depends upon the survival of remains that can be uncovered by archaeology, but because given what seems to be Collingwood's inordinate emphasis upon rethinking one might expect that intellectual history—construed as broadly as you like—might have been the branch of history that would best exemplify what he takes history to be. If it can be shown that even the treatment of such stuff as archaeology deals with can be treated in accordance with Collingwood's conception of historical method,

[1] It is certainly not the immediate, intuitive grasping that so many critics have imputed to Collingwood.

[2] Cf. William Dray, *Laws and Explanation in History* (Oxford, 1957), ch. 5.

[3] When speaking for myself, I obviously do not feel that there is anything compelling about Collingwood's usage with respect to this word.

then it is clearly the case that his critics have construed Collingwoodian history far too narrowly, and there is no branch of
historical scholarship that Collingwood's view requires us to
abandon.[1]

Having presented a detailed account of Hadrian's Wall and the
frontier-defence system of which it was the key element, Collingwood thinks it 'puzzling to find that by 140, two years after Hadrian
was succeeded by Antoninus Pius, drastic changes were being made
in the British frontier-system'.[2] This is revealed by the character
of a new wall built in Antoninus's reign. Like the wall of Hadrian
it was continuous, stretching from sea to sea, but it was remarkably
different from the earlier wall in a number of ways, having a
'simpler design and less elaborate structure'.[3] Collingwood goes
on to detail the ways in which the Antonine Wall appears to be
inferior to its predecessor—absence of milecastles and turrets,
small size of the forts, and such like—but we need not be concerned
with the details of his account. I take it that Collingwood is trying
to answer the question, 'What was Antoninus doing here?'—trying
to determine what it is that this thing being examined is—and at
this point we get at least a partial answer: 'Evidently, then, the
forts of the Antonine Wall were not meant to be occupied each
by a complete regiment'.[4] To this extent, at least, he was doing
something different from what Hadrian had done. Hadrian had
built a wall with fortifications that could be manned by larger
units than those Antoninus seems to have had in mind. We shall
come back to this question and its answer in just a moment.
Having reached his initial conclusions about the nature of the units
for which the fortifications were designed, Collingwood turns to
what he takes to be evidence of economy in the construction.
Presumably, the size of the forts is also evidence of economy,

[1] Which is entirely what one expects when one realizes that Collingwood's is
a theory about what the discipline of history is and how it carries out its work;
it does not purport to say what historians ought to do, other, of course, than to
say that they ought to do historical work to the best of their ability. See my
'Collingwood's Theory of Historical Knowing', *History and Theory*, ix (1970),
pp. 3–36.
[2] 'Roman Britain', p. 140.
[3] Ibid.
[4] Ibid., p. 141.

but in addition the choice of materials—'the rampart itself, instead of stone, is made of turf in the western and central part, of clay in the eastern' and 'the official central buildings in the forts were not uniformly of stone, and the barracks were of the cheapest, wooden hutments which in some cases had thatched roofs'[1]—underscores this still more. Summing up his conclusions about the Antonine Wall, Collingwood says the following:

Both in construction and in organization, then, the Antonine Wall bears the marks of a deliberate effort after cheapness, at the cost of a serious decrease in efficiency. The same thing is to be seen if we consider its strategic position. Both its flanks, especially the left, lie unprotected upon narrow estuaries, easily crossed by the smallest craft in almost any weather. If we recollect the care with which Hadrian . . . fortified the whole of the northwest Cumberland coast for thirty or forty miles beyond the terminus of the Wall, the complete absence of Roman posts on the Clyde below Old Kilpatrick becomes so striking that we cannot put it down to negligence. These various features of the Antonine Wall when considered together, seem less like a series of oversights than parts of a deliberate policy, based on the assumption that a powerful frontier-work on that line was not needed. [2]

This conclusion is reinforced by comparing the wall we have been discussing with the same emperor's fortifications made only five years later in Germany, where, presumably, stronger defence was deemed necessary.

At first appearance, what Antoninus did seems obvious: he built a wall. That thing there which presents itself to the sight of the archaeologist is what was done in the second century, and historians of the period must explain it. But I very much doubt that this is Collingwood's view. That thing there is just something inert, and just seeing it there does not tell us what it is. To be sure, we recognize it as a wall or a fortification, but without wishing to raise all manner of issues tangential to our present interest, I would suggest that so to identify it as a member of a class is not to know what it is as a particular historical construction. Even to know that it was built during the reign and, presumably upon the instruction

[1] Ibid., p. 142.
[2] Ibid., pp. 142 f.

of Antoninus Pius is not really to know what it is. What, after all, does the statement, 'That is the Antonine Wall', tell us about the object it designates? To know what it is as something historical is to know what purpose it served, what thoughts—policies—it embodies. Short of that, one really does not know what that thing stretched across Scotland from sea to sea is. One might look at the thing and say: 'There is Antoninus's Wall; note the shabbiness of its construction. Standards had certainly declined since Hadrian's day.' Or, 'Notice the cheapness of that wall's construction; Antoninus was certainly not as munificent as Hadrian.' But neither of these would be right if Collingwood's re-enactment of the thought of which the wall is an expression is correct. For this is not just a wall; a cheap wall; a shabby wall. It is a wall erected as part of a certain policy which is based upon some determinate assumptions. To call it inferior to Hadrian's presumes that Hadrian's is a standard in terms of which such walls are to be judged. But that is not Collingwood's view. Collingwood thinks that the adequacy of the wall is not to be judged in terms of its semblance to some standard wall, but, rather, as to whether or not it is adequate to the policy it is intended to help carry out. Without that policy—which Collingwood expects that his re-enactment has brought out—we simply do not know what confronts us at the site of the wall, other than merely the member of a class. The answer to the aforementioned question, 'What was Antoninus doing here?' turns out not to be 'Building a wall', to which we then respond 'Why?' It turns out, rather, to be carrying out a certain defensive policy, on the basis of these and those assumptions, requiring, *inter alia,* the construction of a wall having certain minimal characteristics, and so on.

All this is established by means of the re-enactment of thought—together, of course, with evidence, the wall itself, to be sure, but all manner of other sources about Roman administrative and military policy. As I understand Collingwood, thus far we have been learning what happened, but not why. That is, Collingwood has been constituting a past historical event, but he has not yet attempted to explain it. This conception of what he was about is somewhat strengthened by his own words. After presenting the

outcome of his re-enactment of the thought involved in the decision to build the wall and making the brief comparison, mentioned
above, of the Antonine Wall with the frontier-line constructed by
Antoninus in Germany, he adds the following: 'It is evident, then,
that the new features of the Antonine Wall are not due to any
general cause, such as a cheeseparing policy on the part of Antoninus
Pius, or a decline in the efficiency of Roman military engineering,
or a less exacting conception of what was demanded in frontier-
works. Their explanation must be sought in conditions peculiar to
Britain.'[1] The last sentence makes it clear that Collingwood does
not yet consider himself to have offered an explanation for the
event he has been presenting. In the pages which follow, he attempts
to do that. He goes back to the situation in Hadrian's day, traces
the development of the frontier situation and brings the matter
up-to-date, as that would be in Antoninus's time. To some extent
there is repetition in that certain of the elements which entered into
Antoninus's thought must now appear as elements which affected
that thought: Antoninus, obviously, had to consider the situation
in terms of its actual features. I cannot offer a detailed account of
Collingwood's explanation, and I do not wish to decide at all as
to whether there is a consistent carrying out of the distinction
between constitution and explanation in Collingwood's text.
But I do believe that on the whole, the material preceding the
passage I have just quoted is generally taken up with the task of
determining what happened by use of the historian's technique of
re-enacting past thought, and that the material which follows the
passage is for the most part taken up with explaining why it
happened by dealing with the circumstances which Antoninus
and his advisers must have taken in account, that is, with the
circumstances which must have conditioned[2] their thinking to
begin with.

We have so far discussed two kinds of historical reconstruction,
one involving a military campaign and the other an artifact, and
I should like to present one more, an example of strategy. I do not

---

[1] 'Roman Britain', p. 143.
[2] I do not mean by this 'caused' or any other term or notion which suggests
that thought and thinking are not taken seriously on their own terms.

wish to argue that strategy is something distinct from a campaign. I think it is, but there is nothing to be gained here from an attempt to distinguish conceptually between them. Anyone who does not sense or feel that there is a distinction here will simply conclude that I have offered two examples of the same sort. The main value I should think, of adding still another example of whatever sort is to reinforce the claim that re-enactment functions in Collingwood's history in the way I have been saying. It would be interesting, given the historical importance of Julius Caesar, to present in detail Collingwood's account of the strategy of his invasion of Britain,[1] but that would require a good deal of effort and a good deal of space. Instead, I shall discuss just one small point of the strategy of Aulus Plautius who commanded an invasion during the reign of Claudius. Existing evidence makes it clear that the invading fleet left Gaul in three divisions each under a separate commander. It has been suggested that this was so that each fleet could land at one of three ports which it is known were used by the Romans later in history and then, according to their orders, converge at Canterbury. Collingwood thinks there are two reasons why this cannot be so. To begin with, Plautius's campaign was modelled upon that of Caesar, and the latter's account of his campaign gives no reason to believe that good routes were to be had from two of those ports since he only explored one. The other is an a priori argument based upon 'a maxim of strategy', namely, 'that forces should not be divided in face of the enemy'. The point is that any one of the separate units might encounter an enemy force large enough to cause it to suffer a serious setback at the very start of the campaign.[2]

In Collingwood's view, what Plautius had in mind was as follows:

It is more likely that when Plautius divided his forces 'in order that they might not be prevented from landing anywhere' his intention was to confuse the Britons by making feints at two other possible landing-places . . . while intending actually to land at one only. Recent excavations have proved that this one was Richborough, where the remains of a

[1] 'Roman Britain', ch. 3.
[2] Ibid., pp. 79 f.

large camp of Claudian date have been found . . . The discovery of this large land-locked harbour . . . was a triumph for the intelligence service of Claudius's army. It suggests that his staff realized where lay the fundamental weakness of Caesar's campaign, namely, in his failure to find a safe and commodius harbour . . .[1]

Some might think that what Plautius did was distribute his ships and troops in a certain way, and that what Collingwood now does is explain the distribution. But this would seem to require that the mere physical arrangement of people can be treated as human action. That is not Collingwood's view: given his conception of action no historical analogy to behaviourism[2] could possibly be acceptable to him. The arrangement of the invading forces represents or embodies a plan, a well-thought-out piece of military strategy, and the task of the historian is to determine what that is. It is the arrangement of the forces *as embodying* Plautius's strategy that is the human action Collingwood seeks to reconstruct. The procedure is to try to take account of the sorts of thing that Plautius had in mind—the earlier campaign of Caesar as a model, the need to overcome the limitations of that earlier campaign that led to its failure,[3] the particular goal of Claudius, and so on. The passing remark about the archaeological discoveries at Richborough underscores Collingwood's view that rethinking must take into account everything the historian can think of which may be relevant—rethinking must be rooted in knowledge of historical evidence. And it is, I think, worth reiterating the point that this whole procedure, the piecemeal way it is carried on, the need to take up each bit of relevant information, and the taking up if only to refute other views that historians have offered, all make evident that rethinking is systematic and conceptual. All those critics who

[1] Ibid., p. 80.
[2] I say 'analogy to behaviourism' because the historian does not ever observe the overt behaviour of the people he deals with, but simply postulates it as required by the evidence he has. Far from being based upon observation—in the crude sense—historical reconstruction depends upon intellectual operations which completely defy analysis in behaviouristic terms, namely, the operations of historical research.
[3] Caesar's failure to state what the objective of his invasion of Britain was, leads Collingwood to conclude that it was not fully achieved; see 'Roman Britain', p. 33.

have treated rethinking as a species of empathy or intuition have simply no idea at all of what it involves.[1]

III

Nothing is rarer in the critical literature on Collingwood's philosophy of history than consideration of his actual work as an historian; indeed, one almost never sees even the slightest citation of his historical writings.[2] Alan Donagan is one of the very few writers to take seriously Collingwood as historian,[3] and it is thus with some regret that I must take issue with his account of one of the very interesting chapters of 'Roman Britain', one which, as Donagan reminds us, Collingwood himself so esteemed that he described it as 'a chapter which I would gladly leave as the sole memorial of my Romano-British studies, and the best example I can give to posterity of how to solve much-debated problems in history, not by discovering fresh evidence, but by reconsidering questions of principle'.[4] The chapter in question is the one called 'Art', and the problem is set by what appears to be the sudden disappearance of Celtic styles of art during the period of the Roman occupation of Britain only to return in full bloom when that period comes to its end. I shall attempt to show that what Collingwood does in that chapter is the same sort of thing we have seen in the examples of re-enactment we have just been examining. That is, I shall try to

---

[1] Among others, the following may be cited; Patrick Gardiner, *The Nature of Historical Explanation* (Oxford, 1952), pp. 39 and 48; Fred D. Newman, *Explanation by Description* (The Hague and Paris, 1968), p. 51; W. H. Walsh, *An Introduction to Philosophy of History* (New York, etc., 1951), p. 58; L. Jonathan Cohen, 'A Summary of Work in Philosophy of History, 1946–1950', *Philosophical Quarterly*, ii (1952), 172–86, at pp. 173–7; and G. J. Renier, *History: its Purpose and Method* (Boston, Mass., 1950), see Index under 'Collingwood.'

[2] In a footnote to the Introduction to his edition of F. H. Bradley, *The Presuppositions of Critical History* (Don Mills, Ont., 1968), p. 72, n. 83, Lionel Rubinoff writes, 'Examples of the reduction of universal principles to concrete individuals can be found throughout the historical writings of R. G. Collingwood.' But *instead* of telling us where, he adds: 'See, for example, Collingwood's discussion of the "principle of Incapsulation" in the *Autobiography*, ch. XI ...' (To make matters worse, the chapter in question is X.)

[3] Alan Donagan, 'The Verification of Historical Theses' *Philosophical Quarterly*, vi (1956), 193–208.

[4] Ibid., p. 198; quoted from *A*, 144 f.

show that what Collingwood tries to do in his treatment of this problem is to determine *what happened* with respect to art in Britain during the period in question. Donagan, on the other hand, thinks that Collingwood's problem is one of explanation, that he has already an idea of what happened, and is now faced with the need to render what happened intelligible. This is quite clear from the way he formulates the question that he thinks Collingwood sought to answer: 'There are two problems: why, if pre-Roman British art was of such high quality, was Romano-British art so bad? And why did Celtic art revive after its apparent extinction?'[1] I take it that the use of 'why' in both of these formulations makes it apparent that what is taken to be wanted is an explanation of something already known. A bit further on in his discussion, Donagan says the following: 'To re-think significant past thoughts is part of the end an historian strives to accomplish; it is not even the whole of it, for he must also both demonstrate that he has re-thought them, and use them to explain past actions.'[2] The first of these two additional tasks means simply that the historian must take pains to ensure the reasonableness of his claim that rethinking of *past* thought has actually taken place and that he is not imposing upon past actors what is simply his own conception of what might have been or ought to have been thought. Collingwood was himself very much aware of this danger and discusses it in his account of re-enactment in *The Idea of History* (*IH*, 292 and 296). But it is the second of the tasks which interests us here, and it is unambiguously clear that Donagan believes that rethinking is used in historical research in order to explain historical events. If he could show that this was the case, the consequence for what I have been saying so far would be very grim indeed. On the one hand, what we have seen to be Collingwood's conception of an historical action, as distinguished from what he takes to be merely an event, would be very hard to accommodate to what Donagan would have succeeded in demonstrating. And, on the other, the three examples presented in the previous section of this paper would perhaps be in jeopardy, for if re-enactment is, indeed, a technique of explanation

[1] Donagan, op. cit., p. 198.
[2] Ibid., p. 199.

what I have been saying about it may turn out to be all wrong. Thus, it becomes obviously imperative to re-examine the chapter on art in order to determine for ourselves whether Collingwood's problem there is one of explanation or, as I incline to suspect, one of the actual constitution of the historical past.

Of the situation to which he addresses himself, Collingwood says: 'At its lowest terms, the history of Romano-British art can be told in a couple of sentences. Before the Roman conquest the Britons were a race of gifted and brilliant artists: the conquest, forcing them into the mould of Roman life with its vulgar efficiency and lack of taste, destroyed that gift and reduced their arts to the level of mere manufacturers.'[1] This rather terse account, rather more judgemental than descriptive, is followed by an attempt to tell us something about the sorts of thing one sees when examining examples of the art-work of the periods being considered, but that will not actually concern us here. Perhaps it should, but we have no alternative to ignoring it short of digging up the reports cited in Collingwood's footnotes, for his account is not graced with any sort of plate, figure, or illustration. In fact, nowhere in the entire volume is such a thing to be found, surely a serious defect in a work so much concerned with and heavily dependent upon the results of archaeological exploration. In any event, since Collingwood does not present the problem with which he is here concerned in any but judgemental terms—good art and bad art—and has not provided us with the means of doing anything about it, the discussion which follows will simply continue to use his own manner of presentation. So far as our present problem is concerned, namely, to decide what Collingwood himself is attempting to accomplish in his discussion, it really does not matter. His problem is set by the situation characterized in the brief passage quoted in the beginning of the present paragraph with one additional matter: 'we find the same Celtic art which disappeared at the beginning of the Roman period rising mysteriously from its grave, enfeebled and uncertain of itself, but unmistakable, when that period is over.'[2] One would have expected

---

[1] 'Roman Britain', p. 247.
[2] Ibid., p. 250.

that after a period of more than three centuries for which archaeology has not uncovered any evidence of the preservation of old Celtic art that kind of art must have been fairly well extirpated; yet, we are now told, that as soon as the Romans left Britain it begins again to find expression. 'Where have its seeds been preserved? And why have they been hidden so completely for three centuries and a half?'[1] Immediately after this, Collingwood sums up the perplexities which confront him in the form of two questions to be answered: 'Why did anything so well established and well developed as British La Tène art fail to survive the Roman conquest?' And since 'the artistic talent that had produced it was not extinguished: why did it not turn its powers to the production of works in the Roman style' and produce a local school of art in that style of a better sort than what Collingwood thinks actually was produced?

I have been quoting somewhat repetitiously, but not inadvertently. As I have been making the distinction, I want to argue that Collingwood's task in the present chapter is not to explain what happened but to tell us what in fact did happen, yet it might well appear from the language in which he sets his problem that explanation is what he is after. Indeed, just before the passage quoted above about the re-emergence of Celtic art-forms after the departure of the Romans, he uses the expression: 'The thing demands explanation.' That, and the frequent use of 'why' in the passages quoted all make it seem that I must surely be mistaken in insisting that explanation is not the problem here, and I would not wish anyone to think I was not aware of Collingwood's language, much less that I hoped to keep attention away from it. The language is plainly there. It is a straightforward language not easily avoided—short of some effort at conscious circumlocution —in expositions of the sort we find in works like 'Roman Britain'. Yet, for all that, I think that when we look closely at what Collingwood actually does in the attempt to answer his questions, we find historical constitution and not explanation.

As in all instances of historical reconstruction and fully in accord with Collingwood's explicitly stated views, the occasion for

[1] Ibid.

re-enactment or rethinking of the relevant past thought is provided by a body of historical evidence. In the present case, this is mainly the remains of artistic work, and Collingwood tells us about what has been discovered and something about its geographical distribution. In addition, of course, he tells us about the sudden disappearance of Celtic art-forms after the Roman conquest and its subsequent return after the Romans depart. With respect to the question of why the seemingly gifted Celtic artists did not continue to produce fine work albeit in a Roman or Romano-British idiom, Collingwood notes that artistic talent is not something biologically transmissable, but, rather, what is handed down over the generations is a tradition of work in a certain way and in a certain field. We have, he thinks, to do with a tradition and not with an artistic school, and he draws this distinction in the following way:

The continuity of a school is a conscious continuity: it depends on one person's teaching another, explicitly, what to do and how to do it. The continuity of a cultural tradition is unconscious: those who live in it need not be explicitly aware of its existence. The continuity of tradition is the continuity of the force by which past experiences affect the future; and this force does not depend on the conscious memory of those experiences.[1]

I think that this conception of the unconscious of tradition, quite apart from its role in understanding the survival of the Celtic manner of art through the centuries of Roman domination of Britain, is very important for the light it sheds on Collingwood's own conception of thought, as I shall indicate a little further on. But first, I wish to follow Collingwood's attempt to pursue his problem to its first major climax. This can best be done in Collingwood's own words, for while it means I must quote at length, I doubt that I could summarize the points I believe are embedded in his text in any better or clearer fashion.

After his remarks about tradition, we find the following:

The British people had achieved its first great artistic experience through the intensely abstract curvilinear design of the middle La Tène school. It was bound, therefore, to respond to contact with a new art in one of

[1] 'Roman Britain', p. 252.

two ways. If that new art provided opportunity for the perpetuation and development of this particular experience, it would welcome it, converting the traditional motives of the new art into means for continuing that line of artistic growth to which it had already committed itself. If no such opportunities were offered, it would accept the new motives, if forced to accept them, in a dull and uncomprehending manner . . . and do stupidly and blunderingly what it was told to do, not from stupidity, but because it was preoccupied with its own thoughts betraying this preoccupation from time to time by doing work, crude and childish, no doubt, quite unlike what it was wanted to do, but expressive of its own desires, and therefore bearing the stamp of conviction. The one thing it could never do is to behave as if its own great experience had not happened to it, and learn its new lesson with an open mind. A people, like a single human being, is what the past has made it.

Of these two reactions, the first would make for healthy artistic development . . . . The British people would have incorporated the Roman tradition in its own artistic experience, and would be able to go on to the next stage in its development. The second would be in the main a waste of time . . .; Roman art teaching the Briton nothing but what he was glad to forget, Britain contributing to Roman art nothing of which it could be proud. After the end of the contact, Britain would be left to take up her own artistic problem where she had been forced to lay it down.[1]

While I have been trying to discuss the role of the re-enactment of past thought in historical research, I have not attempted to offer an account of what Collingwood takes thought and thinking to be. And, obviously, so difficult a task could not be undertaken as a parenthesis to something else. But I should like to suggest that what Collingwood is doing in the paragraphs just presented is a form of the re-enactment of past thought, though it obviously differs from the examples of re-enactment presented before. In those examples, in order to know what the historical action was which left the evidence which occasioned the historian's rethinking, we found ourselves considering the thoughts of individual agents whose intentions, plans, and purposes were being carried out on the historical stage. Here we have to do with thought—the 'inside'—in some other way. I cannot here work out the details of just what

[1] Ibid., p. 253.

that other way is. But I do think it clear that what is involved is not human behaviour in the sense of what is merely the 'outside'. As we have seen, Collingwood believed that the 'continuity of a cultural tradition is unconscious', but that surely in no way is intended to suggest that the carrying out of the tradition is mere behaviour uninformed by thought. There are meanings—in some relevant sense—which receive expression in the carrying on of a tradition, even if the self-conscious sort of reflection we find in the working-out of a course of action, say, in military strategy, is not to be found. While, as I say, this is no place to work out the theory of the nature of thought implicit in Collingwood's work, I feel certain that readers with any degree of familiarity with his thought will recognize that this must be so, that Collingwood would never turn over the 'continuity of a cultural tradition' to the tender mercies of the behaviourists. I think it is reasonable to suggest that any effort to work out Collingwood's conception of thought entirely from his philosophical writings alone without careful examination of passages such as those just quoted is no more likely to yield satisfactory results than the attempts to construe his sense of re-enactment from *The Idea of History* alone without attention to the actual examples of that procedure with which his 'Roman Britain' abounds.

Now let us see what Collingwood has done in the passages quoted. He has tried to determine the character of the course of Romano-British art by attending to the alternatives the situation offered to a tradition which suddenly confronts or is confronted by a new situation. To this extent, there is a resemblance to the sort of rethinking we saw above since in those cases, too, the point of departure for the course of action is the need of a general or an emperor to deal with a situation he confronts or confronts him. Collingwood knows on the basis of the archaeological record what sorts of art followed in what sequence. And so he is able to determine which of the alternatives he specifies in the first of the two quoted paragraphs was followed. He started with archaeological remains. But after the course of his re-enactment of past thought, he is able to tell what happened, what sort of human action the history of art in the period discussed was. What happened was what is characterized as the second of the two ways in which an art tradition may respond to a new situation. The Roman tradition was not one, he tells us, to which the traditional practices of Celtic artists could be adapted successfully. And so the Celtic artists adopted the Roman style—apparently there was nothing else to be done—but could never really work well at it. The art that was closest to their hearts would be worked at occasionally, apparently with scant success. But that enabled them to preserve a tradition, to which, when times were again propitious, they could devote their full energies. With that, of course, we get the resurrection of the old Celtic tradition which had neither died out completely nor was something embedded in their genetic constitution. Anyone who wants the details of this development will have to consult the last half of Collingwood's chapter. I believe, however, that what I have just sketched is a fair account of what he attempted there to do.

Thus, in the sense that is usually intended, Collingwood has not offered an explanation of anything in that chapter he would leave as a monument to his Romano-British studies. Rather, what he tries there to do is present an account of what took place, based upon evidence and using the method of re-enacting past thought. To deny this, one must ask oneself what it is that Collingwood has been explaining. In light of what I have already said when this sort of thing came up earlier in our discussion, the answer is clear enough: if this chapter does in fact contain an explanation it would have to be about the outside of the action taken by itself. The re-enactment could be said to provide an explanation only if outside and inside could stand alone, each independent of the other. But that is precisely what Collingwood, in his conception of human action, denies. Until the historian has gone through the course of re-enactment, he knows what evidence has survived the depradations of time, but he does not know what human actions have taken place. With re-enactment, we get a conception of what human action must have or might have—I need not choose between these here—taken place. It might be noted again, that one happy by-product of our discussion is a sharpened awareness that Collingwood's conception of both thought and action are not so narrow as some might suppose and that a considerably wider swath of history—actually, I think all of history—is quite compatible with his view of them. In any event, where we had a perplexing body of evidence, we now have a conception of *what* happened. *Why* that sort of thing could happen in a situation of the sort that existed, is something else again.

IV

The final chapter of 'Roman Britain' tells the story of the gradual fading away of the Roman element in Britain. Saxon settlements had been established and were growing in strength. What was an outpost of Roman civilization had retrogressed into a Celto-Roman one, with Celtic elements increasingly prevalent. In the course of his account, Collingwood writes that,

This backwash of Celticism over the romanized regions, both attested and dated by the story of Vortigern,[1] is traceable by archaeological evidence. At Silchester a tombstone was found, with an inscription in Ogams containing the name of a certain Ebicatos and written in the Irish, as distinct from the British, form of Celtic. An Irishman who died in Silchester and left friends able to make him an epitaph in his own language must have been a member of an Irish colony in the town. The Scotic raids, as we saw, had died away; the Silchester inscription shows a state of things in which parties of Scots[2] are settling down peacefully in the lowland zone, and retaining their own language and customs.[3]

This is an interesting paragraph for a number of reasons. To begin with, there are still numbers of people who think that the historian discovers what happened by reading old texts and copies out—to be sure, in a critical spirit—what he finds in them. But there are no texts of that sort which tell about an Irish colony in Silchester in the fifth century. The fact is, the possibility that such a colony existed we owe entirely to the working of the historical imagination. And so we discover still another kind of passage which ought to be mastered for the light it may throw on still another of Collingwood's well-known conceptions, that of

[1] A local Welsh king of the fifth century who was supposed to have invited Horsa and Hengist to settle in Kent.
[2] 'The Scots . . . were the inhabitants of Ireland'; 'Roman Britain', p. 282.
[3] 'Roman Britain', p. 316.

the historical imagination, instead of the more usual practice of trying to tease out its meaning from the text of *The Idea of History* alone.[1] Too, a full appreciation of what the quoted paragraph—and many others in 'Roman Britain', and the body of historical literature altogether—does would make it evident that historical realism—which I take to be the view that statements about past events mean and refer in the same way that statements about present events do and that, in consequence, the correspondence theory of truth is at least plausible for history—cannot possibly do justice to the epistemological idiosyncrasies of history. Given the way in which the account presented in the paragraph is introduced—about which I shall have more to say in the sequel—it clearly does not have the same epistemic status as the report of a witness or the description of something which lies before me in my field of vision. Of course, some will want to say that if the account is true then anyone who might have been present at the time would see certain things and could describe what he experiences. Be that as it may, and without raising the question of what it is one would see or experience—being an Irish colony being rather a different kind of being than being a red chair[2]—the fact of the matter is that *as* the event is constituted in historical research it is not something witnessed and the verification or confirmation of the claim that such a colony existed in Silchester is not done in such a way as to implicate the correspondence theory. The claim is historically true if it makes best sense of our evidence. To assert that it is historically true only if in fact the real past corresponds to what it asserts is to assert a criterion of historical truth which can have no application in the practice of history.[3]

[1] 'The historical imagination' is simply Collingwood's way of referring to the techniques and autonomy of history in the reconstruction of the historical past. It is surely not a category in any sense; cf. the contrary opinion of Brevard S. Childs, *Memory and Tradition in Israel*, Studies in Biblical Theology No. 37 (London, 1962), p. 87.

[2] Most of the philosophical discussion of statements about past events makes the tacit assumption that the two are rather the same. Were the assumption made explicit and then rejected, no small amount of the difficulties we find in such discussions would disappear.

[3] Cf. my 'Evidence and Events in History', *Philosophy of Science*, xxix (1962), pp. 175–94; Pt. I.

18

But there is still a third way in which the quoted paragraph is of interest, and I should like to devote some space to that, namely, to what it indicates about the relation between the historical event there described and the historical evidence upon which it is based. In the present case, it is rather easy to deal with this because Collingwood specifies just what his evidence is—a single tombstone in Silchester. Of course, a single tombstone without any sort of context might not get an historian too far,[1] and a really full account of the relevant evidence would presumably have to include all of the evidence on the basis of which the general circumstances within which the tombstone is located was established. But we need not bother about that here. It does seem plain enough that Collingwood's view that an Irish colony existed in Silchester in the fifth century is based entirely upon the discovery of the tombstone. An entire Irish colony seems like rather a weighty structure to erect upon so frail a foundation, and if there were any truth at all to the widely held opinion that the historical past is *inferred* from historical evidence it is hard to see how Collingwood's Irish colony could at all be taken seriously. But clearly, there is never a relationship of logical entailment—and what else could 'inferred' mean?—between historical evidence and historical events. Rather, the event is postulated by the historian as most likely given what evidence he has and what general information he has about the period. After writing about King Arthur and his military campaigns, Collingwood says:

These are conjectures. But they are based on the facts of fifth-century warfare; and the probability that they may be correct is at least slightly increased by the fact that the traditions which first appear at a much later date, and are embodied so far as we are concerned in the twelfth-century romance of Geoffrey of Monmouth, revolve around the conception of Arthur as the creator of a band of knights. [2]

[1] Yet it is surprising how far the skilful application of the historical imagination can go with very little evidence. See, for example, Hjalmar R. Holand, *Norse Discoveries and Explorations in America, 982–1362* (originally published as *Westward from Vinland: An Account of Norse Explorations and Discoveries in America, 982–1362*) (New York, 1969), Pt. II.
[2] 'Roman Britain', p. 323.

Why that should be so is of no interest here, and anyone who is curious about it may look it up for himself. The point to be made in the present context has to do with the conjectural character of the event Collingwood had been proposing or postulating before the passage quoted, an event based upon some evidence and rendered somewhat more plausible than the evidence itself might suggest by its conformity with what is otherwise known about fifth-century warfare.

Although the interest that brings both scholars and readers to history is the human past, a curiosity about what happened in days gone by, in terms of its strict logical function in the context of historical research, the purpose of the historical event is to explain historical evidence. Collingwood tells us that an Irish colony existed in fifth-century Silchester because in his view only that renders intelligible the presence there of a tombstone inscribed in the Irish form of Celtic. Even if one must admit that interest in the period or some such thing led Collingwood to his studies of the Roman period of British history, surely no one can say that he was particularly interested in that Irish colony and for that reason paid some special attention to the remains of Silchester. Quite the contrary! He had no interest in such a colony at all until he had virtually to call it into existence[1] in order to explain the tombstone. No serious reflection on the genesis and function of the statement, 'An Irishman who died in Silchester and left friends able to make him an epitaph in his own language must have been a member of an Irish colony in the town', in the context in which it appears in 'Roman Britain', leaves room for any alternative view of its epistemic status. It is all well and good to say that Collingwood's statement is true only if there really was such a colony, but that is to say something that has no consequence for historical inquiry; it simply expresses the hope that the historical past is identical with the real past. But Collingwood himself had no illusions about the relevance of that hope to the methodology of historical practice: 'The game is won not by the player who can reconstitute what really happened, but by the player who can

[1] Here the reader may add any qualifications he deems necessary to avoid having an apoplectic sputter.

show that his view of what happened is the one which the evidence accessible to all players, when criticized up to the hilt, supports.'[1]

The point, of course, is entirely general. The logical function of any constructed historical event, understood strictly in terms of its function in historical inquiry and without reference to the hopes and interests of both historians and those who read what they produce, is to explain the body of evidence deemed relevant to the investigation being undertaken. In particular, all of the examples we have considered earlier in this paper do the same thing. If Collingwood is right about Celtic art, he has explained the remains that archaeologists have uncovered. That is, he has explained to us why it is that the art remains of the various periods of British history involved have the character they have, why excellent work in one style should have been succeeded by inferior work in another style, and why, when there seemed every reason to think the first style had vanished completely, instances of it should suddenly appear once again. Likewise, to mention only one more, if his account of the Antonine Wall is sound, Collingwood has explained why it is the wall has certain characteristics, that is, why the surviving evidence has the features it does. But in all of the examples we considered above, the central technique used by Collingwood in his attempt to constitute the historical past was the re-enactment of past thought. Since the re-enactment of thought results in historical constitution, and historical constitution has the function of explaining evidence, it would seem that my insistence that the re-enactment of past thought is not done for the purpose of offering historical explanations was mistaken after all.

Not really. It is clear enough that to talk about explaining historical events and explaining historical evidence is to talk about two rather different things. I do not wish to review the literature here, but I think few will argue with the assertion that those critics of the covering-law conception of historical explanation who have claimed to be working in the spirit of Collingwood—taken as loosely as you like—have usually meant to say that Collingwood's

[1] Collingwood, *Essays in the Philosophy of History*, ed. W. Debbins (Austin, Tex., 1965), p. 97.

theory of re-enactment or rethinking was a way of taking seriously the relevance of rational intentions in the explanation of historical events. Such critics generally contend that the covering-law conception is incapable of doing justice to explanation by rational intention. In addition, since the covering-law position is virtually always presented as a theory about the nature of the explanation of events—the peculiarities of a queen's signature or the migrations of farm workers from blighted to better land—one expects that a critical stance in opposition to it is directed at the same sort of problem. It is hard to avoid the conclusion that it is the general lack of interest among philosophers of history in the intellectual procedures whereby the historical past is constituted in historical research, and their virtually exclusive preoccupation with the nature of the explanation of historical events, that have made it so difficult for the true purport of Collingwood's idea of the re-enactment of past thought to be understood. But, surely, it is by now obvious that the constitution of the historical past and the explanation of past events are two different concerns of historical inquiry. And while each involves some kind of explanation, they are markedly different in kind. While the re-enactment of past thought is central to the constitution of the historical past with its function of explaining historical evidence, that it is to be used in the explanation of past events is something else again. So far as Colling-wood is concerned, we have discovered three bases for claiming that this last is not the position to which he subscribed: (1) it is not compatible with his conception of human action; (2) it is not the way he actually uses the technique in 'Roman Britain'; and (3) we have found a perfectly good instance of the explanation of an historical event in 'Roman Britain' that does not make use of re-enactment.

XIII

COLLINGWOOD'S PHENOMENOLOGY OF EDUCATION: *PERSON* AND THE SELF-RECOGNITION OF THE MIND

SHERMAN M. STANAGE

NO SERIOUS exploration of R. G. Collingwood's philosophy of education has yet been undertaken. In the light of Collingwood's increasingly important place in contemporary philosophy, his thoughtful and carefully argued accounts of many areas of philosophy which tell the story of the human mind at work, e.g., aesthetics and the philosophy of history, and the rich and plentiful lode of other material available to those interested in Collingwood's philosophy, the absence of such an investigation is surprising.

Almost everything he ever wrote presents at least an implicit or heuristic philosophy of education.[1] From first to last, his writings articulated the philosophical life for him as the life of the mind perpetually at work on the problems of moral philosophy which arise during the course of a man's attempt to account, on both practical and theoretical grounds, for the phenomena of his conscious life, the forms of experience which are generated throughout the life of the mind.[2] Indeed, these concerns predated any of his writings, for at the age of eight, as he writes in his *Autobiography*, he began to read Abbott's translation of Kant's *Grundlegung zur Metaphysik der Sitten*, and '. . . felt that the contents of this book, although I could not understand it, were some-

---

[1] Cf., e.g., *SM*, 50–1, 316–17; 'The Place of Art in Education', (1926), in Alan Donagan, ed., *Essays in the Philosophy of Art* (Bloomington, Ind., 1964), pp. 187–207; 'Aesthetic', in R. J. S. McDowall, ed., *The Mind* (London, 1927), pp. 214–44; *A*, 1–167; *EM*, 60, 134–6; *NL*, pp. 308–17.

[2] See *SM*, esp. pp. 12, 15, 36, 317; *NL*, pp. 130–341.

how my business: a matter personal to myself, or rather to some future self of my own . . . I felt as if a veil had been lifted and my destiny revealed' (A, 3-4).

The aim of this brief essay is to bring some of the rudiments of Collingwood's philosophy of education to a more explicit statement primarily by reference to what he says about the notion of person as speaker-hearer and the origination of linguistic relations which both construct, embody, and express the self-recognition of the mind. In this attempt I shall: (1) offer a phenomenological analysis and commentary for a number of pages drawn from *The Principles of Art* which offer an account of *person*, and which bear the title 'Speaker and Hearer' (*PA*, 247-53); (2) briefly develop the grounds for showing how a number of the themes in these pages are directly related to several of the most important developments in his systematic philosophy, among them insights for which he has received widely acknowledged praise in the eyes of many contemporary philosophers; (3) draw from this discussion of themes a number of principles of an explicit philosophy of education.

Collingwood begins the section entitled 'Speakers and Hearers' by writing:

In its most elementary form, language is not addressed to any audience. A child's first utterances are so completely inaddressed that one cannot even describe them as addressed to the world at large or to itself. The distinction between speaking to oneself, speaking to the world at large, and speaking to a particular person or group, is a later differentiation introduced into an original act which was simply the act of speaking (*PA*, 247).

In many places Collingwood is preoccupied with language and its crucial structure and function in the odyssey of the mind.[1] Language is both that inclusive system of bodily movements through which a person intends both meaning and signification and the more specific speaking activity. It is language in the latter

[1] Cf., especially: *EPM*, 199-200; *PA*, 225-69; *NL*, pp. 40-6. Although Collingwood's philosophy of language is absolutely fundamental to his philosophy of education, this essay presents an analysis of a very small portion of it, only so much as seems necessary to lay the foundation for his philosophy of education.

sense which brings the odyssey or the life of the mind into more and more orderly and systematic discourse. Through the expressive acts of speaking the world is brought into life and into view. Thereby the mind is both educa*tive* and educa*ted*.

Collingwood had affirmed similar theses much earlier, in his paper 'The Place of Art in Education'. There he suggested that thought, before its utterance, lay obscured 'and unrealized in the dark places of the soul, in the chaos of preordination and the night of its forebeing.'[1] Language and thinking are overlapping notions and activities.[2] To speak is already to create and to express thinking, and thinking already presupposes language activity.

There is no audience, surely, in the sense of an assembly of listeners or spectators. Nor is there an audience in the sense of a formal hearing. Thus in its most elementary identifiable form the use of language is not an addressing usage, nor is language directed 'straight to' a hearer. Indeed, for Collingwood, these first utterances come forth freely within the civilizing conditions of the family.

The child's first utterances are so unaddressed to the world at large or to itself that adults often do not dwell upon and identify these with the serious care they deserve in Collingwood's view. They are most often characterized as too spontaneous to be serious and meaningful. Adults, to their detriment, miss the point of the child's play with language. They will pick up the child's utterances at the stages where distinctions are already being made through a congeries of eye, head, hand, and other bodily movements. Where addressing distinctions become clear, speaking, in Collingwood's sense, has already been going on for a long time.

---

[1] 'The Place of Art in Education', p. 196.
[2] See Sherman M. Stanage, 'The Role of the "Overlap" in Collingwood's Philosophy', unpublished Ph.D. Dissertation, the University of Colorado, Department of Philosophy, 1959. Cf. p. 105: What Collingwood means by an 'overlap of concepts' is a serial arrangement of concepts. Each of these overlap, i.e., are successive modifications of previous concepts, where 'previous' means 'both logically prior to', and 'logically less inclusive than'. The fundamental relation between any two adjacent overlapping concepts is that one is 'higher than the other on a scale of forms, such that any 'higher' concept must be comprehended through reference to the 'lower' concepts on the scale, and as a culmination of all previous concepts on the scale. This serial arrangement of overlapping concepts on a scale of forms is a purely logical relation.

Only after this early process of unaddressed speaking, are the later processes of distinguishing between speaking to oneself (as children often do when alone), speaking to the world, and speaking to a particular person or group manifested. Collingwood's presentation of this view was founded primarily on his own life experiences and on his principle that learning is a process of coming to know better and better what we have always known in part.[1] Thus learning is partly a process of making more and more careful distinctions. But these are distinctions without a difference or separation, distinctions not based upon the mutually exclusive classes of different kinds of scientific knowledge which psychology, for example, would purport to have. Compartmentalized, fragmentized, specialized facts are not knowledge for Collingwood, but these are all the corrupting wares which the specialist or professional educator will offer his innocent victims. Thus, professional educators 'deracinate' the young and leave them 'emotionally disoriented' for the rest of their lives.[2]

The child as speaker is his own first listener. This is a personal activity, and it bespeaks the priority of the overlap and fusion[3] of the speaking and listening activities. In this stage, speaking and listening are both the same (they form a unity) and different. They can be distinguished, but they are largely undifferentiated. Speaking and hearing must be defined in terms of each other. Speaking, in this early stage of a child's development (and for Collingwood this is not merely language development, but the development and the growing life of the child's mind) *invokes* hearing, and it logically *commits* the hearing function as well. Speaking and hearing here are co-related and appositely placed together, although these are characteristics which come to be distinguished little by little.

Collingwood continues:

Now, speech is a function of self-consciousness; therefore, even at this early stage, a speaker is conscious of himself as speaking, and is thus a

---

[1] Cf. *EPM*, 3, 176–98.

[2] See *EPM*, esp. pp. 26–51, for a discussion of scientific method. See, also, *NL*, p. 310, for his account of professional educators.

[3] See p. 270, n. 2, above, and *EPM*, esp. pp. 64–9, 74.

listener to himself. The experience of speaking is also an experience of listening (*PA*, 247).

Self-consciousness is the personal center of a person. It is not a genetic, logical, or ontological *first placing* of a person, but it can be focussed upon, or bracketed, as a phenomenon to be analysed. It is what can be called a 'first-order consciousness', and 'a whole here-and-now of feeling is raised to consciousness by a linguistic act.' It can be analyzed through the language through which the self is articulated. The self 'consciouses'[1] or 'knows-with'. This transitive verbal form is apt since Collingwood here is not dealing with a state of being but with a functioning, an activity. It is a reflecting and reflexing activity, *viz.*, the self knows *that* it speaks because it listens to *what* is said, and what is said is said because it is listened to. The two functions are not coordinate functions, and neither precedes the other.

An experience is literally a trying-out. To experience is to participate actually, to be in direct contact with someone or something. Thus, in the phrase 'the experience of listening', we have Collingwood's claim that when we try to speak in direct personal terms we are at the same time trying to listen to what we say. The first attempts, unaddressed, unaddressing, and unchannelling are confused, but surely these are pre-predicative, pre-logical utterings. This important point in Collingwood's phenomenology of education is that speaking and listening are personal activities which overlap, and this point is a logical consequence of his philosophical presupposition of concepts overlapping on a scale of forms. The educative significance of discourse with even the very young is thus manifested.

Experience and experiment have the same etymological root; we usually reserve the word 'experience' for those attempts when we speak of our own trying-out, whereas we tend to use the term 'experiment' when we focus upon what someone else is experiencing, or when we *experience* our own experience.

---

[1] Here and in other places *conscious* and its various forms, e.g., *consciousing*, are used as a reminder that, in accordance with the derivation of the word, I am using it to express an intentional 'knowing-with'.

In this sense it can be said that experimentation is reflexive experience.[1]

This may be another name for self-consciousness, and it is another way of saying that 'the experience of speaking is also an experience of listening'. My experience of speaking is being looked at, viz., I am also experimenting. I begin to see *that* I am doing something, and thus beginning to know *what* I am doing, viz., what I am saying, for to know *that* I am saying is to know *what* I am saying, at least in the earliest stages. In this experience, theory and practice are born, distinguishable but inseparable. Again, a principle in Collingwood's philosophy of education follows directly from his presupposition of the overlap of concepts on a scale of forms.

The origin of self-consciousness, whether that phrase is understood psychologically, to mean the stages by which it comes into existence, or metaphysically, to mean the reasons why it begins to exist, is a problem I shall not discuss. There is one thing, however, which ought to be said about it. Consciousness does not begin as a mere self-consciousness, establishing in each one of us the idea of himself, as a person or centre of experience, and then proceed by some process, whether of 'projection' or of argument by analogy, to construct or infer other persons. Each one of us is a finite being, surrounded by others of the same kind; and the consciousness of our own existence is also the consciousness of the existence of these others (*PA*, 247-8).

Collingwood's criticisms of psychology are familiar to his readers,[2] and these criticisms reveal his view of psychology as a science necessarily incapable of articulating the stages of the

---

[1] An experiment commonly is considered to be an act or an operation designed to discover, test, or illustrate some 'truth(s)'. Even this common view carries with it the meaning above. An *experience* has already occurred, e.g., an observation of some phenomenon has taken place, and an *experiment* is devised as a more 'public' experiencing of this experience under controlled conditions. (An early experiment conducted by R. G. Collingwood must have been instructive, for in a poem entitled 'To R. C.', his father writes: 'You've seized my copy and revised, /Absorbed the proofs, devoured the pages,/Retold the tale in travesties,/And sketched and played the personages/In many a quaint disguise.' See William M. Johnston, *The Formative Years of R. G. Collingwood* (The Hague, 1967), p. 7.)

[2] Cf. *RP*, 39-42; *SM*, 168, 181, 195, 247-8, 274-8, 280, 298, and 302; *EM*, especially pp. 101-42.

development of self-consciousness in the life of a person. Still, any account of a philosophy of education in Collingwood's philosophy must suffer from his own failure, to show how psychology properly so called (a science of feeling) can show how self-consciousness comes to be.

Consciousness is a generic concept,[1] and my consciousness of myself and my consciousness of other finite beings are species of the generic concept of consciousness, I both know-with myself and know-with others of whom I have become aware.[2]

But consciousness is a form of thought, and

... Being a form of thought, consciousness is liable to error (Chapter X, Section 7); and when first a child discovers its own existence it simultaneously discovers the existence not only of its mother or nurse but of other persons like a cat, a tree, a firelight shadow, a piece of wood, where errors in admitting this or that neighbour to the category of person are no doubt correlative to errors in its conception of its own personality. But, however much the discovery (like any other discovery) is at first involved in error, the fact remains that the child's discovery of itself as a person is also its discovery of itself as a member of a world of persons (PA, 248).

Collingwood had previously written that 'In its primary form, thought seems to be exclusively concerned with (feeling).' We attend to certain feelings that we have, e.g., as we might say 'I am tired', or 'It is hot today.' He means that our thoughts wait upon, stretch toward, and then grasp our feelings. Feelings have *flowed* into the forms of thinking. In this process, when feelings become embodied in thoughts, a child begins to discover his own existence. His discovery is the embodiment of his feelings through the expressive creativity of language. The child may be in error, a wandering away from what really is; his error may be a case of

[1] Cf. p. 270, n. 2, above, and Stanage, 'The Role of the "Overlap" in Collingwood's Philosophy', p. 74: 'The generic essence of a philosophical generic concept is the full meaning of a generic concept as this meaning is expressed by the individual meanings of the totality of specific concepts which are on the scale of forms into which the generic concept is specified.' Feeling becomes consciousness.

[2] I am not conscious *of* myself or others. I *conscious* myself and others. I actively *intend* myself and them. The implications of this view are crucial in any philosophy of education.

incorrect and mistaken identity. Mistakes of this kind are normal to children, but too many of them lasting over extended periods of time may be correlated with personality disorders in the child's life.[1] Still, thought in this primary form is the child's discovery of himself as a person and also the discovery of himself as a member of a world of persons.

Self-consciousness makes a person of what, apart from that, would be merely a sentient organism. The relations between sentient organisms as such are constituted by the various modes of sympathy which arise out of psychical expression of their feelings. Since persons are organisms, they too are connected by relations of this kind. But, as persons, they construct a new set of relations between themselves, arising out of their consciousness of themselves and one another; these are *linguistic relations*.[2] The discovery of myself as a person is the discovery that I can speak, and am thus a *persona* or speaker (*PA*, 248).

Some sentient organisms become conscious of themselves and thereby come to be more than sentient organisms. They feel-with one another, but as self-conscious they 'construct a new set of relations between themselves and one another'. Language relates them. Collingwood invokes his scale of forms again at this point.[3] These two self-conscious, sentient organisms are not be be understood as mutually exclusive, or as coordinates within a class. One sentient organism already 'overlaps' another sentient organism. The overlap of the two, viz., sentiency or feeling, gives rise to what we intend by person. Such organisms feel-with one another, are sympathetic, and express this through language. Persons, not merely sentient organisms, are expressive of pathos, sympathy, empathy, etc. A given, specific emotion is expressed by that person who is conscious of it. His consciousness of it converts the emotion from 'an emotion into idea', and this expression is the act of speaking. One who speaks first hears himself, and he is conscious of the idea being spoken-of, or expressed. Such is Collingwood's position on linguistic relations.

---

[1] And of course lead to a corrupt consciousness. See p. 288, n. 1, below.
[2] My italics.
[3] See p. 270, n. 2, above.

But how are these to be investigated? How are they to be explored and analyzed? I suggest that they can be investigated phenomenologically, once the given phenomenon can be focussed upon. The phenomenon in this case is any given linguistic relation, and the first stage of the phenomenological investigation is to *intuit* the phenomenon.[1]

Intuition has had a wide variety of meanings in the history of both eastern and western philosophy. In its root sense it evidently means 'to see' something or someone. I am using the term to try (1) to capture in their *togetherness* the first approximations of 'seeing', 'hearing', 'smelling', 'tasting', and 'touching' when we focus or concentrate upon a subject-matter, and (2) to move through to the further, deeper sense of *'really* seeing', *'really* hearing', etc. Our first approximations, or sensings of a linguistic relation are intuitive, 'seeings' in the broad sense of relating, focussing, concentrating 'seeings'.

Unlike various methods of 'objective' analysis which reduce a phenomenon to parts already known and make it depend upon something other than itself, in intuiting the phenomenon we focus upon its uniqueness, upon itself as reducible to nothing by itself. The method of phenomenology thus is particularly appropriate to the exploration of a linguistic relation.

We note that when we hear someone speak to us, or when we read selections from someone's writings, in this case Collingwood's, we discover this other person either for the first time, or again; and if again, in a different way. There is uniqueness, novelty, in this 'seeing', or this intuiting. However we 'see' the person, we must do so in some sense through our feeling, our experiencing, or our consciousing of (i.e., knowing and understanding) him. But in doing so, we are at the same time feeling, experiencing and consciousing *ourselves* as well. To the degree that I understand this other person as speaker, both *that* he is saying something and *what* it is, I am discovering this person either for the first time, or anew. I am also discovering myself.

---

[1] Cf. Sherman M. Stanage, 'The Personal World', *Pacific Philosophy Forum* (now *The Philosophy Forum*), vi, No. 4 (May 1968), 3–46, esp. pp. 26–40.

The richest ways of intuiting a person rest upon such notions as 'feeling' a person, 'experiencing' a person, or 'consciousing' a person. Each of these is the person's being, being *who* he is, *what* he is, *where* he is, *when* he is, etc. These bespeak a sharing somehow with the other person, for feeling, experiencing, and consciousing all connote a relating. For example, feeling is necessarily a relating of a person, and something in addition, to the focussing of his immediate self (e.g., 'I feel the stone', or 'I feel pain'). Experiencing is a doing, an encountering, which is both a giving and a receiving of oneself in relation to someone or something in addition. Consciousing is a knowing-with. Thus feeling, experiencing, and consciousing persons are made possible only by the initial assumption of relatedness. And this relatedness is conveyed through (or as) linguistic relations. But this is already built into the notion of person. Thus, two or more human beings are required for one to speak as and of persons, or to speak of either one as a person; or as Collingwood expresses the matter,

In speaking, I am both speaker and hearer; and since the discovery of myself as a person is also the discovery of other persons around me, it is the discovery of speakers and hearers other than myself. Thus, from the first, the experience of speech contains in itself in principle the experiences of speaking to others and hearing others speak to me. How this principle works out in practice depends on how, in detail, I identify persons among my surroundings (*PA*, 248–9).

That one speaks to a person or is spoken to by a person is the primitive phenomenon which we intuit. These are speaking-acts and hearing-acts. No notion of either 'subjectivity' or 'objectivity' alone can express these intuitions or even the grounds of the possibilities of person. We may say that our intuiting presents us not only with persons but also with the richest of all possible subject-matters, *ourselves*, for as ourselves we are present in sharing with another who speaks of himself.

The relation between speaker and hearer, as two distinct persons, is one which, because of its very familiarity, is easily misunderstood. We are apt to think of it as one in which the speaker 'communicates' his emotions to the hearer. But emotions cannot be shared like food or drink, or handed over like old clothes. To speak of communicating an emotion, if it means anything, must mean causing another person to have emotions like those which I have myself. But independently of language neither he nor I nor any third person can compare his emotions with mine, so as to find out whether they are like or unlike. If we speak of such comparison, we speak of something that is done by the use of language; so that the comparison must be defined in terms of speaking and hearing, not speaking and hearing in terms of such comparison (*PA*, 249).

To communicate is to share in common, and one may characterize this sharing in two ways. In one sense a communication of something, an emotion here, is thought to be a causing, as if we could *cause* another to have that emotion which I am telling him that I have. An emotion, however, intends a moving-out, a strong surge of feeling marked by an impulse to outward expression, and it is often accompanied by complex bodily reactions. 'A *feeling* consists of two things closely connected: first, a *sensuous* element such as a colour seen, a sound heard, an odour smelt; secondly what I call the *emotional charge on this* sensation' (*NL*, p. 18).

Food can be handed over to a person, but a feeling—a colour seen and the moment of pleasure at (in?) seeing the colour—cannot be handed over, cannot be caused to be present in another person. Emotions cannot be communicated in this *first* sense.

In the *second* sense, we may speak of communication as being a fellowship, or a community of discourse. This meaning is carried by our use of the word communion. There is already an overlap of two or more persons in this sense, a fusion, a coalescing, of their feelings, viz., both of the closely connected elements, the sensuous element and the emotional charge. But this sense is expressed as a *logical* relationship like that one articulated in chapter III of *An Essay on Philosophical Method*.[1] Neither in this sense are the emotions communicated as directly expressed through the speaking which is heard. But the logical grounds for Collingwood's next statement are available to him.

Emotions, he says, are not communicated, but they can be compared. Emotions can be examined to see whether they are

[1] Cf. Stanage, 'The Role of the "Overlap" in Collingwood's Philosophy', pp. 77–105, esp. p. 104.

similar or dissimilar, whether they resemble or differ. Comparison, ideally, would determine with precision the equality of the emotions examined. The logical ground for this examination has been provided by the principle or presupposition of the overlap,[1] but the examination can only take place through language. Hence, as Collingwood says, the 'comparison must be defined in terms of speaking and hearing, not speaking and hearing in terms of such comparison.'

An impression and an idea, through their expression, are turned together. An expressive act is already a conscious act, and the conscious act already has built within it a knowing-with. An expressive act is an intentional act with two intended objects in this case, the impression to be expressed, and the idea to be expressed. Thus the expressive act, in its intentional function *presses* one of its intended objects into (or *turns* it into) another of its intended objects. Since the expressive act of consciousness functions generically here, and since the two intended objects already overlap (are fused in a way), and are on a scale of forms combining both degrees and kinds, Collingwood's account suffers from no discontinuity here. It is consistent with a phenomenological account of what takes place in language. It is also an important principle in his philosophy of education, since the grounds are available to Collingwood to show how and why one's emotions, and not merely emotionless 'facts' (if there are any), are necessarily explorable in the educative process.[2]

The implicit is made explicit in the expressive, speaking act. We come to know better and better what we have already known in part.

... If, however, the relation between emotion and language has been correctly described (in paragraph 3 above), sense can be made of these phrases. They will then be analysed as follows.

When language is said to express emotion, this means that there is a single experience which has two elements in it. First, there is an emotion of a specific kind, not a psychic emotion or impression, but an emotion of which the person who has it is conscious, and which by this consciousness he has converted from impression into idea. Secondly, there is a

---

[1] Cf. above: p. 270, n. 2; p. 274, n. 1; p. 278, n. 1.   [2] Cf. *NL*, p. 310.

controlled bodily action in which he expresses this idea. The expression is not an afterthought to the idea; the two are inseparably united, so that the idea is had as an idea only in so far as it is expressed. The expression is speech, and the speaker is his own first hearer. As hearing himself speak, he is conscious of himself as the possessor of the idea which he hears himself expressing. Thus two statements are both true, which might easily be thought to contradict each other: (1) it is only because we know what we feel that we can express it in words; (2) it is only because we express them in words that we know what our emotions are. In the first, we describe our situation as speakers; in the second, our situation as hearers of what we ourselves say. The two statements refer to the same union of idea with expression, but they consider this union from opposite ends (*PA*, 249–50).

The above passage in Collingwood follows easily as an explication of the relation between emotion and language. There is a single generic experience with two overlapping species. One specific form of the experience of speaking the emotion is the consciousness that the person in fact has an emotion and that through this act of consciousness, he 'has converted an impression into an idea.' This specific form overlaps the other specific form of the experience, the person's 'controlled bodily action in which he expresses this idea', viz., usually a speaking-hearing act.

The impression and the idea are, in typically Collingwoodian terms, 'inseparably united', but distinguishable, i.e., overlapping species of the generic concept speaking-hearing act, and 'the idea is had as an idea only insofar as it is expressed.' An expression is a pressing-out, an outward indication or manifestation of something, an idea, but 'outward' to whom? Since the speaker is his own first hearer, this 'outward' manifestation does not reach-out to another person at first. The outwardness is only—and this is an important qualification—a way of calling attention to the overlap, a previously and logically bridged gap, between speaker and hearer.[1] A speaker hears himself speak, and thus 'he is conscious of himself as the possessor of the idea which he hears himself expressing'.

The person to whom speech is addressed is already familiar with this double situation. If he were not, it would be useless to address him.

[1] See p. 279, n. 1, above.

He, too, is a speaker, and is accustomed to make his emotions known to himself by speaking to himself. Each of the two persons concerned is conscious of the other's personality as correlative to his own; each is conscious of himself as a person in a world of persons, and for the present purpose this world consists of these two (*PA*, 250).

Here is a 'double situation' in which every person participates. One first makes his emotions known to himself, but each person is conscious of another's person as co-relative to his own. As person, a sentient organism must always be relative to, referred to, in terms of another sentient organism as person.

The hearer, therefore, conscious that he is being addressed by another person like himself (without that original consciousness the so-called communication of emotion by language could never take place), takes what he hears exactly as if it were speech of his own: he speaks to himself with the words that he hears addressed to him, and thus constructs in himself the idea which those words express. At the same time, being conscious of the speaker as a person other than himself, he attributes that idea to this other person. Understanding what someone says to you is thus attributing to him the idea which his words arouse in yourself; and this implies treating them as words of your own (*PA*, 250).

Recall that Collingwood said that 'each one of us is a finite being, surrounded by others of the same kind', and the consciousness of our own existence is also the consciousness of them. This is the original consciousness he speaks of, and it too must be understood as a generic concept with a subordinate intension of overlapping forms.[1] A person, who has first heard his own speaking, takes the other person's speaking 'exactly as if it were speech of his own: he speaks to himself with the words that he hears addressed to him and thus constructs in himself the idea which those words express' (*PA*, 250). This is one conscious act that he performs as hearer. He is thus addressed, conscious *that* he is hearer, and he builds up together *what* he hears. This building process brings together the impression expressed intentionally as an idea. He has come to understand himself as always being in a double situation, i.e., as

[1] Cf. Stanage, op. cit., pp. 43 and 44–75. A subordinate intensional overlap is an overlap of intension between concepts which are the subordinate intension of a proximate generic concept.

speaker and hearer, and he has come to know himself as surrounded by other persons like himself. Hence, he attributes, assigns, or gives over this idea to someone else. This attributing is itself one's demonstration that he understands the idea. To understand is to show that you can (as hearer) rightly assign an idea to another person as speaker, 'attributing to him the idea which his words arouse in yourself; and this implies treating them as words of your own', or putting it another way, you have folded his words back to him.

This might seem to presuppose community of language between the speaker and hearer; for unless they were accustomed to use the same words, the hearer in using them to himself would not mean the same thing by them. But community of language is not another situation independent of the situation we have been describing, and prior to it: it is one name by which we refer to that situation itself. One does not first acquire a language and then use it. To possess it and to use it are the same. We only come to possess it by repeatedly and progressively attempting to use it (PA, 259).

Collingwood's point is that there is no community of language in the sense that language must first have a being and an existence among or with a *communitas*. Language must be used in common—its sense must be common—but this common sense usage of language first by the speaker with himself as his hearer, and later by other speakers and hearers is itself the community of language. This is Collingwood's version of the view that the meaning of language is itself its own use and employment. But this employment must also include the history of persons' attempts at correct usage; this is what we term the etymology of the words employed in a language. Thus, the use of a language includes necessarily the history of its use. 'Hence, to possess it and to use it are the same. We only come to possess it by repeatedly and progressively attempting to use it.' And the *Oxford English Dictionary*, for example, contains much of the English-speaking world's tracings of this history of usage.

The reader may object that if what is here maintained were true there could never be any absolute assurance, either for the hearer or for the speaker, that the one had understood the other. That is so; but in fact there is no such assurance. The only assurance we possess is an empirical and relative assurance, becoming progressively stronger as conversation proceeds and based on the fact that neither party seems to the other to be talking nonsense. The question whether they understand each other *solvitur interloquendo*. If they understand each other well enough to go on talking, they understand each other as well as they need; and there is no better kind of understanding which they can regret not having attained (*PA*, 250–1).[1]

Consciousness has progressed only so far at a given moment in analysis, or in the investigation of what is being said. A mind has only lived so long, and a person has only become what he has become at a given moment. There is no assurance that complete understanding has taken place between speaker and hearer, even when the speaker hears himself, if by assurance one means arrival at a truth forever safe from falsity or from error. And there is never to be absolute assurance of this. Indeed, all truth is seen to present error in some sense as well, and error is necessary in some degree for something to be known to be true. Collingwood's point can be re-stated by saying that truth and falsity overlap within the generic concept and generic essence *understanding*.[2] Literally, for Collingwood, error, falsity, and negation, stand underneath truth and affirmation, and to learn something, then, is at least to expose errors about it.

There is empirical and relative assurance. A person experiences a relative safety in the truth of what he speaks or hears through conversation and discourse with another person. Two persons

---

[1] The process never ceases. Why? Cf. Collingwood, 'The Devil', (1916), in Lionel Rubinoff, ed., *Faith and Reason* (Chicago, 1968), pp. 212–33, esp. p. 232: 'Man's life is a becoming; and not only becoming, but self-creation. He does not grow under the direction and control of irresistible forces. The force that shapes him is his own will. All his life is an effort to attain real human nature. But human nature, since man is at bottom split, is only exemplified in the absolute spirit of God. Hence, man must shape himself in God's image, or he ceases to be even human and becomes diabolical. This self-creation must also be self-knowledge; not the self-knowledge of introspection, the examination of the self that is, but the knowledge of God, the self that is to be. Knowledge of God is the beginning, the center, and end of human life.'

[2] Cf. *EPM*, esp. pp. 90–1 and 104–6.

repeatedly turn their subject-matters in many directions as they speak and hear, and run about with their words, so to speak. The test of successful understanding is whether either person 'seems to the other to be talking nonsense' or not. In any event, the method according to which both the test is run and the process takes place is what we normally think of as a dialogue at one stage and a dialectic of questions and answers at a higher stage.[1]

The possibility of such understanding depends on the hearer's ability to reconstruct in his own consciousness the idea expressed by the words he hears. This reconstruction is an act of imagination; and it cannot be performed unless the hearer's experience has been such as to equip him for it. We have already seen (Chapter X, Section 4, end) that, as all ideas are derived from impressions, no idea can be formed as such in consciousness except by a mind whose sensuous-emotional experience contains the corresponding impression, at least in a faint and submerged shape, at that very moment. If words, however eloquent and well chosen, are addressed to a hearer in whose mind there is no impression corresponding to the idea they are meant to convey, he will either treat them as nonsense, or will attribute to them (possibly with the caution that the speaker has not expressed himself very well) a meaning derived from his own experience and forced upon them in spite of an obvious misfit. The same thing will happen if, although the hearer has the right impression in his mind, he suffers from a corruption of consciousness (Chapter X, Section 6) which will not allow him to attend to it (PA, 250).

How is it possible to reconstruct in one's own consciousness the idea expressed by the words which he hears? Expressing is an intentional activity with two intended objects, an impression and an idea which, in the act of expression itself, are turned together, with the former leaving its mark in the form of the latter. In the expressive act, the speaker in and through his very language is constructing the idea. He is fashioning it out of a repertoire, but

[1] Stanage, 'The Personal World,' pp. 23–5. Dialogue and dialectic share the same etymological root. They both mean 'to speak through' or 'across'. Dialogue is the actual encounter, the real involvement, the full commitment. Dialectic is the closest approximation of dialogue as actually in process and known re-flexively as being in process. It is a re-creation, re-interpretation, and trans-formation of dialogue, Cf. Collingwood, PA, especially pp. 273–336; A, 29–43; EM, 21–48; Stanage, 'The Role of the "Overlap" in Collingwood's Philosophy', esp. pp. 154–94 passim, and pp. 194–5.

not in the sense of bringing parts together to create a whole. He is choosing the whole already made and coming to know it better in the act of saying it. His expressive act, then, is constructive,[1] and having an idea he must already have had in mind that sensuous-emotional experience which contains the corresponding impression, at least in a faint and submerged shape, at that very moment.

Through this expressive act, the hearer, however, does not merely construct the idea expressed to him. The hearer must re-construct[2] the idea, and this reconstruction can only take place in consciousness. In being spoken-to he is conscious *that* an idea has been expressed, *that* an impression has left its mark in the form of an idea, and then he must build up again this same idea in his own consciousness. In order to do so he must have a mind of his own which has 'an impression corresponding to the idea' expressed to him. He cannot be sure that he does, but he can only find out by a conversational process, a dialectic, a question-answer-question process.[3] This process actually is both the speaker's construction of the idea and the hearer's reconstruction of it, for questions literally both seek and search, whereas answers pledge a direction for the search, to stake out a claim for what is sought. Answers, to be sure, give rise to additional questions in the dialectical process, so construction and reconstruction of ideas can be seen as distinguishable, but inseparable, forms of the generic concept of understanding ideas.

If a hearer does not have in his own mind an 'impression corresponding to the idea' the speaker has attempted to convey, and cannot imagine such an impression in his own consciousness through question-answer-question conversation, then, as Collingwood states, 'he will either treat them as nonsense, or will attribute to them . . . a meaning derived from his own experience and forced upon them in spite of an obvious misfit' (*PA*, 251). That there is a misfit and what it is, however, can still only be adduced

---

[1] Collingwood, 'Aesthetic', pp. 214–44.

[2] This process of *re*-construction is crucial to the educative process, and, of course, for Collingwood's philosophy of history. In the latter case, see *IH*, esp. pp. 282–302.

[3] Cf. p. 284, n. 1, above.

by the question-answer-question process through which the construction of the idea is expressed by the speaker and the *re*-construction of this idea is attempted by the hearer.[1]

The hearer's *re*construction may be an erroneous one, and is perhaps always erroneous in some degree and kind (with the special exception of the case Collingwood makes for the historians' work). Collingwood affirms that many errors, especially persistent ones, contain much, and often important truth. They are a part of the rich texture with which the imagination works. Each of the first four forms of experience (art, religion, science, history) is an error in the sense that no one of these ever succeeds in performing its promise as being a co-ordinate species of knowledge to all the rest. They are 'each valid and autonomous in its own sphere but each limited to a single aspect of reality, each constituting a single aspect of the mind' (*SM*, 251). When the mind cashes in on the pledge to perform in this way, error is discovered and itself proves to be one of the foundations upon which a higher form on the scale of forms may be analyzed through a phenomenology of the forms of experience.[2] For example, 'art fails us because it does not assert', and 'the error of science is its abstractness . . . (but) the discovery by science of its own abstractness is the correction of that abstractness and the revelation of the concrete object' (*SM*, 201).

Collingwood formulated a theory of the forms of error in *Speculum Mentis*, a theory of the ways in which we wander into incorrectness as we articulate the life of our mind. 'The dogmatic philosophies are identical with philosophical errors. Every error is a lapse from concreteness into abstraction, and our abstraction is dogmatism. We err because we dogmatize—because we do not criticize our own assumptions—and we dogmatize because we err, because we think they are not assumptions' (*SM*, 288).

Concrete philosophy is what Collingwood always espoused, a unity and a wholeness of the life of the mind, and any selecting out of special ingredients and parts of this life of the mind growing in unity as the person becomes more conscious of the self-creativity of the life of the mind is liable to error precisely because it parts some

---

[1] See p. 285, nn. 1, 2, above.
[2] Cf. *SM*, *passim*, and *EPM*, *passim*.

things away from the whole.[1] The solution of these kinds of problems and their variations, e.g., the question of identity and difference, was the goal of both the scale of forms and the scale of the forms of experience. But the attainment of this goal necessitated his theory of errors. He conceived of a theory of errors as leading to a table of errors, 'the philosopher's personal confession of sin (SM, 291). A philosopher, in thinking through the problem with which he works must re-think the history of these problems and the attempted solutions to them. He must realize that because these problems have a history they are not really the same problems from time to time. A solution to a philosophical problem at a given time historically gave rise to other aspects of the problem which became problematic themselves and often changed the original problem. Even solutions later demonstrated to have been erroneous contribute to the changing nature of the problems in their history; '. . . the criticism of contemporary error is simply the application to modern problems of lessons learned in the school of philosophical history' (SM, 290). Hence, a writer becomes aware of certain tempting ways to approach philosophical problems which appear attractive but personally unsatisfying. But like Jesus, he must face these temptations alone, re-construct them in his own consciousness, discover both their attractiveness and error, and discard them in favour of a higher truth. This 'pain of certain shipwreck, he must absorb into his own philosophy while rejecting the elements which make them unsatisfactory' (SM, 291).

Adducing the erroneous within a subject-matter is the growing edge in one's education. The history of the methods for dealing with a subject clarifies the errors of these ways and suggests the possibilities for their reconstruction. Thus a child must come to understand this process and to know in his own life that education is *for* 'real life', but not *in* it, for during his preparation for life he is allowed to run the risk of error without paying the penalties for this which might be exacted at a later date.

Misunderstanding is not necessarily the hearer's fault; it may be the speaker's. This will be the case if through corruption in his own con-

[1] Cf. especially SM, 30–8, and in many of his works, *passim*. Note especially: EPM, A, and EM.

sciousness the idea which he expresses is a falsified one; certain elements, which are in fact essential to the expressed idea, being disowned. Any attempt on the hearer's part to reconstruct the idea for himself will (unless his own consciousness happens to be similarly corrupted) result in his rediscovering, as an integral part of the idea, this disowned element; and thus speaker and hearer will be again at cross-purposes (*PA*, 251–2).

Collingwood had previously written that '. . . consciousness is thought in its absolutely fundamental and original shape . . .. A true consciousness is the confession to ourselves of our feelings; a false consciousness would be disowning them, i.e., thinking about one of them "That feeling is not mine"' (*PA*, 216). There are three alternatives open to consciousness concerning the ways of converting an impression into an idea. *First*, if a given feeling is recognized it may be converted from impression to idea simply by being attended to. *Second*, if a given feeling is not recognized, it is left unattended, or ignored.

The *third* alternative, if opted for, lays the foundation for Collingwood's theory of the corruption of consciousness.[1] Consciousness may attend to a feeling and recognize it abortively.

First, we direct our attention towards a certain feeling, or become conscious of it. Then we take fright at what we have recognized: not because the feeling, as an impression, is an alarming impression, but because *the idea into which we are converting it proves an alarming idea. We cannot see our way to dominate it, and shrink from persevering in the attempt. We therefore give it up, and turn our attention to something less intimidating* (*PA*, 217).[2]

---

[1] Collingwood called the corruption of consciousness the 'worst disease of the mind' (*PA*, 336). This corruption of consciousness was often the occasion for analysis and comment, whether in direct or indirect terms: Cf., e.g., *SM*, 229, 288–91, and *passim* (under other guises); *EPM*, 137–50; *PA*, 215–24, 273–336, esp. pp. 280–92, and *passim*; 15, 21, 44–52, 147–67, and *passim*; *EM*, 122–80, 338–43; *NL*, pp. 308–87. See, also, Alan Donagan, *The Later Philosophy of R. G. Collingwood* (Oxford, 1962), pp. 126–33, and Lionel Rubinoff, ed., *Faith and Reason*, pp. 12–19.

In the sense in which the processes of consciousness are aborted and broken by a corrupt consciousness, this notion as Collingwood develops it deserves the most careful attention in any subsequent study of his philosophy of education.

[2] My italics.

The corrupt consciousness is a consciousness which has deliberately *broken*, aborted the conversion process whereby an impression becomes an idea, and it has done so for reasons of bad faith. In this case consciousness cannot accept a given idea; it cannot persevere in the process. At least one other feeling (an impression which consciousness can then attend to) is the feeling of shrinking, revulsion, anxiety, or some similar feeling. When consciousness attends to this feeling, wilfully acknowledging that it is attending to this feeling and not to the more originative one which gave use to the break in the conversation process in the first place, consciousness is *corrupt*.

This corrupt consciousness has been described in a variety of ways by psychologists, viz., as repression, projection, dissociation, fantasy-building, etc., depending on the particular pathway the abortion process takes in the mind. Spinoza saw it even earlier (*Ethics*, Part V, prop. 3). But for Collingwood the condition of the corrupt consciousness is far more serious than these psychological diagnoses would suggest; not only is this condition an untruth, 'it is an example of evil' (*PA*, 220). Moreover, 'when consciousness is corrupted, imagination shares the corruption'. When this happens, the corrupted consciousness of a man, a society, or a civilization infests all of the imaginative labours of that man, society, or civilization, and necessarily all of its intellectual products.[1]

Collingwood held that the imagination is the first step in the growth of knowledge, and that the child should be more proficient in the imagination than anything else. Therefore, the child should be encouraged (primarily through the power, resourcefulness, and the versatility of its parents)[2] in the arts, for it is through these

---

[1] Cf. p. 275, n. 1, and p. 288, n. 1, above. The corruption of the imagination leads to the corrupt consciousness, with all of its attendant ingredients of bad faith, and in turn to the many forms of the propaganda of irrationalism. Among these, Collingwood repeatedly listed: the separatist intellectual fruits of the Renaissance, positivism, critical and analytical philosophy; various obscurantist positions arrayed against metaphysics and psychology as the science of feeling; political and economic malfeasance. All of these, in his understanding, have been a falling away from the orderly and systematic processes of reason and have endangered western civilization. All have been fostered and perpetuated by an irrationalist philosophy of education.

[2] Cf., 'The Place of Art in Education', 'Aesthetic', *NL*, pp, 308–17.

imaginative constructions that the mind becomes embodied in what we call *knowledge*. These embodiments constitute the world of the educated person, and although distinguishable, e.g., as specific problems, disciplines, and kinds of study, they must never lose the unity and wholeness through which they came to birth in the imagination. This loss would lead necessarily to the corruption of the imagination and consciousness—the worst disease of the mind.

In Chapter XI, Section 6, of *The Principles of Art*, Collingwood discusses 'Language and Thought'. That section is important to the present essay since in it imagination and intellect are distinguished; the former 'presents to itself an object which it experiences as one and indivisible', whereas the latter 'goes beyond that single object and presents to itself a world of many such relations of determinate kinds between them'.

He presents a phenomenological analysis of an example which has telling consequences for his theory of education. Consider the example:

I listen to a thrush singing. By mere sensation I hear at any given moment only one note or one fragment of a note. By imagination what I have been hearing continues to vibrate in my thought as an idea, so that the whole sung phrase is present to me as an idea at a single moment. I may now go on to a further act, by which I imagine alongside of this present May thrush-song the thrush-song of January. So far as the entire experience remains at the level of imagination, as distinct from that of intellect, these two songs are not imagined separately as two things with a relation between them. The January song coalesces with the May song, and confers upon it a new quality of mature mellowness. Thus what I imagine, however complex it may be, is imagined as a single whole, where relations between the parts are present simply as qualities of the whole (*PA*, 253).

Imagination articulates itself through the intellection, and in this streamlike process the mind comes to recognize itself through consciousness of itself. This is very much the essence of the educative process for Collingwood. Through linguistic relations, persons (speakers-hearers) attend to phenomena and constitute their world in community; civilization is education, Collingwood affirmed.

In this light, consider his example in more precise, exploratory terms. It is possible to describe both *what* the phenomenon (the continuing vibration) is as it appears and the *ways* of its appearing.

In describing what the phenomenon is Collingwood has invoked a temporal distinction when speaking of 'one note or one fragment of a note', at a given moment which, by imagination, 'continues to vibrate . . .'. Then, as he says, by imagination he may go on to a further act, by which he imagines 'alongside of this present May thrush-song the thrush-song of January'. But his temporal distinctions are not in terms of three modes of time, viz., past, present, and future. Even if such were invoked, 'The January song coalesces with the May song, and confers upon it a new quality of mature mellowness.' Here is a generic, essential thrust, for the coalescence of these songs and 'a new quality of mature mellowness' may be explored as a whole through its temporal lines.

Another way through which the method of phenomenology focusses upon what the experience is (as imagined) is to describe the process of discovering the phenomenon of listening to the thrush-song. Collingwood has done so, and he has shown how we discover this in the ways in which it appears to us. It appears to us in three ways.

In the first *sense* of focussing upon the appearings of this whole, we come to feel, to experience, and to conscious (know-with) better and better what we have already felt, experienced, and conscioused previously in part. Sometimes, even, a whole appears to us 'as a whole', we say. He said, 'so far as the entire experience remains at the level of imagination, as distinct from that of intellect, these two songs are not imagined separately as two things with a relation between them.' This is a way of saying, surely, that the coalescence appears as a whole.

The *second* sense requires that we recognize modifications of the thrush-singing as 'perspectives shading-off', or the phenomenon as it reaches toward its own outer, exploring edges. Collingwood, in calling attention to the 'new quality of mellowness', seems to recognize this.

The *third* sense in which we may describe the relations of the appearings of the coalescence of the January song and the May song may be stated as the 'modes of clarity', or the degrees of clarity and distinctness in which the phenomenon appears to us: 'What I have been hearing continues to vibrate in my thought as an idea, so that the whole sung phrase is present to me as an idea at a single moment.'

Each of these three examples of focussing upon the appearings of a phenomenon like this one in Collingwood's discussion manifests the sort of experience we ordinarily have in mind when we affirm that we have come to know in imaginative, generative ways. But there is still one final sense in which we can describe the relatings of this phenomenon. This way consists in 'the determination of the typical structure of a constitution of a phenomenon by means of an analysis of the essential sequence of its steps.'[1] This kind of description requires that we place together in sequence some of the essential steps through which a phenomenon is constituted in our consciousness. This Collingwood has done clearly in the above passage.

Moreover,

If, starting from the same experience of listening to a bird-song, I now begin to think about it, in the narrower sense of that word, I analyse it into parts. From being an indivisible unity it becomes a manifold, a network of things with relations between them. Here is one note, and here another, higher or lower, softer or louder. Each is different from the other, and different in a definite way. I can think of these qualities by themselves, and reflect that a note might be higher and louder than another, or higher and softer. I can describe the difference between two songs by saying that one has a sweeter tone than the other, or is longer, or contains more notes. This is analytic thought (PA, 253).

Through use of a phenomenological method it will also be possible to describe the particularizings of the experience of listening to a birdsong. There may be at least two ways of particularizing this experience. One of these ways deals with a part of the experience as distinct, but not separate, from the whole, e.g., as one speaks of the one note *heard* higher than another note. Thus, to particularize this phenomenon of listening or hearing is to

[1] See Herbert Spiegelberg, *The Essentials of the Phenomenological Method* (The Hague, 1965), p. 688.

focus upon some one (or more) of its individual constituents, ingredients, and configurations, to *take* the higher note, and to concentrate upon it for special investigation and exploration.

The other way through which the experience of listening to the birdsong might be particularized is to describe the experience, or to portray, represent, and communicate directly, by means of properties and qualities, the uniqueness of the phenomenon which is experienced. This description may begin with a question like, 'How much higher is that note than the other one?' or 'How much softer is the second note?' Each of these ways of describing the particularizings is literally a writing-down, a selection, and a firming-up of central or decisive characteristics of this individual and particular experience, and no other.

Collingwood's example is the thrush-song, but it could be any phenomenon which consciousness intends, and the latter would be, *mutatis mutandis*, another constitution and embodiment of the mind at work in self-recognition. Most of his writings contain explorations and investigations into particular phenomena which, when gathered together under appropriate generic concepts, constitute his scale of the forms of experience (art, religion, science, history, philosophy).[1] These are the structurings of his philosophy of education and the exfoliations in the education of persons.

The intuiting, describing, and relating which belong to his phenomenology of education bespeak an unfinished and un-finishable investigation, for the exact dimension of the overlap of all the forms of experience on the scale presupposed cannot be precisely specified. This openness requires that we suspend all questions pertaining to the existence or non-existence, possibility or impossibility, and even questions of the possible origins of the phenomenon.[2] Whatever else may be involved, this commitment to openness is a plea that the phenomenon not be reduced, but only that educators pay the greatest attention to imaginative con-structions and reconstructions and never entirely leave them behind.

---

[1] See *SM*.

[2] Cf. Collingwood: *SM, passim*, and consider the relevance of the theory of errors with this openness in mind; *EPM*, esp. pp. 1–23, 176–98, *passim*. Cf., also, Stanage, 'The Personal World,' pp. 38–40.

In this brief essay I have tried to stake out the claim that Collingwood's philosophy does offer a philosophy of education, and to chart some of the principal markings within this claim. The major focus has been squarely upon what Collingwood has offered as a theory of persons as speaker-hearer and upon the generation of the linguistic relations and the articulation of the self-recognizing mind through these. In the philosophical sense (although not strictly in the metaphysical and psychological sense) persons discover themselves in and through the constructive and expressive uses of language. Education consists in this and in the perpetuating embodiments in the world of these constructions of language.

Finally, while not dealing directly with Collingwood's many practical suggestions concerning the specifics of a child's schooling, this discussion of his philosophy of education has found it necessary to show how the language of the imagination and the language of thought can be seen as overlapping forms comprising the subordinate intension of the generic concept of language *qua* speaking-hearing act. The method of phenomenology has provided a means for conducting an exploration of this subordinate intension whereby the implicit meanings have become more explicit.

A speaking-hearing act expresses our feelings, and this speaking-hearing act is an imaginative activity first. These acts are fundamental in all education. All of the forms of our experience are born in these imaginative activities, and all of these forms of experience have educative dimensions. But the educative dimensions of the experience of art, the constructing process of the mind through the embodiments of its own self-recognition are the most crucial.

Thus, Collingwood's phenomenology of education has founded for us the most primitive identifiable ways in which the mind comes to cognize and *re*-cognize itself better and better through the ways in which it comes to embodying life through its constructions and reconstructions. Thereby the mind itself constitutes and reconstitutes its worlds, and becomes embodied in them. This embodying mind, constituting and reconstituting itself, and thereby coming to its own self-recognition, is *person*, both speaker and hearer. The process by which it does so is called both civilization and education. And to articulate the principles by which it does so is to do a philosophy of education.

To articulate these principles in the detailed manner necessary would be to present Collingwood's philosophy of education far beyond this rudimentary, claim-staking stage. This more important labour remains to be done by all who are interested, and who in their own ways find in Collingwood's philosophy rich treasures like those I continue to find there.

Finally, the reader who is familiar with Collingwood's philosophy should be able to draw many principles of a philosophy of education from what has been presented throughout this essay. In closing, I will briefly state several of the more significant ones which emerge from what I have said.

1. Education is preparation for life pursued through the orderly and systematic investigation of any subject-matter conceived as a unity.
2. The construction and reconstruction of the embodiments of the mind comprise a scale of the forms of human experience, each a distinguishable but inseparable species of the entirety of identifiable human experience.
3. Persons both discover themselves and others and embody their worlds through the construction and expression of linguistic relations.
4. Although the discovery, embodiments, and construction of persons and their worlds never ends these begin in the family and must be directed and encouraged almost entirely by the parents.
5. The educative process consists fundamentally in the discovery and correction of errors within the linguistic relations which embody persons' worlds and in maintaining and encouraging a healthy consciousness.
6. All persons must be encouraged in the imaginative pursuits (of art, primarily) as the only antidote to a corrupt consciousness which leads to all forms of irrationalist propaganda.

XIV

COLLINGWOOD'S ETHICS
AND POLITICAL THEORY

A. J. M. MILNE

COLLINGWOOD TOUCHED briefly on ethics in *Speculum Mentis* and in his *Autobiography* had some hard things to say about contemporary British politics. But it is to his last completed book, *The New Leviathan*, that we must go for a systematic exposition of his ideas in ethics and political theory. These ideas had apparently been maturing long before the writing of *The New Leviathan* was begun soon after the outbreak of the Second World War. In the Preface, speaking of his return to Oxford after the First World War, Collingwood wrote:

It was now that I began to think out the fundamental ideas of the present book, thereafter revising and elaborating them year after year in experimental form, accumulating as time went on I will not say how many thousands of pages of manuscript on every problem of ethics and politics, and especially on the problems of history which bore on my subject; and imparting my results, when I seemed to reach any which were worth imparting, in lectures to my juniors and in manuscripts to such of my colleagues as seemed interested (*NL*, Preface).

Collingwood describes *The New Leviathan* in the opening chapter as: 'an inquiry into civilization and the revolt against it which is the most conspicuous thing going on at the present time' (*NL*, 1.12). This inquiry is the context in which his ideas in ethics and political theory are expounded. He goes on:

Civilization is a condition of communities; so to understand what civilization is, we must first understand what a community is. A community is a condition of man in which are included women and children; so to understand what a community is we must first understand what men are. This gives us the scheme of the present book: Part 1, an inquiry into man; Part 2, an inquiry into communities; Part 3, an inquiry into civilizations; and Part 4, an inquiry into revolts against civilization (*NL*, 1.13–.15).

And he adds: 'About each subject we need to understand only so much as we need to understand what is to be said about the next' (*NL*, 1.16).

All this, like Collingwood's title, suggests that he is consciously following in the footsteps of Hobbes. That was certainly his intention. He had said in the Preface: 'My own book is best understood as an attempt to bring *The Leviathan* up-to-date in the light of the advances made since it was written, in history, psychology, and anthropology' (*NL*, Preface). An essay might well be written about Collingwood's relation to Hobbes but that is not my purpose here. I shall confine myself to his leading ideas in ethics and political theory, and I shall discuss them under two heads: (A) Freedom and Practical Reason; and (B) The Body Politic. That means that I shall be concerned mainly with the latter part of Part 1 of *The New Leviathan* and with Part 2. But in a brief concluding section, C. Civilization, I shall have something to say about the later stages of Collingwood's enterprise. The thesis which I shall try to develop is briefly this. Collingwood's ideas in ethics and political theory need to be criticized, revised, and reformulated, if what is of value, and I think there is much of value, in his account of civilization is to stand.

Collingwood says that: 'Civilization is a thing of the mind and a community too is a thing of the mind' (*NL*, 1.21). An inquiry into civilization therefore belongs to what he calls 'the sciences of mind'. A discussion of his conception of sciences of mind and of their relation to the natural sciences would also need an essay to itself. Two things however need to be said about it here. The first is that for him psychology is not a science of mind but a natural science. The second, that what he is interested in is not the human mind at large but the modern European mind. 'Whatever I need to know about mind is about the modern European mind; for that is what has produced in itself the thing called modern European civilization, or civilization for short, and also the revolt against it' (*NL*, 9.21). I shall have something to say about this at the end of my essay, but at the outset it is enough to say that Collingwood is engaged in a conceptual inquiry of much the same sort that in the years since the Second World War has come to be regarded by many British and American philosophers as their main business. The concepts in which he is interested are those which he considers to lie at the centre of modern European thought and action in moral, social, and political contexts.

I have already said that my discussion of Collingwood's ethics and political theory will be critical. The kind of criticism in which I shall engage is best understood in terms of the Platonic distinction between 'eristic' and 'dialectic', a distinction which Collingwood himself appropriated and which plays a central role in his whole argument. 'What Plato calls an eristic discussion is one in which each party tries to prove that he was right and the other wrong. In a dialectical discussion you aim at showing that your own view is one with which your opponent really agrees even if at one time he denied it; or, conversely that it was yourself and not your opponent who began by denying a view with which you really agree' (NL, 24.58–.59). In eristic, there is disagreement, in dialectic, 'non-agreement', and the essence of the dialectical attitude is a 'constant endeavour to convert every occasion of non-agreement into an occasion of agreement' (NL, 39.15). There will be a number of occasions of non-agreement between Collingwood and myself in what follows, but I shall do my best to convert them into occasions of agreement.

(A) Freedom and Practical Reason

1. According to Collingwood, men are not born free. They have to achieve freedom and this can be done only at a relatively advanced stage of mental development. What is achieved is freedom of the will. 'The freedom of the will is, positively, *freedom to choose; freedom to exercise a will;* and negatively *freedom from desire;* not the condition of having no desires but the condition of not being at their mercy' (NL, 13.25). If you are at their mercy, you can act from preference but not make choices. 'A man who prefers A. to B. does not choose at all; he suffers desire for A. and aversion towards B.: and goes where desire leads him' (NL, 13.14). Freedom,

or freedom of the will, is achieved by an involuntary act of self-liberation. '*Liberation from what?* From the dominance of desire. *Liberation to do what?* To make decisions' (*NL*, 13.22). If voluntary acts are those which issue from decisions, the act of self-liberation which makes voluntary acts possible cannot itself be a voluntary act. But while the act of self-liberation is involuntary, its occurrence is not inevitable. 'This achievement of free will marks the stage at which, in modern Europe, a man is supposed to reach intellectual maturity. If anything interferes with the course of his mental development, this step may never happen; he will then become a man who is incapable of growing up; perhaps a man who hates the thing (mental maturity) he does not possess' (*NL*, 13.57 and 13.58).

But the freedom of the will which any man can achieve is always a matter of degree. 'On certain questions and in certain circumstances an agent may be capable of decision, or free; on other questions or in other circumstances the same agent may be utterly unable to prevent a certain passion or a certain desire from taking charge' (*NL*, 21.8). Collingwood calls this breakdown of freedom 'a cracking of the will' and he adds: 'for any man, I suppose, there are conditions under which a crack of the will would happen' (*NL*, 21.81). Collingwood distinguishes between physical and mental force, and argues that when a man yields to mental force, he undergoes a crack of the will. 'When a man suffers force, *the origin of the force is always something within himself,* some irresistible emotion which makes him do something he does not intend to do' (*NL*, 20.59); and he goes on: 'If B. suffers force at the hands of A., it is A. who excites in B. this irresistible emotion' (*NL*, 20.59).

Choice is of the essence of freedom but choice in its simplest form is identical with caprice. Collingwood describes caprice as: 'Mere choice or mere decision, uncomplicated by any reason why it should be made in this way and not in that' (*NL*, 13.12). From this he concludes that a completely capricious act is a completely irrational act while a completely rational act is one from which all caprice has been eliminated. It follows that absence of caprice is the test of the rationality of action or of 'practical reason'. The greater the rationality the less the caprice and the greater the caprice the less the rationality. But what kinds of reason are there for choosing in one way rather than in another? What are the forms of practical reason? According to Collingwood, there are three. 'It is not because three is in my eyes a magical number; but I find that people talking about practical reason distinguish various types of it, and that these types, under inspection, resolve themselves into three falling in a certain order' (*NL*, 14.64). The three in ascending order of rationality are: Utility, Right, and Duty. Collingwood says that: 'On any occasion when a modern European answers the question: "Why did you do that?" he will answer: 1. "Because it is useful." 2. "Because it is right." 3. "Because it is my duty"' (*NL*, 14.65).

To do an act because it is useful is to do it as a means to an end. Utilitarian action therefore involves two decisions: one about the end and another about the means. There has to be what Collingwood calls an 'ends plan' and a 'means plan' (*NL*, 15.8). The rationality of utilitarian action lies in: 'the abstract conformity of the means plan to the abstract specifications of the ends plan' (*NL*, 15.8). He calls both the ends plan and the means plan, 'indefinite individuals' and goes on: 'Everything except the conformity of these indefinite individuals to one another is, from the utilitarian point of view, irrational' (*NL*, 15.8). He says of an indefinite individual that it is 'required to satisfy certain specifications but free to vary so long as those specifications are satisfied' (*NL*, 15.72). What he has in mind seems to be this. The ends plan must specify a state of affairs in sufficient detail for it to be envisaged and brought about by human action. The means plan must specify a course of action in sufficient detail for it to be deliberately undertaken as a way of bringing about the state of affairs specified in the ends plan. The detail in each case is incomplete, being no more than is necessary for utilitarian action to get under way. With respect to the detail which it specifies, each plan is an individual plan. But with respect to what it leaves unspecified, each is indefinite or capricious. The unspecified details are free to vary, that is, are decided capriciously as action proceeds. Utility is therefore imperfectly rational owing to the element of caprice in both the ends plan and the means plan. It is also capricious in another way which Collingwood does not mention, although it is perhaps implicit in his account. This is in the decision about what state of affairs is to be the end for utilitarian action. So far as utility is concerned, there is no reason for choosing one end rather than another.

Right is the second form of practical reason. Collingwood contrasts it with utility. 'A thing is useful or the opposite in relation to the end it achieves; it is right or the opposite in relation to the rule it obeys' (*NL*, 16.23). Practical reason in the form of utility gives rise to utilitarian action. Practical reason in the form of right gives rise to regularian action. Collingwood says that: 'A man may, and often does, make rules solely for himself: this, indeed, is regularian action in its simplest form and unless we understand this we shall never understand the complex case in which a man makes rules for others to obey' (*NL*, 16.35). He says that a rule is a generalized purpose which he describes as: 'a purpose to do things of a certain kind on all occasions of a certain kind' (*NL*, 16.31). But 'a rule is only one part of a regularian action. There is also the decision to obey or disobey it' (*NL*, 16.33). Two kinds of decision are therefore involved in regularian action: decisions about what rules to obey; and decisions to obey them in situations which they cover. According to Collingwood, regularian action is infected with caprice although not to the same extent as utilitarian action (cf. *NL*, 16.61). This is because 'a rule only specifies *some* act of a certain kind. The application of it to a given occasion bids me perform one, and only one, of the acts which would conform to its specifications. The acts which so conform may be many or few; which they are, depends not on the rule but on the circumstances; if they are many, I have got to choose between them, but the rule cannot tell me how. From the regularian point of view my choice between the alternatives is a matter of caprice' (*NL*, 16.62). So for that matter, although Collingwood does not mention it, is my initial decision about what rule to obey.

Duty is the third form of practical reason. According to Collingwood, duty is the discharging of an obligation which the agent has already incurred (cf. *NL*, 17.16). His doctrine seems to be this. The incurring of an obligation is a free act. One chooses to give an undertaking to do something. Having given the undertaking one must then carry it out. This is what duty is: the carrying out of undertakings freely given, or the discharging of obligations freely incurred. Collingwood asks what is meant by the phrase 'his duty' when a man says that something is his duty and answers: 'A man's duty on a given occasion is that act which for him is both possible and necessary: the act which at the moment character and circumstance combine to make it inevitable, if he has a free will, that he should freely will to do.' (*NL*, 17.8). Unlike utilitarian and regularian actions, 'dutiful' actions are definite individuals. Duty is in principle free from caprice. It is the only one of the three forms of practical reason which is completely rational. 'Any duty is a duty to do *this* act and only *this*, not *an act of this kind*' (*NL*, 17.53). But judgements about what one's duty is are never incorrigible. The most that a man can say is 'I have considered, X, Y and Z, as claimants for the title of my present duty; X is a better answer than Y, and Y than Z; but there may be a better answer than any which I have overlooked' (*NL*, 17.81).

2. In all this, there are a number of occasions of non-agreement between Collingwood and myself. To begin with his account of mental force: he says that what forces a man is always something within himself. This is not necessarily so. A man may yield to a threat not from panic, but because he judges it to be the lesser evil. His will does not crack. He makes a rational decision. Asked 'Why did you do that?' (for instance, hand over the money) his answer is: 'Because it was prudent.' *Pace* Collingwood, this is an answer in line with modern European ways of thinking and speaking. But although the man's action is rational, is it free? According to common sense: no, because it is done under constraint. According to Collingwood: yes, because he freely decides to yield. He might have resisted the threat. Both are partly right: Collingwood in that the man decides or wills to yield; common sense in that what he does in obeying whoever is threatening him is decided for him, not by him. He is obeying the will of another. The difficulty can be resolved if freedom is thought of in terms of 'self-determination', rather than merely in terms of 'will'. You are free to the extent that you determine your conduct for yourself. To the extent that

it is determined for you, not by you, you are not free. This allows for different kinds and different degrees of freedom in a way that Collingwood's account does not.[1] At the same time it preserves what is true in his account. A man who panics is not free. His action is determined by what he is afraid of. A man who acts from preference is free in the sense that he determines his conduct. But a man who acts from a rational decision is free in a different and wider sense. He determines his conduct in the light of an assessment of the alternatives open to him. But more about this later.

Collingwood says that Right and Duty are different forms of practical reason. But in terms of his account, they are not really different. According to him, to say 'I did X because it was right', is to say: 'I did X because there is a rule which prescribes that X should be done.' To say 'I did X because it was my duty', is to say: I did X because I had freely undertaken to do it.' But why should I do what I have freely undertaken to do? Collingwood does not say, but there can be no doubt about the answer. Not to do so would be wrong. It would be to break the moral rule which says that people ought to keep their word. It follows that on Collingwood's account, Duty is a special case of Right. A duty is a certain kind of right act: namely an act of the kind which meets the requirements of the moral rule that people should always do what they have freely undertaken to do. This means that both the higher forms of practical reason are regularian in character. But Collingwood's account of regularian action is unsatisfactory. Although he distinguishes between 'willing the rule' and 'willing the particular act which obeys it', he does not seem to have grasped the significance of this distinction. 'Willing' or making a rule is not itself a case of regularian action: not, that is to say, a case of obeying a rule. Obeying a rule means deciding to do an act of the kind prescribed by it in a situation of the kind which it covers. You do not have to decide what to do. The rule tells you that. You only have to decide that you will do it. Making a rule means deciding what kind of situations are to be covered and what kind of act

---

[1] I have developed this idea of freedom more fully elsewhere. See A. J. M. Milne, *Freedom and Rights* (London and New York, 1968), especially chs. 5 and 9.

is to be done in them. You have to decide not only what is to be done, but when.

According to Collingwood, the simplest case of regularian action is that of a man making rules for himself. Making rules for others to obey is a 'more complex case'. This betrays his failure to grasp the significance of the distinction between making rules and obeying them. According to his own definition, in regularian action, acts are either right or wrong. They either obey or disobey a rule. But making a rule means deciding what rule to make and while this decision can be better or worse, it cannot be right or wrong. There cannot be a rule telling you what rule to make, although there can be a 'second-order' rule conferring on you authority to make one, but leaving it to you to decide what rule it should be. The simplest case of regularian action is that of obeying rules which you do not make but find already there. This begins early in life. A child learning to talk learns to obey linguistic rules. About the same time he begins learning how to behave which means learning to obey elementary rules of good manners and moral conduct. This priority of regularian action is logical as well as temporal. You must learn how to obey rules before you can make them either for yourself or for other people. The conclusion which follows is that the higher forms of practical reason are not regularian in character. They include the more sophisticated activity of making rules but this is not regularian. Regularian action properly so called belongs to a level below practical reason.

Collingwood arrived at the three forms of practical reason by considering how modern Europeans answer the question: 'Why did you do that?' He has neglected one kind of answer: 'I did it because it was prudent.' For instance, obeying the orders of a gunman. There is also another kind of answer he has not considered 'I did it because it was wise.' 'Why did you change your job?' 'For the sake of better prospects and more interesting work.' 'Why did you take up sailing?' 'Because it would add to my enjoyment of life.' It is wise for me to better my prospects and make my life more interesting and enjoyable. It is prudent for me to provide for my safety and security and avoid unnecessary danger. The common factor here is the idea of personal well-being. Modern

Europeans think that it is rational for a man to act wisely and prudently because they think that it is rational for him to do what he can to maintain and develop his personal well-being. There are good reasons for this conviction. They lie in the fact that while circumstances play a large part in shaping the course of a man's life, he can himself influence it through his choices and decisions. What sort of life he has depends upon what he does in the face of the opportunities and limitations confronting him. He therefore has good reason to make the maintenance and development of his personal well-being a leading consideration in the determination of his conduct. If he does not concern himself with it, why should anyone else? If Collingwood had reflected on the meaning of acting wisely and prudently he might have seen that personal well-being is a form of practical reason. To say 'I did it because it was wise', or 'because it was prudent', is to say: 'I did it because in some way, it contributed to my personal well-being.'

Personal well-being must be distinguished from utility. Utility is a rational basis for the choice of means but so far as utility is concerned, the choice of ends is capricious. Personal well-being is a rational basis for the choice of ends. If a new job has better prospects and more interesting work, getting the job is a rational end of utilitarian action. But personal well-being is also relevant to the choice of means. A particular course of action may be expedient as a means, but tedious or dangerous. It may then be wise or prudent to find some other means, or, failing that, to abandon the end to which the tedious or dangerous course of action is the means. But this is not all. The perspective of utility is confined to action done as a means. The perspective of personal well-being is wider. It includes not only utilitarian action but leisure activities like sailing which are undertaken not as the means to further ends, but because they are interesting or enjoyable in themselves. As a form of practical reason, personal well-being is on a higher level than utility which is properly subordinate to it.

3. According to Collingwood, the third form of practical reason is Duty. But on his own showing, Duty is only a special case of Right. Doing my duty means obeying the moral rule that people

should always do what they have freely undertaken to do. This is not an adequate account of duty, much less of the wider idea of morality. Consider the moral virtue of honesty. If there are any moral duties at all, there is certainly one to cultivate and practice this virtue. But it does not fit Collingwood's account of duty. My duty to be honest does not arise from any undertaking I have freely given. Rather it is presupposed in all such undertakings. Instead of: 'I ought to keep my word because I ought to be honest,' Collingwood is in effect maintaining: 'I ought to be honest because I ought to keep my word.' But why ought I to be honest? More generally: why does there have to be any morality at all? Collingwood ignores this question. But it must be answered if the claim that Duty is a form of practical reason is to be justified.

Morality has a rational basis in certain conditions necessary for human co-operation. People who co-operate together become dependent upon one another. Each must do his part if the common enterprise is not to break down. This means that there can be co-operation only if there is trust, and trust presupposes honesty. Other moral commitments besides honesty are also necessary. They include self-control, justice, and responsibility. A man who cannot control himself cannot be trusted. People who co-operate must deal justly with each other if destructive disputes are to be avoided. Each must be responsible to the rest for making the best contribution he can to the common enterprise. But is there an inescapable commitment to co-operation? Yes, if there is an inescapable commitment to social living, because co-operation is of the essence of social living. I can rationally reject the commitment to co-operation and therefore to morality only if I am prepared to withdraw from social living altogether. That means either committing suicide or becoming a hermit, if the latter is still a live option in the modern world. The answer to our question then is this; there has to be morality if there is to be social living, because without it there could be no co-operation and therefore no social living.

Self-control is the most elementary moral virtue. The duty to cultivate and practice it must be inculcated in early childhood because it is a necessary condition for any coherent activity:

regularian and rational, moral and non-moral. Being honest means obeying certain rules: keeping your word, not lying, deceiving, or stealing. This suggests that over and above the elementary duty of self-control, morality is regularian in character. But justice and responsibility suggest that it is also something more. They are principles rather than merely rules. Acting on a principle involves deciding how best to implement it in the particular circumstances of a given situation: deciding what is most just or least unjust, having regard to all the interests involved; deciding how best to fulfil your responsibilities in the face of particular problems and exigencies. All this points to a distinction between two levels of moral development: a lower regularian level and a higher rational level. The lower level is that of childhood. Being moral consists of obeying established moral rules and in cases which these do not cover, or in which they conflict, relying on the guidance of parents or others to whose authority children are subject. The rational level is that of mature adult life. Being moral now means acting responsibly and justly, obeying moral rules in the spirit rather than the letter and, if doing so on a particular occasion is the lesser evil, breaking them. An important part of the process of growing up consists in making a gradual transition from the lower to the higher level. But there is nothing inevitable about this transition and, for most of us, it is never wholly completed.

At the lower level, morality is a form of regularian action, at the higher level a form of practical reason. But as a form of practical reason, it is best described as Social Morality. This brings out its rational basis. The drawback of the term 'duty' is that it is not confined to practical reason. There is a duty to act responsibly and also to act justly. But self-control and honesty are duties, and there is a general duty to obey moral rules. The question; 'Why did you do that?' can be answered in terms of social morality: 'I did it because it was the best way in which I could fulfil my responsibility', or: 'I did it because in the circumstances, it was more just than any alternative open to me.' It follows that, *pace* Collingwood, the three forms of practical reason are: Utility, Personal Well-Being, and Social Morality.[1] Regularian action belongs to a level below

[1] Cf. Milne, op. cit., especially chs. 3 and 4.

practical reason but is an indispensable preparation for it and continues within it, being, however, subordinate to its requirements. To answer the question: 'Why did you do that?' by 'Because it was right', assumes that the rule which the right act obeys has a rational justification and that on the particular occasion there are no special circumstances which would justify breaking it.

Like personal well-being, social morality is a rational basis for the choice of ends in utilitarian action. 'It is my responsibility to see that the safety precautions are adequate.' 'If we are not to be unjust, we must give him a chance to state his case and make the necessary arrangements.' Social morality is also relevant to the choice of means. No matter how expedient an action may be, if it is unjust or socially irresponsible, it ought not to be chosen as a means. Social morality and personal well-being can sometimes conflict. There is no pre-established social harmony which guarantees that the maximum personal well-being of each is always and everywhere compatible with the maximum personal well-being of all. Acting responsibly or justly can sometimes mean personal sacrifice, hardship, or even death. When this happens, there are good reasons for giving priority to the demands of social morality. Not to do so would be to abandon the commitment entailed in social living. I am not entitled to the benefits of social living unless I am prepared to pay the price and the price is meeting the demands of social morality, not that social morality and personal well-being are always in conflict. What is responsible and just is for the most part usually what is wise and prudent, but not invariably. The perspective of social morality is wider than that of personal well-being. It takes into account the nature and significance of the social dimension of human life. As a form of practical reason, it is on a higher level than personal well-being, which is properly subordinate to it.

According to Collingwood, a completely capricious act is completely irrational. He concludes from this that the less the caprice, the greater the rationality. Right is a higher form of practical reason than Utility, because it is less capricious. Duty is higher than Right, because in principle it is devoid of caprice altogether. But since Duty is only a special case of Right, and since his account of Right is vitiated by his failure to distinguish between regularian action properly so called, and the more sophisticated activity of making rules, his exposition of practical reason gets no further than Utility. I agree that a completely capricious act is completely irrational, or perhaps better, non-rational. I also agree that utility is infected with caprice, but what makes personal well-being a higher form of practical reason than utility is not that it is less capricious, although it is, but that its perspective is wider. The same is true of social morality in relation to personal well-being. One form of practical reason is higher than another, that is to say, because it embodies a better understanding of the character and conditions of human action. According to Collingwood, a rational act is always an individual act. But the point which seems to have eluded him is that in practical reason you have to deal with an individual situation, not as in regularian action merely with a situation of a particular kind. The problem is to decide what is most responsible, prudent, or expedient, in this situation now confronting you with its peculiar circumstances and features. A just or wise act is likely to contain elements of caprice.[1] But that does not matter so long as they do not impair its justice or wisdom. A rational act must be as devoid of caprice as the situation being dealt with requires. It does not have to be a completely 'definite individual' but only as definite as is necessary for it to be responsible, wise, or expedient.

I suggested earlier that thinking of freedom in terms of self-determination, rather than merely in terms of will, brings out more clearly the sense in which freedom is a matter of degree. The relation of regularian action to practical reason bears this out. Regularian action is the first step towards the fuller self-determination involved in practical reason. A child who can follow rules is no longer completely dependent upon adults to tell him what to do. But he is still dependent on rules. He emancipates himself from this dependence and becomes more self-determining to the extent that, as he grows up, he becomes capable of acting in terms of practical reason. A man who is capable of pursuing his personal well-being wisely and prudently achieves personal freedom. Practical reason

---

[1] Cf. A. Donagan, *The Later Philosophy of R. G. Collingwood* (Oxford, 1962), pp. 243–6.

in the form of social morality is moral freedom. A man who acts responsibly and justly is self-determining as a moral agent. Finally, a brief word on dialectic and eristic. The thinking involved in regularian action is essentially eristical. A regularian act is either right or wrong. There is no room for discussion, for reconsideration and modification of decisions about what to do. The rule must be obeyed and that is the end of the matter. The thinking involved in practical reason is essentially dialectical. A rational act is better or worse, rather than simply right or wrong; for instance, more or less just, more or less prudent, more or less expedient. There is room for discussion, re-consideration, and revision of provisional decisions. The question is what would be the most responsible, the wisest, the most efficient course, and second thoughts are always possible. As we shall see later, this has a bearing on Collingwood's ideas about civilization.

(B) *The Body Politic*

1. Collingwood's theory of the body politic has two components: a theory of community and a theory of ruling. Of central importance in the theory of community is a distinction between a social and a non-social community. The theory of ruling is the key to this distinction. According to Collingwood: 'Ruling is either *immanent* or *transeunt*. It is immanent when that which rules, rules itself, the same thing being both agent and patient in respect of the same activity. It is transeunt when that which rules, rules something other than itself: when in respect of the same activity of ruling there is one thing which is agent, the ruler, and another thing which is patient, the ruled' (*NL*, 20.37). Immanent rule is an aspect of freedom. A free man rules himself. Those who have not yet reached the stage of freedom or who are incapable of reaching it, are incapable of immanent rule and, if they are to be ruled, must be subjected to transeunt rule at the hands of those who can exercise immanent rule over themselves. Transeunt rule is a form of mental force. It operates by means of reward and punishment. This is the basis for the distinction between a social and non-social community. A social community or society is made up of free persons and rules itself through the immanent rule of its members. A non-social

community is made up of persons who, being not free and therefore incapable of immanent rule, have to be subjected to transeunt rule. But before saying more about this distinction, let us see what Collingwood's general theory of community is.

He says that: 'By a community I mean a state of affairs in which something is divided or shared by a number of human beings. This state of affairs I call the *Suum Cuique* of the community. What matters to the existence of a community is that it should have a suum cuique. Its taking one form rather than another makes no difference to the things being a community; though much to what kind of a community it is' (*NL*, 20.12–.14). In addition to a *suum cuique*, something else is also necessary. 'Thus any community must have a home or place in which corporately it lives' (*NL*, 20.18). He goes on to say that: 'A community must be ruled if it is to exist' (*NL*, 20.42). This is because: 'A community depends for its existence on something which makes it a community and keeps it a community; that is, alots to its members their respective shares in whatever is divided between them, and causes them to remain faithful to this alotment: maintains the *suum cuique* which is the essence of its communal character. The establishment and maintainance of the *suum cuique* is called *ruling*' (*NL*, 20.34 and 20.35). The difference between a society or social community and a non-social community is that: 'A society is a *self-ruling* community. A non-social community needs for its existence to be ruled by something other than itself' (*NL*, 20.36).

What Collingwood has in mind can be seen in the case of the family. The parents, being adults, are in some measure free persons. They exercise immanent rule over themselves and maintain between them the life of the family as a social community. But for their children who are not yet free persons, the life of the family is the life of a non-social community. This non-social community of the 'Nursery' is kept in being by the parents who exercise transeunt rule over their children who are its members. Since all human beings begin life as children, all human beings begin by being members of non-social communities. They become fit for social life properly so called only when they develop mentally to the point of achieving freedom. Collingwood finds the key to

21

social living in the idea of partnership. Becoming a free person means *inter alia* becoming capable of entering into partnerships with other free persons for the sake of carrying on joint activities with them. 'People become partners by deciding to behave like partners. A society or partnership is constituted by the social will of the partners, an act of free will whereby the person who thereby becomes a partner decides to take upon himself a share of the joint enterprise' (*NL*, 20.22). Partnerships or societies are originated and kept in being by the 'joint will' of the partners or members. There are as many forms of partnership or society as there are kinds of enterprise which free persons can undertake together. One distinction however, is of special importance for the theory of the body politic. 'This is a distinction between two kinds of enterprise, one intended to terminate within a length of time, planned to reach a conclusion at some definite period in the future; this I call a *temporary enterprise*; the other intended in Stevenson's words *to travel hopefully but not to arrive*; no time of termination being stated or implied; this I call a permanent enterprise. Every society is formed for the prosecution of some enterprise. Where it is a temporary enterprise, I call the society a temporary society; where permanent, a permanent society' (*NL*, 21.92–.95). Two men going for a walk together constitute a temporary society. A society for studying the antiquities of a district is a permanent society.

According to Collingwood, a body politic is like a family 'writ large'. 'The simplest body politic differs from the simplest family only at one point. Each is divided into a social part and a non-social part; but whereas the family society is a temporary society, the political society is a permanent society' (*NL*, 25.21). The members of a body politic consist of two classes. 'The first class is a society and rules itself. Its members are *persons* or agents possessed of free will. It also rules the second class which is a community only because it is ruled. Members of the second class are devoid of free will' (*NL*, 25.13–.16). He goes on: 'Let us call the first class the *Council* of the body politic; the second, its *Nursery*. It recruits the council by promotion from the nursery; it recruits the nursery by breeding babies and taking the consequences' (*NL*, 25.17 and 25.18). The body politic *qua* society is permanent because: 'In a body politic new babies are always being born; the nursery is always being replenished and the work of imposing order upon it is never concluded. Equally the work of establishing relations between it and the council is never concluded, nor the work of ordering the council itself, for that, too, is constantly being recruited' (*NL*, 25.24 and 25.25). The council is therefore faced with three never-ending tasks. It must define and maintain a way of life for itself, define and maintain a way of life for the nursery, and maintain the relation between itself and the nursery (cf. *NL*, 25.26).

All this is summarized by Collingwood in three propositions which he calls the 'three laws of politics'. Of them he says: 'They are meant to hold good of every body politic without exception, irrespective of all differences between one kind and another. All good political practice is based on grasping them, and most bad political practice is based on failing to grasp them as rules of political activity' (*NL*, 25.61 and 25.62). They are normative, not descriptive laws, comparable in status to the laws of thought of traditional logic. The first law of politics is that: '*a body politic is divided into a ruling class and a ruled class.*' The second that: '*the barrier between the two classes is permeable in an upward direction.*' The third that: '*there is a correspondence between the ruler and the ruled* whereby the former become adapted to ruling these as distinct from other persons, and the latter to being ruled by these as distinct from other persons' (*NL*, 25.7–.9). To this, however, he adds: 'But the third law also works inversely from the ruled class upwards and determines that whoever is to rule a certain people must rule them in a way in which they will let themselves be ruled' (*NL*, 25.92).

There are two other things in Collingwood's theory of the body politic about which a word must be said: his idea of political action, and of the 'dialectical' character of political life. Of the former he says: 'Political action pure and simple is will pure and simple; but differs from will as such in being, first, the joint will of a society, the rulers of a body politic; secondly, that will exercised immanently upon those who exercise it as the self-rule of that society; and thirdly, the same will exercised as force in transeunt rule over a non-social community, the ruled class of a body politic' (*NL*, 28.1)

Political action, that is to say, is the action of free persons in their capacity as members of the council of a body politic not in their capacity as private persons. Like the action of an individual free man, political action can be capricious. It can also be rational in any one of the three forms of practical reason. Capricious political action is expressed in decrees. 'A decree is the simplest form of political action because it represents the simplest form of will, namely caprice, transposed into the key of politics' (*NL*, 28.3). He goes on to say that political action in the form of Utility is 'policy', in the form of Right, it is 'Law', while in the form of Duty, it is what he calls 'Political Duty' (cf. *NL*, 28.5 ff.). The trouble with this attempt to 'transpose practical reason into the key of politics' is that the defects of his account of practical reason reappear in his account of political action. But more about that later.

According to Collingwood: 'The world of politics is a dialectical world in which non-social communities (communities of men in what Hobbes called a "state of nature") turn into societies' (*NL*, 24.71). Whether or not he is right to interpret Hobbes in this way, what is there which is dialectical about this world of politics? The answer lies in his view of the body politic as a mixed community made up of a social and a non-social element. 'Such a community might be described by attending to the positive element as a society; by attending to the negative element as a non-social community; yet it might be one community which was being so described; the difference being only a difference in *point of view*, a *dialectical* difference'(*NL*, 24.67). The non-agreement between these points of view is converted into agreement when it is realized that the body politic is a mixed community, that it is always in process of becoming a society, and therefore ceasing to be a non-social community but that this process, because the nursery is always being replenished, never ceases. According to Collingwood, things whose existence is a process of transition from one state to another, a process which can never be completed and which never begins, but is always already under way, must be thought of in dialectical terms. To think of them eristically, that is as either being in the state from which they are turning or as being in the state into which they are turning, would be to fail to understand their nature. They are never wholly in either state but are always in the course of transition from one to the other, and this form of 'process' existence is best described as dialectical.

2. Collingwood regarded his theory of the body politic as an amendment to what he called the 'Classical Politics', that is, the political theories of Hobbes, Locke, and Rousseau. The amendment was the replacement of 'the doctrine of the State of Nature' in these theories by his theory of the non-social community. But there is also a clear Platonic strain in his theory of the body politic. A central thesis of *The Republic* is that those who are to rule others must first be able to rule themselves, and this is also the central thesis in Collingwood's theory. The resemblance between his ruled class and Plato's class of 'Producers' is obvious. So too is the resemblance between Collingwood's theory of mind and Plato's 'doctrine of the Soul'. But that is a matter which I cannot pursue here. Granted that those who are to rule others must first be able to rule themselves, is Collingwood's account of ruling in terms of the distinction between immanent and transeunt rule acceptable? I do not think that it is.

Immanent rule, like freedom, is a matter of degree. It is part and parcel of the capacity for self-determination. Its most elementary form is self-control which is a necessary condition for regularian action. For practical reason, something more than merely self-control is necessary, namely the ability to control and determine one's conduct in the light of purposes which have been freely chosen. Transeunt rule need not necessarily be a matter of force. People can and do obey rules which have been made by others for them, and which they could not have made for themselves, without having to be forced to do so. Civil law largely consists of such rules. People obey them for the most part because they recognize the need for them, although they could not have made them and do not understand in detail the particular reasons for their taking one form rather than another. Collingwood is maintaining that only those who can make rules for themselves can freely obey rules made by others, a view which repeats the error in his account of regularian action discussed in the last section.

All this has implications for his theory of the non-social community. Its members are said to be incapable of immanent rule and hence of freedom. They are at the mercy of their desires and passions, and act only from preference, not from choice. Could such people constitute a community at all? Any community must be a regularian community in the sense that its members must be capable of obeying rules and must therefore be capable of enough immanent rule to enable them to do so. They cannot therefore be wholly at the mercy of their desires and passions. No doubt there are cases, for instance a community of prisoners, in which the threat of force plays a large part in securing obedience. But the effective operation of such a threat presupposes some degree of prudence on the part of those who are threatened, not simply uncontrolled fear. According to Collingwood, non-social communities are always dependent on something else which rules them. In fact, he is not wholly consistent about this. In the course of his discussion of political action, he refers to international law as 'the customary law of a very ancient non-social community' (*NL*, 28.79), and likens this customary law to the law of the Iceland of the Sagas. Presumably a community which maintains a customary law is not dependent on something else to rule it, and is best described as a regularian community. What would he say about the so-called 'traditional societies' studied by social anthropologists, that is tribal communities? These are regularian communities, or at least predominantly so. There may be the rudiments of practical reason in the form of utility, but little or nothing of free partnership or 'society' in his sense. Yet tribal communities are not dependent on something else for their existence. They maintain their own largely customary life from generation to generation. They can hardly be called non-social communities in his sense.

A tribal community may not be a social community, but it is a self-sufficient community in the sense of being sufficient for the maintenance of human life. Human life is and always has been carried on in self-sufficient communities. At different times and in different places these have taken very different forms. Tribes, kingdoms, city-states, the principalities and duchies of Medieval Europe, and the nation-states of the modern world, are instances.

Collingwood's theory of the body politic is a theory of the essential characteristics which every self-sufficient community must possess. He is saying, in effect, that if a community is to be self-sufficient for human life, it must be a body politic. But as the case of a tribal community shows, he is wrong. A regularian community can be self-sufficient for human life. It does not have to be a social community as well. Moreover, since there can be no community without regularian action, every self-sufficient community must at least be a regularian community. But it need not be merely a regularian community, it can also be something more. It can become a social community to the extent that its adult members are able to make the transition from regularian to rational morality, that is, become capable of practical reason in the forms of personal well-being and social morality. After making this transition, they are still members of the self-sufficient community, but rational, not merely regularian members. They have become free persons and free moral agents in the sense of being self-determining in both capacities.

This suggests that something can be salvaged from Collingwood's theory of the body politic. The theory of the non-social community must go and be replaced by the theory of the regularian community, which unlike the non-social community, can be a self-sufficient community. But his theory of the social community based on the idea of partnership is compatible with the revised account of practical reason of the last section, and can be combined with the theory of the regularian community to yield a theory of the typical form of self-sufficient community in modern Europe: the nation-state. It is after all with modern Europe that he is primarily concerned. But while this is all right so far as it goes, there is another objection to be reckoned with. In what sense is this revised theory a theory of modern European bodies politic, as distinct from modern European self-sufficient communities? It may be acceptable as a theory of community and society, but in what respects, if any, can it be regarded as a political theory? The short answer is that with the removal of the theory of the non-social community, the political element, what I called earlier the Platonic strain, in his theory of the body politic has gone.

Modern European self-sufficient communities are political communities. They are not only nations but 'States'. Their political character comes from the institution of government. This institution is not essential to the existence of a self-sufficient community as such. Tribes have existed without it and it is absent from the Icelandic community of the Sagas. But it is clearly indispensable to modern European nations. Their ways of life would not be what they are without it. The key to its role lies in distinguishing between the 'public' and 'private' aspects of the ways of life of modern European nations.[1] From one point of view, the life of a modern European nation is a life of 'private enterprise', not merely in economic activity, but in domestic and cultural spheres as well. It embraces many varieties of 'partnerships 'in Collingwood's sense, or voluntary associations, undertaken by people who in some measure at least are free persons and free moral agents. But from another point of view it is a public life, that is a life subject to public regulation, supervision, and direction, the purpose of which is to establish and maintain conditions under which the members of the national community who may number many millions, can all of them participate in the life of private partnerships and voluntary associations. The role of government is to be the custodian of the public life of the nation. While this is only a hint of the complex character of the institution of government, it is enough to bring out the inadequacy of Collingwood's theory of the body politic as a theory of the modern European nation-state. His concept of the 'council' of the body politic throws no light on the distinction between 'public' and 'private'. To think of the body politic as a family 'writ large' is to miss the significance of the institution of government for the life of free partnership and voluntary association.

Of his three laws of politics, only the third contributes anything to the understanding of modern European political life. 'A people can only be governed in the way in which it will let itself be governed'. The first two turn on his distinction between the ruling class and the ruled. But this is only a distinction between those who

[1] This does not, of course, apply to totalitarian states where the distinction is obliterated.

are and those who are not capable of practical reason, a distinction which is a matter of degree, and which blurs the distinction between the public and private aspects of a nation's life. His account of political action fails to distinguish between political and social action. So far as 'transposing practical reason into the key of politics' is concerned, all that needs to be said is this. If the work of governing is to be well done, it must be in the hands of persons capable of practical reason in the form of social morality, that is, persons who can act responsibly and justly as 'custodians of the public interest', as well as wisely and prudently in determining in detail what must be done to promote it.[1]

Collingwood argued that the world of politics is a dialectical world because a body politic is always in the course of a transition from being a non-social community to being a society. It is never wholly the one nor wholly the other. There is a sense in which this might be applied to the public and private aspects of the life of a modern European nation. Its life is never wholly private nor wholly public but always partly one and partly the other, and the line between the two is never fixed. But that is not all. There is another sense in which political life can be dialectical; when the form of government is democratic. However, more about that later. What is false in Collingwood's contention is that the life of a self-sufficient community is dialectical, simply in virtue of its being a self-sufficient community. A tribal community with a predominantly regularian way of life is not in any meaningful sense always in the course of turning from one state into another. The fact that there is always a new generation in the course of growing up makes no difference. This is one of the most stable characteristics of the community. On the other hand, in a self-sufficient community like a modern European nation which is a social as well as a regularian community, the idea of a dialectical character is more plausible. Whether much is to be gained by thinking of modern European communities in this way is another question. Perhaps more important is the sense in which their lives are historical in character, that is, change from generation to generation through the cumulative and largely unforeseen actions in each generation. Collingwood

[1] Cf. Milne, op. cit., ch. 8, for the development of this idea.

would not have denied this, although he did not discuss it in *The New Leviathan*. But the matter cannot be pursued further here.

3. The Modern European Mind has produced 'the thing called Modern European Civilisation'. It has also produced the Modern Democratic State. While Collingwood has something to say about democracy and aristocracy in *The New Leviathan*, it is in connection with his doctrine of the ruling class in a body politic. He does not undertake any sort of examination of democracy as a form of government specially characteristic of Modern European Civilization. The omission is surprising in view of his declared intention to 'inquire into civilization and the revolt against it'.[1] I shall try briefly to fill the gap. The modern democratic state, or 'Western Democracy', rests upon four main principles: the rule of law; representative government; constitutional opposition; and equality of citizenship. I do not say that these principles are fully implemented in self-professing Western democracies: far from it. But I think that thoughtful adherents of Western democracy would agree that they are morally committed to them. Let us look more closely at them.

The rule of law involves three things: the supremacy of law, that is, that legal obligations are paramount; equality before the law, that is the equal subjection of all including the government to the law, and the equal protection for all of the law; and freedom under the law, that is that where the law is silent, all are free to act according to their own volition. A representative government is one which is chosen from and accountable to a wider citizen body, this being secured by periodic free elections. Hence the necessity of the rule of law: electoral procedure must be provided for by law. But without the opportunity for choice and criticism, there can be no free elections: hence the necessity for constitutional opposition. The composition of the citizen body is determined by the fourth principle. Its membership must be co-extensive

---

[1] In the last chapter of his *Autobiography* Collingwood had something to say about the 'democratic tradition' but did not enlarge on it in *The New Leviathan*, perhaps because of the disillusionment with British politics which he went on to express in the former work.

with the entire adult population. This guarantees not only 'one man, one vote', but the equal right of all to participate in politics.[1] The principle of constitutional opposition means what it says. Opposition must be within the limits of the law. You are free to criticize and oppose the government of the day but not to undermine its authority to govern. This presupposes that the great majority of the citizen body has a clear practical understanding of the difference between opposition and rebellion. But they must not only understand the difference. They must be able and willing to act on it. That means acknowledging and fulfilling the paramount obligation to obey the law, and eschewing all forms of revolutionary political action.

Two preconditions are necessary for the successful working of democracy: one social, the other cultural. The social precondition is the absence of fundamental conflict. The members of the democratic body politic must be in broad agreement about the fundamental character of their way of life. It must not matter too much who wins the next election. People must be willing to accept the verdict of the ballot-box. Where this precondition is absent, for instance, in a self-sufficient community deeply and painfully divided along racial or religious lines, the best that can be managed is a government drawn from and accountable to the members of the dominant racial or religious group. Members of the subordinate group will be 'second-class citizens' whose voice can become effective only through revolutionary political action. The cultural precondition is a well-established and widespread tradition of discussion and argument, based on the recognition that to most questions there is more than one side, and that those who are on the opposite side are not for that reason either knaves or fools. This cultural precondition presupposes the social precondition. Both are necessary for the effective working of democracy.

In view of this, it is hardly surprising that democracy has taken root and lasted in only a minority of the nations of the modern world. It is only in Western Europe, North America, and Australasia that both the social and cultural preconditions are to be found. The majority of mankind have never known democracy, and for

[1] Cf. Milne, op. cit., ch. 8.

the foreseeable future will have to manage without it. It is not the best form of government if that means best for everyone always and everywhere. But there is no one form of government which is best in this sense. What is true, however, is that where the social and cultural preconditions are present, democracy is better than any other form of government. This is so for two reasons: one negative, the other positive. The negative reason is that democracy more than any other form of government takes account of and provides protection against human fallibility. It recognizes that no individual and no group has a monopoly of virtue or wisdom. The positive reason is that through the principles of constitutional opposition and equality of citizenship, democracy gives more scope and encouragement to more people to advance from regularian to rational morality than any other form of government. It enables practical reason 'to be transposed into the key of politics', which is another way of saying that it makes possible dialectical rather than merely eristical politics. Under a democratic form of government, occasions of political non-agreement have at least a better chance of being converted into occasions of political agreement, instead of hardening into disagreement. To be fair to Collingwood, an understanding of this is implicit in his discussion of aristocracy and democracy although he did not relate it to an examination of the principles underlying democracy.

(C) *Civilization*

Collingwood distinguishes between the generic and the specific meaning of 'civilization'. According to the generic meaning: 'Civilization is a *process of approximation to an ideal state*. To civilize a thing is to impose on it or promote in it a process; a process of becoming; a process in something which we know to be a community; whereby it approximates nearer to an ideal state which I will call *civility* and recedes farther from its contradictory, an ideal state which I will call *barbarity*' (NL, 34.5–.52). No community is ever simply barbarous, or completely civil. It is always in a condition of turning from the one into the other. To discover the specific meaning, it is necessary to determine the specific character of the process, to know what happens to a community as it becomes more civilized. Discussing the specific meaning, Collingwood says: 'According to the view I find expressed in books I have looked at, and in the mouths of persons I have questioned to find out what the thing called civilization is commonly thought to involve, civilization has something to do with the mutual relations of the members within a community; something to do with the relation of these members to the world of nature; and something to do with the relation between them and other human beings not being members of the same community' (NL, 35.34). The clue to what this something is, lies in the idea of civil behaviour.

'Behaving *civilly* to a man means respecting his feelings: abstaining from shocking him, annoying him, frightening him, or (briefly) arousing in him any passion or desire that might diminish his self-respect; that is, threatening his consciousness of freedom by making him feel that his power of choice is in danger of breaking down and passion or desire likely to take charge' (NL, 35.41). People who treat one another civilly act in a dialectical, not an eristical spirit. '*Being civilized* means living so far as possible, *dialectically*, that is, in constant endeavour to convert occasions of non-agreement into occasions of agreement. (NL, 39.15). What Collingwood means is clear. He is equating the process of civilization with the process by which a community becomes a social community. Civility equals sociality. 'Civilization is the process in a community by which the various members assert themselves as will; severally as individual will, corporately as social will (the two being inseparable)' (NL, 36.89). So far as relations with other communities are concerned, civilization means acting civilly towards their members. So far as the natural world is concerned, civilization means 'a spirit of intelligent exploitation' (NL, 36.25). This is possible only in a community whose members already treat one another civilly since that is necessary for development, conservation, and transmission of the knowledge and experience which is itself necessary for the intelligent exploitation of nature.

What about 'revolts against civilization', the fourth part of Collingwood's inquiry? It is important to distinguish between lack of civilization and the repudiation of civilization.

I distinguish two ways of being uncivilized. I call them savagery and barbarism and distinguish them as follows. Savagery is a negative idea. It means not being civilized, and that is all. In practice, I need hardly say, there is no such thing as absolute savagery; there is only relative savagery, that is, being civilized up to a certain point and no more. By barbarism I mean hostility towards civilization; the effort, conscious, or unconscious, to become less civilized than you are, either in general or in some special way, and, so far as in you lies, to promote a similar change in others. (*NL*, 41.11 and 41.12).

Relative savagery is equivalent to relative barbarity in his account of the generic meaning of civilization. Barbarism is the attempt to reverse the process of civilization and move back towards the ideal state of barbarity, and away from civility. It is the paradoxical attempt by members of a social community to revert to non-social community from which they have emerged, paradoxical because free persons are choosing to abandon freedom, choosing to give up choosing. Collingwood describes the will to barbarism as: 'a will to acquiesce in the chaotic rule of emotion, which it began by destroying. All it does is to assert itself as will and then deny itself as will' (*NL*, 36.94).

If my argument in this essay is sound, Collingwood's account of civilization needs amending. Civilization is a process which is undergone by a self-sufficient community. Such a community is always at the very least a regularian community. It becomes civilized to the extent that it becomes more than merely a regularian community, that is to the extent that practical reason, not merely regularian action, plays a part in its way of life. But practical reason means utility, personal well-being, and social morality. Collingwood's account of it gets no further than utility. The thinking involved in practical reason in terms of my revised version is dialectical, so Collingwood is right to say that 'being civilized means, so far as possible, living dialectically'. But he has failed to give a coherent account of how this manner of living is embodied in practical reason. To say that civilization is a process towards an ideal state of civility and away from an ideal state of barbarity is misleading. It fails to allow for the case of tribal communities which are not in any meaningful sense social communities, and which are untouched by civilization so far as the higher forms of practical reason are concerned. Finally, Collingwood's idea of the body politic leaves no room for a distinction between civilized and uncivilized forms of political life, since he is committed to holding that every self-sufficient community must be a body politic without differentiating between the social and political aspects of its life. He has failed to see that democracy, because more than any other form of government it makes dialectical politics possible, is more civilized than any other form of government.

His conception of barbarism is really a conception of irrationality, as distinct from non-rationality and imperfect rationality. To what extent the historical examples of barbarism which he discusses in Part 4 of *The New Leviathan* are really examples of irrationality I am not competent to judge. But he is certainly right that irrationality, in the sense of the repudiation of practical reason by those who are capable of rational conduct, is a revolt against civilization. Whether he is right in contending that this always takes the form of 'acquiescing in the chaotic rule of emotion' is another matter. It may take the form of ideological commitment in the face of rational misgivings which are repressed or 'rationalized' away. It may take the form of a reaction against what Popper called 'the strain of civilization'.[1] This might be described in Collingwood's terms as a relapse from dialectical into eristical thinking. Collingwood limited himself to revolts against civilization. Equally important is an inquiry into its 'strains' and into the obstacles which impede or arrest it. The social precondition for democracy, the absence of social conflict, is not something which can be created by good will. Dialectical thinking cannot end social divisions since it can flourish only where they are absent.

Collingwood regarded his inquiry into civilization as an essay in the science of mind. I suggested at the beginning of this essay that what he was engaged in was a conceptual inquiry of much the same sort as about a decade later were undertaken by many British and American philosophers. Both Collingwood and his postwar successors seemed to have thought of their task as essentially descriptive rather than critical. Collingwood was led to this

[1] K. R. Popper, *The Open Society and its Enemies* (London, 1945).

conclusion by his ideas about the relation of philosophy to history, postwar philosophers by their views about philosophy and language. In the end perhaps these two views are not really different, since language is essentially a historical phenomenon. Be that as it may, a philosophical study of concepts which eschews criticism is failing to carry out its proper task. Not only 'What can be meant by . . . ?' but 'How should we think of . . . ?' concerns the philosopher. The defects in Collingwood's account of freedom and practical reason, and in his account of the body politic, stem as much from lack of critical appraisal as from incomplete descriptive analysis. But this is not the note on which to end. The impression given of *The New Leviathan* in this essay is misleading because of its concentration upon defects in certain parts of the argument. To do justice to the book as a whole would need more space than is available to me.[1] In his autobiography Collingwood expressed his attitude towards potential critics by saying: 'Let them write, not about me, but about the subject' (*A*, 81). The measure of his achievement in *The New Leviathan* is that if the subject is civilization and the writer a philosopher, he can hardly avoid writing about Collingwood.

[1] Cf. Donagan, op. cit., for a fair appraisal of the merits of Part I of *The New Leviathan*.

COLLINGWOOD BIBLIOGRAPHY

I: WORKS OF R. G. COLLINGWOOD[1]

I. PHILOSOPHICAL BOOKS, ARTICLES, AND REVIEWS

1916   *Religion and Philosophy*. London: Macmillan & Co. 'The Devil', in L. Dongall, ed., *Concerning Prayer: Its Nature, Its Difficulties and Its Value*. London: Macmillan.

1920   Review of *King's College Lectures on Immortality*, ed. W. R. Matthews. *Theology*, i, (November), 299f.
'What is the Problem of Evil?' *Theology*, i.

1921   'Croce's Philosophy of History'. *Hibbert Journal*, xix.

1922   'Are History and Science Different Kinds of Knowledge?' *Mind*, xxxi, *Ruskin's Philosophy*, an Address Delivered at the Ruskin Centenary Conference, Coniston, 8 August, 1919. Kendal: Titus Wilson & Son.

1923   'Can the New Idealism Dispense with Mysticism?' *Aristotelian Society, Supplementary Volume*, iii.
'Sensation and Thought'. *Proceedings of the Aristotelian Society*, xxiv (1923–4).

1924   *Speculum Mentis*. Oxford: Clarendon Press.

1925   'Economics as a Philosophical Science'. *International Journal of Ethics*, xxxvi.
'The Nature and Aims of a Philosophy of History'. *Proceedings of the Aristotelian Society*, xxv (1924–5).
Outlines of a Philosophy of Art. London: Oxford University Press.
'Plato's Philosophy of Art'. *Mind*, xxxiv.
Review of *A Theory of Monads* by H. Wildon Carr. *Hibbert Journal*, xxiii, No. 2 (January), 380–2.

1926   'The Place of Art in Education'. *Hibbert Journal*, xxiv, No. 3, 434–48.
'Religion, Science and Philosophy'. *Truth and Freedom*, ii, No. 7.
Review of *Theory of History* by F. J. Teggart, *Journal of Philosophical Studies*, i (April), 255–6.

[1] For a bibliography of Collingwood's writings in history and archaeology, see I. M. Richmond, *Proceedings of the British Academy*, xxix (1943), pp. 481–5.

'Some Perplexities about Time: with an Attempted Solution'. *Proceedings of the Aristotelian Society*, xxvi, No. 8 (February), 135–50.

1927   'Aesthetic', in J. S. McDowall, ed., *The Mind*. London: Longmans.

'Oswald Spengler and the Theory of Historical Cycles', 2 parts, *Antiquity*, i.

'Reason is Faith Cultivating Itself'. *Hibbert Journal*, xxvi, No. 1, 3–14.

Review of *Epicurus: The Extant Remains*, ed. Cyril Bailey, and *Epicurus: His Morals*, ed. Walton Charleton, *The Criterion*, vi, 369–72.

Review of *Plato: The Man and His Work* by A. E. Taylor, and *Étude sur le Parmenide de Platon* by Jean Wahl, *The Criterion*, vi, 65–8.

Review of *The Social and Economic History of the Roman Empire* by M. Rostovtzeff. *Antiquity*, i, 367–8.

1928   *Faith and Reason*, a pamphlet in the Affirmation Series. London: Ernest Benn. Reprinted in A. A. David, ed., *God and the Modern World*. New York: Dutton, 1929.

'The Limits of Historical Knowledge'. *Journal of Philosophical Studies*, iii, No. 10 (April), 213–22.

'Political Action'. *Proceedings of the Aristotelian Society*, xxix (1928–9).

Review of *Art and Instinct* by Samuel Alexander, *Journal of Philosophical Studies*, iii (July), 370–3.

Review of *Hedonism and Art* by L. R. Farnell, *Journal of Philosophical Studies*, iii (October), 547–8.

Review of *Plato's Theory of Ethics* by R. K. Lodge. *The Criterion*, viii, No. 30 (September), 157–9.

1929   'Form and Content in Art'. *Journal of Philosophical Studies*, iv, No. 15 (July), 332–45.

'A Philosophy of Progress'. *The Realist*, i.

1930   *The Philosophy of History*. Historical Association Leaflet, No. 79. London: G. Bell & Sons.

Review of *The Intelligible World* by W. M. Urban, and *The Idea of Value* by John Laird. *The Criterion*, ix, No. 35 (January), 320–7.

Review of *The Meaning of Beauty: A Theory of Aesthetics* by W. T. Stace. *Journal of Philosophical Studies*, v (July), 460–3. (See rejoinder by Stace in *Journal of Philosophical Studies*, v, 653–4.)

1931 Review of *The Philosophy of Art* by C. J. Ducasse. *Philosophy*, vi (July), 383–6.
Review of *Philosophy of the Good Life* by Bishop Gore. *The Criterion*, x, No. 40 (April), 561–2.
Review of *Selected Essays of J. B. Bury*, ed. Harold Temperley. *English Historical Review*, xlvi (July), 461–5.

1932 Review of *The Nature of Belief* by M. C. D'Arcy. *The Criterion*, xi, No. 43 (January), 334–6.
Review of *A Study in Aesthetics* by L. A. Reid. *Philosophy*, vii (July), 335–7.

1933 *An Essay on Philosophical Method.* Oxford: Clarendon Press.

1934 'The Present Need of a Philosophy'. *Philosophy*, ix, 262–5. (Reprinted in part in N. P. Stallknécht and R. L. Brumbaugh, eds., *The Spirit of Western Philosophy*. New York: Longmans, 1950, pp. xliii–xx.)

1935 *The Historical Imagination*, an inaugural lecture. Oxford: Clarendon Press.

1936 'Human Nature and Human History'. *Proceedings of the British Academy*, xxii. Reprinted, London: Humphrey Milford.

1937 Review of *The Issue in Literary Criticism* by Myron F. Brightfield. *Philosophy*, xii (January), 114–16.

1938 *The Principles of Art.* Oxford: Clarendon Press.
'On the So-called Idea of Causation'. *Proceedings of the Aristotelian Society*, xxxviii (1937–8).

1940 *An Essay on Metaphysics.* Oxford: Clarendon Press.
'Fascism and Nazism'. *Philosophy*, xv.

1941 *The Three Laws of Politics.* L. T. Hobhouse Memorial Trust Lectures, No. 11. London: Oxford University Press.

1942 *The New Leviathan.* Oxford: Clarendon Press.

1945 *The Idea of Nature* (T. M. Knox, ed.). Oxford: Clarendon Press.

1946 *The Idea of History* (T. M. Knox, ed.). Oxford: Clarendon Press.

II. MEMOIRS

1939 *An Autobiography.* London: Oxford University Press. Reprinted by Penguin Books Ltd., 1944.

1940 *The First Mate's Log.* London: Oxford University Press.

III. TRANSLATIONS

1913 B. Groce, *The Philosophy of Giambattista Vico*. London: Latimer. Reissued by Allen & Unwin in the Library of Philosophy Series.

1921 With A. H. Hannay, G. de Ruggiero, *Modern Philosophy*. London: Allen & Unwin.

1927 B. Croce, *An Autobiography*, with a preface by A. J. Smith. Oxford: Clarendon Press.

G. de Ruggiero, *The History of European Liberalism*. Oxford: Clarendon Press.

1928 B. Croce, 'Aesthetic', in the *Encyclopaedia Britannica*, 14th edition.

IV. SELECTED BIBLIOGRAPHY OF HISTORICAL WRITINGS

1923 *Roman Britain*. London: Oxford University Press. (Revised edition, Oxford: Clarendon Press, 1934.)

1930 *The Archaeology of Roman Britain*. London: Methuen & Co. Ltd.

1936 *Roman Britain and the English Settlements* (with J. N. L. Myres). Oxford: Clarendon Press (2nd edition, 1937).

1937 'Roman Britain', in T. Frank, ed., *An Economic Survey of Ancient Rome*. Baltimore, Md.: Johns Hopkins Press (London: Oxford University Press), iii, 1–118.

1947 *A Guide to the Roman Wall*, 4th edition, revised by I. A. Richmond. Newcastle upon Tyne: A Reid, 1947.

1965 *The Roman Inscriptions of Britain* (with R. P. Wright). Oxford: Clarendon Press.

V. EDITIONS AND TRANSLATIONS OF COLLINGWOOD'S WRITINGS

W. Debbins, ed., *Essays in the Philosophy of History by R. G. Collingwood*. Austin: University of Texas Press, 1965.

A. Donagan, ed., *Essays in the Philosophy of Art by R. G. Collingwood*. Bloomington: Indiana University Press, 1946.

Gertrude Herding, trans., *Philosophie der Geschichte*. Stuttgart: Kohlhammer, 1955.

M. L. Rubinoff, ed., *Faith and Reason: Essays in the Philosophy of Religion by R. G. Collingwood*. Chicago: Quadrangle, 1967.

Domenico Pesce, ed. and trans., *Tre saggi di filosofia della storia* ('Human Nature and Human History',) 'Progress as Created by Historical Thinking' [from the *Idea of History*], 'Croce's Philosophy of History'), with an introduction by Pesce. Padova: Liviana editrice, 1969.

VI. UNPUBLISHED MANUSCRIPTS AND CORRESPONDENCE

Correspondence with Gilbert Ryle, 9 May and 6 June 1935, concerning the Ontological Argument; deposited in the Bodleian Library in 1964: Ms. Eng. lett. d. 194.

Lectures on ethics, currently being edited by Mrs. K. Collingwood in collaboration with Mr. J. Rusk, to be deposited in the Bodleian Library. (Professor L. Rubinoff claims that a copy of Collingwood's cosmology also is in Mrs. Collingwood's possession.[2] No mention of this was made by her to the present editor.)

'Libellus de Generatione, An Essay in Absolute Empiricism', in the estate of G. de Ruggiero. This material may not be examined, according to the terms of Collingwood's Will.

Correspondence with G. de Ruggiero, in the care of literary executor Professor Renzo de Felice, Institute di storia moderna, Università di Roma. This material is available for examination.

Correspondence with B. Croce, in care of Alda Croce. This material may now be released for publication.

Correspondence to W. Von Leyden of a personal nature, dated 20 July 1940, 31 May 1941, and 13 June 1941. Available for inspection.

Letter to a Professor Rothenstein, 24 February 1929, deposited in the Houghton Library of Harvard University.

Correspondence with Macmillan of London as Delegate of the Press. Some thirty letters deposited in the Macmillan Archives of the British Museum; available for examination.

II: WORKS ON THE PHILOSOPHY
OF R. G. COLLINGWOOD

ACTON, H. B. Review of A. Donagan, *The Later Philosophy of R. G. Collingwood. Listener* (27 June 1963), p. 1085.

ALBRIGHT, W. F. *History, Archaeology and Christian Humanism.* New York: McGraw-Hill, 1964.

AMBROSIO, GEORGES. 'Ce que signifie la Nature pour la Science, à propos de R. G. Collingwood, *The Idea of Nature'. Critique*, iii (1947), 546–52.

ANONYMOUS. Review of *Outlines of a Philosophy of Art. Times Literary Supplement* (6 April 1925), p. 269.

ANONYMOUS. Review of *Outlines of a Philosophy of Art. Boston Transcript* (1 August 1925), part 6, p. 2.

[2] Rubinoff, L. *Collingwood and the Reform of Metaphysics* (Toronto, 1970), p. 397.

ANONYMOUS. Review of *An Essay on Philosophical Method. Times Literary Supplement* (1 March 1934), p. 136.

ANONYMOUS. Review of *Principles of Art. Times Literary Supplement* (13 April 1938), p. 533.

ANONYMOUS. Review of *An Autobiography. Times Literary Supplement* (5 August 1939), p. 464.

ANONYMOUS. Review of *An Autobiography. Manchester Guardian* (15 August 1939), p. 5.

ANONYMOUS. Review of *An Essay on Metaphysics. Manchester Guardian* (6 May 1940), p. 7.

ANONYMOUS. 'Metaphysician's Faith', review of *An Essay on Metaphysics. Times Literary Supplement* (18 May 1940), p. 240.

ANONYMOUS. Review of *The Idea of History, Times Literary Supplement* (17 August 1946), p. 385.

BAILEY, JOHN A. 'A Reply to Mischel's "Collingwood on Art as 'Imaginative Expression'"'. *Australasian Journal of Philosophy*, xli (December 1963), 372–8.

BALDWIN, B. M. Review of *An Essay on Metaphysics. Nature*, cxlvii, No. 1 (January 1941), 7–8.

BARKER, ERNEST. 'Man and Society', review of *The New Leviathan. Oxford Magazine*, lxi, No. 11 (4 February 1943), 162–3.

BEARD, C. A. Review of *The Idea of History. American Historical Review*, lii (July 1947), 704–8.

BOUCH, C. H. L. 'In Memoriam (R. G. Collingwood)'. *Transactions of the Cumberland and Westmorland Antiquarian and Archaeological Society*, xliii (1943), 211–14.

BOYCE-GIBSON, A. Review of A. Donagan, *The Later Philosophy of R. G. Collingwood. Australasian Journal of Philosophy*, xli (December 1963), 412–17.

BRANDON, S. G. F. 'Modern Interpretations of History and their Challenge'. *Modern Churchman*, xxxix, No. 3 (1949), 238–52.

BROWN, Merle Elliott. *Neo-Idealistic Aesthetics: Croce-Gentile-Collingwood*. Detroit: Wayne State University Press, ed. Barbara Woodward, 1966.

BUCHDAHL, G. 'Logic and History': An Assessment of R. G. Collingwood's *Idea of History'. Australasian Journal of Philosophy*, xxvi (September 1948), 94–113.

—— 'Has Collingwood been Unfortunate in his Critics?' *Australasian Journal of Philosophy*, xxxvi (August 1958), 327–39.

BUCHLER, JUSTUS. Review of *An Essay on Metaphysics*. *Sunday New York Times* (1 December 1940), p. 47.

BULTMANN, R. *History and Eschatology*. Edinburgh: Edinburgh University Press, 1957, ch. ix.

BURGH, W. G. de. Review of 'Human Nature and Human History'. *Philosophy*, xii (April 1937), 233–6.

BURNS, A. E. 'Ascertainment, Probability, and Evidence in History'. *Historical Studies: Australia and New Zealand*, ci, No. 4 (1951), 327–39.

BURNS, CECIL DELISLE. Review of *Speculum Mentis*. *International Journal of Ethics*, xxxv (April 1925), 323.

CARRIT, E. F. Review of *The Principles of Art*. *Manchester Guardian* (27 May 1938), p. 7.

—— Review of *The Principles of Art*. *Philosophy*, xiii (October 1938), 492–6.

CASSERLEY, J. V. L. *The Christian in Philosophy*. London: Faber and Faber, 1949, pp. 200 ff.

CATLIN, GEORGE. Review of *The New Leviathan*. *Political Science Quarterly*, lviii, No. 3, 435–6.

CEBIK, L. B. 'Collingwood: Action, Re-enactment, and Evidence'. *Philosophical Forum*, ii, No. 1 (Fall 1970), 68–89.

CHILD, ARTHUR N. 'History as Imitation'. *Philosophical Quarterly*, ii (July 1952), 193–207.

COHEN, L. J. 'A Survey of Work in the Philosophy of History'. *Philosophical Quarterly*, ii (April 1952), 172–86.

—— 'Has Collingwood been Misrepresented?'. *Philosophical Quarterly*, vii (April 1957), 149–50.

COURNOS, JOHN. Review of *The Principles of Art*. *Sunday New York Times* (17 July 1937), p. 4.

CROCE, BENEDETTO. Review of *Speculum Mentis*. *La Critica: Rivista di litteratura, storia, e filosofia*, xxiii (1925), 55–9.

—— 'In commemorazione di un amico inglese, compagno di pensiero e di fede R. G. Collingwood'. *Quaderni della 'Critica'*, ii, No. 4 (1946), 60–73 (including text of letter to Croce dated 29 January 1939, p. 67).

CROSSMAN, R. H. S. 'When Lightning struck the Ivory Tower: R. G. Collingwood'. *New Statesman and Nation*, xvii (1939), 222–3: reprinted in R. H. S. Crossman, *The Charm of Politics and Other Essays in Political Criticism*. London: Hamish Hamilton, 1958, pp. 105–9.

DEBBINS, W. Introduction to R. G. Collingwood, *Essays in the Philosophy of History*. Austin: University of Texas Press, 1965, pp. ix–xxxiv.

DERFER, GEORGE E. Review of A. Donagan, *The Later Philosophy of R. G. Collingwood. Journal of the History of Philosophy*, iii (April 1965), 143–6.

DONAGAN, A. 'The Verification of Historical Theses'. *Philosophical Quarterly*, vi (July 1956), 193–208.

—— 'Explanation in History'. *Mind*, lxvi (April 1957), 145–64.

—— 'The Croce-Collingwood Theory of Art'. *Philosophy*, xxxiii (April 1958), 162–7.

—— *The Later Philosophy of R. G. Collingwood*. Oxford: The Clarendon Press, 1962.

—— Introduction to R. G. Collingwood, *Essays in the Philosophy of Art*. Bloomington: University of Indiana Press, 1964, pp. ix-xx.

—— 'Does Knowing Make a Difference to What is Known? A Rejoinder to Mr. Post'. *Philosophical Quarterly*, xvi (1966), 352–5.

—— Article on Collingwood in the *Encyclopedia of Philosophy*, ed. Paul Edwards. New York: Macmillan & Co. and the Free Press, 1967, pp. 140–4.

—— Review of L. Rubinoff, ed., *Faith and Reason: Essays in the Philosophy of Religion by R. G. Collingwood. Dialogue: Canadian Philosophical Review*, vii, No. 4 (March 1969), 678–81.

—— Review of W. M. Johnston, *The Formative Years of R. G. Collingwood. Journal of the History of Philosophy*, vii (April 1969), 219–31.

—— Review of Louis O. Mink, *Mind, History and Dialectic: The Philosophy of R. G. Collingwood. History and Theory*, ix, No. 3 (1970), 363–75.

—— 'Comment' (on Watkins's 'Imperfect Rationality') in R. Borger and F. Cioffi, *Explanation in the Behavioural Sciences*. Cambridge: Cambridge University Press, 1970, pp. 218–27.

DRAY, W. H. 'R. G. Collingwood and the Acquaintance Theory of Knowledge'. *Revue Internationale de Philosophie*, xi, No. 42 (1957), 420–32.

—— *Laws and Explanation in History*. London: Oxford University Press, 1957, chs. iv, v.

—— 'Historical Understanding as Re-Thinking'. *University of Toronto Quarterly*, xxvii (January 1958), 200–15.

—— 'R. G. Collingwood on Reflective Thought'. *Journal of Philosophy*, lvii (3 March 1960), 157–63.

—— 'Historical Causation and Human Free Will'. *University of Toronto Quarterly*, xxix, No. 3 (April 1960), 357–69.

—— *Philosophy of History*. Englewood Cliffs, N.J.: Prentice-Hall, 1964.

—— Review of A. Donagan, *The Later Philosophy of R. G. Collingwood*. *Canadian Historical Review*, xlv (1964), 130–2.

DRUMMOND, J. Review of *Concerning Prayer*. *Hibbert Journal*, xv (1917), 327–31.

DUCASSE, C. J. 'Mr. Collingwood on Philosophical Method'. *Journal of Philosophy*, xxxiii (13 February 1936), 95–106.

—— Review of *An Essay on Philosophical Method*. *Journal of Philosophy*, xxxiii (1936), 95–106.

DYKSTRA, VERGIL H. 'Philosophers and Presuppositions'. *Mind*, lxix (January 1960), 63–8.

ELIOT, T. S. Review of *Religion and Philosophy*. *International Journal of Ethics*, xxvii (July 1917), 543.

EMBLOM, W. J. Review of A. Donagan, *The Later Philosophy of R. G. Collingwood*. *Journal of Aesthetics and Art Criticism*, xxii (Fall 1963), 84–5.

EMMET, DOROTHY. Review of A. Donagan, *The Later Philosophy of R. G. Collingwood*. *Philosophical Quarterly*, xiii (October 1963), 371.

ENGLE, MORRIS S. 'An Early Nietzsche Fragment on Language'. *Journal of The History of Ideas*, xxiv (1963), 279–86.

ERDMANN, KARL DIETRICH. 'Das Problem der Historismus in des neuren englischen Geschichtswissenschaft'. *Historische Zeitschrift*, clxx (1950), 73–88.

FAIN, HASKELL. *Between Philosophy and History*. Princeton, N.J.: Princeton University Press, 1970.

—— 'History and Science'. *History and Theory*, 9, No. 2 (27 May 1970), 154–73.

FERRATER MORA, JOSE. Article on Collingwood in *Dictionaris de Filosofia*, 5th ed. Buenos Aires: Sudamericana (1958), 243.

FLENLEY, R. 'Collingwood's Idea of History'. *Canadian Historical Review*, xxvii (1947), 68–72.

FRUCHON, P. 'Signification de l'historie de la philosophie selon l'auto-biographie de Collingwood'. *Les Études philosophiques*, xiii (1958), 143–60.

Gadamer, Hans Georg. *Wahrheit und Methode: Grundzüge einer philosophischen Hermeneutik*. Tubingen: J. C. B. Mohr, 1960, pp. 352 ff.

GALLIE, W. B. *Philosophy and the Historical Understanding*. London: Chatto & Windus, 1964, pp. 56 ff., 213–25.

GALLOWAY, G. Review of *Religion and Philosophy*. *Mind*, xxviii (July 1919), 365–7.

GARDINER, P. *The Nature of Historical Explanation*. London: Oxford University Press. 1952.

—— 'The "Objects" of Historical Knowledge.' *Philosophy*, xxvii (July 1952), 211–20.

GENNARO, ANGELO A. DE. 'Croce and Collingwood'. *Personalist*, xlvi (April 1965), 193–202.

GINSBERG, MORRIS. 'The Character of an Historical Explanation'. *Proceedings of the Aristotelian Society, Supplementary Volume*, xxi (1947), 69–77.

GOHEEN, JOHN. Review of *An Essay on Metaphysics*. *Journal of Philosophy*, xxxviii (January 1941), 48–50.

GOLDSTEIN, L. J. 'Collingwood's Theory of Historical Knowing'. *History and Theory*, ix, No. 1 (1970), 3–36.

—— Review of L. Rubinoff, *Collingwood and the Reform of Metaphysics; a Study in the Philosophy of Mind, Man and World* (forthcoming).

GRANT, C. K. 'Collingwood's Theory of Historical Knowledge'. *Renaissance and Modern Studies*, No. 1 (1957), 65–90.

—— Review of A. Donagan, *The Later Philosophy of R. G. Collingwood*. *Philosophical Books*, iv (May 1963), 3–4.

HANNAY, H. A. Review of *An Autobiography*. *International Journal of Ethics*, li (April 1941), 369–70.

HARRIS, E. E. 'Mr. Ryle and the Ontological Argument'. *Mind*, xlv (October 1936), 474–80.

—— 'Collingwood on Eternal Problems'. *Philosophical Quarterly*, i (April 1951), 228–41.

—— *Nature, Mind and Modern Science*. London: Allen & Unwin, 1954, pp. 29–42.

—— 'Objectivity and Reason'. *Philosophy*, xxxi (January 1956), 55–73.

—— 'The Mind Dependence of Objects'. *Philosophical Quarterly*, vi (1956), 223–35.

—— 'Collingwood's Theory of History'. *Philosophical Quarterly*, vii (January 1957), 35–49.

—— *The Foundations of Metaphysics in Science*. London: Allen & Unwin, 1965.

—— Review of *Essays in the Philosophy of History by R. G. Collingwood*, ed. William Debbins. *History and Theory*, v (1966), 202–7.

—— *Hypothesis and Perception: The Roots of Scientific Method*. London: Allen & Unwin, 1970.

HARRIS, H. S. Introduction to G. Gentile, *Genesis and Structure of Society* (trans. H. S. Harris). Urbana: University of Illinois Press, 1960, pp. 14–20.

HARRIS, R. W. 'Collingwood's *Idea of History*'. *History*, xxxvii (February 1952). 1–7.

HARTSHORNE, C. Review of *An Essay on Philosophical Method*. *International Journal of Ethics*, xliv (April 1934), 357–8.

HARTT, JULIAN N. 'Metaphysics, History and Civilization: Collingwood's Account of their Interrelationships'. *Journal of Religion*, xxxiii (1953), 198–211.

—— Review of *Faith and Reason: Essays in the Philosophy of Region* by R. G. Collingwood, ed. Lionel Rubinoff. *Journal of Religion*, xlix, No. 3 (July 1969), 280–94.

HARVEY, VAN A. *The Historian and the Believer*. New York: Macmillan, 1966, especially Parts II–VIII.

HEARNSHAW, L. S. 'A Reply to Professor Collingwood's Attack on Psychology'. *Mind*, li (April 1942), 160–9.

HEINEMANN, F. H. 'Reply to Historicism'. *Philosophy*, xxi (1946), 245–7.

HEPBURN, R. W. 'A Fresh Look at Collingwood'. *British Journal of Aesthetics*, iii (July 1963), 259–61.

HODGES, H. A. *Philosophy of Wilhelm Dilthey*. London: Routledge & Kegan Paul, 1952.

HOPKINS, J. 'Bultman on Collingwood's Philosophy of History'. *Harvard Theological Review*, lviii (1965), 227–33.

HOSPERS, J. 'The Croce-Collingwood Theory of Art'. *Philosophy*, xxxi (October 1956), 291–308.

HICKS, G. DAWES. Review of *An Autobiography*. 'Survey of Recent Philosophical Literature'. *Hibbert Journal*, xxxviii (October 1939), 128–31.

ILLANES, FELIPE PARDINAS. 'Dilthey y Collingwood'. *Filosofia y letras: Revista della facultad de filosofia y letras* (Mexico), xix (February–March 1950), 87–105.

JOHNSTON, W. M. *The Formative Years of R. G. Collingwood*. The Hague: M. Nijhoff, 1969.

JONES, PETER. 'Collingwood's Debt to his Father'. *Mind*, lxxviii (July 1969), 437–9.

—— Review of *Collingwood and the Reform of Metaphysics* by Lionel Rubinoff. *Dialogue*: March 1972, xi, No. 1.

KAUFMAN, GORDON. *Relativism, Knowledge and Faith*. Chicago: University of Chicago Press, 1960.

KENNEDY, D. E. 'The Wood and the Trees: the Philosophical Development of R. G. Collingwood'. *Australian Journal of Politics and History*, x (1964), 245–8.

KIRK, G. S. 'A Problem in Historical Technique: Collingwood and Ionian Physics'. *Cambridge Journal*, vi (June 1963), 515–33.

KNOX, T. M. 'Collingwood, Robin George (1889–1943)'. *Encyclopedia Britannica*, 14th ed (1929), vi, 19.

—— 'Notes on Collingwood's Philosophical Work: with a Bibliography'. *Proceedings of the British Academy*, xxix (1943), 469–75.

—— 'Professor R. G. Collingwood, F.B.A.' *Nature* (6 February 1943), 163.

—— Editor's preface to R. G. Collingwood, *The Idea of History*. London: Oxford University Press, 1946, pp. v–xxiv.

—— 'R. G. Collingwood'. *Hamburger Akademische Rundschau* 2 (March/April 1947–8) Heft 9–10, 491–6.

—— 'Collingwood, Robin George (1889–1943)'. *Dictionary of National Biography 1941–1950*. Oxford: Oxford University Press, 1959, 168–70.

—— 'Hegel in English Speaking Countries Since 1919'. *Hegel-Studien*, i (1961), 315–18.

—— Review of L. O. Mink, *Mind, History and Dialectic. Mind*, lxx (January 1971), 150–2.

KRAUSZ, MICHAEL. Review of L. O. Mink, *Mind, History and Dialectic: The Philosophy of R. G. Collingwood. Dialogue: Canadian Philosophical Review*, x, No. 1 (March 1971), 151–4.

KRONER, RICHARD. 'Mure and Other Hegelians'. *The Review of Metaphysics*, vii (1953–4), 64–73.

LAIRD, J. Review of *Speculum Mentis. Mind*, xxxiv (April 1925), 235–41.

—— Review of *The New Leviathan. Philosophy*, xviii (1943), 75–80.

—— Review of *The Idea of History. Mind*, liv (1945), 274–9.

LAMPRECHT, STERLING P. Review of *An Autobiography. Journal of Philosophy*, xxxvi (21 December 1939), 717–18.

LANGER, SUSANNE. *Feeling and Form*. New York: Scribner's, 1953, pp. 380–90.

LEWIS, H. D. 'On Poetic Truth'. *Philosophy*, xxi (1946), 147–66.

LION, ALINE. Review of *An Essay on Metaphysics*. *Philosophy*, xvi (January 1941), 74–8.

LLEWELYN, J. 'Collingwood's Doctrine of Absolute Presuppositions'. *Philosophical Quarterly*, xi (January 1961), 49–60.

—— 'Collingwood's Later Philosophy'. *Philosophy*, xxxix (April 1964), 174–7.

LOCAS, CLAUDE. Review of *R. G. Collingwood, Philosophe et Historien*, par Albert Shalom. (1967; Paris, P.U.F.) *Dialogue:* September 1971, x, No. 3, 628–31.

—— 'R. G. Collingwood: 1889–1943'. *Proceedings of the British Academy*, xxix (1943), 463–8.

MACCORMAC, JOHN. Review of *The New Leviathan*. *The Sunday New York Times* (1 August 1943), p. 16.

MACDONALD, MARGARET. 'Art as Imagination'. *Proceedings of the Aristotelian Society*, liii (1952–3), 205–26.

MACIVER, A. M. 'The Character of an Historical Explanation'. *Proceedings of the Aristotelian Society. Supplementary Volume*, xxi (1947), 33–50.

MACIVER, R. M. Review of *The New Leviathan*. *Annals of the American Academy of Political and Social Science*, ccxxix (1943), 181–2.

MACKAY, DONALD S. 'On Supposing and Presupposing'. *Review of Metaphysics*, ii (September 1948), 1–20.

MACKINNON, D. M. Review of *The Idea of History. Journal of Theological Studies*, xlviii (1947), 349–53.

MACQUARRIE, JOHN. *Twentieth-Century Religious Thought: the Frontiers of Philosophy and Theology 1900–1960*. New York: Harper & Row, 1963, esp. pp. 131 ff.

MANDELBAUM, M. Review of *The Idea of History. Journal of Philosophy*, xliv (27 March 1947), 184–8.

MARCHAM, F. G. Review of *An Autobiography. Philosophical Review*, i (September 1941), 546.

MAYO, BERNARD. 'Poetry, Language and Communication'. *Philosophy*, xxix (1954), 131–45.

—— 'Art, Language and Philosophy in Croce'. *Philosophical Quarterly*, v (1955), 245–60.

MCCALLUM, R. B. 'Obituary: R. G. Collingwood (1889–1943)'. *Oxford Magazine*, lxi (1942–3), 160–1.

MEILAND, JACK. *Scepticism and Historical Knowledge*. New York: Random House, 1965, esp. pp. 63–82.

MEYERS, E. D. 'A Note on Collingwood's Criticism of Toynbee'. *Journal of Philosophy*, xliv (28 August 1947), 485–9.

MINK, LOUIS O. 'Comment on Stephen Toulmin's "Conceptual Revolutions in Science"', in R. S. Cohen and M. W. Wartofsky, eds., *Boston Studies in the Philosophy of Science*, iii. New York: Humanities Press, 1963–4, pp. 348–55.

—— 'Collingwood's Dialectic of History'. *History and Theory*, vii, No. 1, (1968), 3–37.

—— *Mind, History and Dialectic: the Philosophy of R. G. Collingwood*. Bloomington: University of Indiana Press, 1969.

—— Review of L. Rubinoff, ed., *Faith and Reason: Essays in the Philosophy of Religion by R. G. Collingwood*. *Journal of the American Academy of Religion*, xxxviii (March 1970), 118–20.

MISCHEL, THEODORE. 'Bad Art as "Corruption of Consciousness"'. *Philosophy and Phenomenological Research*, 21 (1960–1), 390–6.

—— 'Collingwood on Art as "Imaginative Expression"'. *Australasian Journal of Philosophy*, xxxix (1961), 241–50.

—— 'A Reply to Bailey's Defence of Collingwood'. *Australasian Journal of Philosophy*, xlii (1964), 391–3.

MOFFAT, J. Review of *Religion and Philosophy* by R. G. C., 'Survey of Recent Theological Literature'. *Hibbert Journal*, xv, No. 4 (1917), 677–82.

MOLINA, FERNANDO R. 'Collingwood on Philosophical Methodology'. *Ideas y Valores*, vi (1957), 1–15.

MORRIS-JONES, H. 'Art and Imagination'. *Philosophy*, xxxiv (July 1959), 204–16.

MUIRHEAD, J. H. Review of *An Autobiography*. *Philosophy*, xv (January 1940), 89–91.

MURE, G. R. G. 'Benedeto Croce and Oxford'. *Philosophical Quarterly*, iv (October 1954), 327–31.

—— *Retreat from Truth*. Oxford: Basil Blackwell, 1958.

MURPHY, A. E. Review of *The Idea of Nature*. *Philosophical Review*, lv (1946), 199–202.

—— Review of *The Idea of History*, *Philosophical Review*, lvi (1947), 587–92.

MYERS, E. D. 'A Note on Collingwood's Criticism of Toynbee'. *Journal of Philosophy*, xliv (1947), 485–9.

MYRES, JOHN L. Review of *The Idea of Nature*. *Man*, v, No. 45 (November–December 1945), 133.

NORBURN, G. 'The Philosophical Quest, II: Philosophy as Historicism'. *Church Quarterly Review*, cli (October–December 1950), 51–62.

NYE, RUSSEL. 'On Philosophy and History: Work that Reconciles the Two Disciplines'. *Chicago Sun Book Week*, v, No. 5 (1 December 1946), 12. Contains a review of *The Idea of History*.

PASSMORE, J. B. *A Hundred Years of Philosophy*. London: Gerald Duckworth & Co. Ltd., 1957, pp. 304–9.

—— 'The Idea of a History of Philosophy'. *History and Theory*, v (1965), 1–32.

PATON, H. J. 'Fifty Years of Philosophy'. in J. H. Muirhead, ed., *Contemporary British Philosophy*, third series. London: Allen & Unwin, 1956, p. 345.

PAUL, LESLIE. *The English Philosophers*. London: Faber & Faber, 1953, pp. 351–2.

PESCE, DOMENICO. Introduction to *Tre saggi di filosofia della storia*. Padua: Liviana Editrice, 1969, pp. 3–11.

POLANYI, MICHAEL. *The Study of Man*. London: Routledge & Kegan Paul, 1959, pp. 100 ff.

POPPER, SIR KARL. 'On the Theory of the Objective Mind'. *Proceedings of the 14th International Congress of Philosophy*. Herder. Vienna: University of Vienna, 1968, pp. 25–53, especially pp. 45–7 and notes.

—— 'A Pluralist Approach to the Philosophy of History'. *Roads to Freedom: Essays in honour of F. A. Von Hayek* ed. Eric Streissler, Gottfried Hebler, Friedrich Lutz, and Fritz Machlup. London: Routledge & Kegan Paul, 1969, pp. 181–200.

POST, JOHN F. 'A Defense of Collingwood's Theory of Presuppositions'. *Inquiry*, viii (1965), 332–54.

—— 'Does Knowing Make a Difference to what is Known?' *Philosophical Quarterly*, xv (1965), 220–8.

POWELL, ANTHONY. Review of *The Idea of Nature*. *Spectator*, clxxvii (1946), 172.

PRICE-JONES, G. Review of *Principles of Art. Burlington Magazine*, 73 (October 1938), 185.

PYLKKÄNEN, PAULI. 'R. G. Collingwood in historian filosofia'. *Historiallinen Aikakauskirja*, No. 3 (1961), 197–211.

RADER, MELVIN. 'Art and History'. *Journal of Aesthetics and Art Criticism*, xxvi (Winter 1967), 157–68.

READ, HERBERT. 'The Poet and His Muse'. *Franos Jahrbuch*, xxxi (1962), 217–48.

REEVE, E. GAVIN. 'Does Fichte's View of History Really Appear so Silly?' *Philosophy*, xl(January 1965), 57–9 (A reply to Collingwood's discussion of Fichte in *The Idea of History*, pp. 106–11).

RENIER, G. J. *History: its Purpose and Method.* London: Allen & Unwin, 1950, esp. pp. 40–8.

RESCHER, NICHOLAS. 'On the Logic of Presuppositions'. *Philosophy and Phenomenological Research*, xxi(June 1961), 521–7.

RICHMOND, I. A. 'Appreciation of R. G. Collingwood as an Archaeologist' (with 'R. G. Collingwood: Bibliography of Writing of Ancient History and Archaeology', pp. 481–5). *Proceedings of the British Academy*, xxix(1943), 476–80.

—— 'Obituary Notice: Robin George Collingwood: Born 1889, Died 9 January 1943'. *Antiquaries Journal*, xxx(1943), 84–5.

—— 'Robin George Collingwood'. *Archaeologica Aeliana, or Miscellaneous Tracts Relating to Antiquity*, xxi(1943), 254–5.

RITCHIE, A. D. 'The Logic of Question and Answer'. *Mind*, lii(January 1943), 24–38.

—— *British Philosophers.* London-New York-Toronto: Published for the British Council by Longmans, 1950, pp. 57–8.

ROBERTS, T. A. *History and Christian Apologetic.* London: S.P.C.K., 1960, especially chapter I and pp. 91–2.

ROBLIN, RONALD. Review of L. Rubinoff, ed., *Faith and Reason: Essays in the Philosophy of Religion by R. G. Collingwood. Philosophy and Phenomenological Research* (March 1972), xxxii (32), No. 3.

RONAYNE, C. F. Review of *An Essay on Philosophical Method. American Review*, iv (March 1935), 627–33.

ROSEN, STANELY H. 'Collingwood and Greek Aesthetics'. *Phronesis*, iv (1959), 135–48.

ROTENSTREICH, N. 'Historicism and Philosophy. Reflections on R. G. Collingwood'. *Revue internationale de philosophie*, xi, No. 42 (1957), 401–19.

—— *Between Past and Present.* New Haven, Conn.: Yale University Press, 1958.

—— 'From Facts to Thoughts: Collingwood's Views on the Nature of History'. *Philosophy*, xxxv (April 1960), 122–37.

—— 'History and Time: A Critical Examination of R. G. Collingwood's Doctrine'. *Scripta Hierosolymitana* (Jerusalem, 1960), pp. 41–104.

ROWSE, A. L. *The Use of History*. London: Hodder & Stoughton, 1946, pp. 147–9.

—— Review of *An Autobiography*. *Spectator*, clxiii (August 1939), 262.

RUBINOFF, LIONEL. 'Collingwood and the Radical Conversion Hypothesis'. *Dialogue: Canadian Philosophical Review* (1966), 71–83.

—— Review of A. Donagan, *Essays in the Philosophy of Art by R. G. Collingwood*. *Dialogue: Canadian Philosophical Review*, v (December 1966), 467–70.

—— Review of W. Debbins, *Essays in the Philosophy of History by R. G. Collingwood*. *Dialogue: Canadian Philosophical Review*, v (December 1966), 471–5.

—— 'Collingwood's Theory of the Relation between Philosophy and History: A New Interpretation'. *Journal of the History of Philosophy*, vi (October 1968), 363–80.

—— Introduction and Commentary to *Faith and Reason: Essays in the Philosophy of Religion by R. G. Collingwood*. Chicago: Quadrangle, 1968.

—— Introduction and Commentary to *The Presuppositions of Critical History by F. H. Bradley*. Toronto: J. M. Dent-Chicago: Quadrangle, 1968, pp. 1–74.

—— *Collingwood and the Reform of Metaphysics; A Study in the Philosophy of Mind*. Toronto: University of Toronto Press, 1970.

—— 'History and Perception: Reflections on R. G. Collingwood's Theory of History'. *Philosophical Forum*, ii, No. 1 (Fall 1970), 91–107.

—— Review of W. M. Johnston. *The Formative Years of R. G. Collingwood*. *Dialogue: Canadian Philosophical Review*. (forthcoming).

—— Review of L. O. Mink, *Mind, History, and Dialectic*, and A. Shalom, *R. G. Collingwood: Philosophe et historien*. *Journal of the History of Philosophy*. (forthcoming).

RUGGIERO, GUIDO DE, *Filosofia del Novecento*, vol. x of *Storia della filosofia*. 3rd ed. Bari: Editori Laterza, 1963, 92–104.

RUSSELL, L. J. Review of *An Essay on Philosophical Method*. *Philosophy*, ix (July 1934), 350–2.

RUST, ERIC C. *Towards a Theological Understanding of History*. New York: Oxford University Press, 1963, pp. 9–10, 58, 268–9.

—— *Evolutionary Philosophies and Contemporary Theology*. Philadelphia, Pa.: Westminster Press, 1969.

RYLE, G. 'Mr. Collingwood and the Ontological Argument'. *Mind*, xliv (April 1935), 137–51.

23

—— 'Back to the Ontological Argument'. *Mind*, xliv (January 1937), 53–7.

—— *Philosophical Arguments*. Oxford: Clarendon Press, 1946, 3–5.

RYNIN, DAVID. 'Donagan on Collingwood: Absolute Presuppositions, Truth, and Metaphysics'. *Review of Metaphysics*, xviii (December 1964), 301–33.

SCHILLER, F. C. S. Review of *An Essay on Philosophical Method*. *Mind*, xliii (January 1934), 117–20.

SCHLENKE, MANFRED. Review of *The Idea of History*. *Historische Zeitschrift*, clxxxiv (1957), 594–7.

SCHNEIDER, F. O. 'Collingwood and the Idea of History'. *University of Toronto Quarterly*, xxii (1953), 172–83.

SHALOM, ALBERT. 'R. G. Collingwood et la metaphysique'. *Les Études philosophiques*, x (1955), 693–711.

—— *R. G. Collingwood: philosophe et historien*. Paris: Presses Universitaires de France, 1967.

SHIPLEY, JOSEPH T. 'More things in this Philosophy than were Dreamt by Horatio'. *Library Review* (9 May 1925), 5.

SIBLEY, MUMFORD Q. Review of *The New Leviathan*. *American Political Science Review*, xxxvii (August 1943), 724.

SMART, HAROLD. *Philosophy and its History*. La Salle, Ill.: Open Court, 1962, pp. 62–84.

STEBBING, L. S. Review of *Speculum Mentis*. *Hibbert Journal*, xxviii, No. 3 (1925), 566–9.

—— Review of *An Essay on Metaphysics*. *Mind*, l (April 1941), 184–90.

STEWART, H. F. Review of *Concerning Prayer*. *Journal of Theological Studies*, xviii (1917), 79–80.

STRAUSS, L. 'On Collingwood's Philosophy of History'. *Review of Metaphysics*, v (June 1952), 559–86.

SYKES, N. 'Some Current Conceptions of Historiography and their Significance for Christian Apologetic'. *Journal of Theological Studies*, l (January–April 1949), 24–37.

THOMPSON, JUDITH JARVIS. Review of A. Donagan, *The Later Philosophy of R. G. Collingwood*. *Journal of Philosophy*, lxi (24 December 1964), 784–6.

TILLICH, PAUL. 'E. Troeltsch: Historismus und seine Probleme'. *Journal for the Scientific Study of Religion*, i (October 1961), 109 ff.

TOMLIN, E. W. F. *R. G. Collingwood*. Writers and Their Works, series No. 42. London: Published for the British Council by Longmans, 1953.

—— 'The Philosophy of R. G. Collingwood'. *Ratio* i (December 1958), 116–35.

—— *The Western Philosophers*. New York: Harper & Row, 1963, pp. 336–7.

TOULMIN, STEPHEN. 'Conceptual Revolutions in Science', in R. S. Cohen and M. W. Wartofsky, eds., *Boston Studies in the Philosophy of Science*, iii. New York: Humanities Press, 1963–4, pp. 332–47.

TOYNBEE, A. *A Study of History*, vol. ix. London-New York-Toronto: Oxford University Press, 1954, 718–38.

TURNER, JOHN. 'Diachronic Understanding'. *Philosophy*, xliii (July 1968), 284–6.

URMSON, J. O. Article on Collingwood in *Encyclopedia of Western Philosophy*. New York: Hawthorn Books, 1960, pp. 81–2.

VIVAS, ELISEO. Review of *The Principles of Art*. *Nation*, cxlviii (1939), 98.

VOEGLIN, ERIC. 'The Oxford Political Philosophers'. *Philosophical Quarterly*, iii (April 1953), 97–114.

WAGNER, FRITZ. *Moderne Geschichtsschreibung Ausblick auf eine Philosophie der Geschichtswissenschaft*. Berlin-Munchen: Duncherund Humbolt, 1960.

WALPOLE, H. R. *R. G. Collingwood and the Idea of Language*. Wichita, Ark.: Kansas University Studies, No. 55, 1963.

WALSH, W. H. 'The Character of an Historical Explanation'. *Aristotelian Society, Supplementary Volume*, xxi (1947), 51–68.

—— 'R. G. Collingwood's Philosophy of History'. *Philosophy*, xxii (July 1947), 153–60.

—— *Reason and Experience*. Oxford: Clarendon Press, 1947.

—— 'The Limits of Scientific History', *Historical Studies*, 3 (1961), 45–57.

—— 'Historical Causation'. *Proceedings of the Aristotelian Society*, lxiii (1962–3), 217–36.

—— *Metaphysics*. London: Hutchinson University Library, 1963, pp. 160–6.

—— Review of A. Donagan, *The Later Philosophy of R. G. Collingwood*. *Philosophical Review*, lxxiv (January 1965), 119–22.

—— 'Categories', in *Kant*, ed. R. P. Wolff. New York: Doubleday Anchor Books, 1967, pp. 54–70.

—— *Introduction to the Philosophy of History*. 3rd rev. ed. London: Hutchinson's University Press, 1967.

WATKINS, J. W. N. 'On Explaining Disaster'. *Listener* (10 February 1963), 69–70. See also responses to this article in Letters to the Editor section, 24 January 1963, 171; 31 January 1963, 209; and 7 February 1963, 251.

—— 'Imperfect Rationality' and 'Reply', in R. Borger and F. Cioffi, eds., *Explanation in the Behavioural Sciences*. Cambridge: Cambridge University Press, 1970, pp. 167–217 and 228–30.

WEBB, C. C. J. Review of *The Idea of Nature*. *Journal of Theological Studies*, xlvi (1945), 248–51.

—— Review of *The Idea of History*. *Hibbert Journal*, xlv (October 1946), 83–6.

WELLS, G. A. *Herder and After: A Study in the Development of Sociology*. New York: Humanities Press, 1959.

WHEELER, MORTIMER. Review of *Roman Britain*. *Journal of Roman Studies*, xxix, No. 1 (1939), 87–93.

WHITE, HAYDEN V. 'Collingwood and Toynbee: Translations in English Historical Thought'. *English Miscellany*, ix (1957), 147–78.

—— Review of A. Donagan, *The Later Philosophy of R. G. Collingwood*. *History and Theory*, iv, No. 2 (1965), 244–52.

WHITTAKER, EDMUND. Review of *The Idea of Nature*. *Philosophy*, xx (November 1945), 260–1.

WILKINS, BURLEIGH TAYLOR. 'Collingwood Reconsidered', review of A. Donagan, *The Later Philosophy of R. G. Collingwood*. *British Journal for the Philosophy of Science*, xv (1964–5), 72–8.

WINDLE, BERTRAND. Review of *Speculum Mentis*. *Catholic World*, cxxii (1925), 128.

WUNBERG, G. 'Robin George Collingwood: *The Idea of History*'. *Philosophischer Literaturanzeigen*, ix, No. 4 (1956), 156–61.

III: DOCTORAL DISSERTATIONS

COE, WILLIAM J. 'Metaphilosophy and Absolute Presupposition'. Pennsylvania State University, 1967.

COLVER, ANTHONY W. 'Evidence and Point of View in the Writing of History'. Harvard University, 1957.

CRAGG, ROBERT C. 'Collingwood's Logic of Question and Answer: a Study of its Logical and Philosophical Implications, and its Bearing on Historical Method'. University of Toronto, 1949.

CROM, SCOTT E. 'Collingwood and Metaphysics'. Yale University, 1952.

DEBBINS, WILLIAM. 'The Philosophy of R. G. Collingwood'. Syracuse University, 1959.

DeLong, Howard. 'The Development of R. G. Collingwood's Theory of History'. Princeton University, 1960.

Emblom, W. J. 'The Theory of Reality in the Philosophy of R. G. Collingwood'. University of Illinois, 1962.

Ficarra, Francis-Thomas. 'Collingwood's *New Leviathan*'. University of Illinois, 1961.

Flanagan, Sister Thomas Marguerite, C. S. J. 'Collingwood on the Nature of Metaphysics'. St. Louis University, 1964.

Grant, G. K. 'Professor Collingwood's Conception of the Relations between Metaphysics and History, and its Consequences for the Theory of Truth'. University of Oxford, 1950.

Hopkins, Jasper S. 'Epistemological Foundations of R. G. Collingwood's Philosophy of History'. Harvard University, 1963.

Johnston, W. M. 'The Formative Years of R. G. Collingwood'. Harvard University, 1965–6.

Kamins, Herbert. 'Aesthetic Claims: a Criticism of Collingwood's, Lewis's and Richards's Theories and an alternative Analysis of Critical Evaluations'. Cornell University, 1955.

Kaufman, Gordon. 'The Problem of Relativism and the Possibility of Metaphysics: a Constructive Development of Certain Ideas in R. G. Collingwood, Wilhelm Dilthey and Paul Tillich'. Yale University, 1955.

Krausz, Michael. 'A Critique of R. G. Collingwood's Theory of Absolute Presuppositions'. University of Toronto, 1969.

Martin, Rex. 'Collingwood's Critique of the Concept of Human Nature'. Columbia University, 1967.

Mathers, D. M. 'Historical Knowledge in the Philosophy of R. G. Collingwood'. Columbia University, 1954.

Mischel, Theodore. 'R. G. Collingwood's Philosophy of Art'. Columbia University, 1958.

Nelson, Sherwood Mathis. 'The Role of History in the Philosophy of R. G. Collingwood'. University of California, Berkeley, 1954.

Roblin, Ronald. 'R. G. Collingwood's Philosophy of History'. University of North Carolina, 1969.

Rubinoff, Lionel. 'The Relationship between Philosophy and History in the Thought of R. G. Collingwood'. University of Toronto, 1964.

Sayles, Edward M. 'A Critical Evaluation of R. G. Collingwood's Views on Metaphysics'. University of California at Los Angeles, 1956.

SCHNEIDER, HANS. 'Die Geschichtsphilosophie R. G. Collingwood's'. University of Bonn, 1950.

STANAGE, SHERMAN M. 'The Role of the 'Overlap' in Collingwood's Philosophy'. University of Colorado, 1959.

STORMER, GERALD D. 'The Early Hegelianism of R. G. Collingwood'. Tulane University, 1970.

SURANYI-UNGER, NORA. 'Die Politische Philosophie von R. G. Collingwood'. Inaugural doctoral dissertation. University of Munich, 1960.

WEBSTER, GLEN ALBERT. 'R. G. Collingwood's Conception of Philosophy'. University of Washington, 1967.

WILLIAMS, D. E. 'The Metaphysical and Political Theories of R. G. Collingwood'. London School of Economics, 1960.

ZIFF, ROBERT P. 'The Notion of a Work of Art with Special Reference to the Aesthetic Theory of R. G. Collingwood'. Cornell University, 1951.

NAME INDEX

SUBJECT INDEX

Absolute, the, 18, 119–20, 123, 127–8, 133

absolute presuppositions, *see* **Presuppositions,** absolute

abstraction: in philosophy, 8–18; and 'the science of pure being', 136, 189

action, *see* thought: in relation to action

activity, theoretical and practical, 51, 125–6

aesthetic philosophy, *see* **Art, Philosophy of**

anthropology, 108, 297

appetite, 22, 165, 174; *see also* **Consciousness:** orders (levels) of

Art: 2, 3, 7, III, IV, 86–7, 110, 124, 158–9, 176, 254–9; as 'form of experience', 2, 7, 16–17, 87, 89–93, 130, 134, 143–4, 146–9, 168–9, 286, 293; and language, 43–4, 55, 62, *see also* **Expression;** and morality, 45, 65; and feelings, 43–4, 47–8, 53–4, 63, 65; and imagination, 45–6, 55–7, 63, 65; and expression (q.v.), 47–8, 63, 66–7; and technique, *see* **Art, Works of**

Art, Philosophy of: III, IV, 143; and philosophical realism, 9; and imagination, 41; C's early views on, 44–6; C's later views on, 46–50; and philosophy of mind, 45–6, 49–57, 65–7; and philosophy of language, 57–63, 66–7.

Art, Works of: as objects of imagination, 56, 68–9, 70–2, 76–7; as products of technique, 63–5; relation of audience to, 68, 69–70; as products of internalized or externalized art-activity, 72–8; as type or particular, 74–7; the task of defining, 159

atomism, logical, 116–17

attention: and feeling (sensation), 24, 51–2, 59; and consciousness, 26–7, 32; and imagination, 34, 36–7, 39; and thought, 36–7, 50; and art, 55

behaviourism, 242, 245n, 247, 253, 260

being, *see* **Metaphysics**

body politic, C on the, 310–22

Cartesian *cogito*, the, 14

causation, 115, 137–8, 139–42, 193, 198, 207, 223; in history, 151–3, 156

causes and reasons, 48–9, 210–15, 217–18, 220

Christianity, *see* **Religion**

civilization, 296–7, 322–6

classes, overlap of, 4–7, 106–7; *see also* overlap

colours, 216–17

conceptual revolutions, 172, X

conceptual systems, 171, X, esp. 203–6, 208

concrete universal, 118–21, 123, 128, 135–6

Consciousness: II, 49–52, 94–6, 148, 164–8, 195, 271–95 *passim*; orders (levels) of, 20, 22–8, 32, 36, 165–7, 174; in relation to preconscious and unconscious, 20, 26–9; as constituent of mind, 21, 49; and feeling (sensation), 22, 25–8, 49–54; corrupt and uncorrupt, 27, 47–8, 58–9, 62, 66, 275n, 287–9; and language (q.v.), 28, 32; self-c., 10–11, 31–2, 66–7, 125–9, 271–5, *see also* self-knowledge; and imagination, 32, 36, 55–6; identity of subject and object of, 127–8, *see also* thought; 'law of', 183, 185; and speech, 271–2

INDEX OF REFERENCES
TO COLLINGWOOD'S WRITINGS